The African Past

The African Past

Chronicles from Antiquity to Modern Times

BASIL DAVIDSON

With Illustrations

An Atlantic Monthly Press Book

Little, Brown and Company • Boston • Toronto

Second Printing

ATLANTIC–LITTLE, BROWN BOOKS
ARE PUBLISHED BY
LITTLE, BROWN AND COMPANY
IN ASSOCIATION WITH
THE ATLANTIC MONTHLY PRESS

PRINTED IN THE UNITED STATES OF AMERICA

TO

THOMAS FOX-PITT

in friendship

and affection

It is a marvelous country. What is its spell? I cannot tell you, nor wherein lies its strange and unfathomable charm. It lays its hand upon you, and, having once felt its compelling touch, you never can forget it.

PRINCESS MARIE LOUISE *in* 1925

Africa is no vast island, separated by an immense ocean from other portions of the globe, and cut off through the ages from the men who have made and influenced the destinies of mankind. She has been closely connected, both as source and nourisher, with some of the most potent influences which have affected for good the history of the world.

EDWARD WILMOT BLYDEN *in* 1880

History acquires meaning and objectivity only when it establishes a coherent relation between past and future.

EDWARD HALLETT CARR

Author's Note

THIS BOOK IS CONCERNED WITH THE STORY OF AFRICA FROM antiquity to modern times, as told in the chronicles and records of chiefs and kings, travelers and merchant-adventurers, poets and pirates and priests, soldiers and men of learning.

Framed and introduced as a continuous narrative based on what men wrote and thought at the time, *The African Past* is designed to illustrate the drama and variety, challenge and achievement that play so great a part in Africa's long history.

Like its two predecessors, *The African Past* is offered as a contribution to the fuller understanding of Africa today, as well as a guide to the Africa of yesterday and of long ago.

Contents

Author's Note   xi

Introduction: AFRICA IN HISTORY   1

The Stages of the Past   7
African and Asian Records   20
The Western Contribution   27
Unity and Continuity   39

ANTIQUITY   41

HARKHUF: Four Journeys to the Unknown South   47

PEPI-NAKT: Early Empire-Building   49

TUTHMOSIS III: Trade and Tribute   50

PIANKHI: Kush in Egypt   51

HERODOTUS: A City Named Meroë   52
    Carthage Trades South 53

EZANA: The Fall of Meroë   54

DESMOND CLARK: Stone Age Art   57

EARLY WEST AFRICA   61

BERNARD FAGG: The Nok Culture   65

FRANK WILLETT: Two Thousand Years of Sculpture   66

MUHAMMAD BELLO: Where the Yoruba Came From 67

SAMUEL JOHNSON: Yoruba Traditions 68

SABURI BIOBAKU: Yoruba Origins — A Modern View 70

TAMSIR NIANÉ and SURET-CANALE: Foundations of Ghana 70

AL YAKUBI: The King of Ghana 71

AL BEKRI: Ghana in 1067 72
   Royal Finances 72

ANONYMOUS: Sundiata's Triumph 73

AL OMARI: Mali in the Fourteenth Century 75
   Traveling through Cairo 75 The Empire of Mali 77
   Reception at Court 78 The Importance of Horses 78
   Royal Bureacracy 79

IBN BATTUTA: Travels in Mali 79
   Pomp and Circumstance 81 Security and Justice 82

KANO CHRONICLE: The Hausa States 84
   Diplomacy 84 Warfare 85

AL MAGHILI: Social Reform in Songhay 86
   The Seventh Question 86 The Answer 87

AHMED IBN FARTUA: Kanem and Turkey 89

KATI: Bound and Free in 1508 90
   The Duty of Vassals 93 Decline and Fall 94

ES-SA'DI: Djenné 94

EGHAREVBA: The Empire of Benin 95
   Origins 96 Legend and Fact 96 A Ruler from Ife 97
   A Discontented Prince 97 Brass-casting 98 Ewuare the
   Great 99 Guns and Coconuts 99 Missionaries 99

EARLY EAST AFRICA 101

AL MAS'UDI: The Country of the Zanj 107
   The Ivory Trade 109

FREEMAN-GRENVILLE: The Ivory Trade, a Modern View   110

IDRISI: The Export of Iron   111

FREEMAN-GRENVILLE: Money Talks   112

YU-YANG-TSA-TSU: The Blood-Drinkers   114

CHAO JU-KUA: Slaves from Madagascar   114
    Early Zanzibar 115

CHANG HSIEH: Advice to Traders   115

KILWA CHRONICLE: Emergence of Kilwa   116

IBN BATTUTA: Kilwa in 1331   116

MEDIEVAL ETHIOPIA: A Strong Ruler   117

KILWA CHRONICLE: Vasco da Gama   119

PATE CHRONICLE: Seafaring   120

VASCO DA GAMA'S LOGBOOK: The End of an Epoch   122
    Mossel Bay: The Hottentots 122   Quilimane: First Im-
    pact 124   Mozambique: A New World 124   Malindi:
    An Offer of Pilots 127   Journey to India 127

DUARTE BARBOSA: Swahili Civilization   128
    Sofala 128   The Zambezi Mouths 130   Angoya 130
    Mozambique Island 130   Kilwa 131   Mombasa 132
    Malindi 133   Pemba, Mafia, Zanzibar 134   Pate and
    Lamu 134   Brava 134   Mogadishu 135

HANS MAYR: The Sack of Two Cities   135
    Kilwa 136   Mombasa 136

DIOGO DE ALCANÇOVA: Kilwa Tariffs   137

AN INLAND EPIC   139

D. P. ABRAHAM: Conquest and Challenge   144
    Changa Succeeds 145

DIOGO DE ALCANÇOVA: "Kings and Barons"   146

PEDRO VAZ SOARES: Peace at Last   150

DUARTE BARBOSA: Monomotapa   151

JOÃO DE BARROS: Mines and Fortresses   152

JOÃO DOS SANTOS: South-central Africa in 1590-1600   153
    Sofala 154   Kingdom of the Quiteve 154   Far Up the
    Zambezi 158   The Kingdom of Monomotapa 160

ANTONIO BOCCARRO: The Deal with Portugal   163

ADVICES FROM GOA: Destruction of Monomotapa   164

KING OF PORTUGAL: Civilities   166

MANOEL BARRETO: Realities   167
    The Gold Fails 169

WEST AFRICA MEETS EUROPE   171

RUY DE PINA: The Building of El Mina Castle   180
    Portuguese Reach Benin 185

DUARTE PACHECO PEREIRA: Inland Kingdoms   186

DUARTE PIRES: The King of Benin   187

ALONSO DE PALENCIA: A Spanish Raid   188

AFFONSO OF CONGO: Evils of the Trade   191
    The Origins of Slaving 192   A Call for Aid 193

ABREU DE BRITO: Angolan Currency   194

JOHN LANDYE: Guinea Cargoes   195

RICHARD EDEN: English at Benin   196
    Gold and Ivory 197

WILLIAM TOWERSON: Metal Goods   198

JOHN HAWKINS: Towards the Slave Trade   199

RICHARD JOBSON: Mandingo Towns   201
    Lords and Vassals 202   Gambia Craftsmanship 202

OLIVEIRA CADORNEGA: A Million Slaves   203

THE EIGHTEENTH CENTURY 205

JOHN BARBOT: The Trade in Captives 211

JOHN CASSENEUVE: Docile Slaves? 214

"BOSTON POST BOY": Revolt at Sea 215

JAMES BARBOT: Slaving Manners 216
The System in Angola 216 An Angolan "Zimbabwe" 217

WILLIAM BOSMAN: A Report on Gold 217
The Guinea Partnership 218 Guns for Africa 220

MICHEL ADANSON: A Scientific Traveler 221

JOHN ATKINS: Ouidah in 1721 222

WILLIAM SMITH: The Palace of Benin 224

RICHARD BREW: A Dearth of Victims 225

CAPTAIN HEATLEY: The Reverence of Kings 226

JAMES PENNY: The Business of Kings 227

COMPANY DIRECTORS: Abuses of the Trade 228

JOHN JOHNSTON: The Price of Slaves 230

C. B. WADSTRÖM: An Enlightened Ruler 231

ARCHIBALD DALZELL: Rise of Dahomey 234

ROBERT NORRIS: Oyo and Dahomey 235

ABBÉ PROYART: Congo Government 237

OLAUDAH EQUIANO: In Iboland 241

THOMAS WINTERBOTTOM: A Wider Picture 243
Nicotine and Kola 245

JAMES BRUCE: Ethiopian Encounters 246
Adventure at Gondar 247 The Civil Wars 252 Cavalry of Sennar 257 Ruins of Meroë 258

ANDREW SPARRMAN: The Hottentots 259
The Bushmen 261

THE NINETEENTH CENTURY 265

FRÉDÉRIC CAILLAUD: Rediscovering Kush 277

JOHN BARROW: Beyond the Orange River 278

HENRY FYNN: Shaka the Zulu 281

EDOUARD CASALIS: In the Wake of Many Wars 283
 Moshesh of the Basuto 284

ROBERT MOFFAT: Chief Moselekatse 286

ANTONIO GAMITTO: The Land of Kazembe 291
 Marave Bridges 292 Metallurgy 292 Devastation 294
 King Kazembe 294

DAVID LIVINGSTONE: Central Africa in the 1840s 297
 The Roots of Apartheid 297 Boer Policy 298 African
 Justice 299 Security 300 Gold and Iron 301

JAMES PRIOR: Kilwa in Ruins 303
 Songo Mnara 304

W. F. W. OWEN: After the Deluge 306

ABDULLAH BEN NASIR: Lament for Greatness 307

ARNAULD D'ABBADIE: On the Meaning of Gifts 309

MUNGO PARK: To the Niger 310
 The King of Bondou 311 "Broad as the Thames at
 Westminster" 314 Segu 318 A Slave Coffle 321

UTHMAN DAN FODIO: Reformation 322
 The Old Habe Kingdoms 323 Five Rules of Government 325

ABDULLAH IBN MUHAMMAD: Against Bad Rulers 325

MUHAMMAD BELLO: Jihad 326

AL HAJJI SA'ID: Muhammad Bello 327

THOMAS BOWDICH: At Kumasi 328

BRODIE CRUICKSHANK: Political Background 330

HEINRICH BARTH: The Western Sudan 332
   Kano in Mid-Century 333 Finding the *Tarikh es-Sudan*
   335 Timbuktu 336 Industry and Trade 344

MARTIN DELANY: On Slavery 347

ROBERT CAMPBELL: Yoruba Government 349

WINWOOD READE: In the Oil Rivers 350

EDWARD BLYDEN: A West African Spartacus 351

MARY KINGSLEY: In the Gaboon 353
   Ascent of the Ogowé 354 Adventures in the Forest 355
   Advantages of Wearing a Skirt 356

MACEMBA: Facing Invasion 357

THE TWENTIETH CENTURY: A *Few Signposts* 359

K. SCHWABE: Colonial Conquest 363

LEO FROBENIUS: Leopold's Congo 364

R. MEINERTZHAGEN: White Man's Country? 365

CHARLES DOMINGO: The African Awakening 366

THÉODORE MONOD: Rediscovering Africa 367

PLACIDE TEMPELS: Bantu Philosophy 369

VINIGI GROTTANELLI: Points of Arrival 370

ONWUKA DIKE: African History 371

Acknowledgments 373

Index 377

Illustrations

(Between pages 234 and 235.)

Three men of Punt attend their king in a welcome to Egypt's mariners
Late Meroitic inscription from a cemetery on the Middle Nile
Statue in schist from Melazo excavations near ancient Ethiopian capital of Axum
Axumite funerary inscription from Melazo
Page from old prayer book in Ge'ez
Ethiopian illuminated manuscript of the reign of Dawit II
The legend of King Solomon and the Queen of Sheba
Carta del Cantino: 1507 mariner's map of western Africa
Letter from the Western Sudan written by Sultan Bello of Sokoto
Letter from the Sultan of Bornu
Chief Moshesh of the Basuto
King Kazembe
Exploring the Western Sudan

INTRODUCTION

Africa in History

GOOD WINE, THEY WISELY SAY, SHOULD BE LEFT IN THE BOTTLES
that first contained it: pour it afresh, and the flavor will spoil. To
this warning the maker of a selection of historical writings will reply, as I do here, that good old books, unlike good old wine, really
need putting into new covers from time to time, for otherwise they
become forgotten or unreasonably hard to find (let alone to buy);
and that if the work is done with care and affection the loss of
flavor will after all be small and easy to forgive. Indeed, the balance of advantage can well lie with the new, for what was previously set about with antique verbosity and obscureness of reference
may now shine forth in fresh and even unsuspected clarity of
meaning. It is along these lines that I defend — and all makers of
anthologies, it is well known, must defend themselves — my se-
lective pourings from more than a hundred authors, a few of them
new but most of them old and many of them hard or very hard
to find in the original. But I have another and more solid justification; and this I hasten to advance.

There are many anthologies of African exploration. Yet with
one or two exceptions, which I shall mention in a moment, they
are all built to the same pattern. They are anthologies of the European discovery of Africa, conceived as companion books to a
study of Africa which has regarded that subject as no more than an
extension to the study of Europe or the New World. Keeping to
sources which are largely from the nineteenth century, they aim to
show why and how it was that Europe "opened up" a continent
which was soon to become a European possession. Their attitude
is therefore strictly European in standpoint, and their value lies less

in any light they may throw on African life than in the movement they reveal of European penetration and conquest.

Thus the best modern anthology of West African exploration begins with the year 1600, and its introduction is entitled *The Opening of West Africa.* Yet much of West Africa had been "opened" to the outside world — or to a significant part of it — many hundreds of years earlier, and these earlier years are not without important records of their own. To make this point is not to belittle the learned editors of that particular selection, for they could certainly have made it for themselves. As it was, they were concerned with producing an anthology which reflected the colonial situation and met its peculiar requirements. One of these requirements was that no serious consideration of Africa could properly start before the beginning of European (but more especially English and French) exploration: to go back earlier would merely be to plunge into a fruitless mythology. The late Sir Reginald Coupland, writing some thirty years ago of British penetration into the Zambezi valley, put the point quite clearly when he affirmed that up to the middle of the nineteenth century "the main body of the Africans" had had no history, but had "stayed, for untold centuries, sunk in barbarism . . . [so that] the heart of Africa was scarcely beating." African history could be no fit subject for scholarly investigation because no such history existed: hence anthologies would necessarily begin with the arrival of Europe on the scene.

Now this approach is out of date. The last ten or twenty years have promoted an entirely different attitude to the African past. They have displaced what may be called the "colonial stereotype" — that all in Africa was social chaos and stagnation before the time of European conquest — by a view of the subject altogether to the contrary. These years have raised the study of African history from a mere act of eccentricity, perverse, foolish or positively harmful, to a scholarly discipline pursued by institutes of learning in many non-African as well as African countries. It is now accepted by a great and growing number of scholars of many nations that the study of Africa's past is not only possible, but is also useful, and even indispensable, to a closer understanding of the general condition of mankind.

This being so, a new kind of African anthology becomes necessary. Given the obscurity and difficulty and *newness* of the subject, what we need now, evidently, are guides to the whole of African history, or to long periods of it, not only in narrative form but also in relation to the pre-European and European records. We need the kind of anthology which will reflect the deeper truths of African life, its long passage and unfolding through the years, its valid part in the still wider story of human development throughout the world, its distinctiveness from the rest of history as well as its interdependence with the rest of history: an anthology, moreover, which will also shadow forth the limits of prejudice and knowledge within which the old writers wrote.

What follows here, accordingly, is an attempt to meet this need. In this respect, of course, it has an old heritage. Ramusio had the same idea in the middle of the sixteenth century; Guillain, with his *Documents sur l'Histoire de l'Afrique Orientale,* came still nearer to it in the middle of the nineteenth. But the man to whom this fertile concept of "documentary history" owes most in Africa is a great American historian, James Henry Breasted, whose *Ancient Records of Egypt* put all subsequent endeavors in his debt. Other valuable anthologies published in the last few years include Thomas Hodgkin's *Nigerian Perspectives,* a model of its kind, and Greville Freeman-Grenville's documentary selection in his *East African Coast.*

It goes without saying that only the merest outline is possible within the limits of one volume; and a wish to make this as full as possible is one reason why I have limited myself to Africa south of the Sahara: another is that although the division from North Africa is essentially unreal, the history of the latter is fairly well known. Records about Africa south of the Sahara were always thought to be copious; now they are seen to be more plentiful than any but a wild optimist could have supposed a few years ago. More and more purely African documents are coming to light. "The field of written documents," H. F. C. Smith has written of the Western

Sudan in a recent issue of the *Journal* of the Historical Society of Nigeria (itself no mean sign of the times), "is also very rich and astonishingly neglected. The region [has been] fairly well served by European travelers, though even their journals have not yet been studied in the detail required. Most important, however, are the Arabic manuscripts. A very small number of these have been printed in recent times, but the vast majority have never been studied by scholars from the historical point of view . . . The total mass of nineteenth-century Western Sudanese writing . . . is probably very great indeed. Big collections exist in Paris, and there are others in Dakar, Ibadan, Kaduna and Sokoto. But they are also very widely dispersed in the private hands of notables and other *mallams* . . ." Something of the same may be said for the Swahili literature of the East Coast, while fuller publication and modern reassessment of many important Arab writings about Africa, especially for the medieval period, will undoubtedly enlarge the frontiers of understanding.

All this is to be expected. We are only at the beginning of a coherent study of the African past, and, consequently, of the documents concerned with it. This is why it may be useful, I hope, to offer an outline guide to the wealth of material that exists for Africa south of the Sahara, and to present this, as far as practicable, so as to be read as a continuous story. To that end I have drawn on one hundred and thirteen authors of whom nearly a third are African, including some who are famous and others who are not, but generally avoiding the very obscure or the very well known — the first because they are liable to need a great deal of editorial explanation, for which space lacks, and the second because they can be quickly found elsewhere.

There is thus comparatively little from the nineteenth century and almost nothing from the twentieth. Denham and Clapperton, Stanley and Speke, Burton, Krapf and many other well-known travelers are altogether absent: not because they do not deserve inclusion, but because their writings are widely available in other anthologies or in their own books. Yet Mungo Park is here, if in attenuated form, because he marked a turning point in European exploration; and so is Heinrich Barth, the greatest of the nineteenth-century travelers though curiously unknown even to-day. All choices of this sort are personal, of course, but I have tried not to be eccentric. Everything here centers, or is intended to center, on the concept of African historical growth and change. Readers who may be moved to look further into the records (an exercise they will certainly enjoy) will find the main omissions mentioned at least by title in various editorials throughout the book. Meanwhile it may be useful to begin by setting the scene.

The Stages of the Past

Most historical writing has reflected man's disunity. In spite of the liberal example of Herodotus, whose sympathies and interests far outleaped the borders of the Greek world, historians have generally written (and no doubt it could not be otherwise) from a firmly and even narrowly national standpoint. The good ones made the best of this limitation; the bad ones, becoming xenophobic, made the worst of it: with few exceptions none achieved or desired to achieve, or even thought they could achieve if they had wished, what is now called a world view. This is why great segments of historical experience have often become lost or under-valued. The Ancient World failed to remember the Hittites, for example, just as a recent Europe largely forgot the brilliant skills of Islamic civilization in North Africa and Spain: with this last case, indeed, to the point that we still lack full translation and publication of many medieval Arab works.

The world of our own day has begun to see beyond this national limitation. The general reasons are obvious enough. The particular reasons certainly include the achievements of archeology and the wide audience these have won. More and more clearly, as narrow beliefs about the past give way before the startling evidence of spade and trowel, the interdependence of ancient cultures makes this or that exclusive claim ridiculous. Less than a century ago the well-educated man would think of antiquity in terms of Greece and Rome but little else. There was of course the Old Testament, with its disturbing hint of a wider background; and there were also the old Egyptians. Yet these appeared so remote from Greece and Rome as not really to belong to the same category of historical truth. Then archeologists laid bare the great civilizations of the Fertile Crescent, of Sumer and Akkad and Babylon. They displayed the magnificence of Pharaonic Egypt, explained the Phoenicians, explored the ruins of Minos and Mycenae; and with all this the civilizations of Greece and Rome progressively acquired new and splendid depths of meaning. Other archeologists went further afield. China and India were drawn into this revitalized picture of the past. Europe dwindled to the mere segment of a worldwide mosaic.

And as Europe ceased to occupy the center of the picture, the passing of the imperial epoch made way for an ever-quickened impulse of inquiry into the character of the non-European lands. This impulse has now carried us far and wide. It has drawn within the frontiers of history — of the history of mankind considered increasingly as a single though infinitely varied process — almost every quarter of the globe. The generous belief that no people is an island entire of itself, but all are part of the main, has become fulfilled.

Until lately, as we have seen, this large advance had failed to make a landfall on Africa and its peoples. What Melville Herskovits called "the myth of the Negro past" in his pioneering work of that name — the belief which taught that the Negro is "a man without a past" — continued to hold sway, rationalizing "discrimination in everyday contact between Negroes and whites," as Herskovits wrote, and "influencing the shaping of policy where Negroes are concerned." Africans were not thought to have entered the grand circuit of world development. Having no history of their own, they were manifestly "children who had failed to grow up." Being "retarded children," they necessarily forfeited any claim to equality of treatment with other men. Possessing no such claim, they must be taken in hand by superior peoples and shown the path they should tread. Beliefs of this kind underpinned the whole ethos of colonial "trusteeship" and often seemed to do so, what was more, with an appearance of good sense. In terms of its own mythology, the general non-African view of Africa had shifted little since the Middle Ages. It had become more sophisticated, but it had also become more contemptuous. If medieval Europeans thought that monsters inhabited Africa, they none the less respected the Africans they knew, and they respected them as equals: an attitude that was first engulfed and then forgotten during the furious years of the oversea slave trade.

Today the position is otherwise. The myth of the Negro past has joined a number of others of its kind. An intelligent view of human change and progress in Africa must now reach back to the most remote antiquity.

The ancestors of man came of stocks related to the ancestors of apes. But when and where did the lines divide? An island in East Africa's Lake Victoria has lately offered an answer. In a geological bed which is dated to about twenty-five million years ago, Dr. Louis Leakey discovered the fossilized fragments of a creature which lived on the ground but walked erect. Even if *Proconsul,* as Leakey named this creature, was not a man, it was quite probably an ancestor of man. Scanty evidence, indeed: but it so happens that many other manlike fossils have been found in East Africa. Another of Leakey's finds, *Zinjanthropus,* lived in northern Tanganyika about two million years ago; and he, if Leakey's attributions are correct, was certainly a kind of man, for he made crude stone tools. After that the story of man's first faltering movement in the direction of civilization becomes a little less obscure, and merges into what is known as the Old Stone Age, a period of enormous length during which various types of man appeared and disappeared, failed or survived, found slightly better ways of living, and eventually, by selection through unnumbered generations, gave birth to our own ancestors, whether in Africa or elsewhere.

After the Old Stone Age had persisted for many hundred thousand years there came the crucial invention of agriculture, a gradual but nonetheless definite process of experiment and technical gain. This decisive social revolution was neither a sudden nor a soon-completed thing. It followed many centuries of primitive and part-time farming — the collecting and sowing of seeds and tubers — and grew into what may properly be called *agriculture* at different times in different places. If the peoples of the Lower Nile were certainly practicing agriculture some six thousand years ago, and possibly earlier, scholars are not yet agreed upon the dating of the Neolithic — the New Stone Age — in Africa south of the Sahara. It may conceivably be true that this vast region of the continent developed rudimentary forms of farming as early as anywhere else, but the probability is that it did not. What seems clear is that agriculture and stock-raising began later than in northern Africa, and took directions of their own. These facts — if that is what they really are — may doubtless be explained by continental Africa's relative isolation from the rest of the world, after the desiccation of the Sahara, and its poverty in highly fertile river valleys. Yet Africa south of the Sahara began to acquire two distinctive and "mature" Neolithic systems during the fourth millenium B.C.: a cereal system in the forest-fringe lands of western Africa, and a stock-raising system in the East African highlands.

So much for *prehistory*. Taking the term narrowly — as of prehistory continuing until the appearance of written records — this continues in Africa for many centuries after the ending of the Neolithic period. Most rock paintings and engravings belong to the Neolithic cultures, yet many of these are recent and even modern, being the work of still surviving Bushmen and other minorities. Yet *history* in Africa may none the less be said to start with the general ending of the Neolithic and the beginning of an Age of Metals — an Iron Age, as I shall prefer to call it, since iron was by far the most important of the metals in question — for it is then that the origins of modern Africa begin to emerge and acquire historical identity. This is not, of course, because the Iron Age revolution was sudden or universally effective, but because the introduction of ferrous technology set in motion a series of changes that were crucial and cumulative in their effects, and paved the way for the fully historical Africa of medieval times. It is also true, as we shall see, that the earliest written records of Africa (aside from those of Pharaonic Egypt and the Phoenicians of Carthage

or the Sabaeans of Ethiopia) belong to the opening years of the
Iron Age. Even within a narrow use of the term, we are justified in
saying that the history of Africa begins with the coming of iron.

Knowledge of how to obtain and use iron reached the valley of
the Nile at about the same time as it was penetrating northward
into non-Mediterranean Europe. Old Egypt had been content
with bronze, and awakened to its disadvantages only when iron-
shod Assyrian armies appeared in 666 B.C. Thereafter iron tools
and weapons became less rare in Egypt. The Phoenicians began
using them in Carthage at about the same time. So did the Kushites of the Middle Nile, and later their Axumite neighbors in
northern Ethiopia. Kush, Carthage and Axum all played some part
in passing the knowledge of iron southward into the main body of
Africa. But of these three channels of communication, Kush was
much the most important.

Horse or donkey-drawn carts and chariots crossed the western
and central Sahara, between North Africa and the regions of the
Niger River, throughout a long period before the middle of the
first millenium B.C. Another important route lay between the Middle Nile and the region of Lake Chad, passing across Africa by way
of Kordofan, Darfur and Zaghawa. Possibly the peoples of west-
central Africa discovered iron mining and smelting for themselves,
independently of others; the likelihood is that these techniques
followed iron tools and weapons along the trans-African trails
from north and northeast. In any event, archeologists now agree
that at least one West African culture — that of the central area of
modern Nigeria — had passed from a Late Stone Age to an Early
Iron Age civilization by about 500 B.C. or perhaps a little later; and
that iron-making techniques, from about this time, spread rapidly
across the land.

Rapidly: yet among comparatively few people. Humanity was
sparse in Africa. At this period, one may think, the whole great
mass of country from the northern limits of the Congo Basin to
the Cape of Good Hope was peopled only by scattered groups
who lived by hunting game, gathering wild vegetables and also,
but not always, practicing a little agriculture. Some of them,
mainly in the East African highlands, were stock-breeders as well.

These groups had sufficiently mastered their environment to be able to survive, but not so successfully as to create any kind of "population explosion" and its consequent social upheavals. They had worked out their way of life over countless generations. Left to themselves, they would probably have continued to live in that way. Indeed, this is more or less how the Bushmen and a few other rare African peoples still live in our own time.

Rather more than two thousand years ago this ancient stability was upset by two new factors. Both made life a little easier. One of them, the knowledge of how to make iron spears and tools, came from a northerly direction (probably by way of west-central Africa southward through the highlands on either side of the Congo Basin); the second, a better variety of food, seems to have arrived along the coast of southeast Africa in the ships of Indonesian or other Asian seafarers. This wider choice of food consisted in the addition to the African diet of the banana and the yam, both of them ideal for tropical and subtropical conditions such as existed in the broad central belt of Africa. These two factors, better tools and new types of food, appear to have promoted just that "population explosion" which the old ecology had failed to produce.

This "explosion" is closely associated with the emergence of the Bantu-speaking family of African peoples who now dominate the whole central and southern region of the continent. They may be taken to have been the product of indigenous populations of the Neolithic period intermarried with Iron Age migrants from the African regions to the north of them. Here we meet with a constant and baffling process of weaving and interweaving between migrant and local populations, with the newcomers arriving generally from the north and northwest.

Why did early Iron Age groups in western and eastern Africa begin to move into the unknown south? There are two central explanations. The first is that the highly fertile regions of the Lower Niger now gave rise to a certain degree of overpopulation (a factor that would continue to be present in this region during historical and even very recent times); this pressure of land shortage sent men southward because, thanks to the Sahara, they could not go northward. The second explanation is that the iron-pointed spear was undoubtedly a great social and political innovator. Like the musket later on, the iron spear promoted new ideas and needs of government. The old tribal communities had managed with little or no government at all (as a few African peoples still do), but a strong and ambitious group could now impose its will on weaker groups, and could see, increasingly, an advantage in so doing. We begin to get the emergence of centralized political organization, of kingship and a rudimentary bureaucracy, of a systematic social differentiation between masters and servants, rulers and ruled. We are out of the Garden of Eden: a process of social fracturing has been set in motion.

It was this process which divided the "ancestral stocks" into a great variety of distinct peoples — "tribes" as they are often though misleadingly called — through the revolt of chiefs' sons against their fathers, of "junior groups" against "senior groups," of migrant rebels against parent clans and loyalties. In this long and complex disintegration of the Neolithic pattern and its reconstruction within an Iron Age framework we can find the origins of modern African societies, showing as these do, in a multitude of ways, a diversity that is none the less rooted in a profound and ancient unity. This large theme of unity-in-diversity runs throughout subsequent African history. Little about the African past (and therefore about the African present) can be understood apart from it. Pan-African unity is a political ambition of modern times, but its roots go far back into the past.

On the whole Neolithic period, needless to say, the written records are almost entirely silent, for the Egyptians tell us disappointingly little. But with the beginning of the Iron Age we begin to get a little documentary light. We might have had a great deal more if only the Phoenicians had worried less about their commercial secrets, and we may still hope for a little more when the cities of Kush are properly examined and their written language fully studied and explained. As it is, we have to rely on scattered memoirs and geographies written by Greeks who were mostly working with secondhand information. But with every Iron Age century we approach a more historical context. The written documents multiply. So do the archeological records. All the same, the first thousand years of the African Iron Age — which broadly means, as it happens, the first thousand years of the Christian era — remain teasingly vague and mysterious. They are least so, however, in the West African grasslands.

The Iron Age in West Africa took its rise, as we have seen, rather more than two thousand years ago. Working out a new social and political synthesis, important peoples in the grasslands (and somewhat later in the great evergreen forests which border the western coast and the Congo basin) began to evolve new and more complex forms of government. Ghana emerged, earliest of the great West African imperial systems. Traditionally, this happened as early as about A.D. 300, but the date is little more than guesswork based on semilegendary king lists written down many centuries later. As a coherent and important state — a form of centralized organization probably not known before in this vast region of Africa, or not in a pronounced form — Ghana may be safely dated to about A.D. 600 or somewhat later, with the reservation, of course, that it will already have had behind it a long experience of early growth. And as with all other known civilizations, Ghana seems initially to have been the product of immigrant pressure on an established local stability. The makers of ancient Ghana were authentic West Africans, but they were also influenced by ideas and pressures from North Africa and probably from the Nile as well. These ideas and pressures were those of the Iron Age coupled with a growing interest in trans-Saharan trade. The fortunes of Ghana flourished on an intelligent local exploitation of a nonlocal demand for West African gold and other products.

Ghana is said to have emerged from the ambitions of a small but evidently vigorous people called the Sarakolle. For reasons that we do not know and probably shall never know, they made a bid to control their neighbors: according to an eleventh-century Arab source, no doubt drawing on much older information, they were able to succeed because they fought with iron weapons while these neighbors fought with ebony. They needed and acquired a central organization under a divine ruler, the *ghana*, whose title became the name of their state and empire. By the ninth century, if not earlier, they had won control over the westerly part of the West-

ern Sudan in respect of two great items: they or their ruler con-
troled the import of salt from the desert fringes, and also the export of gold towards the north. By the eleventh century, when the
first clear record of Ghana becomes available, a large part of the
Western Sudanese grassland was enclosed within a single system
of imperial tax and tribute. This empire, we may note, was more
or less contemporary with that of the Franks in Western Europe,
and the essential organization of the first, allowing for many differences of attitude and detail, was evidently not much different
from that of the second. Charlemagne and his Ghanaian contemporary, had they ever met each other, could have talked with
keen understanding of each other's political and economic ar-
rangements.

The old Ghanaian pattern set the course of Western Sudanese
history for more than a thousand years: time after time a strong
central authority strove to impose its will on rival authorities and
to hold these vassals in obedience, drawing its military strength
from feudal levies and its financial power from the proceeds of the
export trade in gold and other goods and of the import trade in
salt, copper, and the manufactures of Egypt, North Africa and
Europe. Now and then the pattern was disturbed by foreign invasion, as from Morocco in the eleventh and sixteenth centuries,
but generally the great system held firm. This is one of the grand
periods of African history. It runs from about A.D. 600 to 1600, and
with the passing of the years its documentary sources become increasingly copious and full of pith and meaning. To it belong the
rise and fall of Ghana, Mali, Kanem-Bornu, Songhay and the
Hausa states, and others no less famous and successful in the forest
lands to the immediate south, Oyo and Benin, Akwamu, Denkyira
and their like.

The other main center of growth, the eastern Rift Valley and
its peripheral lands, has a somewhat different story. An Iron Age
began here at about the same period as in West Africa, or not
much later, but for a long time there is no corresponding development of large states and trading systems, or none that we know
of at present. The peoples of the East African interior lacked contact with the world beyond the Sahara, cut off from this as they

largely were by the swamps and marshes of the Upper Nile. Perhaps more tellingly, they lacked the desirable trading metals. Their historical interest rests not so much in what they achieved themselves as in the achievements of migrants whom they sent off towards the south. These Iron Age pioneers mingled with the folk whom they found, and the resultant peoples, using iron and growing rapidly more numerous, became the foundation for two new centers of political and economic growth.

The first of these new centers lay in the region of the modern Katanga, and was based on the smelting and trading of copper; the second was in the plateau lands of the Rhodesias, founded there on the smelting and trading of gold. This, of course, is a simplification. At least two complicating factors should be kept in mind. One was that there is no clear distinction, so far as the central-southern Iron Age is concerned, between the influences that came from West Africa and those that came from East Africa. The other is that there were other stimulants to growth besides an outside demand for copper and gold.

The fact remains that any general survey of the African societies of the last thousand years in east and central-south Africa will show many points of similarity in growth and technique. Much has still to be explained, for the archeology of this area is as yet imperfectly known. But already one can point to close affiliations of language, thought, belief and social organization, to related methods of using stone, to terrace-building for hillside cultivation and soil conservation, and to many other links between nearly all these peoples. From early Iron Age societies in East Africa men developed mature though nonliterate cultures and civilizations which spread southward across the continent as far as the middle of modern South Africa. All this forms another great period of African history, that of the Bantu Iron Age; and here too, as in West Africa, there emerged important states and imperial systems of government and trade.

These seem to have begun in Uganda in about the fourteenth century, but somewhat earlier in the "mining states" of the south. Archeologists at present divide the mature Iron Age of central-southern Africa into two large periods, one starting in about the twelfth century, when the first walls were raised at Great Zimbabwe, and the other in the fifteenth century, when the Karanga people under their Rozwi kings set about founding their notable empire of Monomotapa — named after the title of their king, *mwana-mutapa,* just as Ghana had been. These systems were native to the lands where they emerged but owed much, like those of West Africa, to ideas and influence from other African lands. Their technology in metals and in stone, beliefs and customs, notions of god and government, all go back to a common source which became, with time, an infinitely varied fabric of daily life, religion and behavior.

To this process the course of history along the East African seaboard makes a peculiar and exciting contribution. This was a coast of ancient trading intercourse, being the western shore of the Indian Ocean and drawn thereby into the whole wide community of Indian Ocean commerce. Traders from Arabia settled here more than two thousand years ago, choosing convenient islands or mainland harbors, intermarrying with the local peoples, and producing as time went by a civilization that was distinctive to the seaboard. As new political organizations took shape and trade grew more important, these small Arabo-African colonies underwent a double and in some ways contradictory change. They accepted Islam and Arabic culture, but they became emphatically African in their population and their outlook. This Swahili civilization never penetrated more than a few miles from the coast, but along the coast itself there grew up cities and settlements whose accumulating wealth was drawn from the export of gold and ivory and the import of textiles, porcelain and other manufactured goods from Arabia, India and China.

Among these cities Kilwa became the queen of the south, dominating the gold and ivory trade along the whole southern segment of the shoreline. Their contacts with the inland country of East Africa have yet to be fully classified. In this field there remain some major mysteries. Perhaps the most intriguing of these is that of Engaruka, a late Iron Age town of several thousand stone houses whose ruins, unexplained and almost unexplored, lie on a scorching hillside in the Rift Valley not far south of the Kenya-Tanganyika border.

A larger question consists in the precise relationship which linked the many Iron Age cultures of East Africa, traceable in a long string of ancient settlements from the southern borders of Ethiopia to the head of Lake Nyasa, with their affiliated cultures to the south. In general, though, we may safely conclude that all these cultures — from the borders of the Congo basin through Angola and the Congo to southern Africa, and from East Africa through Tanganyika and Mozambique to the slopes of the Drakensberg Mountains in South Africa — belong to the same broad and many-sided community of Iron Age ideas and organization. Often in isolation from the outside world, usually bereft of any fertilizing help from the high civilizations of the Nile and the Near East, facing a continent of great physical discouragement or poverty in food-giving crops and yet repeatedly solving the problems of their environment, these African pioneers settled and tamed one of the world's most extensive lands.

Such was the general reality when the history of Africa was thought, conventionally, to be about to begin. Coming from industrial societies, the explorers and conquerors of Europe easily assumed — and they could really have known no better — that they were marching into a zone of immemorial stagnation. It has taken more than a hundred years to assure the falseness of this implication of a natural African inferiority. The records easily show why. Here and there, true enough, the incoming expeditions from Europe came upon strong societies and stable governments. Stanley, for example, was deeply impressed by the rule and order that prevailed in Buganda. But generally they found little of that sort. And they explained the internecine warfare and confusion they so often met by Africa's natural inability to govern itself in peace and prosperity.

Today we can assign perfectly clear historical reasons for the social and political disintegration which had overcome a large part of Africa by the middle of the nineteenth century. The great systems of the Western Sudan had never recovered from the shock of the Moroccan invasion of the Songhay empire at the end of the sixteenth century, accompanied and followed as this had been by the political and economic decline of North African civilization when the trans-Saharan trade gave way, increasingly, to a sea-borne trade between West Africa and Europe. A brave effort was indeed put forth by Western Sudanese leaders during the nineteenth century to restore the systems of the past, but it came too late and was swept away by European invasion.

To the southward the peoples of the forest had built new states and governments, such as those of Ashanti and Dahomey, but these, more often than not, were linked fatally to the oversea trade in slaves, a commerce which sowed disorder wherever it touched. In East Africa, meanwhile, those Iron Age cultures which had produced settlements such as Engaruka had suffered disastrous invasion by nomads from the north. The Portuguese had wrecked the Indian Ocean trade on which the coastal cities had built their wealth and welfare. The Boers were pushing up from the Cape of Good Hope. These set in motion other pressures, notably the northward-moving migrations of the Nguni and Zulu peoples who ruined the Iron Age states of Rhodesia and opened the way for later European conquest. Even in Central Africa, where stable government generally continued to prevail, the Arab-Swahili slave trade from the East Coast had gone far to disrupt traditional security and peace. But the invaders of the nineteenth century, as the records show, understood little or nothing of all this.

It will be obvious, no doubt, that even without European intervention — whether through the slave trade or invasion — the African Iron Age would have produced many upheavals out of its own inner dynamic. The founding of states led directly to the conquest of other states, just as the enthronement of kings made infallibly for dynastic strife. In all these ways the lord-and-vassal organization of many African states brought stresses and strains no different in kind from those of feudal Europe. Yet arguing from what we know of Iron Age development, and from the not incomparable history of other lands, we may reasonably suppose that one phase of centralizing organization in Africa would have continued to give rise to another and more advanced phase. The crucial point to bear in mind here is that European invasion arrived in the midstream of a tide of transition. It struck Africa at a moment of great confusion that was itself the product of previous events.

Thereafter nothing could ever be the same. Looking back, one may see now that the colonial period was no more than a large episode in the onward movement of African life: in another sense, however, it was an unexampled means of revolutionary change. At huge cost to many peoples, and with a social and human wastefulness that was characteristic of the nineteenth century, the colonial system shattered the traditional molds of Iron Age society, opened Africa to all the winds that blow, and left her peoples to the enormous task of building entirely new ways of life. This last is the stuff of history in very recent years, and is here outside our scope. Yet these modern happenings cannot be grasped in their fuller meaning unless the story of the past is understood. And to understand the story of the past we must also look at the records of the past, in all their illuminations and their limitations, with a new and thoughtful eye.

African and Asian Records

To the early periods of the African odyssey the inscriptions of Egypt and the geographies of the Hellenic world and Byzantium give us few guides, and these of doubtful value. What the Greek writers show is that the whole central mass of Africa was completely unknown but for stray travelers' tales and myths. Nothing exact is said about anything south of the Nile until a Greek Egyptian seafarer published a mariner's handbook to the northerly regions of the Indian Ocean in about A.D. 60, or possibly a little later. This is the famous *Periplus of the Erythraean Sea*.

The anonymous and unhappily unique author of the *Periplus*

was evidently a merchant of Alexandria or perhaps of one of the Egyptian ports on the Red Sea. He describes the carrying-trade between his home harbors and those of northwestern India with convincing detail that may have come from personal observation; but his great value for African historiography lies in his having added a few sections — sparse but of much interest — on the southern extension of the Indian Ocean trade that carried ships down the East African coast as far as Tanganyika. He offers a tantalizingly brief guide to the hazards and advantages of this East African run, noting that it should normally take twenty-three days' sailing from Opone (Ras Hafun, just south of Cape Gardafui on the Horn of Africa) as far as Rhapta, "the last market town of the Azanian [East African] mainland."

Where was Rhapta? Possibly near the modern Tanganyikan towns of Pangani or Bagamoyo, or further south on Kilwa Island: unless archeology discovers a major settlement of that period, we shall never know. But Rhapta was certainly of great local importance, mainly for the export of ivory to India; and Claudius Ptolemy, another Greek Egyptian of the second century, knew of it as "a metropolis of the barbarians." The relevant passage from the *Periplus*, though famous among africanists, is perhaps worth giving again:

Two days' sail beyond [the unidentified island of Menouthias] there lies the very last market-town of the continent of Azania, which is called Rhapta, which has its name from the sowed boats already mentioned; and in which there is ivory in great quantity, and tortoise shell.

The men who lived along this coast are described as being "of very great stature." They have "separate chiefs for each place." But Rhapta itself is not quite independent, for "the Mapharitic chief [one of the contemporary rulers of southern Arabia] governs it under some ancient right that subjects it to the sovereignty of the state that is become the first in Arabia. And the people of Muza [Mocha?] now hold it under his authority, and send thither many large ships, with Arab captains and agents. These are familiar with the inhabitants, and both dwell and intermarry with them; they know all their villages and speak their language." Here were the humble origins of the Swahili civilization that was to flower so brilliantly more than ten centuries later.

After the seventh or eighth century the Chinese contribute a few scraps of information from their capacious experience of the Indian Ocean and its trading ways, while their famous fifteenth-century admiral, Ch'ang-lo, led two large expeditions to the coast of East Africa. As will be seen, these Chinese records yield little of value. For the whole of medieval times we should be almost completely lost without the Arabs. By Islamic times their merchants were firmly established from southern China to eastern Africa, and gradually they built up and published a body of knowledge which is often of decisive value. Until the tenth century, however, their writers worked mostly from hearsay, mingling probable fact with manifest legend. "The land of Zanj [East Africa] is vast," wrote Suleiman the Merchant: "Its plants are all black in color."

We catch the echo of many unrecorded voyages in writings of this kind, transmuted often into fabulous adventures. It was of the Sea of the Zanj that Sindbad the Sailor recounted his perilous tales in *The Thousand and One Nights*. Thus Sindbad recalls how on his second voyage, "aided by a favorable wind, we voyaged for many days and nights from port to port, and from island to island, selling and bartering our goods, and haggling with merchants and officials wherever we cast anchor"; and how on his fourth voyage "we sped on the foamy highways of the sea, trading from port to port and from island to island." Such was the distant memory of seamen who went down to Kilwa and Sofala a thousand years ago.

From the tenth century the knowledge of the Arabs began to be placed on a less tenuous foundation. Four great names stand out in this work: those of al Mas'udi, al Bekri, Idrisi and Ibn Battuta. Unhappily, we are still without good modern editions of the first three of these, and the case with Idrisi is worst of all. He wrote from hearsay, true enough, but his methods were systematic, intelligent and based on determined efforts to learn the truth. Yet much of his work remains unpublished.

Apart from the major annalists of medieval Islam who dealt with Africa there were others — notably Ibn Said and al Biruni —

who have interesting references to our subject, together with a large number of lesser writers who contribute stray bits of information. The only full review of these appears in Yusuf Kamal's extremely rare *Monumenta Cartographica Egyptae et Africae,* but Yusuf Kamal was interested principally in geography and selected his extracts accordingly. An historical survey of these lesser writers remains to be made from the African standpoint, although two Soviet Africanists have lately contributed a valuable beginning with selections from twenty-three Arab writers of the seventh to tenth centuries who wrote on Africa.* Similar research and publication are also needed for such records of India and Ceylon as may bear on African subjects.

What of Africans themselves? Here, as I have mentioned, there is much more to be published than anyone had suspected even a few years ago. Indeed, there is already a great deal of published material that is generally ignored, and I have taken account of some of this in my selections. Literacy was one of Islam's gifts to Africa, and the gift was used. For East Africa, admittedly, it was not used in an African language, Kiswahili, until fairly late, so that the earliest known manuscript in that language, the *Utendi wa Tambuka,* an epic poem written in an Arabic script, dates only from 1728. Yet a Swahili poem is embedded in the traditional chronicle of the kings of the island of Pate, off the coast of Kenya, that may belong to the fourteenth century. Even if medieval Swahili documents are never discovered — either because Swahili was not yet a written language or, more probably, because they have vanished forever — we still have a large body of Swahili writing for the eighteenth and nineteenth centuries, and some of it has clear historical value.

Western Sudanese literacy in Arabic — the scholarly language that corresponded to Latin in Western Europe — goes back at least eight hundred and fifty years, a fact which was proved for the first time in 1939 with the discovery of a number of royal tombstones at Sané, near the old trading city of Gao on the Middle Niger. "Here lies the tomb of the king who defended God's re-

---

* L. E. Kubbel and V. V. Matveev, *Arabski Istochniki, VII–X Vekov* (Leningrad: 1960).

ligion, and who rests in God, Abu Abdullah Muhammad," runs the inscription on one of these handsome plaques of Spanish marble, offering a statement of somewhat narrow interest were it not for the added date, which is A.H. 494, or 1100 of the Christian era. There is every reason to believe that learned men in the empire of Mali, and just possibly of the last phases in the empire of Ghana, wrote about their beliefs and their condition; no such works, unhappily, have come down to us. Among the earliest known documents, there is one that dates from the Muslim year 913 (May 1507-May 1508), but even this (a safe-conduct issued by the Songhay ruler, Askia Muhammad, from which I give an extract below) comes to us at second hand; although I am glad to be able to include, thanks to the generosity and scholarship of J. O. Hunwick, a little of the famous interchange between Askia Muhammad and the North African theologian al Maghili, who died in 1504 but whose works are still well known in West Africa. Up to the nineteenth century the only major works of West African scholarship to have survived, unless others are yet discovered, are a few of those of the great schools of Timbuktu and Djenné in the sixteenth to eighteenth centuries. But these remain important.

Ahmad Baba, who was born in 1556, became the best known of these writers of Timbuktu. He must have been a man of grand strength of character as well as learning, for he refused to serve the Moroccan invaders of his city and country, and was taken in chains across the Sahara on charges of fomenting rebellion. He is known to have composed some fifty works on the law of the Malikite tradition of Islam, as well as a biographical dictionary which constitutes his principal claim to a place in history. He also collected a library that was held in such esteem by his successors that it has still not been, according to the *Encyclopaedia of Islam*, entirely dispersed. Thirteen of Ahmed Baba's writings, of varying length and value, are at present known; two of these were discovered recently in Northern Nigeria, and there is a fair hope that still others will be found. None has yet been published in translation. (See J. O. Hunwick, "Ahmad Baba and the Moroccan Invasion of the Sudan," in *Journal* of the Historical Society of Nigeria, 1963.)

Early Christianity promoted literacy in the three Christian kingdoms of Nubia and in Ethiopia, but most of the Nubian records, whether in Nubian or Greek, are missing. Monasteries flourished for several hundred years along the Middle Nile in this land that had once been Kush, and even, as recent archeological inquiry has shown, as far west as Darfur and possibly still further west. Little is known of the life that was lived in them. The records of Ethiopia, while occupying a special and rather isolated place in the wider African picture, are fortunately in better case.

These records of Ethiopia may be said to have begun with the Egyptians. There are stray references to "the land of Punt" — the Ethiopian shore of the Red Sea or that of northern Somalia — from very early times, but it is not until the famous expedition of Queen Hatshepsut's sailors in the fifteenth century B.C. that we receive any details of the country and its people. The inscriptions and engravings at Hatshepsut's funeral palace of Deir el-Bahri are rightly famous for their references to Punt. In about the middle of the fourth century the Ethiopian court and state religion became Christian, with Greek for its religious and diplomatic language, but Ge'ez, the language of the country, soon won supremacy. The scriptures were translated into Ge'ez, apparently by erudite monks from Syria, within about a hundred years of the Christian conversion. An ambassador of the Byzantine Emperor Justinian has left a lively description of his arrival at the Ethiopian court, with the king standing on a four-wheeled chariot drawn by four elephants. Another Greek traveler of the sixth century, Cosmas, made some notes on the main Ethiopian port of Adulis. For a long time after this Ethiopia was the scene of invasions and internal wars. The kings were hard-pressed. Now and then we get a shaft of light from these dark ages. Towards the end of the tenth century, according to the *History of the Patriarchs of Alexandria*, the Ethiopian king appeals for aid to George, the king of Christian Nubia. His country is being ravaged by a pagan queen. Churches burn. The people face enslavement.

Things improve with the thirteenth century, a period of literary renaissance. Many books are translated from Greek and Arabic, bearing mostly on the history of Christianity and moral themes.

But now the contemporary life of the country begins to be written down. The legends of the past are also put into new and memorable guise, most notably with the *Kebra Nagast* or *Glory of Kings,* a fourteenth-century panorama of "history" in which the Ethiopian kings are traced back to Moses, and the claim is made that the Ethiopians possess the true Ark of the Covenant together with the Tables of the Law that Moses brought down from the mountain after his interview with God.

For West Africa, the seventeenth century yields two works of central importance from the school of Timbuktu, those of Mahmud Kati and Abderrahman es-Sa'di. This is the latter part of a period celebrated for its high attachment to book learning by Leo Africanus, Hassan ben Muhammad el Wazzan es Zayyati, whose valuable description of the Western Sudan was first published by a Venetian in the middle of the sixteenth century. And with the eighteenth and nineteenth centuries the field of surviving African manuscripts in Arabia becomes broader and includes many West African lands. Some peoples, like the Kotoko of Lake Chad, begin using an Arabic script to write their own languages. None of these writings, perhaps, is more interesting for the light it throws on learning and sophistication than the diplomatic correspondence of 1813 between Sultan Muhammad Bello of Sokoto and his neighbor and opponent, Sheikh Amin ibn Muhammad of Bornu. These two eminent men argued the case for and against the holy war of the Fulani in letters that may still be read with enjoyment. Readers will find them in Charles Smith's English translation of the *Infaq al-Maysur* (London 1951), while Thomas Hodgkin has included several long extracts in his *Nigerian Perspectives* (Oxford, 1960).

From about the seventeenth century a number of West African peoples of the forest zone also began to feel the need for writing, and some more or less rudimentary scripts were invented, beginning with that of the Vai (Liberia-Sierra Leone). It is possible that the Bini of Benin had used a pictographic form of writing in earlier times, but the evidence remains inconclusive. Interesting though they are, none of these scripts has yielded documentary evidence of any value to the study of history. It remains to add that from about the middle of the eighteenth century, or soon after, Africans who had been enslaved and won their freedom began publishing memoirs in Europe, notably Olaudah Equiano of Iboland in southern Nigeria and Ottobah Cugoano of Fantiland in southern Ghana.

The Western Contribution

This begins in late medieval times with the Portuguese voyages down the western coast, but remains very sparse until the end of the fifteenth century. Writers were not yet interested in history, for the concept of social evolution was entirely foreign to the mental atmosphere in which they lived. When that most valiant mariner of Portugal, Diogo Cão, had carried his little ships to the waters of the Congo estuary in 1482, he set up a stone on this distant shore whose inscription (at least according to a later reproduction) declared that the year was also that of "1681 of the creation of the world." The earliest chronicles and memoirs therefore give us little more than tales of mere discovery, often marvelously vivid and convincing, as with Zurara's book of 1453 about the first voyages beyond the Moroccan coast, but never seeking to assess the background of development that lay behind African peoples who were now brought into communication with Europe.

The situation improves with the end of the fifteenth century. Now the king of Portugal enters into an alliance with the king of Congo, and information begins to filter back to Lisbon from envoys and missionaries. Diaz and da Gama pass the Cape of Good Hope, and aboard da Gama's flagship there is a writer who keeps a daily logbook, a *roteiro*, which has most fortunately survived. Some twenty years later a Portuguese priest called Francisco Alvares brings home a detailed description of Ethiopia Other mariners and travelers add their memoirs and reports of Guinea and the

East Coast. Few of these will be published for several hundred years, but these few are valuable in offering Europe its first real insight into the lands beyond the southern skyline.

Some of these early books were lucky to see the light at all. Often enough they told too many commercial secrets or set the explorers in a bad light. Censorship suppressed them. Between 1552 and 1563 the Portuguese annalist João de Barros, working on official archives in Lisbon, published the first three sections of his *Decadas da Asia*, an epic of Portuguese discovery. His work was continued by Diogo de Couto, also an official historian, who brought out four more sections before he died in 1616. One of these, the sixth, found disfavor with those who wished to conceal the course of Portuguese oversea loot and conquest, and was burnt after being printed; later on, permission was given for a somewhat doctored version. The eighth and ninth sections of the *Decadas da Asia* were stolen while still in manuscript, presumably for the same reason as the sixth had been seized and destroyed, and were rewritten in abstract from da Couto's memory. Yet even these versions were not published until much later, the last of them in 1736. The eleventh section was written but has never been found, while five parts of the twelfth section appeared in 1645. The tenth was not published until 1788. All this helps to explain why nineteenth-century historians could so easily overlook the writings of the past. Even to this day many thousands of old Portuguese documents bearing on Africa have still to be published.

Other European peoples besides the Portuguese wanted information which could guide their merchants and seamen. Soon after the middle of the sixteenth century Giovanni Ramusio, secretary to the rulers of the seafaring city of Venice, published in Italian a number of descriptions of Africa and other distant countries. An Englishman called Richard Hakluyt followed after 1597 with his famous *Principal Navigations, Voyages, Traffics and Discoveries of the English Nation*, a labor of collection and publication that was carried on after 1616 by Samuel Purchas.

All through the sixteenth century, moreover, material was piling up in secret archives which have become partly accessible, as we have seen, in recent times. A valuable collection of documents on the old Congo kingdoms, laid away in the Vatican archives, has lately appeared under the editorship of Monsignor J. Cuvelier and Abbé L. Jadin; and other such collections may also appear in the near future. Some curious books came out at the time, notably the tale of an English seaman, Andrew Battell, who spent about eighteen years in Angola during the Yaga invasions, and wrote a lively if somewhat lurid account of what he saw.

But now the period of mere discovery was giving way to that of a systematic commercial and diplomatic intercourse. The seventeenth century saw the final collapse of the Spanish-Portuguese monopoly of control over access to the New World and the West Coast of Africa, the massive intrusion of the English and the French and others into these Iberian preserves, and a vast extension of the oversea carrying trade. This ushered in the period of the slave trade to the Americas. All this had a wide and various impact on European ignorance of Africa. The unknown fate of agents sent to the Guinea Coast, the failure of companies and corporations established for oversea commerce, the fear that rival nations would outpace one's own nation in the race for trade: these were the kind of reasons that promoted a new spirit of inquiry among the politicians and businessmen of Western Europe. From about 1620 onwards the European records swell in ever-growing volume.

The Dutch were the best reporters of the seventeenth century. Of all the maritime nations of that time they were the most advanced in science and the least obstructed by religious superstition: more often than those of other nations, their ships carried men who were capable of describing what they really saw, and of seeing it with the eye of understanding. They were little burdened by a sense of missionary obligation and were therefore less inclined to condemn and despise the ways of strange peoples. It is to them that we owe the best early descriptions of African life.

Solid Dutch reporting goes back, indeed, to the previous century. For Africa it begins with van Linschoten's voyage to India. But the outstanding work of the period was that of a geographer, Olfert Dapper, who published at Amsterdam in 1668 a book that is perhaps the most valuable of all the old anthologies and summaries of travelers' tales. Sixty years earlier, true enough, there had been interesting references to life at Benin in a work by De Bry, who used information from someone called "D. R." (possibly Diereck Ruiters); but it is only with Dapper that we can feel ourselves on the firm ground of far-ranging information. Though never in Africa himself, Dapper (like Idrisi five hundred years before him) collected information from many contemporary sources, though mainly from his own fellow-countrymen, and notably from an otherwise unidentified Samuel Blomert. My only reason for not giving him more space in this selection is that he has been much anthologized and quoted. Borrowing from Dapper is an old habit. John Barbot did it, though without acknowledgment, and so did William Bosman. But these two, so long as they are writing of their own experiences and observation as trading agents on the Guinea Coast (the one in the last quarter of the seventeenth century, the other at the turn of the eighteenth) are full of vivid things to say; and I have drawn accordingly on some of their less well-known passages.

By now, we may observe, two contrary processes were at work in shaping the attitude of Europeans who went to Africa. The brutalizing pressures that were set in motion by the oversea slave trade built up a deep contempt for Africans, just as they certainly encouraged a no less profound African dislike of Europeans. At the same time there were the beginnings in Europe of a genuinely scientific interest in the nature of humanity, including humanity in Africa. These opposing strands of thought and emotional reaction continued side by side throughout the whole period, though it was only with the eighteenth century that the "scientific travelers," of whom the Frenchman Adanson was perhaps the first, began to publish their reports. Meanwhile Europe fed on the coarse and violent stories of the slave trade.

"I sent my pinnace ashore," reports the master of the *James* in 1675, "to know if they would deliver me any slaves and corn. They said they had no orders, but would have had goods, and I had no orders to go into the road. I also sent for 30 pairs of shackles I had lent them and they told my mate they had slaves in them [i.e., in the shackles] and could not let them out lest they [the captives] should run away."

Reporting to his employers three years later, the master of the *Arthur* offered a day-by-day account of the slaves he had bought. On March 6, 1678, for example, "we bought three men and one woman . . . very good negroes not forgetting your honors' orders that none should exceed the age of fourteen, nor be under the age of twelve . . ." Death was common aboard the *Arthur* on that voyage as on so many others: "this day died one man . . . this day died one woman . . ."

"There is put aboard your ship," the English Guinea Company was writing to one of its masters in 1651, "thirty pairs of shackles and bolts for such of your negroes as are rebellious, and we pray you be very careful to keep them under. Let them have their food in due season so that they should not rise against you, as they have done on other ships." No one can read these copious records of slaving and shackling and killing and dying without being steadily amazed at the toll of sorrow in those years; yet somehow the sorrow continued and the toll mounted steadily upward, as though the men and merchants involved were powerless to free themselves from a course of degradation to which, it must have often seemed, there could never be an end.

As to the scientific travelers, they were mostly physicians and surgeons. I have brought in several of them here, my own favorite being Dr. Thomas Winterbottom, an English physician who served the infant colony of Sierra Leone. His good sense and breadth of interest come as a wonderfully sweet relief after the diet of fear, violence and blinkered prejudice in which the records of the seventeenth and eighteenth centuries otherwise abound. Those were times when the notion of Africans as "natural slaves" had gone far to form the general legend and mythology of "backward children" that was to surround the great imperial epoch. Part of this myth was that most Africans were liable to eat each other for choice and diet at almost any time (what many Africans, as it happened, also believed of most Europeans). Winterbottom concluded that cannibalism was nonexistent not only in Sierra Leone "but for many hundred leagues to the northward and southward." He found, however, that the inhabitants of these lands "had no scruple of accusing other nations at a distance, whom they barely know by name, of cannibalism" — a kindliness to neighbors, we may note, in which these peoples were scarcely alone.

With Winterbottom, moreover, we find the first clear picture of the evils of intensive slaving to which many peoples of the Guinea Coast were now subjected. "Although," he wrote, "Europeans have carried on the trade with the natives of the western coast of Africa for many centuries, the latter have no cause to rejoice in the intercourse. Instead of introducing amongst the Africans what they pride themselves in possessing, the boasted arts of civilized life — to say nothing of the slave trade, the natural effects of which in degrading and brutalizing the human character are sufficiently apparent — Europeans have taught them only the vices of their own countries . . ."

This note of condemnation grows stronger with the end of the eighteenth century and the success of the critics of the slave trade. "I need not mention," writes Captain Philip Beaver, a naval philanthropist, in 1805, "the various modes which Europeans also take to overreach the Africans in trade, by light weights, short measure and diminished capacity etc., all of which are now so well known to the natives as to us; and therefore, as before observed, they [the Africans] consider us as a compound of treachery and deceit. There is nothing degrading, nothing base, nothing infamous, but what they consider to form part of the white character." Beaver also had something to say on the subject of racial prejudice, and this too sounded a new note. Of some white women on the West Coast he remarks that these "had been very well treated by the Canabacs, for which they were probably indebted to the national prejudice of these people, who look upon white women rather as objects of disgust than desire. Their devil is white . . ."

The religious travelers and workers, who dealt in souls and not in bodies, were nicer in their language, having less provocation to be otherwise: besides, many of them were traumatically shocked by what they saw and experienced. Even so, the Christianity of this period of Europe had become as firmly fixed in the toils of racial or national discrimination as a great religion well may; and it was widely taken for granted by men and women of good will that an absence of Christianity must mean not only spiritual misfortune but also, and perhaps worse, utter moral darkness. From this notion of a *necessary* heathen or non-Christian immorality there also flowed in later years the grand colonial doctrine of a natural human inferiority among Africans, the notion that was expressed so often by the advocacy of "trusteeship" for Africans who must otherwise remain in misery and chaos.

Even in African national pride, which Europeans of that time might easily have understood from the habits of their own continent, there seemed to be something perverse and ridiculous. Father Cavazzi could not possibly reconcile Congolese self-confidence with a proper attitude to life. These Congolese nations, he was complaining in 1687, "think themselves, with nauseating presumption, the foremost men in the world, and nothing will persuade them to the contrary . . . They think their country is the largest, happiest, most enjoyable and most beautiful there is." No doubt these Congolese attitudes implied an exaggeratedly hopeful view of life in that part of the world. Yet it was one with which a European missionary might have had some sympathy, coming from a continent more arrogant about itself, perhaps, than any other has ever been.

I rather think it is the religious travelers and missionaries who are usually the most disappointing in the records of European reporting on Africa. With a few outstanding exceptions in the nineteenth century, notably Livingstone and Casalis, they were writers who appear to have found it surprisingly difficult to apply the Christian ethic in its teaching about human equality. Time and again their writings are made puny by fits of merely racial prejudice or superstition. Quite frequently, one feels, they are fathers who do not really love their "children," yet who cannot bear, notwithstanding this, that these "children" should grow up and face the world on their own. They demonstrate a kind of "paternalism" that has been common enough in Africa, whether in the regions of Roman Catholic or Protestant influence: a poor sort of parentage where "fatherhood" has imposed on others the obligations of love and respect but rather seldom displayed those qualities itself.

Viewed historically, however, the great weakness of Christianity in Africa, as a force for unity and progress and therefore enlightenment, seems to have been a long failure to emancipate itself from the imperial establishment; and this, too, has diminished the value of missionary records. In this respect its achievements compare unfavorably with those of Islam. Judged by results, Islam has promoted the idea of human equality far more effectively than Christianity, and this has been the case not only between different peoples — conquerors and conquered, immigrants and aboriginals — but also within individual societies. If Islam has continued to make converts in Africa at the expense of Christian endeavor, this may have been in no small measure because Islam has often offered a wider and more practical sense of personal emancipation. Sometimes, as with the Tijaniyya of the Western Sudan in the nineteenth century, branches of Islam have had for Africans the same tremendous appeal as had Nonconformist Christianity for the dispossessed peasants and proletariat of industrial England. So far as the Christian records are concerned — though we shall see that there have been a good many exceptions to this rule — the historians of the future will draw more nourishment from the documents and manifestos of African Christianity over the past fifty years or so, for it has been through these that the authentic voice of Africa has lately spoken.

Another valuable source of light emerges from European and American efforts to establish colonies in West Africa where liberated slaves could find their freedom in a new life. Through these doors there came to Africa not only men and women out of bondage, but ideas as well; and it may yet be found, as the study of African history goes deeper, that some of these ideas became part of the political consciousness of the independent Africa that was to emerge a hundred and fifty years afterwards. Both the French and American revolutions were important in this respect.

Some of the earlier ideas of this kind read strangely now. Consider, for example, the founding ideas of Sierra Leone. Its main promoter, the antislaving champion Granville Sharp, issued a *Short Sketch of Temporary Regulations* which Christopher Fyfe in his *History of Sierra Leone* has summarized as providing "a constitution bound by a social contract rooted in history, in the institutions of the Anglo-Saxon monarchy, and of Israel under the

judges . . . Every ten householders would form a tithing, every
ten tithings a hundred, collectively responsible for preserving order
and keeping watch against outside enemies, each householder
with a voice in the Common Council." The colonists translated all
this into a code of laws which indicated that they took the spirit as
well as the letter of Sharp's advice. They fixed prices, listed fines
for criminal offenses, provided protection against debt, and much
else besides; but they also, in Fyfe's words, "denied the right of
Governor and Council to interfere in anything but the Company's affairs."

This, of course, was premature anticolonialism, and harsh words
were said against it. For these were years of revolutionary ferment
in France (and, though quickly smothered, in England too), and
it was seen that the colonists of Sierra Leone had caught the influence of that. "They have made," opined the famous Wilberforce
in 1800, "the worst possible subjects, as thorough Jacobins as if
they had been trained and educated in Paris." Rather more than a
century later, one may add, the same note would be struck by a
Negro Jamaican who had made Liberia his adopted home. Combining the traditions of the French and American revolutions in
an African synthesis whose fuller workings are visible in our own
day, Edward Blyden declared in 1903 that "every race . . . has a
soul, and the soul of the race finds expression in its institutions,
and to kill those institutions is to kill the soul . . . No people
can profit by or be helped under institutions which are not the
outcome of their own character."

But between the Sierra Leone colonists, practicing their "African
Jacobinism" by insisting on running their own affairs, and Edward
Blyden demanding the liberation of all Africa and the right of all
Africa to find its own way into the future, there lay a whole
momentous century. By the time it was three parts over, African
peoples in almost every corner of the continent had more or less
unwillingly opened their gates and given their trust to European
explorers whose motives varied from pure philanthropy to the
search for loot, but who were all, knowingly or not, the harbin-
gers of colonial invasion. And by the time the nineteenth century
was fully over, the *indirect* subjection of the oversea slave trade

with its framework of relationships and attitudes had become the *direct* subjection of imperial rule exercised from other lands. The "opening up" of Africa was also, in a profound sense, its closure: what men such as Livingstone had intended as the emancipation of the inland continent became, for other and more influential kinds of men, a mere source of material gain. If many of the agents of European penetration were of good faith and high ideals, their paymasters were all too often nothing of the kind. "We must lose no chance," King Leopold II was writing to Baron Solvyns in 1877, "of winning a share in this magnificent African cake." Less than fifty years later a Belgian official commission in the Congo would quietly estimate that the population of the Belgian Congo had been as much as halved since Leopold's cutting of that cake. These new attitudes bore heavily on the nature of the voluminous records that were now sent home.

The literature of exploration and conquest is as vast and varied as those processes themselves. Yet with a few outstanding exceptions the records are built uniquely to a single dominating attitude: they are the journals of men who look at Africa resolutely from the outside. I am not saying that many of them could have been expected to do otherwise: the important point is that the quality of their observation was circumscribed within a cramping limit, and they must be read today with this in mind. If they tried to understand the minds and actions of the Africans they knew, it was by the way and it was rare. Nearly all of them were convinced that they were faced by "primeval man," by humanity as it had been before history began, by societies which lingered in the dawn of time. This point of view marched in step with Europe's overwhelming expansion of power and wealth, with its political strength and resilience and sophistication, with its belief in somehow being the elected continent of God. What otherwise honorable explorers thought and did may be seen in the writings of men like Henry Stanley or in the actions of men like Cecil Rhodes and his mineral-hunting agents, ready as they were to represent themselves as honest allies of their African friends so long as the "treaties" were secured — the treaties through which "effective occupation" could be "proved" to each other by the governments or private interests which they served and formed.

The same distinctive attitude of the nineteenth century may be seen at a more sophisticated level in the approach of early anthropologists, believing as they generally did that Africa was some kind of "human reserve" where the nature and condition of Ancient Man could be studied in all its simplicity and savage innocence: a reserve, moreover, in which the Negroes occupied the lowest place in the hierarchy of achievement, while the "Hamites" (honorary Europeans, being of caucasoid origin) were responsible, in the words of no less an authority than the late C. G. Seligman, for any good thing that might have got itself done. "It would not be very wide of the mark," wrote Seligman some forty years ago, "to say that the history of Africa south of the Sahara is no more than the story of the permeation through the ages, in different degrees and at various times, of the Negro and Bushman aboriginals by Hamitic blood and culture." Racialist declarations such as this will now seem far from the truth — so far indeed that the very existence of ancient "Hamites" in Africa south of the Sahara has become a matter of grave scholarly doubt — but they were the natural outcome of the Europocentrism which accompanied the years of discovery and conquest.

Against this background there is only one sound way of reaching an estimate about the historical value of the greater part of these abundant nineteenth-century writings. This is to place them within the perspective of previous and, when that becomes fully possible, also of subsequent records. Historical anthologies of Africa a hundred years hence will ignore most of them; as it is, I have given them significant room in this selection without allowing them to occupy their usually dominant place. There is a minority who are indispensable. Heinrich Barth, for example, remains of primary importance for the Western Sudan. Some of the explorers of southern Africa, whether lay or missionary, are of the same kind. Without men like Abbadie in Ethiopia, Krapf and Rebmann in the interior and Burton along the coast of East Africa, and a good many others, we should be hard put to "make the joint" between discovery and later invasion or, as it was generally called, "occupation by treaty." But the work of these explorers must now be laid alongside the purely African record, whether known in writing, in orally remembered tradition, in the finds of archeology or in the reports of ethnographers. For while the Victorians may be excused for their many wrong and curious judgments, no such justification for ignorance and prejudice exists today. With the twentieth century the records enter upon an entirely new phase of broad enlightenment.

Quite apart from questions of space, my purpose has not been to anthologize the writings of the twentieth century, and I offer only a handful of extracts to whet the appetite of readers, for the books are quickly available in any good library. Besides, the records of oral tradition, ethnography and archeology make hard reading for all but the specialist. What needs to be remembered is that the conception of African history has become a task for workers in many disciplines. But the documentary basis for this great advance, for this intellectual joining of Africa to the mainland of human development, lies none the less in the kind of materials which will be found in the pages that follow here.

There is another theme that will bulk large in the anthologies of the future. With the passage of time we shall better understand the subtle and often veiled process of growth and change in African ideas about many things, and not least about liberty and equality. We shall better appreciate the important part played by the African diaspora, the Negroes of the New World, in reassessing not only their own position but also that of their parent stocks in Africa itself. We shall more clearly see the interaction of African and non-African thought at many points that are now obscure, especially in the nineteenth century. Even then there were discordant voices in the chorus of European self-congratulation.

> Unutterable mysteries of fate
> Involve, O Africa!, thy future state

declaimed the romantic but perhaps farseeing James Montgomery as early as 1841, offering perhaps the earliest sketch of a united Africa in the distant future:

Dim through the night of these tempestuous years
A Sabbath dawn o'er Africa appears;
Then shall her neck from Europe's yoke be freed,
And healing arts to hideous arms succeed;
At home fraternal bonds her tribes shall bind,
Commerce abroad espouse them with mankind . . .

Unity and Continuity

Africa is still far from realizing that vision, but she is nearer to it by many long and bitter marches. The "yoke" is loosened, even largely cast away. In a deeper sense than ever before, one era ends and another begins. Between the Africa of the Middle Ages and the Africa of colonial rule there is no true dividing line to be found: early partnership with Europe shades off into the massive commerce in captives who were bought for slaves, and the oversea slave trade in turn is slowly merged with imperial conquest. It is impossible to say where the one phase ended and the other began. But Africa today moves into a situation entirely new: a situation wherein large possibilities of independence are combined with worldwide connections and an unprecedented freedom of movement.

In this new situation the impact of challenge may be expected to fall increasingly on the theme of inter-African unity; indeed, the temper and content of contemporary African thought already shows this to be so. Without progress towards unity there will be a failure of nerve and a collapse of liberty. I allow myself to suggest this here because the theme of unity is not in fact strange to African history. On the contrary, the unfolding of African social development as we can now begin to grasp it, from records both old and new, will emphasize repeatedly the inner unities which have underlain the great diversity of African life. It is this unity in diversity, continuity in variety, that may reasonably justify the effort to consider African history as a whole, and to show the records, even if briefly, within their continental framework.

Antiquity

*T*HE RECORDS OF ANCIENT AFRICA BEGIN WITH EGYPT. YET THE
Egyptian contribution has been little studied on its African side.
A familiar habit has considered old Egypt merely and strictly in
her relationship to the civilizations of Asia and the Mediterranean.
We have had, in consequence, a lopsided view of the true position.
Egypt's connections with the Middle East have been lit with bril-
liant clarity; those with the rest of Africa have remained in dark-
ness, rather as though they had never been.

In this aspect, too, a new approach to African history has lately
begun to right the balance. The pendulum swings the other way.
Egypt's influence on old Africa, and Africa's on old Egypt, are
seen to have had a fertile past, even a crucial one: a past, moreover, in which Africa's part may have been the greater, and Egypt
the receiver still more than the giver. "Egyptian art," in the words
of a famous Egyptologist, "is the product of the soil of Africa, like
the rest of Egyptian civilization." If the history of early Africa is
unthinkable without Egypt, so too is the history of early Egypt inexplicable without Africa. Ancient Egypt was essentially an African
colonization.

Here and there, reaction against a purely Asian or non-African
interpretation of Egypt has gone to the other extreme. One recent
writer would have it that Egypt of the Pharaohs was a Negro state;
another would trace the Akan of modern Ghana to ancestral
parents on the banks of the Lower Nile. These are romantic views,
sometimes turning on its head the "white" monopoly of history
that so many Europeans have cherished, distorting the complex
subtleties of human growth; but at least they point to the Afri-

can value of the Pharaonic records. If only as a gesture in the same direction, space lacking for more than that, I begin with some of these. In this I follow a distinguished French Egyptologist, Professor Jean Leclant, in holding that "African studies may draw to their great advantage on the immense documentation comprised in the abundant monuments, texts and graphic descriptions of five thousand years of history; and that perhaps the greatest service Egyptology can offer is to furnish, as no other branch of study can, precious chronological points of departure for the ancient history of Africa."

Four early journeys to the southward are recorded on the tomb of a nobleman of Aswan in the Sixth Dynasty (conjectural opening date: 2340 B.C.); three made under the Pharaoh Mernere and a fourth under Pepi II. "These caravans," writes Dr. Arkell in his *History of the Sudan*, "must have left the Nile at Aswan by the Elephantine road, and one route is likely to have been via the oases of Dunqul and Selima, and so by the Derib al Arba'in to Darfur," the Forty Days' Road which a hardy traveler may still use from Asyut on the Middle Nile to El Fasher in the far west of the modern Republic of the Sudan. "Harkhuf brought back ebony, ivory and frankincense from Yam. All of these could have been obtained in Darfur; and even if the intervening country was as desert as it is now — and it probably was not — it would be possible to travel today by the Derib al Arba'in [as Harkhuf did] with three hundred good donkeys — one hundred carrying goods, one hundred forage and one hundred water." Breasted placed Harkhuf among "the earliest known explorers of inner Africa," and Harkhuf's bare descriptions may still be read with the excitement that attends a good report of hidden places and legendary peoples.

Having discovered, the Pharaohs conquered. Here one must imagine a process of two thousand years of enterprise and effort, failure and success. Under many Pharaohs, through many years, expeditions pushed stubbornly to the interior. Settlements were made. Commerce became systematic. And after the traders and raiders there came the armies. Castles were raised, some of them as formidable as any the world has seen. Much of Nubia, much of the country of the Middle Nile, became vassal to the Pharaohs.

It is not until the eighth century B.C. that we begin to hear the voice of those whom the Pharaohs had placed in tribute. Then the tide of conquest turns upon itself for a while, and sweeps up from the southward. The early kings of a Kushite state whose capital was at Napata (towards the region that had once been Irthet or Wawat for the great imperial Pharaohs of an already distant past) seized and held the land of Egypt for nearly a century. Kashta began this northern enterprise. After his death in about 751, Piankhi continued it. Taharqa completed it. Kush became a world power and Taharqa, by way of the Old Testament, briefly entered the European idea of history. One startling document survives from the Kushite side, though others may yet appear. In the twenty-first year of his reign (conjecturally 731), Piankhi put up a granite stela or tablet of stone at Jebel Barkal, not far from his Kushite capital, on which the details of his conquest are inscribed.

Some two hundred years later the Kushite rulers moved their capital southward to Meroë, whose ruins lie about a hundred miles to the north of modern Khartoum. Here they presided over a distinctive civilization which flourished for seven hundred years. The Greeks called it Ethiopian, confusing later understanding of the matter, for the Kushites were entirely different from the ancestors of those called Ethiopians today. Distressingly little is yet known of this Meroitic civilization. To begin with it used Egyptian hieroglyphics, and later a pictographic form of writing that was partly hieroglyphic; but later still — at the zenith of its power in perhaps 300 or 200 B.C. — the Meroites invented an alphabet of their own. Archeologists have so far collected about eight hundred fifty fragmentary texts in this Meroitic script, but nobody has yet succeeded in reading more than a score of words. As the mystery of Cretan Linear B was to Mediterranean history until Ventris read it, so now is Meroitic to the story of African antiquity.

Early in the fifth century B.C. a wonderful Greek of Asia Minor traveled to Upper Egypt, and heard news of Meroë. It is one of the great sorrows of African historiography that he never managed to go any further. Even so, Herodotus had a little to say on the subject that is still worth repeating. He was profoundly interested in Egypt — and by extension in Kush — because he believed that the Greeks had taken a great deal from that part of the world, especially in religion. He also thought, striking once again a very modern note, that continental Africa's influence on Egypt was both wide and deep. On circumcision, for example, "as between the Egyptians and the Ethiopians [that is, the Kushites], I should not like to say which learned from the other . . ." As to the skin color of the Egyptians, he recalls the story of a dove connected with the Egyptian oracle at Dodona. This bird was said to have been black. Why black? "As to the bird being black," says Herodotus, "they merely signify by this that the woman was an Egyptian." Explaining why the Colchians "are of Egyptian descent," he suggests that they may have descended from Egyptian soldiers who had served under Sesostris, a Pharaoh whose armies had invaded the Near East. But "my own idea on the subject was based first on the fact that they [the Colchians] have black skins and woolly hair (not that that amounts to much, as other nations have the same), and secondly, and more especially, on the fact that the Colchians, the Egyptians, and the Ethiopians [the Kushites] are the only races which from ancient times have practiced circumcision." "Black" notwithstanding, it will be rash to build any "racial" conclusions from this much-commented passage: what interested Herodotus was not the "racial" origins of people but their habits and relationships.

Meroë and its sister-cities declined in the third century after Christ, and perished in the fourth. A final blow was delivered by their old trading rival, Axum in northern Ethiopia. King Ezana of Axum, then a rising power, invaded Kush in about 325, burned towns of straw and towns of stone, and fortunately left a long inscription on the subject. Extracts from it will be found below. Though often obscure, this remains a key document.

Lastly in this brief section, the reader will find a description and discussion by a modern writer of another kind of old African document. Rock paintings and engravings are scattered throughout the continent from the far north to the far south, often in abundance and of high artistic value. They bear witness to peoples and cultures which have long since disappeared, but as well to those surviving peoples of the Stone Age who continue, here and

there, to pursue their life in remote corners of the land. These
pictures also belong, if at second remove, to the records of Africa.

HARKHUF

Four Journeys to the Unknown South

First Journey from Aswan [c. 2300 B.C.]

The majesty of Mernere, my lord, sent me, together with my
father, the sole companion, and ritual priest Iri to Yam, in order
to explore a road to this country [of the south]. I did it in only
seven months and I brought all (kinds of) gifts from it . . . I was
very greatly praised for it.

Second Journey

His majesty sent me a second time alone; I went forth upon the
[Aswan] road, and I descended from Irthet, Mekher, Tereres,
Irtheth, being an affair of eight months. When I descended I
brought gifts from this country in very great quantity. Never before
was the like brought to this land. I descended from the dwelling of
the chief of Sethu and Irthet, after I had explored these countries.
Never had any companion or caravan-conductor who went forth to
Yam before this, done (it).

Third Journey

His majesty now sent me a third time to Yam; I went forth from
—— upon the —— road, and I found the chief of Yam going to
the land of Temeh to smite Temeh as far as the western corner of
heaven. I went forth after him to the land of Temeh, and I pacified
him, until he praised all the gods for the king's sake . . . Now
when I had pacified that chief of Yam . . . I found the chief of
Irthet, Sethu and Wawat . . . I descended with three hundred

From J. H. Breasted, *Ancient Records of Egypt* (Chicago: 1906), vol. 1,
pars. 333-336 and 353.

asses laden with incense, ebony, heknu, grain, (panthers), ivory, (throw-sticks), and every good product. Now when the chief of Irthet, Sethu, and Wawat saw how strong and numerous was the troop of Yam, which descended with me to the court, and the soldiers who had been sent with me, (then) this (chief) brought and gave to me bulls and small cattle, and conducted me to the roads of the highlands of Irthet, because I was more excellent, vigilant, and —— than any count, companion or caravan-conductor who had been sent to Yam before. Now when the servant there [i.e., himself] was descending to the court (of the Pharaoh), one [i.e., the Pharaoh] sent the . . . master of the bath, Khuni, upstream with a vessel laden with date wine, (cakes), bread and beer . . .

Fourth Journey

This time Harkhuf returned with "a dancing dwarf of the god from the land of the spirits, like the dwarf which the treasurer Burded brought from Punt in the time of Isesi." Informed of this, the Pharaoh writes as follows.

Come northward to the court immediately; thou shalt bring this dwarf with thee, which thou bringest living, prosperous and healthy from the land of the spirits, for the dances of the god, to rejoice and (gladden) the heart of the king of Upper and Lower Egypt, Neferkere, who lives forever. When he goes down with thee into the vessel, appoint excellent people, who shall be beside him on each side of the vessel; take care lest he fall into the water. When (he) sleeps at night appoint excellent people, who shall sleep beside him in his tent; inspect ten times a night. My majesty desires to see this dwarf more than the gifts of Sinai and of Punt . . .

PEPI-NAKT
Early Empire-Building

This nobleman of Aswan on the Middle Nile was sent by Pepi II —
late third millenium B.C. — on two imperial expeditions southward
into the Nubian lands of Wawat and Irthet, thus preparing the way for
later conquests. His inscriptions survive.

First Expedition to Nubia

The majesty of my lord sent me, to hack up Wawat and Irthet.
I did so that my lord praised me. I slew a great number there consisting of chiefs' children and excellent commanders . . . I brought
a great number of them to the court as living prisoners, while I was
at the head of many mighty soldiers as a hero. The heart of my lord
was satisfied with me in every commission with which he sent me.

Second Expedition

Now, the majesty of my lord sent me to pacify these countries.
I did so that my lord praised me exceedingly, above everything. I
brought the two chiefs of these countries to the court in safety,
bulls and live (goats) . . . together with chiefs' children, and the
two commanders of ——— who were with them . . .

From J. H. Breasted, *Ancient Records of Egypt* (Chicago: 1906), vol. 1,
pars. 358 ff.

TUTHMOSIS III
Trade and Tribute

From very early times the Egyptians also traded with Punt, which may be placed at the southern extremity of the Red Sea and the north coast of modern Somalia. One great expedition ordered by Queen Hatshepsut (1490-1468 B.C. by Gardiner's conjectural dating) is marvelously recorded in the queen's temple at Deir el-Bahri. Here, together with many inscriptions, are depicted scenes of Punt, a "portrait" of the chief of Punt and another of his wife, who rides upon a donkey: the earliest pictorial records of Africa "south of the Sahara," together with an explicit list of "the loading of the ships very heavily with marvels of the country of Punt." Hatshepsut's coeval, Tuthmosis III, (1490-1436 by conjectural dating) continued this trade.

Marvels brought to his majesty in the land of Punt in this year: dried myrrh, 1685 heket, gold ——— gold, 155 deben, 2 kidet; 134 slaves, male and female; 114 oxen, and calves; 305 bulls; total 419 cattle; beside vessels laden with ivory, ebony, (skins) of the southern panther; every good thing of (this) country ———

(Tribute of conquered Wawat in Nubia): ——— 13 male (negro) slaves; total 20; 44 oxen and calves; 60 bulls; total 104; beside vessels laden with every good thing of this country; the harvest of this place likewise.

From J. H. Breasted, *Ancient Records of Egypt* (Chicago: 1906), vol. 2, pars. 486-487.

PIANKHI
Kush in Egypt

Late in the first half of the eighth century B.C. the kings of Kush invaded and conquered Egypt. An important document on this northward-sweeping enterprise is the granite stela which Piankhi set up at Jebel Barkal, near Napata, in the twenty-first year of his reign, and which is now in the Cairo Museum. Here is its graphic description of the taking of Memphis.

When day broke, at early morning, his majesty reached Memphis. When he had landed on the north of it, he found that the water had approached to the walls, the ships mooring at (the walls of) Memphis. Then his majesty saw that it was strong, and that the wall was raised by a new rampart, and battlements manned with mighty men. There was found no way of attacking it. Every man told his opinion among the army of his majesty, according to every rule of war. Every man said: "Let us besiege it —; lo, its troops are numerous." Others said: "Let a causeway be made against it; let us elevate the ground to its walls. Let us bind together a tower; let us erect masts and make the spars into a bridge to it. We will divide it on this (plan) on every side of it, on the high ground and —— on the north of it, in order to elevate the ground at its walls, that we may find a way for our feet."

Then his majesty was enraged against it like a panther; he said: "I swear, as Re loves me, as my father, Amon (who fashioned me), favors me, this shall befall it, according to the command of Amon . . . I will take it like a flood of water. I have commanded . . ." Then he sent forth his fleet and his army to assault the harbor of

From J. H. Breasted, *Ancient Records of Egypt* (Chicago: 1906), vol. 4, pars. 861 ff.

Memphis; they brought to him every ferryboat, every (cargo) boat, every (transport), and the ships, as many as there were, which had moored in the harbor of Memphis, with the bow-rope fastened among its houses. (There was not) a citizen who wept, among all the soldiers of his majesty.

His majesty himself came to line up the ships, as many as there were. His majesty commanded his army: "Forward against it! Mount the walls! Penetrate the houses over the river. If one of you gets through upon the wall, let him not halt before it, (so that) the (hostile) troops may not repulse you . . ."

Then Memphis was taken as (by) a flood of water, a multitude of people were slain therein, and brought as living captives to the place where his majesty was.

HERODOTUS
A City named Meroë

[c. 430 B.C.] I went as far as Elephantine [Aswan] to see what I could with my own eyes, but for the country still further south I had to be content with what I was told in answer to my questions. The most I could learn was that beyond Elephantine the country rises steeply; and in that part of the river boats have to be hauled along by ropes — one rope on each side — much as one drags an ox. If the rope parts, the boat is gone in a moment, carried away by the force of the stream. These conditions last over a four days' journey, the river all the time winding greatly, like the Maeander, and the distance to be covered amounting to twelve *schoeni*. After this one reaches a level plain, where the river is divided by an island named Tachompso.

South of Elephantine the country is inhabited by Ethiopians who also possess half of Tachompso, the other half being occupied

From the translation of *The Histories* of Herodotus by Aubrey de Sélincourt, Penguin Books, 1954.

by Egyptians. Beyond the island is a great lake, and round its shores live nomadic tribes of Ethiopians. After crossing the lake one comes again to the stream of the Nile, which flows into it. At this point one must land and travel along the bank of the river for forty days, because sharp rocks, some showing above the water and many just awash, make the river impracticable for boats. After the forty days' journey on land one takes another boat and in twelve days reaches a big city named Meroë, said to be the capital city of the Ethiopians. The inhabitants worship Zeus and Dionysus alone of the Gods, holding them in great honor. There is an oracle of Zeus there, and they make war according to its pronouncements, taking from it both the occasion and the object of their various expeditions.

Carthage Trades South

The Carthaginians also tell us that they trade with a race of men who live in a part of Libya beyond the Pillars of Heracles. On reaching this country, they unload their goods, arrange them tidily along the beach, and then, returning to their boats, raise a smoke. Seeing the smoke, the natives come down to the beach, place on the ground a certain quantity of gold in exchange for the goods, and go off again to a distance. The Carthaginians then come ashore and take a look at the gold; and if they think it represents a fair price for their wares, they collect it and go away; if, on the other hand, it seems too little, they go back aboard and wait, and the natives come and add to the gold until they are satisfied. There is perfect honesty on both sides; the Carthaginians never touch the gold until it equals in value what they have offered for sale, and the natives never touch the goods until the gold has been taken away.

EZANA

The Fall of Meroë

A little patience with this famous text from Axum can win from it a good deal of sense. It really offers a vivid report of King Ezana's war against his neighbors on the Middle Nile in the fourth century. By this time Meroë had lost its old power, and the Meroites — the Kushites of Meroë, the Kasu of this inscription — had clearly passed through many troubles. They were still living in "towns of masonry" that were anything but destitute — 'Alwa and Daro in Ezana's report, the former being very possibly Meroë itself — but they had suffered infiltration, and perhaps successful invasion, by the Noba or Nuba. These Noba lived in "towns of straw" — that is, grass-hut settlements — but were evidently at peace with the urban Kasu. However, they were not at peace with Axum, a strong rival for the foreign trade of the region, and they provoked Ezana (or that is what he says) into invading them.

The Noba were of two kinds, the "Red" and the "Black." It was the first of these who most annoyed Ezana. He marched northwest down the Takkaze (the Atbara) and routed them three times, but they were not put down. Then he took the field a fourth time, fought them "on the Takkaze at the ford of Kemalke," and pursued them for twenty-three days. Having got so far, he went further. He "arrived at the Kasu" (the Kushites or Meroites), set up a base at the junction of the Atbara and the Nile, and pushed raiding parties north and south. Those who went south assaulted the "towns of masonry" of the Kasu — their ruins may still be seen near Shendi on the Nile — while those who went north along the Nile (the Seda in Ezana's language) ravished "the towns of straw" of the Black Noba and two towns of masonry of the Kasu which have not been securely identified, but which L. P. Kirwan, whose interpretation I am largely following here,

From L. P. Kirwan, "The Decline and Fall of Meroë," *Kush*, 1960. Mr. Kirwan's translation is from the German of that of E. Littmann in "Äthiopischer Inschriften," *Miscellanea Academica Berolinensia* II/2, 1950, pp. 97 ff.

thinks may have been Kawa and Salam on the Dongola reach of the river.

This is the last sure word we hear of Meroë until the times of rediscovery many centuries later. But the Noba, whether "Red" or "Black," were far from finished. They were the peoples — the Nobatae or the Blemmyes or both of these — who took over much of Meroitic culture, became converted to Christianity in A.D. 543, and built another famous Nubian civilization, Christian and literate, which endured until Islamic conquest many hundreds of years afterwards.

[c. A.D. 325]

Through the might of the Lord of All I took the field against the
    Noba, when the people of Noba revolted,
When they boasted and "He will not cross over the Takkaze," said
    the (people of) the Noba,
When they did violence to the peoples Mangurto and Hasa and
    Barya, and the Blacks
Waged war on the Red Peoples and a second and a third time
    broke their oath and without
Consideration (*Rücksicht*) slew their neighbors and plundered
    our envoys and our messengers
Whom I had sent to interrogate them, robbing them of their pos-
    sessions and
Seizing their lances. When I sent again and they did not hear me,
    and reviled me
And made off, I took the field against them. And I armed myself
    (?) with the power of the Lord of the Land
And fought on the Takkaze at the ford of Kemalke. And there-
    upon they fled
And stood not still, and I pursued the fugitives (?) twenty-three —
    23 — days
Slaying (some of) them and capturing others and taking booty
    from them, where I came; while prisoners and
Booty were brought back by my people who marched out; while I
    burnt their towns,

Those of masonry and those of straw, and (my people) seized
their corn and their bronze and the dried meat

And the images in their temples and destroyed the stocks of corn
and cotton and (the enemy)

Plunged into the river Seda, — and (there were) many who perished in the water,

The number I know not — and as their vessels foundered, a multitude of people

Men and women, were drowned . . .

And I arrived at the Kasu, slaying (some of) them and taking
(others) prisoner

At the junction of the rivers Seda and Takkaze. And on the day
after my arrival

(I) dispatched into the field the troop of Mahaza and the
Damaw(a) and Falh(a) and Sera

Up the Seda (against) the towns of masonry and of straw; their
towns

Of masonry are called 'Alwa, Daro. And they slew and took prisoners and threw (them)

Into the water, and they returned safe and sound, after they had
terrified their enemies and had conquered through the power of
the Lord of the Land.

And I sent the troop Halen and the troop Laken (?) and

The troop Sabarat and Falh(a) and Sera down the Seda (against)
the towns of straw

Of the Noba, 4, Negues, 1; the towns of masonry of the Kasu
which the Noba had taken (were) Tabito (?)

Fertoti; and they arrived at the territory of the Red Noba, and

My people returned safe and sound after they had taken (some)
prisoner and slain (others) and had seized their booty through
the power of the Lord of Heaven.

And I erected a throne at the junction of the rivers Seda and

Takkaze, opposite the town of masonry which is on this peninsula.

DESMOND CLARK
Stone Age Art

One of the most remarkable features of the culture of the Later Stone Age peoples, as we have mentioned, was their pictorial art which, particularly south of the Zambezi, reached an extremely high standard of artistic ability in the naturalistic sphere.

In 1797 Barrow visited a cave in the Bamboesberg, a part of the Stormberg Range, in which a Bushman painter had very recently been disturbed. He had been busy making a drawing of a tortoise, the model for which lay close by, on the floor of the cave. Barrow visited other caves which contained paintings made by the hastily departed occupants. In 1869 Stow attempted to gain an interview with one of the last Bushman painters in the mountains near Tylden in the Kei River Area, but he was unsuccessful. This Bushman was named Gou-wa, and he was then an old man. Stow describes him, from hearsay presumably, as the painter of the family and as still carrying two or three of his horn paint-pots on a belt round his waist. He was the artist who painted the representation of the Boer Commando on the wall of his brother's rock shelter and which was said to commemorate the first attack made by the Boers on this particular band. Stow also says that the last survivors of the "painter tribes" took refuge in the Maluti Mountains in Basutoland, and although he gives no specific date it was presumably in the 1860s that the last of the artists there was killed in the Witteberg Native Reserve. He had ten small horn pots hanging from a belt, each of which contained a different colored paint . . .

One may, very generally speaking, divide the paintings into two main periods, an Earlier Period which is characterized by a "peace-

From J. D. Clark, *The Prehistory of Southern Africa*, 1959. First extract: pp. 255-256; second, p. 265; third, pp. 268-269.

ful" and simple, naturalistic art showing no recognizably modern equipment or peoples, and a Later Period which is essentially that of the Bushmen, when the paintings are less carefully or skillfully executed and show a restlessness of approach and an abundance of complicated scenes of fights, raids, and ceremonies, in which Bushman, Bantu, and Hottentot can all be distinguished. This period might again be subdivided into two parts — an earlier half when the different races appear to be more or less at peace with one another, and a later when the struggle for survival had begun. This last group is for the most part confined to South Africa, in particular the southeastern region.

The beginning of rock art in South Africa is believed by some to date back to the later Middle Stone Age or Magosian times, that is to say to about 10,000-8000 B.C. It is by no means improbable that the artistic tradition goes back to those times, but it is most unlikely that any of the art that survives today is as old as that, unless it be some of the earliest engravings. For example, it is interesting to note that a Magosian industry has been found in the Molopo shelter in Basutoland in a deposit containing a serpentine engraving on the lower part of the cave wall. There is reason to suppose that the paintings and a large part of the engravings date to much more recent times, and it is likely that most of this art dates to a time subsequent to the beginning of the Christian era. Some investigators would put it later still and believe that many of the best paintings in the southeastern group are not earlier than the beginning of the eighteenth century.

Two facts clearly emerge from a study of this art. The first is that there is a continuity running through it which, in spite of the differences of style and technique, holds it together and, in view of its indubitable associations, labels it as essentially Later Stone Age in conception. There is too pronounced a stratigraphical break between the Magosian and the Later Stone Age proper, and often too much exfoliation from the rock surface has taken place between the two, for any of the paintings to date back to Magosian times. Secondly, the earliest examples that have come down to us are much too advanced in conception and execution to represent the first expression of this art and it is certain that earlier, more primitive styles must have existed, though the paintings have now disappeared. It is most probable, therefore, that the origins of this parietal art extend back beyond the beginning of the Later Stone Age proper to the time of the microlithic revolution . . .

A question that is so often asked is, "What was the motive behind this art?" Was it predominantly magical, or was it purely freedom of artistic expression, "art for art's sake," as it were? It would seem that some of the paintings and engravings, in particular the earlier naturalistic ones, were connected with magical beliefs, and especially is this considered to be the case with the geometric art of our Northern Region where the signs and symbols must have had some magical or ceremonial significance. The large animal paintings that constitute some of the earliest art, and the beautifully incised naturalistic engravings, probably followed from the beliefs of many primitive peoples that by drawing an eland, for example, one will be given power to find and kill this animal in the hunt, or that the eland will be drawn towards the hunter so that he may kill it. Or again there is the belief that by depicting a certain beast or by wearing a part of it, the hunter, or perhaps the band, will take on something of its nature. Some of the large and early paintings of elephants in Rhodesia may perhaps be explained in this way as having been made to endow the band with the strength of the elephant.

Other of the animal paintings may represent the totemic ancestor of the group that occupied the site, and Stow has indicated that there is reason to believe that some of the southern group of paintings may have been done for this purpose.

But the bulk of the paintings which represent hunting scenes and ceremonies, and certainly the later ones showing fights with Bantu, cattle raids, dances, representations of everyday events, must be considered primarily as examples of representational art. These are essentially records of events and provide us with most interesting details of the life and habits of the different peoples depicted, and perhaps some day will be the means of filling some of the still blank pages of our history books.

Early West Africa

M ODERN ARCHEOLOGY THROWS LIGHT UPON A DISTANT AND OTHER-
wise silent past. Extracts from two essays by writers of our own
time accordingly open this section. The finding and fixing of the
first Iron Age culture to be clearly assessable in West Africa — the
Nok Culture of the Niger-Benue confluence lands — provides a
starting point for much African history and the likely origins, as
will be seen, of the high art of Ife and its neighbors.

Another wide river of information on preliterate Africa flows
from the tales and genealogies which African chiefs and others
have learned and remembered of their past. But its waves and
spates have to be ridden with care, for the dividing line between
the hazards of genial invention and the safety of navigable fact is
always difficult and sometimes impossible to trace. Yet these remembered traditions must be admitted to the records of history.
Even when their details are doubtful or merely fantastic, the general picture they offer can remain of potent value. Many traditions
reach back usefully into the past, and the reconstruction of history that is now going on takes due account of them, not seldom
finding them surprisingly reliable. It has seemed right to include a
handful of writings drawn from this oral history of Africa. I have
chosen these on the simple plan of illustrating the traditional origins of two or three of West Africa's well-known peoples. Among
these are the Yoruba of Western Nigeria. Did some of their founding ancestors really come from the Nile, from the neighborhood
of Kush, bringing with them the heritage of Meroë, or some of it?
Here, at any rate, is what they have thought about their own beginnings.

With the ninth century the Arab records begin, and with the eleventh we are on the broad high road of accurate notation provided by al Bekri, an Arab of Granada in Spain, whose *Al-Masalik wa 'l-Mamalik* collects with a marvelous clarity and vigor what the Muslim West knew of the lands beyond the Sahara in the same period as Duke William of Normandy was invading Anglo-Saxon England. The position improves again with the rise of the Mandingo Empire of Mali in the thirteenth and fourteenth centuries. Apart from traditions recorded in Arabic by the African scholars of Timbuktu in the sixteenth and seventeenth centuries, we have the eyewitness reports of Ibn Battuta, who sojourned in Mali soon after the death of its greatest ruler, *Mansa* Kankan Musa, as well as the contemporary writings of al Omari and lesser authors. What could be more vividly convincing than Ibn Battuta's tales of the court of Mali, or al Omari's story of a collapse in the value of money when *Mansa* Musa gave the citizens of Cairo so much gold? These memoirs are as good of their kind as anything we have from medieval Europe.

There is a further improvement with the history of the Songhay empire of Gao, for a few of the works of the school of Timbuktu become available. By now, too, there is the long and detailed report of Leo Africanus, especially useful for its account of Songhay political and economic structures, as well as sundry notes from scattered European travelers and collectors of travelers' tales. These last are mainly useful for the peoples of the western coastline, and it is for this reason that I end this section with an extract that is somewhat out of order. Chief Egharevba's justly famous history of Benin sets forth at a point that is much before the rise of Songhay or the arrival of the Portuguese in the Bight of Benin; but it leads on to this last event, and makes a useful link with the early European records.

BERNARD FAGG

The Nok Culture

There can have been few archeological discoveries made as a direct result of open-cast metal-mining which have given such a revealing and intimate picture of a completely unsuspected yet widespread culture as those made at Nok, which is situated very close indeed to the geographical center of Nigeria.

The discovery was only fully appreciated in 1944, when an exceptionally fine head in terra cotta was found twenty-five feet deep during tin-mining in the hills close to Jemaa. This was found to bear a striking stylistic resemblance to a small monkey's head which had been dug up many years before at Nok itself . . .

The area in which the Nok Culture has so far been found, and this we believe may be only a fraction of its actual distribution, has already spread to an area of three hundred miles by one hundred miles lying across the Niger and Benue valleys, mostly north of the confluence . . .

[In 1956] we excavated two large cuts, or "paddocks," in the area reserved for archeological research at Nok and in the second were successful in finding substantial pieces of trunk wood *in situ* in the heart of the gray clay, in the youngest deposits in fact which had so far produced figurines. An analysis of these specimens gave the satisfactory date of approximately A.D. 200. Specimens from the gravels below in which figurine material was found gave a date of approximately 900 B.C. . . .

It is now therefore an acceptable hypothesis that the Nok Culture flourished at least during the latter half of the first millennium B.C. and for some two centuries into the Christian era. How much

From B. A. B. Fagg, "The Nok Culture in Prehistory," *Journal* of the Historical Society of Nigeria, Dec. 1959, p. 288. Mr. Fagg was until recently the Federal Director of Antiquities of Nigeria.

later the style persisted it is not yet possible to say, but evidence is now building up indicating that the art style of the Nok Culture must have survived very much longer . . .

There is now every reason to hope that further finds both in the area of the Nok Culture and in more or less dateable deposits in Yorubaland, Benin and elsewhere on the West Coast will confirm the basic homogeneity of so much of West African sculpture and its derivation from a traditional complex going back at least two thousand years, and at the same time will dispose of the widely held hypothesis that the Ife-Benin complex owes its style and inspiration to origins outside West Africa.

FRANK WILLETT

Two Thousand Years of Sculpture

All the bronzes so far known from Ife (apart from some evidently recent work) are in the naturalistic style, of which far more numerous examples have survived in terra-cotta. A study of the terra-cotta figures reveals stylistic affinities with those of the Nok Culture, already known from a large part of Northern Nigeria, but probably in reality even more widespread. Radiocarbon samples from the type-site suggest that the terra-cotta figures began to be made some time after 900 B.C., probably by a neolithic or early metal-age people; and that the culture may have continued to produce terra-cottas after A.D. 200 . . . It looks very much as if the art of Ife developed from that of Nok . . .

In Ife there are examples of terra-cottas which are almost certainly postclassical, and lead on to the modern Yoruba style. In due time we may hope to find more examples of terra-cottas to illustrate the stages of development from the Nok to the classical Ife style. Some of the sites which have produced Nok terra-cottas

From F. Willett, "Ife and Its Archaeology," *Journal of African History*, 2, 1960.

may be substantially later than the type-site itself, whilst we know that the apogee of the naturalistic style at Ife was not later than the middle of the fourteenth century. The interval between these two dates represents a crucial phase in the history of most of the major peoples of Nigeria, to judge by traditions. In the case of the Yoruba, it seems likely that a small but influential group of people came into Nigeria during this period and established themselves as rulers over an indigenous iron-using population making Nok terra-cottas . . .

As yet there is no direct evidence of who these [newcomers] were, where they came from, or when. They seem to have come from the east or the northeast, possibly from Meroë, which collapsed in the early fourth century, or perhaps they came a few centuries later from Zaghawa or from Christian Nubia. The Yoruba migration legends, both those about their origin and those of diffusion within Nigeria, almost certainly refer only to the ruling group.

Yoruba civilization appears therefore to be the result of a small intrusive ruling class, bringing ideas from outside, with a highly artistic indigenous population. The resulting social pattern seems to have borne some resemblance to that of the City States of Ancient Greece, but the unique achievement of the Yoruba was to have possessed such an evolved urban civilization without the knowledge of writing.

MUHAMMAD BELLO

Where the Yoruba Came From

Sultan Muhammad Bello (1779-1837) was one of a number of distinguished scholars and statesmen of the nineteenth-century Western Sudan (p. 26, p. 322). The English traveler Hugh Clapperton has left

From Muhammad Bello, *Infaq al-maysur*, paraphased and translated by E. J. Arnett in *The Rise of the Sokoto Fulani* (Kano: 1929), p. 16.

an engaging and probably characteristic portrait. "Saw the Sultan this morning," Clapperton wrote (*Journal of Second Expedition into the Interior of Africa from the Bight of Benin to Soccatoo*, London, 1829, p. 198), "who was sitting in the inner apartment of his house, with the Arabic copy of Euclid before him, which I had given to him as a present. He said that his family had a copy of Euclid brought by one of their relations, who had procured it in Mecca; that it was destroyed when part of his house was burnt down last year; and he observed, that he could not but feel very much obliged to the king of England for sending him so valuable a present . . ."

The country of Yoruba is extensive and has streams and forests and rocks and hills. There are many curious and beautiful things in it. The ships of Christians come there. The people of Yoruba are descended from the Bani Kan'an and the kindred of Nimrud. Now the reason of their having settled in the west according to what we are told is that Ya'rub ibn Qahtan drove them out of 'Iraq to westwards and they traveled between Misr and Habash until they reached Yoruba. It happened that they left a portion of their people in every country they passed. It is said that the Sudanese who live up on the hills are all kindred; so also the people of Yauri are their kindred.

SAMUEL JOHNSON
Yoruba Traditions

The origin of the Yoruba nation is involved in obscurity. Like the early history of most nations the commonly received accounts

From Samuel Johnson, *History of the Yorubas* (London: 1921), pp. 3-5. Completed in 1897 but not published until 1921, Johnson's work has been described by Hodgkin as "the most substantial study of Yoruba history yet undertaken," and is based principally upon the oral traditions of the Yoruba Kingdom of Oyo. See also the Benin traditions collected by Chief Egharevba, on p. 95.

are for the most part purely legendary. The people being unlettered, and the language unwritten, all that is known is from traditions carefully handed down.

The National Historians are certain families retained by the King at Oyo whose office is hereditary; they also act as the King's bards, drummers, and cymbalists. It is on them we depend as far as possible for any reliable information we now possess; but, as may be expected, their accounts often vary in several important particulars. We can do no more than relate the traditions which have been universally accepted.

The Yorubas are said to have sprung from Lamurudu, one of the Kings of Mecca, whose offspring were: Oduduwa, the ancestor of the Yorubas, the Kings of Gogobiri and of the Kukawa, two tribes in the Hausa country. It is worthy of remark that these two nations, notwithstanding the lapse of time since their separation and in spite of the distance from each other of their respective localities, still have the same distinctive tribal marks on their faces; and Yoruba travelers are free amongst them and vice versa, each recognizing each other as of one blood.

At what period of time Lamurudu reigned is unknown, but, from the accounts given of the revolution among his descendants and their dispersion, it appears to have been a considerable time after Mahomet . . .

That the Yorubas came originally from the East there cannot be the slightest doubt, as their habits, manners and customs, etc., all go to prove. With them the East is Mecca and Mecca is the East. Having strong affinities with the East, and Mecca in the East looming so largely in their imagination, everything that comes from the East, with them, comes from Mecca; and hence it is natural to represent themselves as having hailed originally from that city.

SABURI BIOBAKU
Yoruba Origins — A Modern View

In our search for the origins of the Yoruba we ought to glance at the Kingdom of Meroë . . .

The modern Yoruba themselves usually confused the Near East with Arabia and owing to the prestige of Islam locate their origin in Mecca. The probable place is Upper Egypt rather than the Yemen . . .

It is almost certain . . . that the Yoruba migrations from the Near East occurred between 600 and 1000 A.D. The Yoruba did not emigrate from their original homes in one mass exodus . . . [but] in successive waves which may be grouped into two major waves with an interval of about three hundred years in between . . .

From S. O. Biobaku in *Lugard Lectures* (Lagos: 1955). Dr. Biobaku is a Nigerian historian who is now in charge of African studies at the University of Ife, and is also the author of *The Egba and Their Neighbours, 1842-1872* (Oxford: 1957).

TAMSIR NIANÉ and SURET-CANALE
Foundations of Ghana

From the third century the Sarakolle kingdom of Wagadu was in full development. The king of Kumbi [its capital] was called *Ghana*, meaning "War Chief," or *Kaya Maghan* meaning "King of the Gold" . . .

From D. T. Niané and J. Suret-Canale, *Histoire de l'Afrique Occidentale* (Paris: 1961), p. 23. Translated here by B. Davidson.

The king of Wagadu early imposed himself on other kings. The kingdoms of Tekrur [in Senegal], Manding [Mali] and Gao recognized his authority; the Berbers of the town of Aoudaghost did the same. The kingdom of Wagadu became a large empire extending from the Atlantic to the Niger.

From the seventh century the Arabs penetrated Black Africa, passing either by way of Egypt or North Africa. Attracted by the gold of Wagadu, the Arabs and Berbers came with many caravans of camels to trade in the towns of Wagadu.

Some of these traders settled at Kumbi where they formed a big residential quarter apart from the royal palace. The Arabs were Muslims, but the emperor and people of Wagadu were pagans . . .

AL YAKUBI

The King of Ghana

. . . the king of Ghana [is] a great king. In his territory are mines of gold, and under him a number of kingdoms, among them the kingdom of Sugham and the kingdom of Sama. In all this country there is gold.

From Yakubi, A.D. 891, translation from Houtsmar Text (Brill, Leyden: 1883) by H. R. Palmer (Sir Richmond Palmer) *Sudanese Memoirs* (Lagos: 1928), vol. 2.

AL BEKRI
Ghana in 1067

Ghana is the title of the kings of this people, while the name of their country is Aoukar [Wagadu in surviving traditions, however]. The king who governs them at present . . . is called Tenkaminen; he came to the throne in A.H. 455 . . . Tenkaminen is the master of a large empire and a formidable power . . . The king of Ghana can put two hundred thousand warriors in the field, more than forty thousand being armed with bow and arrow . . .

When he gives audience to his people, to listen to their complaints and set them to rights, he sits in a pavilion around which stand ten pages holding shields and gold-mounted swords: and on his right hand are the sons of the princes of his empire, splendidly clad and with gold plaited into their hair. The governor of the city is seated on the ground in front of the king, and all around him are his vizirs in the same position. The gate of the chamber is guarded by dogs of an excellent breed, who never leave the king's seat: they wear collars of gold and silver, ornamented with the same metals. The beginning of a royal audience is announced by the beating of a kind of drum which they call *deba*, made of a long piece of hollowed wood. The people gather when they hear this sound . . .

Royal Finances

The king [of Ghana] exacts the right of one *dinar* of gold on each donkey-load of salt that enters his country, and two *dinars* of gold on each load of salt that goes out. A load of copper carries a duty of five *mitqals* and a load of merchandise ten *mitqals*. The

From Abdullah Abu-Ubayd al Bekri, *Al-Masalik wa 'l-Mamalik* (Cordoba: 1067). Above extracts are from French translation of MacGuckin de Slane (Paris: 1859), 2 vols. Translated here by B. Davidson.

best gold in the country comes from Ghiaru, a town situated
eighteen days' journey from the capital [Kumbi] in a country that
is densely populated by Negroes and covered with villages. All
pieces of native gold found in the mines of the empire belong to
the sovereign, although he lets the public have the gold dust that
everybody knows about; without this precaution, gold would become so abundant as practically to lose its value . . . The Negroes . . . known as Nougharmarta are traders, and carry gold
dust from Iresni all over the place . . .

ANONYMOUS

Sundiata's Triumph

In about the year 1240, according to tradition, the Mandingo ruler
Sundiata Keita fought a crucial battle against the Sosso (Fulah) King
Sumanguru, and won. This is generally accounted as the beginning of
the empire of Mali. An anonymous manuscript in Arabic, recovered
and translated by the late Maurice Delafosse, tells the story of this
battle as popular memory recorded it long afterwards.

As Sundiata advanced with his army to meet Sumanguru, he
learned that Sumanguru was also coming against him with an
army prepared for battle. They met in a place called Kirina [not
far from the modern Koulikoro]. When Sundiata turned his eyes
on the army of Sumanguru he believed they were a cloud and
said: "What is this cloud on the eastern side?" They told him it
was the army of Sumanguru. As for Sumanguru, when he saw the
army of Sundiata, he exclaimed: "What is that mountain of
stone?" For he thought it was a mountain. And they told him: "It

From Delafosse, *Traditions historiques et légendaires du Soudan occidental*
(Paris: 1913). Translated here from version in *Notes Africaines*, Institut Français d'Afrique Noire, Dakar, July 1959: French text and valuable notes.

is the army of Sundiata, which lies to the west of us." Then the two columns came together and fought a murderous battle; in the thick of the fight, Sundiata uttered a great shout in the face of the warriors of Sumanguru, and at once these ran to get behind Sumanguru; the latter in his return uttered a great shout in the face of the warriors of Sundiata, all of whom fled to get behind Sundiata. Usually, when Sumanguru shouted, eight heads would rise above his own head.

When they had done this, Sundiata said to Sangaran Danguinia Konnté: "Have you forgotten the taboo?" [A reference to an earlier prophecy of Sumanguru's imminent downfall, and the manner of its bringing about.] As soon as Sangaran Danguinia heard Sundiata's question he came to the front of the army, halted, grasped the arrow (spear?) armed with the spur of a white cock, and threw it at Sumanguru. As soon as it had struck Sumanguru, Sangaran said: "This is the arrow of him who knows the ancient secrets . . ." While he was saying this, Sumanguru vanished and was seen no more. Now he had had a gold bracelet on his wrist, and this fell on that spot [i.e., at Kirina]; a baobab tree grew out of it and carries the mark to this day. [Fifty years ago, it is said, the people of Kirina would still show their visitors a baobab tree which they held to be the same one as grew there on the day of Sundiata's famous victory.]

. . . As for Sundiata, he defeated the army of Sumanguru, ravaged the land of the Susu and subjugated its people. Afterwards Sundiata became the ruler of an immense empire [Mali] . . .

AL OMARI
Mali in the Fourteenth Century

In 1324 the renowned emperor of Mali, *Mansa* Kankan Musa, left his capital on the Upper Niger for a pilgrimage to Mecca, taking with him, it was said, five hundred slaves each bearing a staff weighing five hundred *mitqals* of gold, a *mitqal* being then about one-eighth of an ounce. His passage through Cairo long echoed in memory. Ibn Fadl Allah al Omari, who was in Cairo twelve years after this glittering event, has left a secondhand account which reads with a marvelous veracity, no doubt because he was able to draw on the intimate memoirs of a court functionary whose task it had been to greet the Mali emperor on his arrival at the gates of Cairo. Omari also wrote a description of the empire from information provided by a learned friend who had lived in Mali for thirty-five years.

Traveling through Cairo

During my first journey to Cairo and sojourn there I heard talk of the arrival of the Sultan Musa [*Mansa* Musa, emperor of Mali] and I found the Cairenes very glad to talk of the large expenditures of those people. I questioned the Emir Abu'l 'Abbas Ahmed ben Abi'l Haki, el Mehmendar, who spoke of the sultan's noble appearance, dignity and trustworthiness. "When I went out to greet him in the name of the glorious Sultan el Malik en Nasir [of Egypt]," he told me, "he gave me the warmest of welcomes and treated me with the most careful politeness. But he would talk to me only through an interpreter [that is, his spokesman or linguist] although he could speak perfect Arabic. He carried his imperial treasure in many pieces of gold, worked or otherwise."

From Ibn Fadl Allah al Omari, *Masalik al Absar fi Mamalik al Amsar*, in the French version of Gaudefroy-Démombynes (Paris: 1927). Translated by B. Davidson.

"I suggested that he should go up to the palace and meet the Sultan [of Egypt]. But he refused, saying: 'I came for the pilgrimage, and for nothing else, and I do not wish to mix up my pilgrimage with anything else.' He argued about this. However, I well understood that the meeting was repugnant to him because he was loath to kiss the ground [before the Sultan] or to kiss his hand. I went on insisting and he went on making excuses. But imperial protocol obliged me to present him, and I did not leave him until he had agreed. When he came into the Sultan's presence we asked him to kiss the ground. But he refused and continued to refuse, saying: 'However can this be?' Then a wise man of his suite whispered several words to him that I could not understand. 'Very well,' he thereupon declared, 'I will prostrate myself before Allah who created me and brought me into the world.' Having done so he moved towards the Sultan. The latter rose for a moment to welcome him and asked him to sit beside him: then they had a long conversation. After Sultan Musa had left the palace the Sultan of Cairo sent him gifts of clothing for himself, his courtiers and all those who were with him; saddled and bridled horses for himself and his chief officers . . .

"When the time of pilgrimage arrived, [the Sultan of Egypt] sent him a large quantity of drachmas, baggage camels and choice riding camels with saddles and harness. [The Sultan of Egypt] caused abundant quantities of foodstuffs to be bought for his suite and his followers, established posting-stations for the feeding of the animals, and gave to the emirs of the pilgrimage a written order to look after and respect [the Emperor of Mali]. When the latter returned it was I who went to greet him and settle him into his quarters . . ."

"This man," el Mehmendar also told me, "spread upon Cairo the flood of his generosity: there was no person, officer of the [Cairo] court or holder of any office of the [Cairo] sultanate who did not receive a sum in gold from him. The people of Cairo earned incalculable sums from him, whether by buying and selling or by gifts. So much gold was current in Cairo that it ruined the value of money." . . .

Let me add [continues Omari] that gold in Egypt had enjoyed

a high rate of exchange up to the moment of their arrival. The gold *mitqal* that year had not fallen below twenty-five drachmas. But from that day [of their arrival] onward, its value dwindled; the exchange was ruined, and even now it has not recovered. The *mitqal* scarcely touches twenty-two drachmas. That is how it has been for twelve years from that time, because of the great amounts of gold they brought to Egypt and spent there.

The Empire of Mali

The king of this country is known to the people of Egypt as the king of Tekrur [roughly, inland Senegal]; but he himself becomes indignant when he is called thus, since Tekrur is only one of the countries of his empire. The title he prefers is that of lord of Mali, the largest of his states; it is the name by which he is most known. He is the most important of the Muslim Negro kings; his land is the largest, his army the most numerous; he is the king who is the most powerful, the richest, the most fortunate, the most feared by his enemies and the most able to do good to those around him.

His kingdom consists of the lands of Gana, Zagun, Tirakka, Tekrur, Bambugu, Zarquatabana, Darmura, Zaga, Kabora, Baraguri, Gao-gao. The inhabitants of Gao-gao are of the tribes of Yarten. The region of Mali is that where the residence of the king is situated [in] the town of Niane,* and all the other regions are dependent on it; it has the official name of Mali because it is the capital of this kingdom which also includes towns, villages and centers of population to the number of fourteen.

The honorable and truthful Sheikh Abu Sa'id Otman ed Dukkali, who has lived in the town of Niane for thirty-five years and traveled throughout the kingdom, has told me that this is square in shape, being four months [of travel] in length and at least as much in breadth . . .

The sultan of this country has sway over the land of the "desert of native gold," whence they bring him gold every year. The inhabitants of that land are savage pagans whom the sultan would subject to him if he wished. But the sovereigns of this kingdom

* Near Siguiri on the right bank of the Upper Niger, on the frontier of the Guinea and Mali Republics. A small village still exists there.

have learned by experience that whenever one of them has conquered one of these gold towns, established Islam there and
sounded the call to prayer, the harvest of gold dwindles and falls to
nothing, meanwhile it grows and expands in neighboring pagan
countries. When experience had confirmed them in this observation, they left the gold country in the hands of its pagan inhabitants, and contented themselves with assuring their obedience and
paying tribute.

Reception at Court

The sultan of this kingdom presides in his palace on a great
balcony called *bembe* where he has a great seat of ebony that is
like a throne fit for a large and tall person: on either side it is
flanked by elephant tusks turned towards each other. His arms
stand near him, being all of gold, saber, lance, quiver, bow and
arrows. He wears wide trousers made of about twenty pieces [of
stuff] of a kind which he alone may wear. Behind him there stand
about a score of Turkish or other pages which are bought for him
in Cairo: one of them, at his left, holds a silk umbrella surmounted by a dome and a bird of gold: the bird has the figure
of a falcon. His officers are seated in a circle about him, in two rows,
one to the right and one to the left; beyond them sit the chief
commanders of his cavalry. In front of him there is a person who
never leaves him and who is his executioner; also another who
serves as intermediary [that is, official spokesman] between the
sovereign and his subjects, and who is named the herald. In front
of them again, there are drummers. Others dance before their
sovereign, who enjoys this, and make him laugh. Two banners are
spread behind him. Before him they keep two saddled and bridled
horses in case he should wish to ride.

The Importance of Horses

Arab horses are brought for sale to the kings of this country,
who spend considerable sums in this way. Their army numbers
one hundred thousand men of whom there are about ten thousand horse-mounted cavalry: the others are infantry having neither

horses nor any other mounts. They have camels in this country but do not know the art of riding them with a saddle . . .

The officers of this king, his soldiers and his guard receive gifts of land and presents. Some among the greatest of them receive as much as fifty thousand *mitqals* of gold a year, besides which the king provides them with horses and clothing. He is much concerned with giving them fine garments and making his cities into capitals.

Royal Bureaucracy

It is one of their customs that whenever someone charged with a certain task of important affair reports to the king, the latter questions him on everything that has happened from the time of his departure to the time of his return, and in great detail. Legal cases and appeals also go up to the sovereign who examines them himself. Generally he writes nothing; but gives his orders, most of the time, orally. He has *qadis*, secretaries, offices.

IBN BATTUTA

Travels in Mali

The most traveled of all the Muslim writers of the Middle Ages, Muhammad ibn Abdullah ibn Battuta, was born of a Berber family at Tangier in 1304, spent the greater part of his adult life in wandering about the Muslim world from West Africa to India and China, and died in Marrakesh in 1377. Not long before his sixtieth year he dictated his memoirs to Ibn Juzayy, who made a book of them. A complete text

From Muhammad ibn Abdullah ibn Battuta, *Tuhfat al-Nuzzar fi Ghara'ib al-Amsar wa 'Adja'ib al-Asfar*. The first two extracts are from the English of H. A. R. Gibb, *Ibn Battuta, Travels in Asia and Africa* (London: 1929), pp. 324-325, 326-327, 329; the third from the French of C. Défremery and B. R. Sanguinetti, *Les Voyages d'ibn Battuta* (Paris: 1854), vol. IV, translated by B. Davidson.

of Ibn Juzayy's work was found in Algeria about 130 years ago and translated into French in the middle of the century, since when it has become famous for its unique description of West and East Africa in the fourteenth century. I give a few extracts here as bait for the reader who does not yet know Ibn Battuta, a wonderful teller of tales whose cast of character — whose quiddity — has sting and savor that bring him to life even after six hundred years. With its highly personal mixture of sophistication and simplicity, Ibn Battuta's narrative remains one of the best travel books ever made.

His journey to the Empire of Mali began in 1352. He took the old but still difficult and dangerous caravan route across the western Sahara from Sijilmasa through Teghaza to Walata, crossing, as he says in another famous passage, "a desert haunted by demons" and arriving in Walata two months after leaving Sijilmasa. "[At first] we used to go ahead of the caravan, and when we found a place suitable for pasturage we would graze our beasts. We went on doing this until one of our party was lost in the desert; after that I neither went ahead nor lagged behind."

In Walata our learned friend declared himself shocked by the manners of the women but stayed for fifty days, thence continuing by way of the Middle Niger to the capital of Mali, which was probably at Niane on the left bank of the upper reach of the river. He returned north eighteen months later by way of the Middle Saharan route through the Hoggar mountains, thence westward again to Sijilmasa and so to Fez, "the capital of our master the Commander of the Faithful (may God strengthen him), where I kissed his beneficent hand and was privileged to behold his gracious countenance . . . and settled down under the wing of his bounty after long journeying."

The sultan of Malli is *Mansa* Sulayman, *mansa* meaning [in Mande] sultan, and Sulayman being his proper name. He is a miserly king, not a man from whom one might hope for a rich present. It happened that I spent these two months without seeing him, on account of my illness. Later on he held a banquet in commemoration of our master [the late sultan of Morocco] Abu'l-Hasan, to which the commanders, doctors, qadi and preacher were invited, and I went along with them. Reading-desks were brought in, and the Koran was read through, then they prayed for

our master Abu'l-Hasan and also for *Mansa* Sulayman. When the
ceremony was over I went forward and saluted *Mansa* Sulayman.
The *qadi*, the preacher, and Ibn al-Faqih told him who I was, and
he answered them in their tongue. They said to me, "The sultan
says to you, 'Give thanks to God,'" so I said, "Praise be to God
and thanks under all circumstances."

Pomp and Circumstance

On certain days the sultan holds audiences in the palace yard,
where there is a platform under a tree, with three steps; this they
call the *pempi*. It is carpeted with silk and has cushions placed on
it. [Over it] is raised the umbrella, which is a sort of pavilion made
of silk, surmounted by a bird in gold, about the size of a falcon.
The sultan comes out of a door in a corner of the palace, carrying
a bow in his hand and a quiver on his back. On his head he has a
golden skullcap, bound with a gold band which has narrow ends
shaped like knives, more than a span in length. His usual dress is
a velvety red tunic, made of the European fabrics called *mutanfas*.
The sultan is preceded by his musicians, who carry gold and silver
guimbris [two-stringed guitars], and behind him come three hundred armed slaves. He walks in a leisurely fashion, affecting a very
slow movement, and even stops from time to time. On reaching
the *pempi* he stops and looks round the assembly, then ascends it
in the sedate manner of a preacher ascending a mosque-pulpit. As
he takes his seat the drums, trumpets, and bugles are sounded.
Three slaves go out at a run to summon the sovereign's deputy and
the military commanders, who enter and sit down. Two saddled
and bridled horses are brought, along with two goats, which they
hold to serve as a protection against the evil eye. Dugha stands at
the gate and the rest of the people remain in the street, under the
trees.

The Negroes are of all people the most submissive to their king
and the most abject in their behavior before him. They swear by
his name, saying *Mansa Sulayman ki*. If he summons any of them
while he is holding an audience in his pavilion, the person sum-
moned takes off his clothes and puts on worn garments, removes
his turban and dons a dirty skullcap, and enters with his garments

and trousers raised knee-high. He goes forward in an attitude of humility and dejection, and knocks the ground hard with his elbows, then stands with bowed head and bent back listening to what he says. If anyone addresses the king and receives a reply from him, he uncovers his back and throws dust over his head and back, for all the world like a bather splashing himself with water. I used to wonder how it was they did not blind themselves. If the sultan delivers any remarks during his audience, those present take off their turbans and put them down, and listen in silence to what he says. Sometimes one of them stands up before him and recalls his deeds in the sultan's service, saying "I did so-and-so on such a day" or "I killed so-and-so on such a day." Those who have knowledge of this confirm his words, which they do by plucking the cord of the bow and releasing it [with a twang], just as an archer does when shooting an arrow. If the sultan says "truly spoken" or thanks him, he removes his clothes and "dusts." That is their idea of good manners.

Security and Justice

Among the admirable qualities of these people, the following are to be noted:

1. The small number of acts of injustice that one finds there; for the Negroes are of all peoples those who most abhor injustice. The sultan pardons no one who is guilty of it.

2. The complete and general safety one enjoys throughout the land. The traveler has no more reason than the man who stays at home to fear brigands, thieves or ravishers.

3. The blacks do not confiscate the goods of white men [that is, of North Africans] who die in their country, not even when these consist of big treasures. They deposit them, on the contrary, with a man of confidence among the whites until those who have a right to the goods present themselves and take possession.

4. They make their prayers punctually; they assiduously attend their meetings of the faithful, and punish their children if these should fail in this. On Fridays, anyone who is late at the mosque will find nowhere to pray, the crowd is so great. Their custom is to send their servants to the mosque to spread their prayer-mats in

the due and proper place, and to remain there until they, the masters, should arrive. These mats are made of the leaves of a tree resembling a palm, but one without fruit.

5. The Negroes wear fine white garments on Fridays. If by chance a man has no more than one shirt or a soiled tunic, at least he washes it before putting it on to go to public prayer.

6. They zealously learn the Koran by heart. Those children who are neglectful in this are put in chains until they have memorized the Koran. On one festival day I visited the *qadi* and saw children thus enchained and asked him: "Will you not let them free?" He replied: "Only when they know their Koran by heart."

Another day I was passing by a young Negro, a handsome lad and very well dressed, who had a heavy chain on his feet. I said to my companion: "What's happened to the boy? Has he murdered someone?" The young Negro heard what I had said and began laughing. "They have chained him," I was told, "simply to make him memorize the Koran."

But these people have some deplorable customs, as for example:

1. Women servants, slave women and young girls go about quite naked, not even concealing their sexual parts. I saw many like this during Ramadhan; because it is the custom with the Negroes that commanding officers should break their fast in the sultan's palace, and they are served with food which is brought by women slaves, twenty or more of them who are completely naked.

2. Women go naked into the sultan's presence, too, without even a veil; his daughters also go about naked. On the twenty-seventh night of Ramadhan I saw about a hundred women slaves coming out of the sultan's palace with food, and they were naked. Two daughters of the sultan were with them, and these had no veil either, although they had big breasts.

3. The blacks throw dust and cinders on their heads as a sign of good manners and respect.

4. They have buffoons who appear before the sultan when the poets are reciting their praise-songs.

5. And then a good number of Negroes eat the flesh of dogs and donkeys.

KANO CHRONICLE
The Hausa States

The Kano Chronicle offers precious evidence of the States of the Hausa people that flourished in what is now Northern Nigeria throughout the Middle Ages and for long afterwards, and which were conquered by the Fulani at the beginning of the nineteenth century.

The manuscript of the Chronicle, Sir Richmond Palmer has commented, "is of no great age, and must on internal evidence have been written during the latter part of the decade 1883-1893; but it probably represents some earlier record which has now perished. It is said, and no doubt with some truth, that the Fulani, in their fanatical zeal, destroyed many old records and books, on the ground that they were the books of 'Kafurai,' for their *casus belli* was that the Hausa *Sarkis* [rulers] were infidels, and as such deserved to be destroyed with all their works. The records on which the Chronicle must be based were apparently an exception. The authorship is unknown, and it is very difficult to make a guess . . ."

Diplomacy

The eighth *Sarki* was Shekkarau [who reigned A.H. 689-706 or A.D. 1290-1307]. His mother's name was Auta. When he became *Sarki* his men said to him, "*Sarkin* Kano, what do you see in the talk of the people of this city?" He said, "I see nothing between us except things we can settle without fighting." They replied, "If you try to make peace with the people they will say that you are afraid. If they come to you and make smooth talk, turn away from them; then you would not be acting wrongly. If matters do not fall out thus we will fight them, and if we prevail over them we will cut the throats of all their chief men and destroy their

From the translation in H. R. Palmer, *Sudanese Memoirs* (Lagos: 1928), vol. 3.

god." These counsels prevailed. All the pagans came to the
Sarki with many presents and said: "*Sarki,* and Lord over us, we
come to you to say to you one word: do not take notice of what
we have done, we pray you, but put away the slanderous counsel
of your advisers. If the domains of a ruler are wide, he should be
patient; if they are not so, he will not obtain possession of the
whole country by impatience." The *Sarki* said to them, "Your talk
is true," and left them their customs and power. They said, "Were
it not for fear of what may result we would have told the *Sarki*
the secrets of our god." The chief of them, Samagi, said, "If we
show him the secrets of our god we shall lose all our power, and
we and our generation will be forgotten."

So the dispute continued till the *Sarki* died. Shekkarau was
Sarki seventeen years.

Warfare

The thirty-eighth *Sarki* was Muhammad Kumbari [who reigned
A.H. 1143-1156 or A.D. 1731-1743], the son of Sharefa and Luki.
He was a liberal *Sarki* but quick to anger. His counselors liked him,
but the common people hated him. In his time there was fierce
war between Kano and Gobir.

The name of *Sarkin* Gobir was Soba. If the Gobirawa defeated
the Kanawa one day, the Kanawa defeated them the next. This
state of affairs continued for a long time. In Kumbari's time
Sarkin Bornu Mai Ali came to Kano to war. He encamped at
Faggi for three nights without a battle being fought, since *Shehu*
Tahiru and *Shehu* Bunduu prevented it. He returned to Bornu.
Kumbari went to war with Dussi in the time of *Sarkin* Dussi
Makuri and very nearly entered the town through the fierceness of
his attack, but his advisers prevented him entering the town, saying
to him, "*Sarkin* Kano, you have won the day, go home." He lis-
tened to their advice and went home. In the Dussi war *Sarkin*
Aujera Bugau was killed. Kumbari returned to Kano. In his time
shields were first brought from Nupe, which was then ruled over
by *Sarkin* Nupe Jibrila. Guns were also brought.

AL MAGHILI
Social Reform in Songhay

We know what blistering condemnation was evoked from medieval Christian theologians by the morals and manners of feudal Europe. But what did their Muslin contemporaries think about the habits of the countries beyond the Sahara for which they, in their turn, were required to give advice and precept? One might well despair of finding out. As it is, and by great good fortune, a remarkable answer is to hand; or rather a series of answers.

Some one hundred fifty years after Ibn Battuta had reported on the habits of the Western Sudan, the renowned Songhay ruler, Askia Muhammad ben Abi Bakr Ture (Touré) (r. 1493-1528) put a number of questions to the North African theologian, Muhammad ben Abd al-Karim al Maghili (died 1504). Concerned with everyday things, these questions were designed to elicit a program of social reform. Al Maghili's replies — still well known among the Muslims of West Africa — suggest how strong were the puritanical threads that were early woven into Islam there.

The Seventh Question

[c. 1495] Among the people [of the Songhay Empire, said Askia Muhammad], there are some who claim knowledge of the supernatural through sand divining and the like, or through the disposition of the stars . . . [while] some assert that they can write (talismans) to bring good fortune . . . or to ward off bad fortune . . . Some defraud in weights and measures . . . others adulterate gold and silver with copper, or do not extract the sand

From the translation (1963) by J. O. Hunwick of al Maghili's replies to Askia Muhammad. Mr. Hunwick has established the Arabic text from the two MSS deposited in the Library of the Institut Français de l'Afrique Noire, Dakar, and a manuscript in the Bibliothèque Nationale, Paris.

from gold dust . . . others swell meat (by blowing in air) and mix water with milk . . . Others, when buying goods, take them and go off with them before paying for them. . . . Some will sell a slave-girl and then marry her to the purchaser without caring whether or not she is already pregnant. Then, if it becomes apparent that she is pregnant, they quarrel over the offspring. This happens very frequently.

One of their evil practices [continued Askia Muhammad] is the free mixing of men and women in the markets and streets and the failure of women to veil themselves . . . [while] among the people of Djenné it is an established custom for a girl not to cover any part of her body as long as she remains a virgin . . . and all the most beautiful girls walk about naked among people . . .

So give us legal ruling concerning these people and their ilk, and may God Most High reward you!

The Answer

The answer — and God it is who directs to the right course — is that everything you have mentioned concerning people's behavior in some parts of this country is gross error. It is the bounden duty of the commander of the Muslims and all other believers who have the power [replied al Maghili] to change every one of these evil practices.

As for any who claims knowledge of the supernatural in the ways you have mentioned . . . he is a liar and an unbeliever . . . Such people must be forced to renounce it by the sword. Then whoever renounces such deeds should be left in peace, but whoever persists should be killed with the sword as an unbeliever; his body should not be washed or shrouded, and he should not be buried in a Muslim graveyard . . .

As for defrauding in weights and measures [continued al Maghili] it is forbidden (*haram*) according to the Qur'an, the Sunna and the concensus of opinion of the learned men of the Muslim community. It is the bounden duty of the commander of the Muslims to appoint a trustworthy man in charge of the markets, and to safeguard people's means of subsistence. He should standardize all the scales in each province . . . Similarly, all measures both large and small must be rectified so that they conform to a uniform standard. It is not necessary for the whole country to have uniformity in weights and measures: each province may have its own. But the weights and measures of each province must all be brought into line with the uniform standard of that particular province. It is most necessary that weights and measures be frequently brought out for inspection. Then if anyone appears to be perpetrating a fraud, punish him and turn out of the Muslim's markets . . . It is the duty of the commander of the Muslims to restrain those who defraud and cheat in the most forceful way possible. If anyone obtains wealth by such means, (it should be taken from him and considered) booty which the commander may use for the benefit of the Muslims.

A sale is contracted by spoken agreement and the handing over (of the price and the goods). The purchaser must hand over the money he owes. If he refuses, it must be taken from him by force . . .

The commander of the Muslims must make people observe the practice of *Muwada'a* for ascertaining absence of pregnancy in regard to *all* slave-girls who are normally taken as concubines, even if the seller denies having had intercourse . . . *Muwada'a* means that she is placed under the care of a trustworthy man until she menstruates . . .

Now, what you mentioned about the free mixing of men and women and leaving the pudenda uncovered is one of the greatest abominations. The commander of the Muslims must exert himself to prevent all these things . . . He should appoint trustworthy men to watch over this by day and night, in secret and in the open. This is not to be considered as spying on the Muslims; it is only a way of caring for them and curbing evildoers, especially when corruption becomes widespread in the land as it has done in Timbuktu and Djenné and so on.

The correct and binding thing is that every woman should be taken away from the place where suspicion may arise . . . Anyone whom they [the watchers] see talking to a strange woman or entering her house or gazing at her should be seized and brought (to a judge) . . . [And if no trustworthy man can be found to act as judge in such matters, nevertheless it will be better to appoint someone than merely neglect the evil . . .] However, it is a current practice and State policy in many Muslim countries that, as from the time shortly after the evening prayer, the governor and his helpers patrol the township the whole night long. Anyone they come across in the street is thrown into prison and his case looked into the following day . . .

AHMED IBN FARTUA

Kanem and Turkey

Rising obscurely before the tenth century but continuing long into later times, the Kanem-Bornu empire was the political and economic equivalent in the central Sudan of the great systems of Mali and Songhay further to the west. It had links with these but also with the Fezzan in the north, the Nile Valley in the east, and the peoples of the forest country in the south.

Mai (Sultan) Idris Alooma is remembered as one of Kanem's most successful sovereigns, the probable dates of his reign being 1571-1603. He made many expeditions against his eastern rivals, the Bulala kings, and became the most powerful ruler in the west central Africa of his day. Memoirs of this ruler's life and achievements were written at the time by a man who served and knew him well, the Imam Ahmed ibn Fartua. What follows here is from H. R. Palmer's translation of a copy of Ibn Fartua's *Kanem War of Idris Alooma* obtained by Heinrich Barth a century ago, and sent by him to the British Museum.

. . . We traveled on the Saturday to Bari. The Sultan there gave the order that the troops were not to disperse before reaching Ruwaya . . . On the next day all mounted after arraying themselves and their horses in armor, cuirasses, shields and their best

From H. R. Palmer, *Sudanese Memoirs* (Lagos: 1928), vol. 1.

apparel. When we had proceeded a short distance towards the west we met messengers of the king, the Lord of Stambul, the Sultan of Turkey, who had been sent to our Sultan . . . They were drawn up in order of precedence near the town of Bursalim . . .

The troops of our Sultan were drawn up on the west in rank after rank, leaving sufficient space between the ranks for the wheeling of a restive horse. Our troops charged towards them and they galloped their horses towards us. This continued for a long time until the infantry were tired with long standing. Then the Sultan went westwards and passed through Bursalim and on to Gatawa and then to the river in the neighborhood of Gambaru. He halted there on Friday. Our army rejoiced . . .

O my wise friends and companions! Have you ever seen a king equal to our Sultan or like him at the time when the Lord of Stambul, the Sultan of Turkey, sent messengers to him from his country with favorable proposals . . .

KATI

Bound and Free in 1508

In 1590 a Spanish mercenary led a Moroccan army across the Sahara to the successful invasion of the Songhay empire, then centered on the three notable cities of Gao, Timbuktu and Djenné, and brought to a close the grand epoch of medieval Muslim civilization in the Western Sudan. We are fortunate in having some remarkable testimonies of what that closing period was like.

"Here in Timbuktu," Leo Africanus had written eighty years before the Moroccan conquest, "there are great store of doctors, judges, priests and other learned men, bountifully maintained at the king's cost and charges. And hither are brought divers manuscripts or written books out of Barbary, which are sold for more money than any other merchandize." Of these scholars the best remembered was to be Ahmad

From Mahmud Kati, *Tarikh al-Fettash*, translated here from the French version of the Arabic text by O. Houdas and M. Delafosse (Paris: 1913).

Baba (page 24). But for the history of the Western Sudan in late and postmedieval times we have books by three other men. These cover the large span of 231 years, from 1519 to 1750, while the first two preserve many of the "founding legends" of Ghana and Mali as well as much material from other chronicles, both oral and written. They are the *Tarikh al-Fettash* of Mahmud Kati and one of his grandsons; the *Tarikh es-Sudan* of Abderrahman es-Sa'di; and the *Tedzkiret en-Nisian* of another but anonymous author of Timbuktu.

The first and perhaps most useful of these works came to European knowledge only in 1911 and 1912, when two somewhat dissimilar copies of it were obtained by French administrators at Timbuktu and Kayes. These established that the main author was a Soninke (or Sara-kolle) scholar, Mahmud Kati, who was born in 1468 and lived to the age of one hundred twenty-five, a claim somewhat sustained by evidence in the book itself. Kati belonged to the personal following of the great Songhay ruler, Askia Muhammad (who reigned from 1493 to 1529). He accompanied the Askia on pilgrimage to Mecca, and evidently began work on his book in 1519. His death came in 1593, three years after the Moroccan invasion, but a grandson later worked on his notes and on the notes of his children (scholars, as he had been), and brought the story down to 1665.

The *Tarikh es-Sudan* offers an eyewitness account of a somewhat shorter period but often in more personal detail, while it also adds to stories of the past that are touched on by the *Tarikh al-Fettash*. Its author, Abderrahman es-Sa'di, was born in Timbuktu in 1596, served in Djenné as a notary, became a *kateb* or government secretary, and embarked on a career of official diplomacy after 1629. His book has potted biographies of many scholars of the period, and carries its narrative down to 1655. A note of sadness runs throughout es-Sa'di's writing, for the whole of his life was overshadowed by the disasters he had witnessed as a child.

"I saw the ruin of learning and its utter collapse," he recalls: "and because learning is rich in beauty and fertile in its teaching, since it tells men of their fatherland, their ancestors, their annals, the names of their heroes and what lives these led, I asked divine help and decided to record all that I myself could gather on the subject of the Songhay princes of the Sudan, their adventures, their history, their achievements and their wars. Then I added the history of Timbuktu from the foundation of that city, of the princes who ruled there and the scholars and saints who lived there, and of other things besides . . ." Barth — as shown on page 336 — had the first European knowledge of this book.

The identity of the third author, who composed the *Tedzkiret en-Nisian,* remains unknown. He carried on the story of Songhay, but more especially of Timbuktu, from soon after the ending of the *Tarikh es-Sudan* until 1750, but limited himself to giving little more than the names and principal exploits of the postinvasion pashas of Timbuktu, of whom there were 156 in 160 years.

French translations of the Arabic texts were made by Octave Houdas and published in Paris in 1900 (*Tarikh es-Sudan*), 1901 (*Tedzkiret en-Nisian*), and 1913 (*Tarikh al-Fettash*). No complete English translations have ever been published. I have put these few extracts into this section, rather than a later one, because they seem to fit better here.

The *Tarikh al-Fettash* tells how in A.H. 913 the Songhay emperor, Askia Muhammad, made restitution to three poor scholars who had suffered persecution by *Chi* Ali, a previous and despotic ruler. Having received servants and cattle from the Askia, these men asked for a safe-conduct for all the cities of the empire. Askia Muhammad agreed, "and at once gave order to his secretary to set into writing what he should now dictate." Kati's grandson, who completed this *tarikh,* notes that "I myself have seen this safe-conduct . . . Worms had eaten several lines, and the paper was mutilated by holes at certain points. But here is what it said . . ."

After commanding all whom it may concern to respect and protect the three scholars, the document continues with an illuminating picture of the social relations of the time. The "slaves" should be thought of as serfs or servants within a feudal context and not, of course, as chattel slaves.

We exempt them from all State taxes to the point that no person may demand anything of them, not even hospitality. If any accusation or claim be made against or upon them, none may return a judgment save I myself or those who shall succeed me in my functions. If any of my successors should oppress them or extort the least thing from them, may God refuse His blessing during his reign, may He trouble his empire and bring him to a sorry end . . . I further authorize [these scholars] and their descendants to marry any woman they may wish throughout my empire, from the

Kanta to the Sibiridugu [that is, from modern northeastern Nigeria to the region of Segu in modern Mali] where lies the frontier
between my states and those of the emperor of Mali: children born
of any such marriage shall be free and therefore their mothers also.
We except from this the women of the Sorko and the Arbi: the
women of these [castes] they may not marry, for these are our
property. If any of [these scholars] should disobey this order, the
child born of such a marriage shall be free by reason of its parentage, but the mother shall not be free; as for the mother, none shall
have the right to treat her as a slave so long as she may live within
that marriage, but she shall become our property again as soon as
her husband should renounce her or should die.

The Duty of Vassals

When Askia Muhammad became emperor of Songhay in 1493,
Mahmud Kati explains, he inherited twenty-four tribes or castes of
servile or vassal status.

Three of these were from the pagan tribes of Bambara . . . *Chi*
Baro [the Askia's predecessor] had inherited them from his father,
who had in turn received them by inheritance . . . These tribes
had in fact become vassals of the king of Mali at a time when the
latter was of great power and after having themselves previously
enjoyed authority over the king of Mali . . . They became domestic serfs of the king of Mali . . .

The fourth of these tribes was called Tyindiketa . . . Their
service . . . was to cut fodder for the horses . . .

The fifth were that of the Zanj.* Each Zanj from the Kanta to
the Sibiridugu owed a duty that was exacted every year at the time
of low water on the river. It consisted in ten packets of dried fish
for those who could provide it [or less for those who could not]
. . . And every time the prince was asked for river transport, he
provided it from the canoes of this tribe, together with a crew . . .

The sixth tribe were called Arbi. They were the personal servants and escorts of the prince . . .

* A common Arabic name for Africans south of the Sahara. It applies here to
the riverfolk of Songhay, the fishermen and boatmen of the Middle Niger.

As for the seventh, eighth, ninth, tenth and eleventh tribes, who were blacksmiths, they owed a duty of one hundred spears and one hundred arrows every year for each family of them . . .

Decline and Fall

Kankan Musa set forth [upon his pilgrimage to Mecca in 1324] with large forces, carrying large sums with him and being at the head of a numerous army. A *talib* [disciple] tells me that he heard from our master, the very learned *qadi* Abu'l-Abbas . . . that he [the *qadi*] had asked how many people and in what state the pasha Ali ben Abdelkader departed for Tuat on the outset of his [recent] pilgrimage to Mecca. They told him that the pasha had taken with him about eighty men-at-arms. Whereupon the *qadi*, having rendered praise to God, said: "Everything in this world is perishing. When Kankan Musa left here for the pilgrimage to Mecca [in 1324] he had eight thousand men with him. The Askia Muhammad, who made the pilgrimage later [in 1496], had no more than a tenth of that number, or eight hundred. And now Ali ben Abdelkader, who comes after them, has only eighty, the tenth part of eight hundred . . ."

ES-SA'DI

Djenné

This city is great, flourishing and prosperous . . . one of the great markets of the Muslim world. Here gather the merchants who bring salt from the mines of Teghaza and those who bring gold from the mines of Bitou . . . It is because of this fortunate city that the caravans flock to Timbuktu from all points of the horizon . . .

From Abderrahman es-Sa'di, *Tarikh es-Sudan,* translated here from the French version of the Arabic text by O. Houdas and Edm. Benoist (Paris: 1900).

Djenné is surrounded by a rampart which used to have eleven gates, but three have since been walled up . . . The town was founded by pagans in the middle of the second century after the Flight of the Prophet [i.e., about 850] . . . God has drawn to this fortunate city a certain number of learned and of pious men, strangers to the country, who have come to live here . . .

EGHAREVBA

The Empire of Benin

Like other states in early medieval West Africa, the "forest belt" empire of Benin emerged from the economic and social changes which an onward-moving Iron Age brought in its train. Its earliest beginnings are purely legendary but there is likely to be a core of truth in the legends, for they indicate a probable development as well as a powerful if vague memory of such events. This memory comprises a tradition, an oral history, which goes back more than a thousand years.

Chief Jacob Egharevba, curator of the Benin Museum and a member of the Royal Society of the House of Iwebo, began collecting Benin traditions more than thirty years ago. His *Short History* was published in 1934. Subsequent editions of this indispensable work bear witness to its value. In a foreword to the latest edition, the third (of 1960), Dr. R. E. Bradbury comments on the scholarship and authority of Egharevba's book. "To take one example," Bradbury writes, "it is now extremely difficult to calculate the dates of past *Obas* [rulers of Benin] from sources independent of Chief Egharevba's work, which is relied upon as much in Benin as elsewhere. Nevertheless, his approximate date for the accession of *Oba* Eresoyen has recently been virtually confirmed from Dutch sources which record that an *Oba* died in 1734 or 1735" — the latter being the date which Egharevba gave in 1934. Dr. A. F. C. Ryder is of the same opinion. "Continuing research," he has written,* "will inevitably lead to modifications in any synthesis of oral

From J. V. Egharevba, *A Short History of Benin* (3rd ed., Ibadan: 1960).

* In the *Journal* of the Historical Society of Nigeria, Dec. 1961, p. 288.

and documentary material, but this book will retain a permanent value as the major record of Benin traditional history, and the historian is likely to be continually surprised at the verifiable accuracy of Chief Egharevba's information."

Origins

Many, many years ago, the Binis came all the way from Egypt to found a more secure shelter in this part of the world after a short stay in the Sudan and at Ile-Ife, which the Benin people call Uhe. Before coming here, a band of hunters was sent from Ife to inspect this land and the report furnished was very favorable. Tradition says that they met some people who were in the land before their arrival. These people are said to have come from the Sudan originally.

For over a century the management of the affairs of the country was carried out under different leaders. The Empire of the first period or dynasty was founded about A.D. 900. The rulers or kings were commonly known as Ogiso before the arrival of Odudua and his party at Ife in Yorubaland, about the twelfth century of the Christian era.

Ultimately, one of the prominent leaders, Igodo, was made Ogiso or king. Igodo, the first Ogiso, wielded much influence and gained popularity as a good ruler. He died after a long reign and was succeeded by Ere, his eldest son.

Legend and Fact

It is said that thirty-one Ogisos reigned but very few of their names are known and they are very hard to trace out. Therefore it is wise to make some research into it because some people doubt the existence of the first period of the Benin Empire [up to about A.D. 1200]. This is partly because many mythical and frightful tales have been attached to the people connected with the Ogisos. Whereas, in fact, these people were human beings, ruled by their Ogisos in the same way as we have been ruled by our Obas from Oranmiyan onwards in the second period of the Benin Empire.

A Ruler from Ife

It was some years after Evian's victory over Osogan [tradition-ally, sometime before 1170] that Owodo was banished for misrule by the angry people, who then appointed Evian as administrator of the government of the country because of his past services to the people. When Evian was stricken by old age he nominated his eldest son, Ogiamwen, as his successor, but the people refused him. They said he was not the *Ogiso* and they could not accept his son as his successor because, as he himself knew, it had been ar-ranged to set up a republican form of government. This he was now selfishly trying to alter.

While this was still in dispute the people indignantly sent an am-bassador to the *Oni* Odudua, the great and wisest ruler of Ife, asking him to send one of his sons to be their ruler. For things were getting from bad to worse and the people saw that there was need for a capable ruler.

In order to test the ability of the Binins to look after his son, Odudua first of all sent seven lice to the Benin chiefs to be cared for and returned after three years. This condition was fulfilled and Odudua was greatly surprised to see the lice in increased sizes when they were sent back to him by the chiefs. He exclaimed that "the people who can take care of such minute pests as lice can un-doubtedly take care of my son."

A Discontented Prince

Before he could send his son to Benin, Odudua died, but he left strong orders to his son and successor, Obalufon, that Oran-miyan should be sent there. So Prince Oranmiyan, one of the sons of Odudua of Ife, the father and progenitor of the Yoruba *Obas*, was sent, accompanied by courtiers, including Ogiefa, a native doctor, and he succeeded in reaching the city after much trouble at Ovia River with the ferryman. [The traditional date for the beginning of Oranmiyan's reign, according to Egharevba, is A.D. 1170.]

Ogiamwen, the son and successor of Evian, was much opposed to his coming. He gave it as his reason that it was too difficult to serve a king — "Ogie mianmwen na ga," hence his name Ogiam-wen. But as the need for a proper *Oba* was felt to be so great by the inhabitants, no heed was paid to his advice.

Prince Oranmiyan took up his abode in the palace built for him at Usama by the elders (now a coronation shrine). Soon after his arrival he married a beautiful lady, Erinmwinde, daughter of Osa-nego, the ninth *Onogie* of Ego, by whom he had a son. After some years residence here he called a meeting of the people and renounced his office remarking that the country was a land of vexation, "Ile-Ibinu," (by which name the country was after-wards known) and that only a child born, trained and educated in the arts and mysteries of the land could reign over the people. He caused his son born to him by Erinmwinde to be made *Oba* in his place, and returned to his native land, Ife, leaving Ogiefa, Ihama, Oloton and others at Benin in charge of his son . . .

On his way back to Ife Oranmiyan halted at Ugha, now Okha, in the northwest of Benin Division where the Binis went to him for decisions in their matters for a period of three years . . .

Oranmiyan also halted at Obbah and remained there for over two years before leaving for Ife finally. He did this in order to allow some time for the growth of his son, Eweka I, before going to Ife, so that he might not be sent back to Benin by the then *Oni* of Ife, or, as the Bini say, Oghene n'Uhe. After staying about three years in Ife, he left for Oyo where he also left a son behind on leaving the place, and this son ultimately became the first *Alafin* of the present line, while Oranmiyan himself was reigning as the *Oni* of Ife. Therefore, Prince Oranmiyan of Ife, the father of Eweka I, the *Oba* of Benin, was also the father of the first *Alafin* of Oyo.

Brass-Casting

Oba Oguola wished to introduce brass-casting into Benin so as to produce works of art similar to those sent him from Ife. He there-fore sent to the *Oni* of Ife for a brass-smith and Iguegha was sent to him. Iguegha was very clever and left many designs to his suc-cessors, and was in consequence deified, and is worshiped to this day by brass-smiths. The practice of making brass-castings for the preservation of the records of events was originated during the reign of Oguola. He lived to a very old age.

[The bronzes of Benin are more properly called brasses. While *Oba* Oguola's traditional date is about A.D. 1280 (for the beginning of his reign), there is some reason to believe that the introduction of brass-casting to Benin came from Ife at a later date than Egharevba's account suggests, and perhaps not before about 1400.]

Ewuare the Great

After the murder of Uwaifiokun, Ogun was crowned the *Oba* of Benin with the title Ewuare (Oworuare) meaning "It is cool" or "The trouble has ceased." [His reign traditionally began in about A.D. 1440.] Prior to his accession he caused a great conflagration in the city which lasted two days and nights as a revenge for his banishment.

Ewuare was a great magician, physician, traveler and warrior. He was also powerful, courageous and sagacious. He fought against and captured 201 towns and villages in Ekiti, Ikare, Kukuruku, Eka and the Ibo country on this side of the river Niger. He took their petty rulers captive and caused the people to pay tribute to him.

He made good roads in Benin City and especially the streets known as Akpakpava and Utantan. In fact the town rose to importance and gained the name "city" during his reign . . .

Ewuare was the first *Oba* of Benin to come into contact with Europeans, for Ruy de Sigueira visited the Benin area in 1472 . . .

Guns and Coconuts

A Portuguese explorer named John Affonso d'Aveiro visited Benin City for the first time in 1485-1486. He introduced guns and coconuts into this country.

Missionaries

It is said that John Affonso d'Aveiro came to Benin City for the second time during this reign. [That of *Oba* Esigie, beginning in A.D. 1504]. He advised the *Oba* to become a Christian, and said that Christianity would make his country better. Esigie therefore sent Ohen-okun, the Olokun priest at Ughoton, with him, as an Ambassador to the king of Portugal, asking him to send priests who would teach him and his people the faith. In reply the king of Portugal sent Roman Catholic missionaries and many rich presents, such as a copper stool (*erhe*), coral beads and a big umbrella, with an entreaty that Esigie should embrace the faith. At the same time he also gave presents to the Ambassador and his wife. The king of Portugal also sent some Portuguese traders who established trading factories at Ughoton, the old port of Benin. They traded in ivory, Benin cloths, pepper and other commodities in the king of Portugal's interest. Owing to the unhealthy state of the country their commerce soon ceased.

But John Affonso d'Aveiro with the other missionaries remained in Benin to carry on the mission work, and churches were built at Ogbelaka, Idumwerie and Akpakpava (Ikpoba Road), the last named being the "Holy Cross Cathedral." The residence of the Fathers was situated between the present Roman Catholic School and John Holt's Store. They had another at Idunmwu-Ebo, and the missionary cemetery was where the Government School now stands. The work of the Mission made progress and thousands of people were baptized before the death of the great explorer John Affonso d'Aveiro, who was buried with great lamentations by the *Oba* and the Christians of Benin City.

The missionaries went with Esigie to the Idah war which took place in 1515-1516. [A Portuguese account of life in Benin at this time appears on p. 187.]

Early East Africa

MANY HUNDRED YEARS SEPARATE THE *Periplus of the Erythraean Sea* (pp. 20-21) from the next eyewitness report on East Africa. With the tenth century these eastern harbors and commercial settlements were growing into wealthy towns, links in the whole great network of Indian Ocean trade, to which they sold ivory and gold. To some of these towns there traveled early in the tenth century an Arab of the Hejaz who would be afterwards remembered as one of the outstanding geographers of medieval times. Unfortunately, few of al Mas'udi's works have survived, the best of these being the early sections of an otherwise vanished historical encyclopedia, *Muruj al-Dhabab*, the "Meadows of Gold," which have a reference to the East African coast, disappointingly short of detail but nonetheless of capital importance. The next long account of East African trade and development is in Idrisi's *Kitab Rujar*, still incompletely published, ill translated into French and not at all into English, but valuable as a secondary source.

Archeology has made startling finds along the East African seaboard, notably in Tanganyika, such as the great palace of Husuni Kubwa uncovered by Neville Chittick in 1961. But nothing in this field is more convincing of the breadth and antiquity of this East African coastal civilization than its surviving coins. An extract from Freeman-Grenville's analysis of these will be found below.

China's "discovery of Africa," as Duyvendak called it, merits a little chapter of its own, not because the Chinese records are copious or even very useful — in fact, they are surprisingly meager — but because they too demonstrate the scope and variety of contacts that were enjoyed by Swahili civilization through a long period of time. China had participated in the Indian Ocean trade since remote antiquity, being generally far ahead of any other country in the development of sailing-ship and navigational technology at least until the fifteenth century. Documentary evidence of this refers back to the Early Han Dynasty (202 B.C. to 9 B.C.), although many of the texts are tantalizingly vague in their identification of the countries which they mention. Thus the *Ch'ien-han-shu,* "an extremely curious notice," in Duyvendak's words, about maritime trade in Early Han times, notes that the country of Tu-yuan is five months' sailing beyond Jihnan, which was Upper Annam (modern Vietnam). "Going again by boat about four months, there is the country of Yi-lu-mo. Going by land about ten days, there is the country of Fu-kan-tu-lu." Two months' beyond again, there was Huang-chih; and from Huang-chih the Emperor P'ing (A.D. 1-6) received an envoy who brought a rhinoceros as a present.

How far west were these countries reached by traders and envoys from Peking some two thousand years ago, even if with trans-shipment from one vessel to another? Some scholars think that Han trade reached the Red Sea (just as it certainly went overland to Rome), and certain Meroitic styles of metalware seem to confirm this. But there is no known Chinese document about East Africa until the *Hsin T'ang-shu* of 1060. This contains an extract from a still earlier work, the *Yu-yang-tsa-tsu,* written in 863 (at a time, we may note, when Arab traders were well established at Canton); the full text was published only in the seventeenth century. The *Hsin T'ang-shu* also mentions an East African coastal city called Malin. Then comes the best of all the old Chinese texts on Africa, being part of the *Chu-fan-chi* of Chao Ju-kua, a foreign-trade commissioner of Ch'uan-chou in Fukien, who completed his book in 1226. Lastly, early in the fifteenth century, there were the voyages of the Ming admiral Ch'ang-lo, some of whose many ships reached Mogadishu and Brava (Somali coastline) in 1418 and 1432; the records of these voyages have survived, however, only in the briefest form.

None of the East African city-states was more successful than Kilwa. With its handsome capital at Kilwa Kisiwani (Kilwa Island off the southern coast of Tanganyika), this thrusting commercial polity, a true Venice of the South in all its imperial powers, international connections and comfortable wealth, was strongly in control of the gold trade from southern Africa between the thirteenth and sixteenth centuries. Two traditional histories have outlived Kilwa's ruin, one in an Arabic text and the other in Kiswahili. According to the first of these (written by a native of Kilwa in about 1520 and surviving in a manuscript copy given to Sir John Kirk by the Sultan of Zanzibar in 1872), the founders of Kilwa were sailors from the Persian Gulf. These Persian or Shirazi ancestors have remained in popular memory, although it is clear enough that the culture of Kilwa, as of most of its sister ports and towns and cities along the coast, became Africanized (though Muslim) at an early date, and that Swahili people were soon dominant in them. Indeed, the other traditional history (collected by Velten and published, with four other such chronicles, in *Prosa und Poesie der Suaheli*, Berlin 1907) begins by explaining that the founder of Kilwa, a certain Shirazi (or Persian) called Sultan Ali ben Selimani, married the daughter of the ruling African chief on Kilwa Island, and that the son of this marriage — thus already half-Swahili — was Kilwa's second ruler.

Even today the ruins of Kilwa offer a haunting experience, deepened through intelligent and tactful restoration of walls and pillars by the Tanganyika Antiquities Department, for this had been a great city. More than six centuries ago, as will be seen, the tireless Ibn Battuta found it "one of the most beautiful and best constructed towns"; and he had looked at many. On the early Portuguese it made a profound and disconcerting impression, revealing a wealth and urbanity such as they had not suspected could exist here. To illustrate how they felt, though at the cost of anticipating a little, I have put into this section a number of Portuguese accounts, mainly from the logbook of Vasco da Gama's first flagship on the journey east and from the memoirs of a royal commercial agent called Barbosa.

This man Barbosa came home in 1518, long after Francisco d'Almeida had seized and sacked Kilwa, but he had almost certainly seen the city in its prime, or near its prime, for he had gone out to the east in one of Portugal's earliest fleets. Dames, his translator into English, thought it probable that he had sailed with Pedro Alvares Cabral in 1500, and Cabral, as we know from an anonymous but contemporary narrative of his voyage (in W. B. Greenlee, *The Voyage of Pedro Alvarez Cabral, etc.*, Hakluyt Society, 1938) made rendezvous in the Kilwa roads with five other of his ships. "The houses of Kilwa are high like those of Spain," wrote Cabral's memorialist. "In this land there are rich merchants, and there is much gold and silver and amber and musk and pearls. Those of the land wear clothes of fine cotton and of silk and many fine things, and they are black men." Barbosa says much the same.

These cities fell victim to the piracy of the Portuguese, as the records most dramatically show; but the Portuguese, as the records also explain, failed most dismally to reconstruct in their own interest the commercial prosperity they had ruined. These Portuguese writings are useful to African as distinct from European history so long as one keeps in mind how little their writers really knew and understood about the societies they encountered. Though strongly biased by a sense of crusade against the Muslim infidel, they show an attractive lack of racial prejudice which was not to endure.

I also offer a single extract from a fifteenth-century Ethiopian chronicle, feeling at the same time that some apology may be due to the Ethiopians, for they are sadly underrepresented in this book. Yet the fact is that Ethiopia throughout this medieval period lay in much isolation from her African neighbors, defending her culture and civilization within the ring of her mountains, but impinging little on the beliefs and behavior of other East Africans.

AL MAS'UDI

The Country of the Zanj

Abdul Hassan ibn Hussein ibn Ali al Mas'udi was born of a Hejazi family of Bagdad towards the end of the ninth century and died in Fostat (Old Cairo) in 956 or 957. He wrote many works of erudition of which few have survived; among these, fortunately, is his *Muruj al-Dhabab wa Ma'adin al-Jawhar*, "Meadows of Gold and Mines of Gems," which includes an account of the East African seaboard based at least in part on Mas'udi's own experiences there. Apart from the first short paragraph (which I have taken from Sprenger's English translation of part of the Arabic text, London, 1841), what follows is translated from volume three of the French version entitled *Les Prairies d'Or*, Paris, 1864, nine volumes, by C. Barbier de Meynard and Pavet de Courteille.

When al Mas'udi speaks of the Zanj he means the coastal peoples of East Africa from the Horn to Mozambique. The Island of Kanbalu is sometimes identified with Madagascar, but was more probably one of the smaller and more northerly islands. Yet what the report lacks in geographical precision it more than makes up in other detail. Here, most clearly, we find a picture of traditional African society at a period when the central-southern Iron Age was approaching its major period of state-forming maturity.

Various explanations have been given for the title of their kings, *Waklimi:* the most convincing, perhaps, is that of Freeman-Grenville (*Medieval History of the Coast of Tanganyika*, London, 1961, p. 40), who says that this word "appears to be a corruption of the texts for the Swahili *mfalme*, a king, *wafalme*, kings." This would not necessarily mean, of course, that "the Zanj of the Waklimi" were Swahili, but it would mean they were Bantu-speaking people; and this is what one would expect.

The sailors of Oman . . . go on the sea of the Zanj as far as the island of Kanbalu and the Sofalah of the Demdemah, which is on the extremity of the country of the Zanj and the low countries thereabout. The merchants of Siraf are also in the habit of sailing on this sea. I have made a voyage on it from Sohar, which is the capital of Oman, with a crew of Sirafians . . . And in A.H. 304 I made a voyage from the island of Kanbalu to Oman. . . .

The sea of the Zanj reaches down to the country of Sofala and of the Wak-Wak which produces gold in abundance and other marvels; its climate is warm and its soil fertile. It is there that the Zanj built their capital; then they elected a king whom they called *Waklimi*. This name . . . has always been that of their sovereigns. The *Waklimi* has under him all the other Zanj kings, and commands three hundred thousand men. The Zanj use the ox as a beast of burden, for their country has no horses or mules or camels and they do not even know these animals. Snow and hail are unknown to them as to all the Abyssinians. Some of their tribes have sharpened teeth and are cannibals. The territory of the Zanj begins at the canal which flows from the Upper Nile and goes down as far as the country of Sofala and the Wak-Wak. Their settlements extend over an area of about seven hundred parasangs in length and in breadth; this country is divided by valleys, mountains and stony deserts; it abounds in wild elephants but there is not so much as a single tame elephant . . .

Although constantly employed in hunting elephants and gathering ivory, the Zanj make no use of ivory for their own domestic purposes. They wear iron instead of gold and silver . . .

To come back to the Zanj and their kings, the name of the kings of the country is *Waklimi* which means supreme lord; they give this title to their sovereign because he has been chosen to govern them with equity. But once he becomes tyrannical and departs from the rules of justice, they cause him to die and exclude his posterity from succession to the throne, for they claim that in thus conducting himself he ceases to be the son of the Master, that is to say of the king of heaven and earth. They call God by the name of Maklandjalu, which means supreme Master . . .

The Zanj speak elegantly, and they have orators in their own language. Often a devout man of the country, pausing in the midst of a numerous crowd, addresses to his listeners an exhortation in which he invites them to serve God and submit to His orders. He points out the punishments which disobedience must entail, and recalls the example of their ancestors and their ancient kings. These peoples have no code of religion; their kings follow custom, and conform in their government to a few political rules. The Zanj eat bananas, which are as abundant with them as in India, but the basis of their food is *dorrah*, a plant called *kalari* which they take from the ground like a truffle, and the *elecampane* root . . . They also have honey and meat. Each worships what he pleases, a plant, an animal, a mineral. They possess a great number of islands where the coconut grows, a fruit that is eaten by all the peoples of the Zanj. One of these islands, placed one or two days' journey from the coast, has a Muslim population who provide the royal family; it is the island of Kanbalu . . .

The Ivory Trade

[Tusks from the country of the Zanj] go generally to Oman, and from there are sent on to China and India. That is the route they follow, and were it otherwise, ivory would be very abundant in Muslim countries. In China the kings and their military and civilian officers used carrying-chairs of ivory; no official or person of rank would dare to visit the king in an iron chair, and ivory alone is used for this purpose . . . Ivory is much prized in India: there it is made into handles for the daggers known as *harari*, or *harri* in the singular, as well as for the hilts of curved swords . . . But the biggest use of ivory is in the manufacture of chessmen and other gaming pieces . . .

FREEMAN-GRENVILLE

The Ivory Trade, a Modern View

As far back as the time of the *Periplus* [*of the Erythraean Sea,* first century] the main export [of the East African coast] was ivory, and this merits some digression. Only the "soft" ivory of East Africa can be used for the making of bangles. These have a special ritual significance in the marriage rites of Hindus, and cannot be made from the tusks of the Indian elephant since they are too narrow in gauge. Once used, no other person may wear these bangles, and they are invariably cremated with the married woman who has employed them. Even today [1960] India imports half of the world's supply of ivory, and of this no less than half is employed in the making of bangles for Hindu brides. To the extent of this trade, even further afield as far as China, not only the *Periplus,* but also al Mas'udi bear witness and there can be no doubt that this was the fundamental reason for the continued Arab interest in East Africa, since the Southern Arabs from time immemorial had dominated the carrying trade of the western and northern parts of the Indian Ocean. There were, of course, other articles of commerce, gold, tortoiseshell and slaves, although of the latter literary references are scarce indeed in the Middle Ages. If there were East African slaves in India in the fifteenth century, it is improbable that there were many elsewhere in the Islamic world, since there were other and ample sources, especially in Caucasia and Western Asia, from which they might be derived.

From G. S. P. Freeman-Grenville, "Islam and Christianity in East Africa Before the Mid-nineteenth Century," in *African Ecclesiastical Review,* July 1960.

IDRISI
The Export of Iron

Abu Abdullah Muhammad al Idrisi (1100-1166) was a Moroccan Muslim scholar who lived at Palermo as a member of the court of a Norman king of Sicily, Roger II. There he devoted himself to collecting information about the whole known world, drawing on other writers and using informants who traveled at his royal patron's expense. His *Kitab Rujar* (Book of Roger), or *Nuzhat al-Mushtaq fi Ikhtiraq al-Afaq,* "the recreation of him who yearns to travel the lands," as Freeman-Grenville has translated this title, was completed in 1154. This long work was accompanied by many maps. One of the worst omissions of later scholarship is to have failed to produce a full and reliable edition and translation. Four copies of the manuscript are known to exist, two in Paris and two in Oxford, with possibly a fifth in Istanbul; while an Arabic abridgement was published in Rome in 1592 and again in Latin in Paris in 1619. Several translations exist in French, none of them satisfactory; the brief passage I have reproduced here is from the French of P. A. Jaubert, *La Géographie d'Edrisi*, Paris, 1836, 2 vols., p. 65, but no great reliance can be placed on its accuracy of detail.

The inhabitants [of the coastal land of Sofala in modern Mozambique] are poor and wretched, and have no other means of livelihood than ironworking. There are, in fact, a great number of iron mines in the mountains of Sofala. The people of the Zanedj Islands and other neighboring islands come here for iron, which they carry to the continent and islands of India, where they sell it at a good price, for it is a material of great trade and consumption in India . . .

FREEMAN-GRENVILLE

Money Talks

During the 1950s Freeman-Grenville and others (following in the steps of Walker at the British Museum, who had led the way in 1936) began systematic work on the many coins of various periods which had turned up along the East African seaboard. Much new light has thus been shed on the economy of the Coast. It is now certain that Kilwa and Zanzibar had mints of their own, the former at least from the late thirteenth century, and probable that Mogadishu also had one. So far, about seven thousand coins of the Kilwa sultans are known, about four thousand of the Zanzibar sultans, and about seven thousand from Mogadishu.

Up to April 1959 a total of some 19,600 coins had been examined, although no exhaustive search has yet been made for others; they go back in date, as the following analysis (G. S. P. Freeman-Grenville, *Journal of African History*, 1, 1960) clearly shows, to Ptolemaic times in Egypt.

Native East African coins begin with the late thirteenth century at Kilwa, and greatly help in the fixing of a Kilwa "king list." At the same time they are disappointing, like all the East African coins, in being solely of copper (although Kilwa had much gold available for export), and in bearing neither dates nor values. Another oddity of the known coins is that although they include several hundred Chinese pieces, there are only seven from Portugal and all of copper. The following list refers only to foreign coins of ancient and medieval times, and illustrates the scope and breadth of the old East African connection.

	Kilwa	Mafia	Zanzi-bar	Pemba	Kenya	Somalia	Total
Hellenistic (3rd to 1st centuries B.C.)	—	1	—	2	—	22	25
Parthian (1st to 2nd centuries after Christ)	—	—	3*	—	—	—	3
Sassanian (3rd century)	—	—	2	—	—	—	2
Roman	—	—	—	2	1	6	9
Byzantine	—	—	—	2	—	46	48
Ummayad	—	—	—	2	—	—	2
'Abbasid	—	—	—	7	—	1	8
Saljuq	—	—	—	1	—	—	1
Mamluk	2	—	—	4	—	6	12
Mongol	2	4	—	1	—	—	7
Egypt under the Turks	—	—	—	—	—	7	7
Other foreign Muslim (unidentified)	—	20	3	15	—	—	38
Chinese:							
T'ang Dyn.	—	—	4	—	—	1	5
Sung Dyn.	—	9	185	—	2	16	212
Ming Dyn.	—	—	—	—	—	6	6
Ching Dyn.	—	—	—	—	—	10	10
Ceylon	—	—	—	—	—	4	4
Annam	—	—	—	—	—	4	4
S. India — 13th century	—	—	—	—	—	1	1
India — Bahmanid	—	—	—	—	—	1	1

* possibly Dar es-Salaam.

YU-YANG-TSA-TSU
The Blood-Drinkers

The country of Po-pa-li [generally agreed to be Berbera in the Horn of Africa] is in the south-western sea. [The people] do not eat any of the five grains but eat only meat. They often stick a needle into the veins of cattle and draw blood, which they drink raw, mixed with milk . . . From olden times on they were not subject to any foreign country. In fighting they use elephants' tusks and ribs and the horns of wild buffaloes as lances, and they wear cuirasses and bows and arrows. They have twenty myriads of foot soldiers. The Arabs make frequent raids on them.

From J. J. L. Duyvendak, *China's Discovery of Africa* (London: 1949).

CHAO JU-KUA
Slaves from Madagascar

[In the west] there is an island in the sea on which there are many savages. Their bodies are black as lacquer and they have frizzled hair. They are enticed by [offers of] food and then captured (and sold) as slaves to the Arabic countries, where they fetch a very high price. They are employed as gate-keepers, and it is said that they have no longing for their kinsfolk.

From Chao Ju-kua, *Chu-fan-chi*, trans. F. Hirth and W. W. Rockhill (St. Petersburg: 1911). The identification with Madagascar of the island in the first of these two extracts has not, so far as I know, been questioned.

Early Zanzibar

The Tsöng-po [Zanj-ba, Zanzibar] country is on an island in the sea south of Hu-cha-la [Gujerat in western India]. To the west it reaches to a great mountain.

The inhabitants are of Ta-shi [Arab] stock and follow the Ta-shi religion. They wrap themselves in blue foreign cotton stuffs and wear red leather shoes. Their daily food consists of meal, baked cakes, and mutton.

There are many villages, and a succession of wooded hills and terraced rocks.

The climate is warm, and there is no cold season.

The products of the country consist of elephants' tusks, native gold, ambergris and yellow sandalwood.

Every year Hu-cha-la and the Ta-shi localities along the seacoast send ships to this country with white cotton cloth, porcelain, copper and red cotton to trade.

CHANG HSIEH

Advice to Traders

Coming into contact with barbarian peoples, you have nothing more to fear than touching the left horn of a snail. The only things one should be really anxious about are the means of mastery of the waves of the sea — and, worst of all dangers, the minds of those avid for profit and greedy of gain.

From Chang Hsieh, *Tung Hsi Yang Khao* (1618), translated by J. Needham in *Science and Civilisation in China* (Cambridge), vol. 6, 1963.

KILWA CHRONICLE
Emergence of Kilwa

Historians have said, amongst their assertions, that the first man to come to Kilwa came in the following way. There arrived a ship in which there were people who claimed to have come from Shiraz in the land of the Persians. It is said there were seven ships: the first stopped at Mandakha; the second at Shaugu; the third at a town called Yanbu; the fourth at Mombasa; the fifth at the Green Island (Pemba); the sixth at the land of Kilwa; and the seventh at Hanzuan. They say that all the masters of these (first) six ships were brothers, and that the one who went to the town of Hanzuan was their father. God alone knows all the truth!

From the translation by G. S. P. Freeman-Grenville, *East African Coast, Select Documents* (London: 1962), p. 35.

IBN BATTUTA
Kilwa in 1331

Then I set off by sea from the town of Mogadishu for the land of the Swahili and the town of Kilwa, which is in the land of the Zanj. We arrived at Mombasa, a large island two days' journey from the land of the Swahili. The island is quite separate from the mainland. It grows bananas, lemons, and oranges. The people also gather a fruit which they call *jammun* (*Eugenia jambu*) which looks like an olive. It has a nut like an olive, but its taste is

From the translation of the Arabic text by G. S. P. Freeman-Grenville in *East African Coast, Select Documents* (London: 1962), p. 31.

very sweet. The people do not engage in agriculture, but import grain from the Swahili. The greater part of their diet is bananas and fish. They follow the Shafi'i rite, and are devout, chaste, and virtuous.

Their mosques are very strongly constructed of wood. Beside the door of each mosque are one or two wells, one or two cubits deep. They draw water from them with a wooden vessel which is fixed on to the end of a thin stick, a cubit long. The earth round the mosque and the well is stamped flat . . .

We spent a night on the island [of Mombasa] and then set sail for Kilwa, the principal town on the coast, the greater part of whose inhabitants are Zanj of very black complexion. Their faces are scarred, like the Limiin of Janada. A merchant told me that Sofala is half a month's march from Kilwa, and that between Sofala and Yufi in the country of the Limiin is a month's march. Powdered gold is brought from Yufi to Sofala.

Kilwa is one of the most beautiful and well-constructed towns in the world. The whole of it is elegantly built.* The roofs are built with mangrove poles. There is very much rain. The people are engaged in a holy war, for their country lies beside that of pagan Zanj. The chief qualities are devotion and piety: they follow the Shafi'i rite.

* The MS apparently has "built entirely of wood" but this statement, as Freeman-Grenville says, cannot be correct; he accordingly offers an alternative reading. On this point, controversy remains.

MEDIEVAL ETHIOPIA
A Strong Ruler

The Chronicle of the Emperor Zara Yaqob (1434-1468), from which the following is taken, was written some fifty years after that ruler's death. It offers a glimpse of the vivid pictures of contemporary

From the translation in *The Ethiopian Observer*, 2, vol. 5, 1960.

or almost-contemporary life to be found in these old Ethiopian chronicles.

———————

In the reign of our king Zara Yaqob, there was great terror and great fear in all the people of Ethiopia, on account of the severity of his justice and of his authoritarian rule and above all because of the denunciations of those who, after having confessed that they had worshipped Dasak and the devil, caused to perish many innocent people by accusing them falsely of having worshipped thus together with them . . .

A certain Zara Seyon, nicknamed Zara Saytan, who by his false accusations had caused the death of a large number of monks, canons and men and women, was, when God revealed his crimes, forced to become a monk and exiled to Hayq.

The office of Aqbe Saat [a court official] was then conferred on Amha Seyon, who was greatly esteemed by our king . . . The offices of Beit Wiedad of the right and of the left [court officials] were at that time vacant at the palace. The king conferred them on two of his daughters . . .

The king placed at the head of each province one of his sisters, entrusted with administering the district in his name . . . Later, the king himself took in hand the government of the whole of Ethiopia . . . All the peoples trembled before the undaunted might of the king . . .

When our king Zara Yaqob went into the district of Axum to fulfill the law and the rite of coronation according to the rites followed by his ancestors . . . all of the inhabitants, as well as the priests, went to meet him and welcomed him with a great rejoicing . . . When he entered within the gates of the town, the king had on his right hand and on his left the governor of Tigre and the administrator of Axum who carried and waved according to custom, olive branches . . . After arriving within the walls of Axum, the king had brought to him much gold which he scattered as far as the city gate on the carpets which were spread along his route. This amount of gold was more than a hundred ounces; as for more, I do not know whether it was thirty or forty ounces . . .

During his stay at Axum, our king regulated all the institutions of the Church and prescribed to be recited each day, at canonical hours, prayers which up to that time had been neglected . . .

During the reign of our king Zara Yaqob, there was in the whole land of Ethiopia a great peace and a great tranquility, for the king taught justice and faith . . .

KILWA CHRONICLE
Vasco da Gama

During al-Fudail's reign there came news from the land of Mozambique that men had come from the land of the Franks. They had three ships, and the name of their captain was al-Mirate [Admiral Vasco da Gama]. After a few days there came word that the ships had passed Kilwa and had gone on to Mafia [an adjoining island to the northward]. The lord of Mafia rejoiced, for they thought they [the Franks] were good and honest men. But those who knew the truth confirmed that they were corrupt and dishonest persons who had only come to spy out the land in order to seize it. And they determined to cut the anchors of their ships so that they should drift ashore and be wrecked by the Muslims. The Franks learnt of this and went on to Malindi [a trading city on the Kenya coast]. When the people of Malindi saw them, they knew they were bringers of war and corruption, and were troubled with very great fear. They gave them [the Franks] all they asked, water, food, firewood, and everything else. And the Franks asked for a pilot to guide them to India, and after that back to their own land — God curse it!

From the translation of G. S. P. Freeman-Grenville, *The East African Coast, Select Documents* (London: 1962), p. 34.

PATE CHRONICLE
Seafaring

Pate Island occupied much the same position of preeminence along the northern reach of the Swahili coast as Kilwa along the southern. Local tradition preserved in the Swahili Chronicle of Pate asserts, indeed, that Kilwa was subject to it for a time early in the sixteenth century. Having made alliance with Malindi and overawed Mombasa, "the Pate people passed overland and fought the whole of the Mrima coast [as far as Kilwa and beyond]." The original text of this useful work, which begins its story as long ago as 1204, is said to have perished in the bombardment of Witu in 1890; but several versions have survived. A helpful discussion on these texts is in A. H. J. Prins, "On Swahili Historiography," *Journal of the East African Swahili Committee,* July 1958.

Sultan Muhammad lived in the country of Pate and made it prosper, making plantations and building vessels called *Gharabs* which are now called *Jahazis.* [Deep-sea dhows, lateen-rigged; many such are still in use. The word is from the Hindustani for a ship.]

Now in those days Arab and Indian vessels used to come to Pate harbor.

Sultan Omar had a nephew who was very fond of traveling. On his first journey he set out for India, but was completely lost and his ship sank, and he himself, after meeting with great hardships and difficulties and losing everything, returned home. He remained at home for a year, but the next year he wished to travel abroad again . . . [His parents now vainly attempted to dissuade him.] As they were unable to stop him they made up a fleet of seven ships for him, and he voyaged away and wrecked all his

From the translation in C. H. Stigand, *The Land of Zinj,* 1913.

ships. He returned alone, and he had nothing and no one with him . . . [But still he persisted in his wish to travel the seas, and again prevailed upon his parents and friends.] When his parents found that they were unable to prevent him, they gave him a fleet according to his wishes.

So he set out and arrived in India where he traded and made much profit. During the return they were lost at sea for many days till from the vessel on board of which he was they saw an island near them.

So they disembarked as they were in need of water, and that youth wished to rest from the discomforts he had suffered. He lay under a tree and told his servants to cook his food and bring it to him here.

They sat down to cook, and when the fire blazed up they saw the sand of that place melt and run away. When it had gone a little from the fire it cooled in separate little pieces . . . [This the enterprising young man immediately recognized to be silver. He persuaded his crew to jettison most of the cargo they had bought and to load instead with this silver-bearing sand.]

So they took his advice and unloaded all their goods and filled up with sand for three days till the ship could carry no more . . . [They lost some in a storm but] afterwards they got a safe and favorable wind and arrived home [where he was joyfully received] . . .

He rested for three days and then at dead of night he brought some of the sand and put it in a store in his house. Then he called skilled workmen and showed them a little, and when they had made an ornament out of it they found that it was very pure silver.

Now it was at this time that the Portuguese arrived in Pate, and first they came in friendship. Afterwards he showed the ore to the Portuguese and they asked him where he got it. He told them the story from first to last because of his joy when he knew that it was real ore.

Those Portuguese wanted him to show them the spot, and they went together with the captain and searched for six months and returned again without finding it . . .

VASCO DA GAMA'S LOGBOOK

The End of an Epoch

From the European point of view, da Gama performed three great services. He sailed directly from the West Coast of Africa to the neighborhood of the Cape of Good Hope, Diaz before him having followed the long western seaboard by way of the Congo estuary; he discovered the civilization of the Swahili (though he recognized it, as would other Portuguese explorers, merely as Muslim or "Moorish"); and he reached India. From the African point of view, however, his coming was an unrelieved disaster. It brought to an end the long and flourishing epoch of untrammeled trading intercourse with other lands of the Indian Ocean. It signaled ruin for many of the Swahili cities. Yet da Gama's *Roteiro* can still be useful to African history, if only because it records most graphically the reactions of the Portuguese to an African civilization whose sensitivity and splendor were as impressive as they were unexpected. It will be noticed that Kilwa is missing from the story; on this occasion Kilwa escaped notice, for da Gama's ships — as noted by the Kilwa Chronicle quoted above (p. 119) — were carried past it on the tide.

Mossell Bay: The Hottentots

On Saturday [December 2, 1497] about two hundred negroes came, both young and old. They brought with them about a dozen oxen and cows and four or five sheep. As soon as we saw them we went ashore. They forthwith began to play on four or five flutes, some producing high notes and others low ones, thus making a pretty harmony for negroes who are not expected to be musicians; and they danced in the style of negroes. The captain-major then ordered the trumpets to be sounded, and we, in the

From the translation in *A Journal of the First Voyage of Vasco da Gama,* edited by E. G. Ravenstein, Hakluyt Society, 1898.

boats, danced, and the captain-major did so likewise when he rejoined us. This festivity ended, we landed where we had landed before, and bought a black ox for three bracelets. This ox we dined off on Sunday. We found him very fat, and his meat as toothsome as the beef of Portugal.

On Sunday [December 3] many visitors came, and brought with them their women and little boys, the women remaining on the top of a hill near the sea. They had with them many oxen and cows. Having collected in two spots on the beach, they played and danced as they had done on Saturday. It is the custom of this people for the young men to remain in the bush with their weapons. The (older) men came to converse with us. They carried a short stick in the hand, attached to which was a fox's tail, with which they fan the face. Whilst conversing with them, by signs, we observed the young men crouching in the bush, holding their weapons in their hands. The captain-major then ordered Martin Affonso, who had formerly been in Manicongo [Congo] to advance, and to buy an ox, for which purpose he was supplied with bracelets. The natives having accepted the bracelets, took him by the hand, and, pointing to the watering place, asked him why we took away their water, and simultaneously drove their cattle into the bush. When the captain-major observed this he ordered us to gather together, and called upon Martin Affonso to retreat, for he suspected some treachery.

Having drawn together, we proceeded [in our boats] to the place where we had been at first. The negroes followed us. The captain-major then ordered us to land, armed with lances, assagais, and strung crossbows, and wearing our breastplates, for he wanted to show that we had the means of doing them an injury, although we had no desire to employ them. When they observed this they ran away. The captain-major, anxious that none should be killed by mischance, ordered the boats to draw together; but to prove that we were able although unwilling to hurt them, he ordered two bombards to be fired from the poop of the long boat. They were by that time all seated close to the bush, not far from the beach, but the first discharge caused them to retreat so precipitately that in their flight they dropped the skins with which they were covered and their weapons. When they were in the bush two of them turned back to pick up the articles which had been dropped. Then they continued their flight to the top of a hill, driving their cattle before them.

Quilimane: First Impact

When we had been two or three days at this place two gentlemen [*senhores*] of the country came to see us. They were very haughty, and valued nothing which we gave them. One of them wore a *touca*, with a fringe embroidered in silk, and the other a cap of green satin. A young man in their company — so we understood from their signs — had come from a distant country, and had already seen big ships like ours. These tokens [*signaes*] gladdened our hearts, for it appeared as if we were really approaching the bourne of our desires. These gentlemen had some huts built on the river bank, close to the ships, in which they stayed seven days, sending daily to the ships, offering to barter cloths which bore a mark of red ochre. And when they were tired of being there, they left in their small craft [*almadias*] for the upper river.

Mozambique: A New World

The people of this country are of a ruddy complexion and well made. They are Mohammedans, and their language is the same as that of the Moors. Their dresses are of fine linen or cotton stuffs, with variously colored stripes, and of rich and elaborate workmanship. They all wear *toucas* with borders of silk embroidered in gold. They are merchants, and have transactions with white Moors [i.e., Indians], four of whose vessels were at the time in port, laden with gold, silver, cloves, pepper, ginger, and silver rings, as also with quantities of pearls, jewels, and rubies, all of which articles are used by the people of this country.

We understood them to say that all these things, with the exception of the gold, were brought thither by these Moors; that further on, where we were going to, they abounded, and that precious stones, pearls and spices were so plentiful that there was no need to purchase them as they could be collected in baskets. All this we learned through a sailor the captain-major had with him, and who, having formerly been a prisoner among the Moors, understood their language.

These Moors, moreover, told us that along the route which we were about to follow we should meet with numerous shoals; that there were many cities along the coast, and also an island, one half the population of which consisted of Moors and the other half of Christians, who were at war with each other. This island was said to be very wealthy.

We were told, moreover, that Prester John resided not far from this place; that he held many cities along the coast, and that the inhabitants of those cities were great merchants and owned big ships. The residence of Prester John was said to be far in the interior, and could be reached only on the back of camels. These Moors had also brought hither two Christian captives from India. This information, and many other things which we heard, rendered us so happy that we cried with joy, and prayed God to grant us health, so that we might behold what we so much desired.

In this place and island of Moncobiquy [Mozambique] there resided a chief [*senhor*] who had the title of Sultan, and was like the viceroy. He often came aboard our ships attended by some of his people. The captain-major gave him many good things to eat and made him a present of hats, *marlotas*, corals and many other articles. He was, however, so proud that he treated all we gave him with contempt, and asked for scarlet cloth, of which we had none. We gave him, however, of all the things we had.

One day the captain-major invited him to a repast, when there was an abundance of figs and comfits, and begged him for two pilots to go with us. He at once granted this request, subject to our coming to terms with them. The captain-major gave each of them thirty *mitqals* in gold and two *marlotas*, on condition that from the day on which they received this payment one of them should always remain on board if the other desired to go on land. With these terms they were well satisfied.

On Saturday, March 10 [1498], we set sail and anchored one league out at sea, close to an island, where mass was said on Sunday, when those who wished to do so confessed and joined in the communion.

One of our pilots lived on the island, and when we had anchored we armed two boats to go in search of him. The captain-major went in one boat and Nicolau Coelho in the other. They were met by five or six boats [*barcas*] coming from the island, and crowded with people armed with bows and long arrows and bucklers, who gave them to understand by signs that they were to return to the town. When the captain saw this he secured the pilot whom he had taken with him, and ordered the bombards to fire upon the boats. Paulo da Gama, who had remained with the ships, so as to be prepared to render succor in case of need, no sooner heard the reports of the bombards than he started in the *Berrio*. The Moors, who were already flying, fled still faster, and gained the land before the *Berrio* was able to come up with them. We then returned to our anchorage.

The vessels of this country are of good size and decked. There are no nails, and the planks are held together by cords, as are also those of their boats [*barcas*]. The sails are made of palm-matting. Their mariners have Genoese needles, by which they steer, quadrants, and navigating charts.

The palms of this country yield a fruit as large as a melon, of which the kernel is eaten. It has a nutty flavor. There also grow in abundance melons and cucumbers, which were brought to us for barter.

On the day in which Nicolau Coelho entered the port, the lord of the place came on board with a numerous suite. He was received well, and Coelho presented him with a red hood, in return for which the lord handed him a black rosary, which he made use of when saying his prayers, to be held as a pledge. He then begged Nicolau Coelho for the use of his boat, to take him ashore. This was granted. And after he had landed he invited those who had accompanied him to his house, where he gave them to eat. He then dismissed them, giving them a jar of bruised dates made into a preserve with cloves and cumin, as a present for Nicolau Coelho. Subsequently he sent many things to the captain-major. All this happened at the time when he took us for Turks or for Moors from some foreign land, for in case we came from Turkey he begged to be shown the bows of our country and our books of the

Law. But when they learnt that we were Christians they arranged to seize and kill us by treachery. The pilot, whom we took with us, subsequently revealed to us all they intended to do, if they were able.

Malindi: An Offer of Pilots

On Easter Sunday [April 15, 1498] the Moors whom we had taken in the boat told us that there were at this city of Malindi four vessels belonging to Christians from India [they were, of course, Hindus], and that if it pleased us to take them there, they would provide us, instead of them, Christian pilots and all we stood in need of, including water, wood and other things.

The captain-major much desired to have pilots from the country, and having discussed the matter with his Moorish prisoners, he cast anchor off the town, at a distance of about half a league from the mainland. The inhabitants of the town did not venture to come aboard our ships, for they had already learnt that we had captured a vessel and made her occupants prisoners . . .

[Afterwards they went ashore and were formally received by the Sultan of Malindi who] wore a robe of damask trimmed with green satin, and a rich *touca*. He was seated on two cushioned chairs of bronze, beneath a round sunshade of crimson satin attached to a pole. An old man, who attended him as page, carried a short sword in a silver sheath. There were many players on *anafils*, and two trumpets of ivory, richly carved, and of the size of a man, which were blown from a hole in the side, and made sweet harmony with the *anafils* . . .

Journey to India

On the following Sunday, the 22nd of April, the king's *zavra* brought on board one of his confidential servants, and as two days had passed without any visitors, the captain-major had this man seized, and sent word to the king that he required the pilots whom he had promised. The king, when he received this message, sent a Christian pilot, and the captain-major allowed the gentleman, whom he had retained in his vessel, to go away . . .

We left Malindi on Tuesday, the 24th of the month [of April] for a city called Calecut, with the pilot whom the king had given us . . .

On Friday, the 18th of May, after having seen no land for twenty-three days, we sighted lofty mountains, and having all this time sailed before the wind we could not have made less than six hundred leagues . . .

[They anchored off Calecut and were spoken by boats of the port.] On the following day [May 21] these same boats came again alongside, when the captain-major sent one of the convicts to Calecut, and those with whom he went took him to two Moors from Tunis, who could speak Castilian and Genoese. The first greeting that he received was in these words: "May the Devil take thee! What brought you hither?" They asked what he sought so far away from home, and he told them that we came in search of Christians and of spices.

DUARTE BARBOSA
Swahili Civilization

The value of Duarte Barbosa's memoirs lie in their picture of the East Coast before the full impact of Portuguese intervention had been felt. They summarize the knowledge of a man who first saw the coast in 1500 or 1501, and last saw it in 1517 or 1518. I have modernized the orthography of the place names.

Sofala
And the manner of their traffic was this: they came in small vessels named *zambucos* from the kingdoms of Kilwa, Mombasa, and Malindi, bringing many cotton cloths, some spotted and others white and blue, also some of silk, and many small beads, gray, red,

From *The Book of Duarte Barbosa*, translated by Mansel Longworth Dames, Hakluyt Society (2 vols., London: 1918).

and yellow, which things come to the said kingdoms from the great kingdom of Cambay [in Northwest India] in other greater ships. And these wares the said Moors who came from Malindi and Mombasa [purchased from others who bring them hither and] paid for in gold at such a price that those merchants departed well pleased; which gold they gave by weight.

The Moors of Sofala kept these wares and sold them afterwards to the heathen of the Kingdom of Benametapa, who came thither laden with gold which they gave in exchange for the said cloths without weighing it. These Moors collect also great store of ivory which they find hard by Sofala, and this also they sell in the [Indian] Kingdom of Cambay at five or six cruzados the quintal. They also sell some ambergris, which is brought to them from the Hucicas, and is exceeding good. These Moors are black, and some of them tawny; some of them speak Arabic, but the more part use the language of the country. They clothe themselves from the waist down with cotton and silk cloths, and other cloths they wear over their shoulders like capes, and turbans on their heads. Some of them wear small caps dyed in grain in chequers and other woolen clothes in many tints, also camlets and other silks.

Their food is millet, rice, flesh and fish. In this river as far as the sea are many sea horses, which come out on the land to graze, which horses always move in the sea like fishes; they have tusks like those of small elephants, being whiter and harder, and it never loses color. In the country near Sofala are many wild elephants, exceeding great (which the country-folk know not how to tame), ounces, lions, deer and many other wild beasts. It is a land of plains and hills with many streams of sweet water.

In this same Sofala now of late they make great store of cotton and weave it, and from it they make much white cloth, and as they know not how to dye it, or have not the needful dyes, they take the Cambay cloths, blue or otherwise colored, and unravel them and make them up again, so that it becomes a new thing. With this thread and their own white they make much colored cloth, and from it they gain much gold. This they did as a remedy after they had perceived that our people [the Portuguese] were taking from them the trade of the *zambucos,* and that they can only obtain goods through the hands of the factors whom the King our Lord has there in his factories and forts.

The Zambezi Mouths

Journeying from Sofala forty leagues more or less towards Mozambique there is a very great river which they call Cuama, which leads into the inner country over against the kingdom of Benametapa more than a hundred and seventy leagues. In the mouth of the said river is a town whose king they call Mangalo. By this river comes much gold from Benametapa to this Moorish town, and from this river is formed another which goes to a town called Angoya, and it is here that the Moors have many *almadias* [boats] to convey cloth and much other merchandise from Angoya and others to take abundance of gold and ivory thither.

Angoya

Further on, leaving this Cuama, a hundred and forty leagues from it, skirting the coast, is a very great town of Moors called Angoya (which has its own king). In it dwell many merchants who deal in gold, ivory, silk and cotton cloths and Cambay beads as those of Sofala were wont to do. The Moors of Sofala, Mombasa, Malindi and Kilwa convey these wares in very small craft concealed from our ships, and in this wise they carry great store of provender, millet, rice and flesh of divers kinds. The natives thereof are some black and some tawny, they go bare from the waist up, and below it are clad in silk and cotton cloths and they wear other cloths folded like cloaks on their shoulders; some wear turbans on their heads, and other caps made of squares of silk cloth. They speak the native language of the country, that of the heathen, but some speak Arabic. At times these Moors obey the King our Lord, but at other times, being far from our fortresses, they become rebellious.

Mozambique Island

Going forward towards India, and leaving Angoya, there are three islands very near to the mainland, among which is a Moorish town called Mozambique which has a very good haven, formerly

the resort of the Moors who traded to Sofala and Cuama to repair their ships — "as they found there good depth of water and
wood and provisions." Among the Moors of this isle of Mozambique was a Xarife [sharif] who governed and judged them.
These Moors are of the same tongue and have the same customs
as those of Angoya.

Here the King our Lord has a fortress, so that the aforesaid
Moors are under his rule and governance, and our ships now take
in at this port water, wood and provisions which are found in that
land, and there they mend the ships that need it, in going as well
as in coming, and hence they send supplies to the Portuguese at
Sofala, as well as many things which come from Portugal and from
India also, as it lies on the way thither. On the mainland appertain-
ing to these islands are many very great elephants and other wild
beasts. The land is inhabited by heathen who are like beasts,
going naked and smeared with red clay. Their private parts are
wrapped in strips of blue cotton cloth with no other clothing.
Their lips are bored with three holes, and in each hole three
cowries, and in these they place bones with little stones and other
little pendants.

Kilwa

Going along the coast from this town of Mozambique, there is
an island hard by the mainland which is called Kilwa, in which is
a Moorish town with many fair houses of stones and mortar, with
many windows after our fashion, very well arranged in streets, with
many flat roofs. The doors are of wood, well carved, with excellent
joinery. Around it are streams and orchards and fruit-gardens with
many channels of sweet water. It has a Moorish king over it. From
this place they trade with Sofala, whence they bring back gold, and
from here they spread all over *Arabia Felix*, which henceforth we
may call by this name (even though it be in Ethiopia) for all the
seacoast is well peopled with villages and abodes of Moors.

Before the King our Lord sent out his expedition to discover
India the Moors of Sofala, Cuama, Angoya and Mozambique were
all subject to the king of Kilwa, who was the most mighty king
among them. And in this town was great plenty of gold, as no

ships passed towards Sofala without first coming to this island. Of the Moors there are some fair and some black, they are finely clad in many rich garments of gold and silk and cotton, and the women as well; also with much gold and silver in chains and bracelets, which they wear on their legs and arms, and many jeweled earrings in their ears. These Moors speak Arabic and follow the creed of the Alcoran, and have great faith in Mafamede.

This town was taken by force from its king by the Portuguese, as, moved by arrogance, he refused to obey the King our Lord. There they took many prisoners and the king fled from the island, and His Highness ordered that a fort should be built there, and kept it under his rule and governance. Afterwards he ordered that it should be pulled down, as its maintenance was of no value nor profit to him, and it was destroyed by Antonio de Saldanha.

Mombasa

Further on, an advance along the coast towards India, there is an isle hard by the mainland, on which is a town called Mombasa. It is a very fair place, with lofty stone and mortar houses, well aligned in streets after the fashion of Kilwa. The wood is well fitted with excellent joiner's work. It has its own king, himself a Moor. The men are in color either tawny, black or white and also their women go very bravely attired with many fine garments of silk and gold in abundance. This is a place of great traffic, and has a good harbor, in which are always moored craft of many kinds and also great ships, both of those which come from Sofala and those which go thither, and others which come from the great kingdom of Cambay and from Malindi; others which sail to the Isles of Zanzibar, and yet others of which I shall speak anon.

This Mombasa is a land very full of food. Here are found many very fine sheep with round tails, cows and other cattle in great plenty, and many fowls, all of which are exceeding fat. There is much millet and rice, sweet and bitter oranges, lemons, pomegranates, Indian figs, vegetables of divers kinds, and much sweet water. The men thereof are ofttimes at war but seldom at peace with those of the mainland, and they carry on trade with them, bringing thence great store of honey, wax and ivory.

The king of this city refused to obey the commands of the King our Lord, and through this arrogance he lost it, and our Portuguese took it from him by force. He fled away, and they slew many of his people and also took captive many, both men and women, in such sort that it was left ruined and plundered and burnt. Of gold and silver great booty was taken here, bangles, bracelets, earrings and gold beads, also great store of copper with other rich wares in great quantity, and the town was left in ruins.

Malindi

Leaving Mombasa, and journeying along the coast towards India, there is a fair town on the mainland lying along a strand, which is named Malindi. It pertains to the Moors and has a Moorish king over it; the which place has many fair stone and mortar houses of many stories, with great plenty of windows and flat roofs, after our fashion. The place is well laid out in streets. The folk are both black and white; they go naked, covering only their private parts with cotton and silk cloths. Others of them wear cloths folded like cloaks and waistbands, and turbans of many rich stuffs on their heads.

They are great barterers, and deal in cloth, gold, ivory, and divers other wares with the Moors and heathen of the great kingdom of Cambay; and to their haven come every year many ships with cargoes of merchandise, from which they get great store of gold, ivory and wax. In this traffic the Cambay merchants make great profits, and thus, on one side and the other, they earn much money. There is great plenty of food in this city, rice, millet, and some wheat which they bring from Cambay, and divers sorts of fruit, inasmuch as there is here abundance of fruit-gardens and orchards. Here too are plenty of round-tailed sheep, cows and other cattle and great store of oranges, also of hens.

The king and people of this place ever were and are friends of the King of Portugal, and the Portuguese always find in them great comfort and friendship and perfect peace, and there the ships, when they chance to pass that way, obtain supplies in plenty.

Pemba, Mafia, Zanzibar

Between this island of Saõ Lourenço [Madagascar] and the mainland, not very far therefrom, are three islands, one called Mafia, another Pemba, another Zanzibar; which are inhabited by Moors. They have great store of food, for in them are found rice, millet, flesh-meat in great quantity, oranges, limes and citrons, of which the woods are full, and every other kind of fruit. There is great plenty of sugar cane, but they know not how to make the sugar. These islands have Moorish kings. Some of them deal in their stock of flesh and fruit with the mainland in very small, weak, ill-found and undecked boats having but one mast. The planks are bound and sewn together with a cord they call *cairo*, and their sails are palm-leaf mats.

They are a feeble folk and have but few weapons. The kings of these isles live in great luxury; they are clad in very fine silk and cotton garments, which they purchase at Mombasa from the Cambay merchants. The women of these Moors go bravely decked, they wear many jewels of fine Sofala gold, silver too in plenty, earrings, necklaces, bangles and bracelets, and they go clad in good silk garments. They have many mosques, and honor greatly the Alcoran of Mafamede.

Pate and Lamu

And as soon as they pass Malindi, going towards India, they begin to cross the gulf, for the coast doubles back towards the Red Sea.

Going forward along this coast is a town of Moors named Pate and then another named Lamu. These carry on trade with the inland country, and are well walled with stone and mortar, inasmuch as they are often at war with the heathen of the mainland.

Brava

Yet further along the coast, beyond these places, is a great town of Moors, of very fine stone and mortar houses, called Brava. It has no king, but is ruled by elders and ancients of the land, who are the persons held in the highest esteem, and who have the chief dealings in merchandise of divers kinds. And this place was destroyed by the Portuguese, who slew many of its people and carried many into captivity, and took great spoil of gold and silver and goods. Thenceforth many of them fled away towards the inland country, forsaking the town; yet after it had been destroyed the Portuguese again settled and peopled it, so that now it is as prosperous as it was before.

Mogadishu

Proceeding coastwise towards the Red Sea there is a very great Moorish town called Mogadishu; it has a king over it; the place has much trade in divers kinds, by reason whereof many ships come hither from the great kingdom of Cambay, bringing great plenty of cloths of many sorts, and divers other wares, also spices: and in the same way they come from Aden. And they carry away much gold, ivory, wax and many other things, whereby they make exceeding great profits in their dealings.

In this country is found flesh-meat in great plenty, wheat, barley, horses and fruit of divers kinds, so that it is a place of great wealth.

They speak Arabic. The men are for the most part brown and black, but a few are fair. They have but few weapons, yet they use herbs on their arrows to defend themselves against their enemies.

HANS MAYR

The Sack of Two Cities

Early Portuguese intentions on the East Coast may be fairly summarized as being, first, to plunder the Indian Ocean trade; secondly, to put the seaboard towns in tribute; thirdly, to accumulate personal

From the Portuguese text in E. Axelson, *South-east Africa, 1488-1530*, 1940. This extract is from a translation of the full account in Freeman-Grenville, *The East African Coast, Select Documents* (London: 1962), p. 105.

loot. In one way or another all three designs were briefly realized. The following eyewitness notes on d'Almeida's behavior at Kilwa and Mombasa in 1505 are thought to have been written by a German called Hans Mayr who traveled in the *Sam Rafael*, d'Almeida's flagship. Another and longer account of d'Almeida's expedition was published by de Barros, *Da Asia*, 1st Decade, translated in G. M. Theal, *Records of South-eastern Africa*, 1900, vol. 6.

Kilwa

In Kilwa there are many strong houses several stories high. They are built of stone and mortar and plastered with various designs. As soon as the town had been taken without opposition, the Vicar-General and some of the Franciscan fathers came ashore carrying two crosses in procession and singing the *Te Deum*. They went to the palace, and there the cross was put down and the Grand-Captain prayed. Then everyone started to plunder the town of all its merchandise and provisions. [Two days later d'Almeida fired the town, destroying, as the account in de Barros explains, "the greater part of this city of abomination."]

Mombasa

The Grand-Captain ordered that the town should be sacked and that each man should carry off to his ship whatever he found: so that at the end there would be a division of the spoil, each man to receive a twentieth of what he found. The same rule was made for gold, silver, and pearls. Then everyone started to plunder the town and to search the houses, forcing open the doors with axes and iron bars. There was a large quantity of cotton cloth for Sofala in the town, for the whole coast gets its cotton cloth from here. So the Grand-Captain got a good share of the trade of Sofala for himself. A large quantity of rich silk and gold embroidered clothes was seized, and carpets also; one of these, which was without equal for beauty, was sent to the King of Portugal together with many other valuables.

DIOGO DE ALCANÇOVA
Kilwa Tariffs

The duties, Sir, which the king of Mombasa receives from the merchants who go to Sofala are the following: any merchant who comes to Mombasa and brings a thousand pieces of cloth pays to the king duties of entrance for each thousand pieces of cloth one *mitqal* of gold; and then they divide the thousand pieces of cloth into two halves; and the king takes one half; and the other half remains with the merchant; and, whether he carries them beyond [Mombasa] or sells them in the city, he has to take this half to the king: and the king sends his to be sold at Sofala or at Kilwa.

And the duties which the king of Kilwa has are: that any merchant who wishes to enter the city pays for each five hundred pieces of cloth he brings, no matter what the quality, one *mitqal* of gold as entrance duty; and, after paying this *mitqal* for the five hundred pieces of cloth, the king takes two-thirds of all the merchandise, and the merchant one-third; and the third which remains to the merchant must not be taken from the city, and the whole merchandise remaining in that third is again valued, and pays for each thousand *mitqals* thirty *mitqals* for the king of Kilwa. And from that place the merchant departs for Sofala; and, on arriving there, he must pay for every seven pieces of cloth one piece for the said king of Kilwa. And when any one returns from Sofala, he is obliged to stop at Kilwa; and he must pay to the king for each thousand *mitqals* of gold he carries with him fifty *mitqals* of gold, and at Mombasa going through costs nothing. And, if he passes Kilwa, and does not enter it, he must however go

From Diogo de Alcançova's letter to the King of Portugal of Nov. 20, 1506, in the translation in G. M. Theal, *Records of South-eastern Africa*, 1898, vol. 1, p. 62. It refers, of course, to Kilwa before the Portuguese sacking and subjection.

to Mombasa, and if he does not carry with him a clearance to show that he has paid at Kilwa, there they take these fifty *mitqals* out of every thousand *mitqals*, and send them to the king of Kilwa.

And the duty on ivory which they also pay to the king of Kilwa is: that for each *bahar* he pays twenty *mitqals* of gold in Sofala; and when they come to Kilwa, he pays further for each seven tusks one, and in each *bahar* are twenty *farazulas*, and in each *farazula* there are twenty-three pounds. And since, Sir, this king of Sofala, whom Pedro d'Anaya killed, reigned, no one has ever paid duties to the king of Kilwa out of those collected at Sofala.

An Inland Epic

NOW THAT AFRICAN HISTORY MAY INCREASINGLY BE SEEN FROM its own standpoint, thanks largely to archeology and the collection of oral tradition, the old European records often deepen in value. They stand exposed, true enough, as terribly partial (though the older records generally come through better, in this respect, than the newer), but much that they have to say acquires a broader meaning. This is notably the case with the Portuguese records of Monomotapa, the inland empire of Central Africa (essentially, of Southern Rhodesia and Mozambique) with which the pioneers of Portugal made contact at the beginning of the sixteenth century, and from which, as they rightly believed, much of the gold of the interior was drawn. A later world invested Monomotapa — of *the* Monomotapa, for the name, like that of Ghana, was initially the title of a king and not a kingdom — with a rigmarole of mysteries. Zimbabwe became the land of Ophir. Phoenicians and Ancient Egyptians were named as those who had built the walls and forts of this inland country. Archeology has now exorcized these ghosts from a remote or alien past.

Great Zimbabwe, like all other stone structures of the Rhodesian plateau (of Zimbabwe and Zambia, as their African nationalists call Southern and Northern Rhodesia), was the work of Africans. Its last alterations, but for those of Nature, were made less than three centuries ago. They represented, in stone, the climax of a long process of Iron Age growth which began in this region some two thousand years ago (pp. 16-17). Readers who wish for a detailed description of this process may turn to J. D. Clark, *The Prehistory of Southern Africa*, 1959, especially chapter eleven,

"Mines, Metalworkers, and Builders in Stone"; and to my *Lost Cities of Africa*, 1959. Valuable articles include R. Summers, "The Southern Rhodesian Iron Age," *Journal of African History*, 1, 1961; B. Fagan, "Pre-European Iron-Working in Central Africa, with special reference to Northern Rhodesia," *Journal of African History*, 2, 1961, and, in the same issue, D. P. Abraham's remarkable "Maramuca: An Exercise in the Combined Use of Portuguese Records and Oral Tradition," the first coherent account ever to be published of politics in central-southern Africa during the fifteenth century.

The last great phase of pre-European social change and growth on the central plateau may be said to have owed its stimulus to two external but interwoven factors. The first was a new wave of migration from the north, directly from what is now Northern Rhodesia and the Katanga, though ultimately from somewhat further afield. These migrants, like others before them, were gradually absorbed by the existing peoples of the plateau; so were their habits and ideas, yet these, in being assimilated by existing cultures, nonetheless changed the way men lived. This was the process of movement-and-assimilation that has given an underlying unity of culture to very many of the peoples of eastern and central-southern Africa. In his paper mentioned above, Mr. Abraham puts it in this way:

"At the start of the fifteenth century a group of patrilineal Bantu clans, collectively known as the Vakaranga,* occupied in strength the south and southwest of what is now Southern Rhodesia. The population was mainly composed of small-scale peasant cultivators and cattle-breeders who lived in modest stockaded villages of thatched mud huts and granaries, and who practiced an ancestor-cult introduced by their forebears from the region of the Great Lakes — perhaps during the course of the eleventh and twelfth centuries."

These Karanga clans took their lead from a dominant clan called the Rozwi (Varozwi or Barozwi in the plural), and were cemented in their common loyalty by religious beliefs that were powerful and supposed a divine king. Later on, as Abraham says,

* Va-, like Ba-, being the plural prefix of Karanga.

the power and prestige of this theocentric Rozwi state was to be symbolized by the large stone structure known as Great Zimbabwe. Tall soapstone bird-figures found among these ruins may have represented the spirits of departed rulers.

Now the second stimulus came into play. This was foreign trade. The Swahili cities of the coast, notably Kilwa by way of Sofala, had been exporting metal, especially gold and (if we are to believe the relevent note in Idrisi — see p. 111) a great deal of iron, ever since the tenth or eleventh century. Much of this gold came from the central plateau, as its many thousands of pre-European workings prove beyond question, just as the iron would have gone from workings nearer the coast, and copper undoubtedly went from the workings in pre-European Katanga. Ivory was another staple from the interior; so, perhaps, was tin. This steady demand for valuable goods combined with the growth of central authority, though in ways that cannot yet be traced precisely, to build the Karanga clans into a unified and conquering power. Here we may detect the same process as had been at work in ancient Ghana. There too the trans-Saharan demand for gold had combined with the growth of central authority — itself the product of Iron Age development — to promote another notable trading empire, also theocentric in its structure.

How much gold did these old "mines" — open shafts going down to as much as a hundred feet — send out to India and other eastern countries? "There is scarcely a modern gold mine in Southern Rhodesia," comments Roger Summers, "which is not on the site of an 'ancient working,' so it is clear that the 'miners' had a good knowledge of prospecting. It has been deduced that originally the zone from the surface down to about twenty feet was exceptionally rich in gold, and it seems very probable that immense quantities of gold were exported." The Portuguese, by comparison, got very little, for they were trusted neither by the inland people nor by the coastal traders, and they were never able to make the system "work." Yet even the Portuguese gathered no mean quantity. Reporting on trade through Sofala during 1512-1515, a Portuguese royal agent wrote of an annual average export of 12,500 *mitqals* of gold (perhaps 100 lbs.), as well as of a much larger quantity of ivory and copper, some amber, seed pearls, coral, and six slaves. The last entry is interesting as a confirmation of the view that slaving from these eastern ports was of little or no importance until later times.

United under their Rozwi "kings and barons," the Karanga embarked upon imperial conquests. This evidently reached a decisive phase in about 1440, or nearly half a century before the Portuguese raided up round the Cape of Good Hope. Within ten years, according to tradition, the ruling Rozwi king had fastened his suzerainty over the great part of Southern Rhodesia. He now controlled most of the gold mines of the plateau and all the trading routes to and from the coast. He could use his power to impose commercial duties on all incoming goods — textiles and beads, porcelain, brassware and other items from oversea — as well as on the exports of his empire. This Rozwi king, Mutota, died before he could complete the logic of his policy by securing control of the coast as well, but his son and successor Matope, as Mr. Abraham shows in the passage that follows here, valiantly carried on the work. Yet the seeds of decay were already present: characteristically for this feudal structure, the "barons" began to nourish ambitions of their own. They contested their supreme lord's power, and sought to seize it for themselves.

D. P. ABRAHAM
Conquest and Challenge

Mutota died [c. A.D. 1450] before he could realize his full ambitions, and it fell to his son and successor Matope to fulfill

From D. P. Abraham, "Maramuca: An Exercise in the Combined Use of Portuguese Records and Oral Tradition," *Journal of African History* 2, 1961. Mr. Abraham's work is a brilliant demonstration of the possibility of merging "oral tradition" with available European records, and will be crowned by a full-scale history of the kingdom of the Mwanamutapa from about 850 to 1902.

the complete specifications of the blueprint drawn up by his father. Over a period of thirty years Matope moved singlemindedly from area to area with his armies, until finally he succeeded in conquering unopposed right to the shores of the Indian Ocean, south of the Zambezi Estuary — leaving undisturbed, however, the Arab *entrepôts** at Sena, Kilimani and Sofala. The southern provinces of Mbire and Guniuswa he entrusted to two Rozwi vassals, Torwa and Changa. The newly won eastern and south-eastern provinces — Chidima, Utonga, Barwe, Shiringoma, Man-yika, Uteve and Madanda — he placed in the hands of sons and trusted relatives. The northern provinces, adjoining the Zambezi valley, he retained under the immediate control of his brothers and himself, and thus replaced the Katanga homeland in the south as the center of political authority.

Changa Succeeds

Thus came into being the golden — but short-lived — phase of the vast feudal domain created by Matope and his father Mutota Mwanamutapa, after whom the Arabs called this Bantu empire Wilayatu 'lMu'anamutapah, and the Portuguese, following the Arabs, Imperio do Manamutapa. Overextended lines of com-munication, political intrigue within the ruling circles, and a lack of ethnic and cultural homogeneity in the conquered provinces sufficient to give rise to a sense of community of interest with the central power, were destined rapidly to disintegrate the new empire into its component parts. Already prior to Matope's death, c. 1480, Changa had taken advantage of the virtual isolation of the southern provinces to transform his position imperceptibly, with the cooperation of his colleague Togwa, into that of inde-pendent ruler. On the death of Matope, Changa began openly to flout the authority of his son and successor Nyahuma, and in-spired by the title *Amir* flatteringly accorded him by his Arab advisers, adopted the dynastic title *Changamire* to emphasize his separatist policy vis-à-vis the Mwanamutapa paramountcy. This policy led to a head-on collision, resulting in the death of Nya-

* That is, Swahili *entrepôts.*

huma in battle c. 1490 and the usurpation by Changamire of the seat of empire for a period of four years.

Kakuyo Komunyaka, son of Nyahuma, succeeded in staging a military comeback and killed the usurper, thus regaining formal control of the Empire; however Changamire's son and successor was able to retain control of the southern provinces Mbire and Guniuswa, which became *de facto* independent of the Empire. Furthermore, by a strenuous diplomatic campaign the new Chang-amire was partially able to detach the eastern and southeastern provinces from loyalty to the Mwanamutapa, who was left with effective domain over what would now be the northern half of Southern Rhodesia and a strip of territory varying from one hundred to two hundred miles in depth, running east and then southeast down to the Indian Ocean for a distance of about six hundred miles. This was the political situation which the Portuguese verified after their initial establishment at Sofala in 1505, a situation in which they became progressively involved in pursuit of their policy to supplant the Arab trade monopoly* of the interior.

* That is to say, the monopoly of trade with the interior possessed by the Swahili coastal cities, notably, at this stage, Kilwa by way of its tributary Sofala.

DIOGO DE ALCANÇOVA
"Kings and Barons"

Establishing themselves along the southeast coast during the opening years of the sixteenth century, the Portuguese became at once aware of powers in the inland country upon which they must depend for any hope of gold. They had much trouble in understanding the true situation there, partly because the Swahili merchants whose cities they had seized and subjected were anything but anxious to enlighten them, and partly because they were as yet incapable of going to see for

From Alcançova's letter of 1506 in G. M. Theal, *Records of South-eastern Africa*, 1900, vol. 1, p. 62.

themselves. Alcançova's letter to the king in Lisbon reflects their confusion about the dynastic strife which was then going on between the Monomotapa and his rebellious vassals, notably Changa in the far southwest. Changa having won these wars, in 1513 the Sofala factor duly reports "peace at last."

Barbosa told in 1518 what was known or believed about the interior. De Barros, writing somewhat later and basing himself on the royal archives in Lisbon, added a good deal more. But from the middle of the sixteenth century the factors and captains along the coast began to receive information from their own upcountry agents; by the end of the century, when we have the invaluable reports of dos Santos, these agents were well established along the banks of the Middle Zambezi and as far as Masapa, a trading post they were able to maintain near the court of the Monomotapa himself. In 1573 the ruling Monomotapa had in fact ceded to the Portuguese a large river line area (between Sena and Tete), and much of this area now became settled by Portuguese planters who constantly forwarded their own interests by political and military intervention in the country's affairs. By this time the power of the Monomotapa was limited to the northeasterly districts of Southern Rhodesia and perhaps the northwesterly fringe of Mozambique, while the Rozwi-Karanga empire held sway throughout the southerly regions under the heirs of Changa, and the kings of Quiteve (Chiteve) continued to rule the upland region on the present frontier of Southern Rhodesia and Portuguese East Africa.

This was the period of greatest prosperity for the Rozwi-Karanga state and empire. Never seriously bothered by the Portuguese, much less subjected by them as were the Monomotapas, the Rozwi divine kings embellished Great Zimbabwe, their capital, built its walls still higher, and reigned through two centuries, until they in turn suffered ultimate disaster at the hands of African invaders from the south. There appears to have been great security in the land, for none of the large stone structures associated with the Karanga (with the possible exception of the "acropolis" at Great Zimbabwe) shows much sign of serious fortification. The situation was different on the eastern borderlands, where fortified dwellings appeared in the seventeenth or eighteenth centuries, and it was possibly different in the Northern Transvaal, where the people of the "Mapungubwe Culture" (linked to that of Zimbabwe) lived in many hilltop settlements.

This long epic of inner Africa, a title that is surely well deserved, moves on into the eighteenth and nineteenth centuries. Here I have stopped with the illuminating report of Manoel Barreto in 1667. Having fatally intervened in the affairs of the Monomotapa, the Portuguese proved far too weak to impose a new system of law and order in that far country; they merely opened the gate to a new chaos. They made furious if erratic attempts to find gold and silver, but succeeded only in undermining the dominant social systems which they found. In this they were helped, no doubt, by the point of growth which these inland states had now reached. Crucial fissures repeatedly appeared in the structure of central rule. This fissuring process was of course a common feature of all lord-and-vassal forms of government. Without Portuguese intervention the Monomotapas might have worked out their conflicts to the same stability as the Rozwi kings achieved. As we shall see, they never really had the chance of doing so.

The kingdom, Sir, in which there is the gold that comes to Sofala is called Vealanga, and the kingdom is very large, in which there are many large towns, besides many other villages, and Sofala itself is in this kingdom if not the whole land along the sea. The kings of the interior pay little or no regard to it if the Moors are in possession [of Sofala]; and going along the coast and towards the interior four leagues, because they [the Moors] do not attempt to go farther inland, as the Kaffirs rob and kill them, for they do not believe in anything. And, Sir, a man might go from Sofala to a city which is called Zumubany [Zimbabwe?] which is large, in which the king always resides, in ten or twelve days, if you travel as in Portugal; but because they do not travel except from morning until midday, and eat and sleep until the next morning when they go on again, they cannot go to this city in less than twenty or twenty-four days; and in the whole kingdom of Vealanga gold is extracted; and in this way: they dig out the earth and make a kind of tunnel, through which they go under the ground a long stone's throw, and keep on taking out from the veins with the ground mixed with the gold, and, when collected, they put it in a pot, and cook it much in fire; and after cooking they take it out, and put it to cool, and, when cold, the earth remains, and the gold all fine gold . . . and no man can take it [the gold] out without leave from the king, under penalty of death.

And this king who now reigns, Sir, in Vealanga, is the son of Mokomba, late king of the said kingdom, and he has the name Kewsarimgo Menomotapam, which is like saying king so and so, because the title of the king is Menomotapam, and the kingdom Vealanga. Your Highness is already aware that for twelve or thirteen years there has been war in the kingdom from which the gold came to Sofala . . .

Alcançova describes the struggle for power between the reigning Monomotapa and his chief vassal of the south, Changamire (cf. D. P. Abraham above, pp. 144-146), in which the Monomotapa attempts to slay Changamire, but the latter prevails.

. . . and when the ameer [Changamire] saw that the king [wished to kill him], he made up his mind to kill [the king] in the city where he was, which is called Zimhauhy [Zimbabwe]: and he took with him many people; and when he arrived near the city, the grandees who were with the king knew that he was coming, they went to receive him, and, when they saw him coming in that way [i.e., with many followers], they would not remain in the city and went out of it [i.e., deserted the Monomotapa]; and the ameer went to the houses of the king, which were of stone and clay very large and of one story, and he entered where the king was with his slaves and some other men; and while speaking to the king the ameer cut his head off; and as he killed him, he made himself king; and all obeyed him; and he reigned peacefully four years; and the king Mokomba [i.e., the Monomotapa] left twenty-two children; and the ameer killed them all, except one, the eldest, who was still young, whose name was Kwekarynugo, who is now the king; and this one fled to another kingdom of his uncle; and when he was twenty years old, he took possession of the kingdom with many people of his father, who came to join him; and he marched against the ameer who had killed his father, in a field close to the town.

And, when the ameer saw that he was coming upon him, he sent many people to fight with him; and the son of the king killed many people of the ameer; and when the ameer saw that they killed so many people, he came out to fight with him; and the son of the king killed the ameer in the field; and the battle lasted three days and a half, in which many people were killed on both sides; and, as the ameer was dead . . . [the Monomotapa] had the kingdom to himself, except that the territories of the ameer would not submit to him; and the ameer left a relative who is named Toloa, who now with a son of the ameer wages war with the king . . . And in this way, Sir, the war was originated, and is still today. And for this reason, Sir, the gold does not come to Sofala as it used to . . .

PEDRO VAZ SOARES

Peace at Last

. . . At present [1513] the whole country is at peace as far as Monomotapa, who is the chief king and lord of all this country, and to whom all the other kings and lords are subject and obedient, and where there is the greatest quantity of gold in these parts, according to what all say, who, after he had finished some wars in which he was engaged, sent to make peace through all the country which is obedient to him, in order that all the traders might go and come to carry on traffic wherever they wished in security . . .

From the translation of a letter to King Manuel of Portugal written in 1513 by his factor at Sofala, Pedro Vaz Soares, in G. M. Theal, *Records of Southeastern Africa*, 1900, vol. 1.

DUARTE BARBOSA
Monomotapa

[What the Portuguese along the Mozambique coast had learned by 1517 was that:] Beyond this country [Sofala, etc.] towards the interior lies the great kingdom of Benametapa [Monomotapa] pertaining to the Heathen whom the Moors [i.e., the Swahili] name Cafres; they are black men and go naked save that they cover their private parts with cotton cloth from the waist down. Some are clad in skins of wild beasts, and some, the most noble, wear capes of these skins with tails which trail on the ground, as a token of state and dignity. They leap as they go, and sway their bodies so as to make these tails fly from one side to the other. They carry swords thrust into wooden scabbards bound with much gold and other metals, worn on the left side, as with us, in cloth girdles which they make for this purpose with four or five knots with hanging tassels to denote men of rank. They also carry assagais in their hands, and others carry bows and arrows of middle size; the arrows not so long as those of the English, and not so short as those of the Turks. The iron arrowheads are long and finely pointed. They are warlike men, and some too are great traders . . .

From *The Book of Duarte Barbosa*, translated by M. L. Dames, Hakluyt Society (2 vols., London: 1918), vol. 1, par. 5.

JOÃO DE BARROS
Mines and Fortresses

[Summarizing what Lisbon had heard or understood by 1550, this annalist reports that:] Of the mines of this land from which gold is taken the nearest to Sofala are those which they call Manica, which are in a plain surrounded by mountains having a circumference of about thirty leagues. The place where gold is to be found is generally known from the earth being dry and poor in herbage. The whole of this district is called Matuca, and the people who dig there are called Botongas . . .

There are other mines in a district called Toroa, which by another name is known as the kingdom of Butua, which is ruled by a prince called Burrom, a vassal of Benametapa, which land adjoins that aforesaid consisting of vast plains, and these mines are the most ancient known in the country, and they are all in the plain, in the midst of which there is a square fortress, of masonry within and without, built of stones of marvelous size, and there appears to be no mortar joining them. The wall is more than twenty-five spans in width, and the height is not so great considering the width. Above the door of this edifice is an inscription, which some Moorish merchants, learned men, who went thither, could not read, neither could they tell what the character might be. This edifice is almost surrounded by hills, upon which are others resembling it in the fashioning of the stone and the absence of mortar, and one of them is a tower more than twelve fathoms high.*

The natives of the country call all these edifices Symbaoe, which

From De Barros in G. M. Theal, *Records of South-eastern Africa*, 1900, vol. 6, p. 261.

* No evidence of a *square* structure in medieval Rhodesia, nor of old inscriptions, has ever come to light.

according to their language signifies court, for every place where Benametapa may be is so called; and they say that being royal property all the king's other dwellings have this name. It is guarded by a nobleman, who has charge of it after the manner of a chief alcaide, and they call this officer Symbacayo, as we should say keeper of the Symbaoe; and there are always some of Benametapa's wives therein, of whom this Symbacayo takes care. When, and by whom, these edifices were raised, as the people of the land are ignorant of the art of writing, there is no record, but they say they are the work of the devil, for in comparison with their power and knowledge it does not seem possible to them that they should be the work of man.

JOÃO DOS SANTOS
South-central Africa in 1590-1600

João dos Santos, who wrote the earliest detailed reports of Central Africa, was a Dominican priest who arrived on the East Coast in 1586. From then until 1590 he served at Sofala. In the latter year he traveled up the Zambezi to the trading posts of Sena and Tete, returning a year later to Mozambique Island. He left Africa in 1595 after serving in the Kerimba Islands and again at Sofala, remained eleven years in Portugal, returned to the Coast and went up the Zambezi a second time. His *Ethiopia Oriental* was published at Evora in 1609 and soon afterwards translated into English. When he refers to "Moors," he is speaking of the Muslim inhabitants of the coastal settlements, most of whom were Swahili. Much of what he has to say is of the highest sociological interest.

From João dos Santos, *Ethiopia Oriental*, in the translation of *Purchas His Pilgrimes* (reprinted Glasgow: 1905), vol. 9. Also in J. Pinkerton, *A General Collection of the Best and Most Interesting Voyages and Travels, etc.* (London: 1814), vol. 16.

Sofala

The Fortresse of Sofala stands in 20.30 Southerne degrees, situate on the Coast of Easterne Ethiopia, neere the Sea, and just by a River a league in the mouth, little more or lesse, which riseth higher above one hundred leagues, arising in the Countrey called Mocarangua, and passing by the Citie Zimbaoe where the Quiteve resides, who is King of those parts, and of all the River of Sofala. Up that River the Portugals trade to Manica, a land of much gold, seated within the land above sixtie leagues. Within the Fort of Sofala is a Church, to which belong six hundred Communicants. The Inhabitants usually are Merchants, some to Manica for gold, which they barter for Stuffes and Beades, both to the Captayne and themselves; others to the River of Sabia, and the Iles das Bocicas, and other neere Rivers, for Ivorie, Gergelimspice, Pulse, Amber, and many Slaves.

There is another habitation of Moores two Caliver shot from the Castle, poore and miserable, which live by serving the Portugals. The women performe there the offices of Tillage and Husbandry; as also doe the Moores. They pay their Tithes to the Dominicans Church. The Fortresse was built An. 1505 by Pero da Nhaya, with consent of the Moorish King Zufe, a man blinde of both his eyes (in both senses, externall and internall, religious and politike) who too late repenting, thought to supplant it with trecherie, which they returned upon himselfe and slew him. In old times they had many such petty Moorish Kings on the Coast, few of which now remaine by reason of the Portugall Captaynes succeeding in their places, and in their amitie and commerce with the Quiteve King of those Countries . . .

Kingdom of the Quiteve

The King of these parts [inland Mozambique and frontier with S. Rhodesia] is of curled haire, a Gentile, which worships nothing, nor hath any knowledge of God; yea, rather hee carries himselfe as God of his Countries, and so is holden and reverenced of his Vassals. Hee is called Quiteve, a title royall and no proper name, which they exchange for this so soone as they become Kings. The

Quiteve hath more than one hundred women all within doores, amongst which one or two are as his Queenes, the rest as Concubines: many of them are his owne Aunts, Cousins, Sisters and Daughters, which he no less useth, saying, that his sonnes by them are true heires of the Kingdome without mixture of other bloud. When the Quiteve dyeth, his Queenes must die with him to doe him service in the other world, who accordingly at the instant of his death take a poyson (which they call Lucasse) and die therewith. The successor succeedeth as well to the women as to the state. None else but the King may upon paine of death marry his Sister or Daughter. This Successor is commonly one of the eldest Sonnes of the deceased King, and of his great Women or Queenes; and if the eldest be not sufficient, then the next, or if none of them be fit, his Brother of whole bloud. The King commonly whiles hee liveth maketh the choise, and traines up him to affaires of State, to whom he destines the succession. Whiles I lived there . . . the King had above thirtie Sonnes, and yet shewed more respect to his Brother a wise man, then to any of them, all honoring him as apparent heire.

The same day the King dies, he is carried to a Hill where all the Kings are interred, and early the next morning, hee whom the deceased had named his Successor, goeth to the Kings house where the Kings Women abide in expectation, and by their consent hee enters the house, and seates himselfe with the principall of them in a publike Hall, where the King was wont to sit to heare Causes, in a place drawne with curtens or covered with a cloth, that none may see the King nor the Women with him. And thence he sends his Officers, which goe thorow the Citie and proclayme Festivals to the New King, who is now quietly possessed of the Kings House, with the Women of the King decessed, and that all should goe and acknowledge him for their King: which is done by all the great Men then in Court, and the Nobles of the Citie, who goe to the Palace now solemnely guarded, and enter into the Hall by licence of the Officers, where the new King abides with his Women; entring some, and some, creeping on the ground till they come to the middle of the Hall, and thence speake to the New King, giving him due obeysance, without seeing him or his Women. The King makes answere from within, and accepts their service: and after that drawes the Curtens, and shewes himselfe to them; whereat all of them clap their hands, and then turne behind the Curtens, and goe forth creeping on the ground as they came in; and when they are gone, others enter and doe in like sort. In this ceremonie the greatest part of the day is spent with feasting, musick and dancing thorow the citie. The next day, the King sends his Officers thorow the Kingdome to declare this his succession, and that all should come to the Court to see him breake the Bowe. Sometimes there are many Competitors, and then Hee succeeds whom the Women admit into the Kings House: for none may enter by Law without their leave, nor can bee King without peaceable entrance; forceable entrie forfeiting his Right and Title. By bribes therefore and other wayes, they seeke to make the Women on their side.

Neere the Kingdome of Quiteve is another of Lawes and Customes like thereto, where the Sedanda raignes: both which were sometimes but one Kingdome. Whiles I was in Sofala, the Sedanda being incurably sick of a leprosie, declared his Successor, and poysoned himselfe: which also is the custome there, if any King have any deformitie in his person. The named Successor sought admittance of the Women, but they much distasting him, had secretly sent by night for another Prince whom they better liked, as more valiant and better beloved; whom they admitted, and assembled themselves with him in the publike Hall, and caused Proclamation to bee made to the people of his succession. The other, whom they had rejected, fled for feare of his life, and being mightie assembled a great power, and by force entred the Kings House. But this was strange to all, who therefore forsooke him, and stuck to him whom the Women had chosen; whereupon the other fled, and no more lifted up his head.

Before the New King begins to governe, he sends for all the chiefs in the Kingdome, to come to the Court and see him breake the Kings Bowe, which is all one with taking possession of the Kingdome. In those Courts is a custome then also to kill some of those Lords or great Men, saying, that they are necessarie for the service of the decessed King: whereupon they kill those of whom they stand in feare or doubt, or whom they hate, in stead of whom they make and erect new Lords. This custome causeth such as feare themselves to flee the Land. Anciently the Kings were wont to drinke poyson in any grievous disasters, as in a contagious disease, or naturall impotencie, lamenesse, the losse of their foreteeth, or other deformitie; saying, that Kings ought to have no defect; which if it happened, it was honour for him to die, and goe to better himselfe in that better life, in which he should be wholly perfect. But the Quiteve which raigned whiles I was there, would not follow his predecessors herein; but having lost one of his foreteeth, sent to proclaime thorow his whole Kingdome that one of his teeth were fallen out, and that if (that they might not be ignorant when they saw him want it) his predecessors were such fooles, for such causes to kill themselves, he would not doe so, but awaite his naturall death, holding his life necessary to conserve his estate against his enemies, which example hee would commend to posteritie.

If the Cafars have a suit, and seeke to speake with the King, they creepe to the place where hee is, having prostrated themselves at the entrance, and looke not on him all the while they speake, but lying on one side clap their hands all the time (a rite of obsequiousnesse in those parts) and then having finished, they creepe out of the doores as they came in. For no Cafar may enter on foot to speake to the King, nor eye him in speaking, except the familiars and particular friends of the King. The Portugals enter on their feet, but unshod, and being neere the King, prostrate themselves lying on one side almost sitting, and without looking on him speake to him, at every fourth word clapping their hands according to the custome. Both Cafres and Portugals are entertained by him with wine of Mays, or their wheate, called Pombe, which they must drinke, although against stomacke, not to contemne the Kings bountie; whence the Portugals have had some trouble, and are forced to stay in Towne without leave to returne home, with great expence of time and charges . . .

They use three kinds of Oathes in Judgement most terrible, in accusations wanting just evidence. The first is called, Lucasse, which is a vessell full of poison, which they give the suspected, with words importing his destruction, and present death if he be guilty; his escape, if innocent: the terrour whereof makes the conscious confesse the crime: but the innocent drinke it confidently without harme, and thereby are acquitted of the crime; and the plaintiffe is condemned to him whom he falsly had accused; his wife, children, and goods being forfeited, one moitie to the King, and the other to the defendant. The second Oath they call, Xoqua, which is made by iron heated red hot in the fire, causing the accused to lick it being so hot with his tongue, saying, that the fire shall not hurt him if hee bee innocent; otherwise it shall burne his tongue and his mouth. This is more common, and is used by the Cafres and the Moores in those parts; yea, (which worse is) some Christians give the same Oath to their slaves suspected of stealth; which one in Sofala caused, on suspicion of a stollen garment, a slave to doe three times without hurt. The third Oath they call, Calano, which is a vessell of water made bitter with certain herbs, which they put into it, whereof they give the accused to drinke, saying, that if he be innocent, he shall drinke it all off at one gulp without any stay, and cast it all up againe at once without any harme: if guilty, he shall not be able to get downe one drop without gargling and choaking . . .

Far up the Zambezi

The River Cuama is by them called Zambeze; the head whereof is so farre within Land that none of them know it, but by tradition of their Progenitors say it comes from a Lake in the midst of the Continent, which yeelds also other great Rivers, divers wayes visiting the Sea. They call it Zambeze, of a Nation of Cafres dwelling neere that Lake, which are so called. It hath a strong current, and is in divers places more than a league broad. Twentie leagues before it enters the Sea, it divides it selfe into two armes, each Daughter as great as the Mother, which thirtie leagues distant pay their Tribute to the Father of waters. The principall of them is called Luabo, which also divides it selfe into two branches, one called Old Luabo, the other Old Cuama. The other lesse principall Arme is named Quilimane.

Luabo is sailed all the yeere long, but Quilimane only in the

Winter. They saile up this River West North-west above two hundred leagues, to the Kingdome of Sacumbe, where it makes a great Fall from Rockes, beyond which they goe up the River twentie leagues to the Kingdome of Chicova, in which are Mines of Silver, which cannot be sailed by reason of the strong current: but from Chicova upwards it is Navigable, but how farre they know not. Luabo hath its name of an Iland so called in the Barre thereof in nineteene degrees, which Iland divides old Luabo on the South from Old Cuama, on the North: and in the East each salutes the other by entercourse of a streame five leagues long, which is the length and breadth of the Iland, peopled with Moores and Cafres. The Pangayos or great Barkes of Mosambique here discharge, being too great to passe higher, and carrie their goods in a Fleet of small Boates to the Fort of Sena, which is sixty leagues . . .

Sena is a Fort of Lime and Stone, furnished with Artillery; the Captayne is placed by the Captayne of Mosambique. There were in my time eight hundred Christians, of which fiftie Portugalls. Seven or eight leagues from hence on the other side of the River, is the high Hill Chiri, which may be seene twentie leagues off, the Hill and Valleys exceeding fertile. To this Factory of Sena, they come from Tete to buy Merchandize with their Gold.

Tete is a stone Fort sixtie leagues further up the River in the Kingdome of Inhabaze, under the Manamotapa, the Captayne is placed by the Captayne of Mosambique. In this place were in my time sixe hundred Christians, of them fortie Portugalls. These one hundred and twentie leagues the Portugalls goe up the River, and from thence goe by Land with their Merchandize. The Countrey is very fertile, and Portugall wares are here sold at great prizes. From Tete they goe with their wares thorow a great part of Manamotapa to three Marts, Massapa, Luanze, Manzovo, in which the inhabitants of Sena, and Tete have houses and Factories, thence to store all the Countrey.

Massapa is the chiefe, where resides a Portugall Captayne, presented by the Portugalls, and confirmed by the Manamotapa, which cals him his Great Wife, a name of honour, as before is observed. This Captayne holds jurisdiction over all the Cafres without Appeale, as also over the Portugalls in that Kingdome, granted by the Vice-Royes, as all other Captaynes of those parts have. This Captayne of Massapa treats all businesse with the Manamotapa, whose Customer he is also, taking one cloth of twentie, in which respect the Countrey is free to them. But beyond Massapa, neerer the Manamotapa, [no] one may goe without license from the King or the Captayne. The Captayne hath an Azagay of blacke Wood pointed with Gold, for his Ensigne or Rod of Authoritie. The Captayne of Mosambique payes at his entrance to the Manamotapa, three thousand Cruzados in goods for the three yeares of his Captayne-ship, for free Trade in his Countreyes, which they may travell securely laden with Gold; it beeing never knowne that Theeves assaile them, or any without the Kings authoritie . . .

The Kingdom of Monomotapa

This Kingdome of Manamotapa, is scituate in Mocaranga, which in times past was wholly of the Manamotapan Empire, but now is divided into foure Kingdomes, to wit, this of Manamotapa, that of Quiteve, the third of Sedanda and the fourth of Checanga. This division was made by a Manamotapan Emperour, who not willing or not able to governe so remote Countreyes, sent his Sonne Quiteve to governe that part which runnes along the River of Sofala, and Sedanda another Sonne, to that which Sabia washeth, a River which visits the Sea before the Bocicas: and Chicanga a third Sonne to the Lands of Manica. These three after their Fathers death would never acknowledge their Brother his Successor: and the same not without yeerely warring with each other, continues to their Posteritie. Yet is the Kingdome of the Manamotapa, bigger then the other three together. The Cafres call them all Mocarangas, because they speake the Mocaranga Tongue.

This Kingdome of Manamotapa is above two hundred leagues long, and as much broad. On the North-west he confines with the Kingdome of Abutua (the King and Kingdome have the same name) which they say, stretcheth thorow the Continent to the borders of Angola. I have seene in Sofala a Commoditie bought by a Portugall in Manica, brought thither by the Cafres of Abutua, which had come from Portugall by the way of Angola. In this Kingdome of Abutua is much fine Gold, but the Naturals being farre from the Portugals, doe not much seeke after it, but rather to multiply their cattle of which they have abundance. On the East Manamotapa confineth with the River Zambeze, which the Manamotapans call Empando, which signifieth Rebelling against his King: for say they, were it not for the River, the Manamotapa would bee Lord of the Countrey on the other-side, to which he cannot passe his Armie for want of Boats. On the South-west this Kingdome extendeth to the Ocean, into which it enters with a point of Land of ten or twelve leagues large, from the River Luabo, to that of Tandanculo. The rest of the Lands Southwards to the River Inhanabane, and devided betwixt the three Kings, which rebelled as is said: from Tendanculo to Sofala, the Quiteve reigneth: thence to the South is the Kingdome of Sabia, under the Sedanda, who is Lord also of Botonga to the Region Inhambane: within Land at the head of both these Kingdomes is Manica under the Chicanga, who is on the North-west, some hundreths of leagues remote from the Sea. On the North side of Manica, is Abutua, and on the North-east is the Manamotapa, and to the South is a King called Biri. Those three Kings which rebelled are great, but the Quiteve is the greatest, and richest by trade with the Portugals for Stuffes and Beades (which is the Cafres wealth) and his people are the strongest of the Mocarangas, and the best Archers, and most expert at the Azagay.

Neere to Massapa is a great high Hill, called Fura, whence may bee discerned a great part of the Kingdome of Manamotapa: for which cause he will not suffer the Portugalls to goe thither, that they should not covet his great Countrey and hidden Mines. On the toppe of that Hill are yet standing pieces of old wals, and ancient ruines of lime and stone, which testifie that there have beene strong buildings . . .

In all the Regions of Manamotapa, or the greatest part thereof, are many Mines of Gold; and particularly in Chiroro, where is the most and most fine. They gather it, as is said before, of Quiteve. It is paine of death for any Moore which discovers a Mine to take away any, besides his goods forfeited to the King. And if by

chance any find a Mine, he is bound to cry out aloud, that some
other Cafar may come to testifie that he takes none: and both are
then to cover the Place with Earth, and set a great bough thereon,
to give warning to other Cafares to avoyd the place. For if they
should come there, it would cost them their lives, although there
be no proofe that he tooke any thing. This severitie is used to keep
the Mines from the knowledge of the Portugals, lest covetous desire thereof might cause them to take away their Countrey. It is
found in poulder like sand; in graines like beads; in pieces some
smooth as they were melted, others branched with snags, others
mixed so with Earth, that the Earth being well washed from them,
they remayne like Honiecombes; those holes before full of red
Earth, seeming as though they were also to be turned into Gold.
As for that in stone, we have alreadie spoken . . .

Although the Manamotapa be greater than those three mentioned, yet hath he not other Kings Vassals or Tributaries to him:
only some of his subjects called Encosses or Fumos, are great
Lords, and have Tenants subject to them. Botero therefore in his
Relations, Gusman, and Osorius, were deceived by false information, giving to the Manamotapa, so large a Sea-coast with tributary Kings; which, I doubt, whether ever there was any such thing;
at lest there is now no memory thereof. Philip Pigafetta also from
the Relations of Lopez, hath falsly described these Coasts and
Kingdomes, and hath told a long Tale of Amazons in these parts,
where neither are such, nor any memoriall of them. They tell also
of the Royall Ensignes, a Spade of Gold with an Ivorie head to
intimate his Husbandry; and two Arrowes, the notes of his Justice;
and that he alwayes is accompanyed with Souldiers; but in all they
deceive and are deceived. As for Bows and Arrowes, it is as ordinary with the Cafres as with the Portugalls, to weare a Sword in
their Cities; none of them going out of doores without them. And
in like manner when the Manamotapa goeth forth, hee carries in
his hand his Bow and Arrowes, as likewise doe the Cafres which
accompany him, as a custome and not as Warriours. Before him
goeth a Cafre beating with his hand on a great Cushion, to give
notice that the King is at hand. When the Manamotapa will not
carry his Bow, an Officer called Mascorira (which is as a Page of the

Chamber) carries it; and the King carrieth in his hand an Azagay, or Javelin of blacke wood with the point of pure Gold, like the Iron head of a Lance, or three pieces of wood, called Fimbos, of two spannes and a halfe, wrought and slender. And when hee speakes with a Cafre, whom he will have dye, he lets fall one of these Fimbos, and his infices (executioners) take and kill him with an Azagay; and so dye condemned persons.

He hath many women, and the principall, which is most respected, called Mazarira, is his entire sister a great friend of the Portugals, to whom when they give the King his Curua, they give a Present of Clothes. No man speakes with the King or with his Wife, but hee brings a Present; the Portugals give Beades, the Cafres Kine, or Goats, or Clothes: and when they are able to give nothing else, they bring a Sacke of Earth to acknowledge subjection, or a bundle of straw to thatch the Kings Houses; for all the Houses in Cafraria are thatched. The Manamotapa which now reignes, is called Mambo, and his subjects use to sweare by his life, saying Xè Mambo; and when they speake with him, they say Xè dico, as we, Please your Majestie. The Kings Children are called Manambo. Hee hath given leave to our Religious men in his Kingdomes, to convert and to build Churches; of which they have built three, to wit, at Massapa, Luanze, Bucutu, where live many Portugals . . .

ANTONIO BOCCARRO

The Deal with Portugal

In 1607 the Monomotapa, being faced with the revolt of powerful vassals, called in the Portuguese to help him. They did so with men

From the translation of Antonio Boccarro in G. M. Theal, *Records of Southeastern Africa*, 1900, vol. 3, p. 376. Boccarro succeeded Diogo de Couto as Keeper of the Archives and Chronicler of India (which was taken to include southeast Africa), and died in 1649. His reports were first published in Lisbon in 1876.

from Sena and Tete under Diogo Simões; in return for this the Monomotapa "promised with great liberality to give him all the silver mines
in his kingdom, as being what he [Simões] most valued; and afterwards for these and other greater victories Diogo Simões induced the
emperor to make a donation to his Majesty of all the mines of gold or
other metals which might be in the whole of his kingdom, as will be
hereafter related." This was done formally by the Monomotapa on
August 1, 1607, though it was not in fact the first of its kind, a similar
agreement dating from 1593. The document of 1607 was drawn up by
Simões, and has survived.

"I, the emperor Monomotapa, think fit and am pleased to give
to his Majesty all the mines of gold, copper, iron, lead and pewter
which may be in my empire, so long as the king of Portugal, to
whom I give the said mines, shall maintain me in my position . . ."

. . . Having made this donation [Boccarro reports] the army of
the emperor set out with our Kaffirs, vassals of Tete, in the van,
and the other Portuguese with Diogo Simões in the rear . . . The
army of the Monomotapa went forward in the order aforesaid, of
which the enemies were not informed, and therefore they attacked
it in the van, as they had done before, but finding the resistance
different from what they expected, and that our people were killing them like hens, they turned their backs, and our people pur-
suing them, wounded and killed as many as they overtook . . .

ADVICES FROM GOA

Destruction of Monomotapa

But steady Portuguese encroachment met with resistance. By 1630,
as we learn from "advices from Goa" to the court in Lisbon — all news

From G. M. Theal, *Records of South-eastern Africa*, 1900, vol. 2, p. 249,
for the first extract and vol. 5, p. 290, for the second.

of southeast Africa went via India — the Portuguese used their early alliance as the door to large-scale intervention by force. The independence of Monomotapa was largely destroyed.

The Emperor of Monomotapa having robbed the Portuguese residing in Sena and Tete, and killed the ambassador whom the Captain at Mozambique had sent to him, we took the field with two hundred and fifty Portuguese and thirty thousand Kafirs, their vassals, at two different times — the first in December, 1628, and the second in May, 1629. Their two great armies were destroyed, and on the second day the greater part of the grandees of the empire were killed, and the remainder made Manura* their emperor in place of the former one, who, according to the laws of the country, for certain excesses he had committed in the flight, could no longer reign. Manura at this time became a Christian, and was put in possession by the Portuguese, in the name of and as the vassal of their king, and received and guaranteed all the conditions which the Portuguese considered conformable to the honor of the Gospel, and of the Crown of Portugal.

Following this invasion, the same report of 1630 continues, the Monomotapa Manura signed a new treaty with the Portuguese on May 24, 1629.

First that this kingdom is delivered to him [i.e., to Manura] in the name of the king of Portugal, our lord, of whom he shall acknowledge himself to be a vassal . . .

That he, the said king, shall allow all the religious of whatever order who may be in his *zimbahe* to build churches and in all the other lands in his dominions . . .

That ambassadors who come to speak to him shall enter his *zimbahe* shod and covered, with their arms in their belts, as they speak to the king of Portugal, and he shall give them a chair on which to seat themselves without clapping their hands; and other

* More properly Mavura, according to Abraham, "The Monomotapa Dynasty," in *Native Affairs Department Annual*, Salisbury, Southern Rhodesia, 1959, p. 58.

Portuguese shall speak to him in the manner of ambassadors, and shall be given a *kaross* to sit upon . . .

He shall make his lands free to the Portuguese . . .

Throughout all his kingdom he shall allow as many mines to be sought for and opened as the Portuguese like . . .

Within a year he shall expel all the Moors [i.e., Swahili and Arab traders from the coastal towns] from his kingdom, and those who shall be found there afterward shall be killed by the Portuguese, and their property shall be seized for the king of Portugal . . .

KING OF PORTUGAL

Civilities

Two years after the signature of the above treaty of 1629, the King of Portugal writes politely to the Monomotapa Manura.

———————

Most noble and powerful king of Monomotapa, I, Dom Philipe, by the grace of God king of Portugal, of the Algarves, and of the sea on both sides of Africa, lord of Guinea and of the conquest, navigation, and commerce of Ethiopia, Arabia, Persia, and India, etc., greet you well, as one whom I love and esteem as a brother.

I have seen the letter which you wrote to me by the ships of last year, 1630, and having gathered therefrom, as my viceroy of the State of India also wrote to me, how the wars and disturbances in your kingdom had ended, and how my captains gave you the investitute and possession of it . . . I think fit to inform you that I received great satisfaction from all this . . .

From G. M. Theal, *Records of South-eastern Africa*, 1900, vol. 4, p. 225.

MANOEL BARRETO
Realities

In a valuable report of 1667 to the viceroy in Goa upon the "State and Conquest of the Rivers of Cuama, Commonly and Truly called the Rivers of Gold," Manoel Barreto explains to the viceroy that he is writing after many years spent in the region. He is speaking mainly of the lands of the Lower Zambezi.

As [the empire of] Maravi is beside us up the river [Zambezi] on the eastern side, so is Mokaranga on the northern side. It commences immediately above Tete, and extends towards the west and north about a hundred and fifty leagues, both in length and breadth . . .

Mokaranga is very healthy, fertile and verdant . . . In this kingdom . . . rich in gold, its kings chose for their court, or *zimbaoe*, a site which is dry, sterile and unhealthy, which makes the residence of the chief captain and garrison [i.e., Portuguese] of that court sufficiently difficult. The distance from Tete to Dambarari is about fourteen days' journey, and to the *zimbaoe* twenty.

Dambarari is a noble settlement and good-sized town in the heart of Mokaranga, and has grown to be the center of that conquest, with many rich inhabitants. The Portuguese and even the *mocoques* [chiefs] of Dambarari and of the rest of Mokaranga possess vast lands, or provinces, which they have bought, and buy every day, from the king of Mokaranga. With the people of these lands and their *macamos*, as they call their troops of slaves, they are more powerful than the king of Mokaranga himself. It is a

From the translation of the original (in the Bibliothèque Nationale, Paris) by G. M. Theal, *Records of South-eastern Africa*, 1900, vol. 3, p. 436 for the first extract and p. 490 for the second.

proof of this that while I was there they separated themselves from the poor king, through no fault of his, and declared war against him. Before it came to a battle, when the armies were almost in sight of each other, the *encozes*, who are the lords or chief Kaffirs of that kingdom, killed the poor king (a thing unprecedented among the Kaffirs) for fear of the Portuguese, and came and subjected themselves to them that they might make whom they chose king. They elected a young man of the royal house, but very crafty and cunning, who is now sufficiently feared by them. I fear the punishment of God for the injustice done to the poor dead king, particularly upon Antonio Rois de Lima, who was the head of this unjust rebellion and other great disorders in that conquest.

To keep this new and formidable king in check, Antonio de Mello was obliged to send Antonio Lobo da Silva to Mokaranga as chief captain . . . Antonio de Mello's motive was that he had been told the gold would fail, because the Kaffirs would not dig for it through fear of the Portuguese. It is true that the *encozes* do not wish gold to be dug for in their lands, because upon the report of gold being found the Portuguese buy the land from the king, as frequently happened, and they, the *encozes*, being great lords, counts, dukes and marquises, are despoiled of their lands and become poor *caporros*, which signifies laborers. But this objection is not avoided by the Portuguese giving up the lands they have already, as the *encozes* would retain them from the king again, with many more. It would be sufficient, in order to avoid this obstacle, to pass an inviolable law that the king should not give or sell any more lands to the Portuguese, by which the *encozes* who now hold them would be without fear; but who can tie the hands of a king and prevent him from doing what he pleases in his own kingdom? Besides, this would close the door by which the Portuguese become each time more powerful in that kingdom, and which is very conducive to conquest.

This king of Mokaranga is honored by his Majesty with the title of brother-in-arms, but strictly speaking he is his vassal, for in the time of the rebel king Capracina the Portuguese conquered the kingdom by force of arms, and now they elect and depose kings at their pleasure.

If this king should rise in rebellion it would be proper to conquer the whole of the kingdom, and divide the lands among the Portuguese, by which there would be great favors and rich appointments for the deserving. Then the natives would dig as much gold as their masters, the Portuguese, required . . .

The Gold Fails

There are many reasons to account for the small quantity of gold produced.

First, the repugnance of the *encozes* [chiefs], who will allow no digging in their lands, that the Portuguese may not covet them . . .

Secondly, the want of population, which is great throughout Kaffraria . . .

But the principal cause of the want of population is the bad conduct of the Portuguese, from whose violence the Kaffirs flee to other lands . . .

West Africa Meets Europe

*T*HE MEETING OCCURRED IN THE MIDDLE OF THE FIFTEENTH CEN-
tury, rather more than five hundred years ago. It was brusque and
bloody to begin with, an affair of squalid raids and running fights,
but soon calmed to a more or less regular trading partnership. In
exchange for textiles and metalware, West African gold and ivory
and spice began to reach Europe by sea instead of through the
hands of middlemen across the Sahara. A new period of history
began.

Looking back, we can see that the meeting might well have occurred two or three centuries earlier — Genoese ships had come as
far as Salé in Morocco by 1163 — but for a major climatic obstacle.
Along the Atlantic Coast from Cape Juby to Cape Blanc, a reach
of some four hundred miles, the wind is almost always from the
northward. Not until the early fifteenth century were the ships of
Europe technically capable of sailing into the wind; while their
crews, having neither astrolabe nor compass, were understandably
reluctant to sail "round the wind" by steering boldly westward out
of sight of land. This meant that they could well enough go down
the coast beyond Cape Juby, but could hope to get back again
only with the use of oars against the wind, a very laborious and
perhaps impossible trial of strength. Even so, several attempts are
known to have been made, the most famous being that of Jacme
Ferrer, who voyaged from Mallorca for the Rio d'Oro (the legendary "river of gold") in 1346, as the Catalan Atlas of thirty-one
years later graphically records, but never returned.

Then these nautical problems were solved. Perhaps through the
experience of the Crusades, European seamen learned the use of

the lateen sail, no doubt from Muslim sailors of the eastern Mediterranean who would have had it from their fellow-seamen of the Indian Ocean. Invented in China, the nautical compass also reached Europe by way of the Arabs. So did the astrolabe, a device for measuring latitude. Cartography enormously improved. The fruits of all this were not long in coming. In 1434 a Portuguese crew sailed beyond Cape Bojador and returned safely against the wind. Others followed. Within little more than half a century these hardy and courageous mariners had pushed their discoveries to the Cape of Good Hope. (An admirable discussion of the technical and political background to all this will be found in Professor Raymond Mauny's *Les Navigations Médiévales sur les Côtes Sahariennes antérieurs à la Découverte portugaise*, Lisbon, 1960.)

The early Portuguese and Spanish material is fairly copious but of greatly varying value. After Azurara's (or Zurara's) picturesque *Discovery of Guinea*, completed in 1453 (English translation by C. R. Beazley and E. Prestage, Hakluyt Society, 2 vols., 1896), there are useful if highly partial memoirs collected by Ruy de Pina, who became chief chronicler of Portugal in 1497, as well as a number of lesser works. An Italian in Portuguese service, Ca' da Mosto, sailed to the Gambia in 1456 and published an interesting account of trade along the coast (English translation by G. R. Crone, Hakluyt Society, 1937). Then comes a work of capital importance, the first detailed and reliable description of the geographical outline of the western reaches of the Guinea seaboard: the curiously named *Esmeraldo de Situ Orbis* of Duarte Pacheco Pereira, written probably between 1505 and 1508. Pereira had sailed to India in one of the three fleets of 1503, returning two years later, and therefore knew the route from his own experience. A systematic picture of the coast now became available in Lisbon.

Other Europeans followed where the Portuguese had led, notably the English and the French and, a little later on, the Dutch. Until the seventeenth century — though rarely even then — their writings are seldom more than laconic tales of adventure or bare recitals of trading profit, laced now and then with more or less fantastic speculations on the nature of African humanity. There are some exceptions to this, as the reader will see, but not many. Yet these ships' logs and seamen's tales throw light on two interesting aspects of this European-African connection of the sixteenth century: they reveal the beginnings of a trade that was profitable to both sides, a trade that was still free of slaving so far as the French and English (though not the Portuguese) were concerned; and they show the relationship of equality and mutual respect that held good between the two sides of a promising commercial partnership. Apart from the slaving voyages of John Hawkins, the English (as the French) were not in the least concerned with buying captives. They wanted gold, pepper and ivory in that order of priority, offering hardware and textiles in exchange. This trade was perilous because of the dangers of the voyage and the enmity of the Portuguese, who claimed a monopoly of access to West Africa, yet it prospered. The voyages of Thomas Windham and John Lok, and William Towerson's three remarkable voyages of 1555-1557, were highly profitable to the merchants of London, and, so far as the records show, no less satisfactory to those of Africa. The story is much the same on the French side.

But the Portuguese were already deeply involved in buying captives for slave labor in the Americas. Like the English and the French, they had begun with other intentions; it was the slave trade on the west coast — as it was their piracy on the east — that dragged their connection with Africa into a morass of bloody violence. On this the records are perfectly clear. They can be followed most easily in relation to the African kingdoms that lay round the estuary of the Congo and southward in western Angola. Here we are fortunate in possessing twenty-four letters written by King Affonso (Mbemba Nzinga) to two successive kings of Portugal, a collection that is of unique value to history in that it offers the earliest African commentary on the European connection.

Reading between the lines of these polite and often puzzled letters we can trace the early hopes of this African monarch and his later disillusionment; the determination with which he tried, time and again, to turn the trade with Portugal to constructive ends; his efforts to circumvent the Portuguese monopoly of contact with Europe; the growing ruin of the slave trade; the steady collapse of trust and confidence, and the multiplying signs of early Portuguese imperialism. A fuller examination of all this may be found in my *Black Mother*, 1961. Much parallel material from the Roman Catholic missionary side is in *L'Ancien Congo d'après les Archives romaines* (1518-1640), edited by Monsignor J. Cuvelier and Abbé L. Jadin (Brussels: 1954), while the contemporary records and memoirs of Pigafetta (Rome: 1591) and Resende (Lisbon: 1622) are of major importance.

These contemporary writings were composed, one should remember, against a background of grotesque superstition, especially among the Portuguese, and acute religious prejudice. Their authors were quite without a scientific approach. Even the achievements of Muslim science were largely unknown, or, if known at all, filtered at second or third hand through the private libraries of kings and princes. Such libraries were designed to further national and commercial purposes rather than the pursuit of knowledge, and they were generally barred to public use. No monarch, least of all the king of Portugal, had any interest in sharing what he knew with rivals and competitors; on the contrary, the pioneers and merchants kept their knowledge closely to themselves. It was nearly four centuries before Pereira's book was published, and we have already noted what befell the work of de Barros and de Couto. Not until the end of the imperial epoch was there to be any real chance of seeing "in the round" what Europeans believed or knew of Africa in those early days. But now with fuller knowledge and smaller prejudice it is possible to reassess these memoirs and adventures as a whole, and award them their small but useful place in the records of the continent. What follows here is a brief but representative selection.

This section also takes in the seventeenth century.

If the sixteenth had been a time of European piracy passing into alliance and regular trading intercourse with maritime chiefs and peoples from the Senegal to the Congo, the seventeenth was one of intensive and developing commercial enterprise. For France and England, this was the period of the early "chartered companies," those stumbling experiments in early forms of banking and capital investment; and, on the Coast itself, of the rise of the Dutch with their emergence as commercial and military leaders of the whole European enterprise. It was likewise the period of Spanish decline, and the strong establishment of the English and the French in the Caribbean. Out of these various factors came the oversea slave trade as a *system*. This system was to dominate European-African relations from the middle of the seventeenth century until the middle of the nineteenth.

For Africa the seventeenth century was similarly a time of large and in some respects crucial change. In the Western Sudan it brought the final collapse of the Songhay Empire of Gao; with declining Muslim prosperity in North Africa, it witnessed a dwindling of the trans-Saharan trade, and the consequent impoverishment of trading cities such as Timbuktu and Djenné. Europe having opened West Africa's back door, the gold and ivory (and now, increasingly, the slaves) went northward or westward by way of the sea. For the same order of reasons there were great organic changes in the forest-belt states between the grasslands and the coast. The ground was laid for the rise of new powers, such as Ashanti and Dahomey, which would soon challenge the old mastery of Oyo and Benin. In central and southern Africa (with the Dutch acquiring a toehold at the Cape of Good Hope in 1652) the seventeenth century brought new constellations of power among some of the leading Bantu-speaking peoples, notably in the lands of the southern Congo basin. Ethiopia triumphed over her Muslim neighbors and rivals. The "black sultans" of the Fung built their powerful state on the Middle Nile.

Some of these inner-African changes were the consequence of indirect pressures from the European connection along the seaboard; most took place, however, beyond the probing reach of European influence. On these the European records are entirely silent, or, if not quite mute, greatly misinformed. Here and there, true enough, envoys and missionaries sent home interesting reports or wrote them after retirement; prominent among these were some of the missionaries in the old Congo kingdoms, Father Giovanni Cavazzi and others, who offer highly impressionist but none the less firsthand view of the situation. Generally, however, the records of the seventeenth century (especially by contrast with those of the eighteenth) are of much greater value to European than to African history, being concerned for the most part with internecine rivalry, largely between the English and the Dutch and between the Dutch and the Portuguese.

Characteristic of their type and temper, for example, is a petition of 1662 by the owners of the *Daniell* to the Privy Council. They had commissioned Henry Oake to sail the *Daniell* "Neere the Gold Coast at Guinny" and there to buy ivory, gold, and captives for the West Indian plantations. "He arrived safely, and did barter away part of his Lading for 83 Negroes, a parcel of Elephants' Teeth, and some Gold . . ." All seemed well. But "as he was in his lawful employment, one Jasper Vanhuisen, General for the Dutch West India Company residing at Guinny, first seized his Boat and five of his men, going towards Cormantine and carrying them away prisoners; and some days after, a ship of Amsterdam . . . belonging to the Dutch, being mounted with 30 guns, and the ship *Daniell* having but Four, the said ship of Amsterdam . . . took her and all the Goods and Negroes, stripping and plundering the Company . . ." On this and the immediately following period the magnificent work of Elizabeth Donnan, *Documents Illustrative of the History of the Slave Trade to America* (Carnegie Institution, Washington, D.C.: 1930-1935), has put all subsequent writers and readers deeply in her debt.

Encroaching on each other, the Europeans also encroached on their African partners and were frequently rebuffed. Not for a long time would the power of Europe prove capable of carrying things here with a high hand. As late as 1694 an English captain arriving off Accra "bought a five-hand canoe here of the black general [of Akwamu], who had surprised and seized the Danes' fort here [Christiansborg Castle], forced the Danes' general to fly to the Dutch for his life, murdered his second and several of the soldiers and now trades with the Dutch interlopers," an incident that was typical of African impatience with the arrogantly monopolizing habits so often assumed by the European companies. A little further in his *Journal*, published only in 1732, this Captain Phillips describes how the Akwamu authorities allowed the Danes back into their fort on payment of a weighty fee in gold. The colonial threat was still below the skyline. Manners were accordingly polite. "I saw and spoke to the *Oba* of Benin," the Dutchman van Nyendael would record of this time, "in the presence of his three great counselors. He was seated on an ivory throne under a canopy of Indian silk. He was about forty years old and of lively expression. According to custom I stood about thirty feet away from him. So as to see him better I asked permission to draw closer. He laughingly agreed."

Being commercially and technically more advanced than other Europeans of the seventeenth century, the Dutch were better reporters. In 1668 the efficient and well-informed Amsterdam geographer, Olfert Dapper, published in his immediately famous *Description of Africa* a number of invaluable reports on the condition of Benin and some other African states and cities. For this he drew on compatriots with firsthand experience. He is particularly good on Benin, for which he used eyewitness material by otherwise unknown Dutch merchants who sojourned there. The Empire by that time, according to these witnesses, measured some four hundred fifty miles from west to east and an unknown distance towards the north, having "many towns and an infinity of villages, the capital city itself being enclosed on one side by a wall ten feet high, made of a double palisade of trees" pierced by "several gates eight or nine feet high and five feet wide," each made of a single piece of wood and turning "on a stake."

"The King's palace," these Hollanders reported, "is on the right side of the town . . . [being] a collection of buildings which occupy as much space as the town of Harlem," with numerous apartments and fine galleries "most of which are as big as those on the Exchange in Amsterdam." These galleries "are supported by wooden pillars encased with copper, where their victories are depicted . . ." while the corner of each gallery roof "is adorned with a small pyramidal tower, on the point of which is perched a copper bird spreading its wings." The whole town "is composed of thirty main streets, very straight and 120 feet wide, apart from an infinity of small intersecting streets," the houses being "close to one another, arranged in good order . . ."; and "these people are in no way inferior to the Dutch as regards cleanliness" — no mean tribute from the member of a nation that was probably, in point of cleanliness, the most advanced in the Europe of its day. Dapper's informants also brought him much precious detail on the organization and political system of Benin, then still near the height of its power and influence. Readers who would like to pursue these vivid references will find them conveniently set forth in Thomas Hodgkin's *Nigerian Perspectives* (Oxford: 1960); or, given access to a good library, in Dapper himself.

RUY DE PINA

The Building of Elmina Castle

[1482] The king [of Portugal], considering, as a wise man, the great profit and good health which his subjects would receive in body and soul, and also how his merchandise, and the affairs of his honor, estate, and service would be properly secured, if he were to possess in those parts of Mina [Gold Coast] a fortress of his own, and wishing to know whether such a fortress could or should be built, held a meeting of his council to discuss this matter, and contrary votes and opinions were given there.

While some thought it would be an easy thing to do and very profitable, others believed it would be very dangerous and perilous, and, in fact, impossible, or, even if they allowed it to be built, its upkeep would be very difficult, both on account of the great remoteness of the land and because the climate was very sickening and the Negroes little truthful and less trustworthy. These objections were so considerable, they said, that it ought not to be built. The king, after these arguments had been advanced, nevertheless determined that it should be built.

From the translation of Ruy de Pina's chronicle of John II (*Colleçao de livros ineditos de historia portugueza*, 1792) in J. W. Blake, *Europeans in West Africa* (2 vols., Hakluyt Society: 1942), vol. 1, p. 70 for the first extract and p. 78 for the second. In regard to the latter, compare Benin traditions in Egharevba, pp. 99-100.

For this purpose, he ordered that all the timber and freestones, which would be necessary for the gates, the windows, the corner-rafters of the walls, the tower, and other things, should forthwith be cut and shaped in this country, so that without any delay in the work they could be set in place immediately. Moreover, a great quantity of mixed and compounded lime was made ready, together with tiles and bricks, nails and iron tools, and provisions, and all other things pertinent to the work in great abundance. And six hundred men also were ordered and equipped, one hundred masters of masonry and carpentry and five hundred for defense and service. And it was agreed that the whole should be carried, as it was carried, in *urcas* and great ships with the idea that they might not return or sail any more, and, besides these, there went other ships and caravels, strong and sound, with many provisions, medicines, and rich wares, and very honorable men and dependents of the king were appointed captains of these ships.

After certain persons, to whom this work was assigned, had already provided the king with excuses for themselves for fear of the difficulties and perils involved, the first man to accept it freely and to be willing to undertake it was Fernã Lourenço, who was the secretary of his exchequer and had charge of the treasury and factory of these trades, afterwards being officially appointed. But the king, after praising him highly and profusely thanking him for this offer, as his goodwill deserved, refused him, on account of the same charge with which he was entrusted.

Then, being informed of the virtues, loyalty, great courage and good sense of Diego da Azambuja, a knight of his household, who had already been proved in other affairs of considerable importance and great peril, with words about the singular confidence, which he reposed in him, and promising him that he might expect great rewards and preferments, he entrusted him with the work; and da Azambuja, with others of very praiseworthy obedience and sure loyalty, accepted it with a smiling face and a steady heart. And to put this into execution, he then went to make preparations at Lisbon, from where he departed in December on the eve of the day of Santa Luzia in the year one thousand four hundred and eighty-one . . .

And finally, guided by the Holy Spirit and committing himself to its care, he arrived near the village, which was called das Duas Partes (Village of the Two Parts), where he disembarked on Wednesday, the nineteenth of January, in the year one thousand four hundred and eighty-two, and, examining with great care the lofty situation of the land, which was very suitable for defense and for the health of the people, and having tested and sounded the anchorages of the sea for the ships, he discovered that a better disposition for a fortress could neither be found nor pictured, especially since there was much rock, and a large settlement, which offered hope to the inhabitants of fresh water and other provisions for very long periods.

And on the next day, which was the day of Sam Sebastiam, by the advice of one, Joham Bernaldez, whom he met there bartering, he went on land, clothed in silk and brocade, and with his men in good order. And at the foot of a tree, under its shade, he commanded a mass to be said (which was the first that was said) and he attended; and henceforth that valley was, and shall always be, called the Vale of Sam Sebastiam. Then, after eating, he ordered a richly ornamented platform to be erected; and he sat thereon, accompanied by very honorable men, and with his trumpets, tambourines and drums, and all in an act of peace, in order to receive there, by agreement, the lord of the place, who was called Caramansa, whom the Negroes called king, and to speak with him.

Hither the king came, and before him a great noise of bugles, bells and horns, which are their instruments, and he was accompanied by an endless number of Negroes, some with bows and arrows, and others with assagais and shields; and the principal persons were attended behind by naked page-boys with seats of wood, like stools, to sit upon . . .

Then the principal persons who came with him, followed him, all first wetting their fingers in their mouths and then wiping them on their breasts, before touching those of the captain, which is a courtesy and a rare grace among them that is specially kept for kings and persons of great estate. When all were again seated and a signal for silence given, the captain began his speech, with the aid of a Negro, familiar with the language, who forthwith inter-

preted it, and its substance was: that, on account of the good report which the king, his lord, had received about them, and of the
good treatment which they above all the men of that land gave to
his vassals, who were accustomed to come to trade there, his highness had sent him there to treat with them and for ever to secure
peace and friendship . . . And forasmuch as a house was necessary, because it was reasonable that the merchandise, which they
were now bringing, and would in future arrive, might always remain there continuously, fresh and secure, he asked them to give
place and license and even assistance, so that it might be built at
the mouth of the river, because from such a house and from the
Christians, who would be stationed in it, they would always find
and receive protection, profit and favor.

The king, with his principal persons there, then replied to him,
saying that the people of the Christians, who up to that time had
come there, were few, foul and vile, and that the people, who had
now arrived, were very different, particularly he himself, who by
his clothes and appearance must be the son or the brother of the
king of Portugal . . . Proceeding in their reply, they said furthermore that, judging by his appearance and by his assurance that he
spoke to them in the name of the king, it could not be that he
was hiding the truth from them, or that he was intending trickery
or malice against them by his requests. Accordingly, they gave him
permission then to build the house, as he desired; since, if, when
it was built, he kept his promise, it was certain that the king of
Portugal, his lord, would be better served, and that the Christians,
his subjects, would at all times be treated better; but if he should
do the contrary, they would leave him the houses and the land,
set their own persons free, and in another land would not want for
straws and sticks with which they might soon build other houses.
Then the captain responded to them, by a sign, that they might
always be sure and certain of everything which he had told them;
because Christians were not accustomed to lie; but rather to do
and discharge affairs better than they talked of them . . .

Then the captain, before withdrawing, went at once with the
master-craftsmen, whom he brought, to put together the base of
the fortress, for which they took material from the top of some high

rocks, which the Negroes were accustomed to worship and to hold as very sacred. On that day, the captain then divided the work by shifts and captaincies, so that on the next day, which was the twenty-first of January, they might begin it, as they did. Also in like manner, he sent to the king and his men a good present of many lambres, basins, manillas and other cloth, which was to be given to them first before all else to ensure their good will, and he entrusted Joham Bernaldez with this task, who yet went with it not so early but that already the workmen and quarrymen began the work sooner; because at dawn they were busy laying the foundations of the tower and also breaking the stones and then setting them in place.

The Negroes, upon seeing the destruction and utter ruin of their sacred rocks, meanwhile believed that they were looking upon the loss of all hope of their salvation, and all eagerly and in a great rage took up their arms and so struck hard at the workmen, who, not being able to resist them, retreated in flight to the boats. Whereupon, Diego da Azambuja then hurriedly sent help; and because he knew that the present, which he had ordered, had not yet been delivered, he realized that the cause of the tumult proceeded from the negligence of the messenger. Accordingly, he commanded that there was to be no delay in delivering the present, to which he added some more things owing to the greater need of their favor; whereby all the evil of the Negroes was at once turned into good and their direct refusal into a double consent.

As a result of this incident, no other house was marked out or founded and no foundation laid, until the tower was above one story high. When it had been built up to this level, the surround of the castle was forthwith begun, for which it was necessary to demolish some houses of the Negroes, and to this they and their women consented easily and without taking offense in return for large reparations and the gifts which were given to them. Then they began to need water urgently; for they were unable to make use of the supply in the land and near there, on account of the Negroes guarding it continuously and forbidding them to use it, and because they did not wish to attack them and to take it by force. After having considered many remedies, they were obliged by chance and, as it were, miraculously to provide themselves with a supply elsewhere. Though many of the people sickened and some died, the work was pressed on so fast that within twenty days the walls of the fortress were built up to their full height, and so was the tower, and within many houses were finished. Then the fort was assigned the name O Castello de Sam Jorge, as a mark of respect to him who is the patron and protector of Portugal.

Portuguese Reach Benin

[1486] In this year, the land of Beny beyond Myna to the Rios dos Escravos was first discovered by Joham Affom da Aveiro,* who died there; whence there came to these kingdoms the first pepper from Guinee, whereof a great quantity was produced in that land; and presently samples of it were sent to Framdes [Flanders] and to other parts, and soon it fetched a great price and was held in high esteem. The king of Beny [Benin] sent as ambassador to the king a Negro, one of his captains, from a harboring place by the sea, which is called Ugato [Gwato], because he desired to learn more about these lands, the arrival of people from them in his country being regarded as an unusual novelty.

This ambassador was a man of good speech and natural wisdom. Great feasts were held in his honor, and he was shown many of the good things of these kingdoms. He returned to his land in a ship of the king's, who at his departure made him a gift of rich clothes for himself and his wife: and through him he also sent a rich present to the king of such things as he understood he would greatly prize. Moreover, he sent holy and most catholic advisers with praiseworthy admonitions for the faith to administer a stern rebuke about the heresies and great idolatries and fetishes, which the Negroes practice in that land. Then also there went with him new factors [commercial agents] of the king, who were to remain in that country and to traffic for the said pepper and for other things, which pertained to the trades of the king. But owing to the fact that the land was afterwards found to be very dangerous from sickness and not so profitable as had been hoped, the trade was abandoned.

* Other Portuguese had certainly gone as far as the Bight of Benin by 1471-1472.

DUARTE PACHECO PEREIRA
Inland Kingdoms

You find the first Negroes at the Sanagua [Senegal] River, and this is where the kingdom of Jolof [Wolof] begins . . . The king of Jolof can put ten thousand horsemen and one hundred thousand footmen into the field and all these people go naked save nobles and notables who wear blue cotton shirts and *serouals* (trousers?) of the same stuff . . . None of these people nor their neighbors know where the Sanagua River comes from . . . We have learned from numerous Ethiopians [that is, Africans], fairly well-informed men who know the country for five hundred leagues upstream, various provinces and countries through which it passes, that its source is unknown; but judging by its course and its point of departure we know that it comes from a big lake of the River Nile which is thirty leagues long and ten broad, in such a way that it [the Sanagua River] seems to be a branch that the Nile sends out across lower Ethiopia towards the west. Another branch goes north and reaches the sea through four mouths in Egypt . . . At the head of this lake there is a kingdom called Tambucutu [Timbuktu] which has a big city of the same name near the lake. There, too, is the city of Jany [Djenné], inhabited by Negroes and surrounded by a wall of baked clay; brass and copper are very expensive there, and so are red and blue stuffs and salt, and everything but the stuffs is sold by weight . . . The trade of that region is very great . . .

From Duarte Pacheco Pereira: *Esmeraldo de Situ Orbis*, c. 1505. Translated here from the French of R. Mauny, *Esmeraldo de Situ Orbis* (Bissau: 1956), p. 49. See also G. H. T. Kimble (Hakluyt Society: 1937) for a complete translation in English.

DUARTE PIRES
The King of Benin

[1516] Most high and mighty king and prince, our lord. May God increase your royal estate. Sir, your highness will be pleased to know how Pero Baroso gave me a letter from your highness, which made me rejoice that your highness should be mindful of so humble a man as I; and now I render account to your highness in regard to the letter which you sent me. Sir, with reference to what you say about my being in very great favor with the king of Benin, it is truly so; because the king of Benin is pleased with what I said in favor of your highness, and he desires to be your very good friend and speaks of nothing save what concerns Our Lord and your interest; and so he is very glad, and likewise all his noblemen and his people; and your highness will shortly know about this.

The favor which the king of Benin accords us is due to his love of your highness; and thus he pays us high honor and sets us at table to dine with his son, and no part of his court is hidden from us but all the doors are open. Sir, when these priests arrived in Benin, the delight of the king of Benin was so great that I do not know how to describe it, and likewise that of all his people; and he sent for them at once; and they remained with him for one whole year in war. The priests and we reminded him of the embassy of your highness, and he replied to us that he was very satisfied with it; but since he was at war, that he could do nothing until he returned to Benin, because he needed leisure for such a deep mystery as this; as soon as he was in Benin, he would fulfill

From a letter dated Oct. 20, 1516, in Portuguese royal archives of Torre do Tombo. Original text reprinted in J. R. Coelho, *Alguns documentos do Archivo Nacional,* 1892, p. 33. Translation here is that of J. W. Blake, ed. *Europeans in West Africa* (2 vols., Hakluyt Society: 1942), vol. 1, p. 123.

his promise to your highness, and he would so behave as to give great pleasure to your highness and to all your kingdom.

So it was that, at the end of one year, in the month of August, the king gave his son and some of his noblemen — the greatest in his kingdom — so that they might become Christians; and also he ordered a church to be built in Benin; and they made them Christians straightway; and also they are teaching them to read, and your highness will be pleased to know that they are very good learners. Moreover, sir, the king of Benin hopes to finish his war this summer, and we shall return to Benin, and I shall give your highness an account of everything that happens. Sir, I Duarte Pires, and Joham Sobrynho, a resident in the island of O Principe, and Grygoryo Lourenço, a black man and formerly the servant of Francysquo Lourenço, all remain in the service of your highness, and we have submitted proposals on your behalf to the king of Benin, and we have described to him how your highness is a great lord and how you can make him a great lord. Done in this war, on 20 October 1516.

To our lord the king.

DUARTE PIRES

ALONSO DE PALENCIA
A Spanish Raid

In order to set a bound to these insults and cruelties from the Portuguese [who claimed monopoly of access to West Africa by right of Papal Bull], King Don Fernando sent a strong fleet of Andalucians with orders to break their arrogance, and to humble the pride, which the riches of Guinea had inspired in them. The

From Alonso de Palencia, *Crónica de Enrique IV* (ed. Paz y Melia, 1904-1909), decada (volume) III, bk. 25, chap. 4; translated in J. W. Blake, ed. *Europeans in West Africa* (2 vols., Hakluyt Society: 1942), vol. 1, p. 215.

Andalucians joyfully obeyed, and, while a fleet of thirty ships was being prepared in the port of Seville, some fishermen of Palos, already accustomed to warlike expeditions and fortunate against the Portuguese, joined with other mariners of Puerto (de Santa Maria), and arrived in two caravels at the coasts nearest to Guinea. They call that territory "that of the Azanegas [a Berber people of the Mauretanian Coast]," by which name they distinguish those of citrine color from others of a darker color and of customs even darker.

The condition of these natives, when they feed themselves on fish alone, is very gentle, and as they always walk unarmed by the lagoons, they suffer themselves to be seized without difficulty by warlike and unarmed men. The mariners of the two caravels secured 120 Azanegas and carried them to Andalucia, despising the orders of King Don Fernando, who absolutely forbade fraudulent trade with the men of Guinea, let alone the making captives of them, and commanded them to attach themselves to the royal fleet and to obey the admiral implicitly. The disturbances of the times emboldened the men of Palos to carry out this exploit, and, provoked moreover by the insolent words of Gonzalo de Estuniga, governor of the fortress of Palos, they fitted out three other caravels and put into the coasts of Guinea with the intention of loading slaves.

The king of that region, through his frequent traffic with the Portuguese, to whom he bartered his prisoners of war for trifles, believed that the ships were Portuguese. After signals of peace had been made by both sides, the king with some of his men entered into the first caravel and inquired who commanded it, and the reply in Portuguese confirmed him in his error. Then, he agreed to the barter of slaves for brass rings, small oval leather shields, clothes of diverse colors, and other objects, which the poverty of the inhabitants caused them to covet greatly. To celebrate the exchanges, the king caused one calf and sheep to be brought for the feast of that day, and he accepted for the following day the hospitality of the patron of the caravels. He appeared on the beach surrounded by a great multitude, and mounted to the ship with his brothers, his close friends, and the most powerful of his people. After the feast was ended, the patron invited him to visit the interior of the ship, and then the treacherous mariners closed the hatch-ways, and, having armed, they secured 140 nobles of splendid physique.

Once on the high seas, the king, complaining of the cruel trick, again inquired who owned the ships. They told him Spaniards. He wished to know whether they obeyed any king, and, when he was told that they obeyed a most noble one, he expressed his confidence that he would free him from such an iniquitous captivity.

On arrival at Palos, the Andalucians wished to force him to walk in the crowd amongst the other slaves. But he resisted, and said that they should take him either dragging by a rope or on horseback, because his misfortune must be either terrible or dignified. Gonzalo de Estuniga, moved by this resolution verily of royal spirit, or perchance spurred on by anxiety about the future ransom, ordered a horse to be brought. The king nimbly mounted upon it, and, going before the slaves, he began to march with a majestic air.

When King Don Fernando learned all this, he commanded that the king be immediately restored to his native land. But as the execution of the order was deferred owing to the disturbances of those days, he ordered us, doctor Antonio Rodriguez de Lillo and myself, to intimate to Gonzalo de Estuniga that he must set the king at liberty. He managed to delay the execution of the order, and it was only at the end of some months of captivity that we succeeded in returning the unhappy monarch to his native land, although we were not able to prevent his brothers and other relatives from being sold in Andalucia as slaves.

That savage maintained a certain regal authority during his captivity, and he displayed dignity in his countenance, gravity in speech, prudence in conduct, and courage in adversity. On reaching his country, he exercised such cunning in order to avenge himself on his treacherous oppressors that, in spite of the distrust with which they traveled, he succeeded in securing some and keeping them as hostages for as many others of his relations.

AFFONSO OF CONGO
Evils of the Trade

[1526] Sir, Your Highness [of Portugal] should know how our Kingdom is being lost in so many ways that it is convenient to provide for the necessary remedy, since this is caused by the excessive freedom given by your factors and officials to the men and merchants who are allowed to come to this Kingdom to set up shops with goods and many things which have been prohibited by us, and which they spread throughout our Kingdoms and Domains in such an abundance that many of our vassals, whom we had in obedience, do not comply because they have the things in greater abundance than we ourselves; and it was with these things that we had them content and subjected under our vassalage and jurisdiction, so it is doing a great harm not only to the service of God, but the the security and peace of our Kingdoms and State as well.

And we cannot reckon how great the damage is, since the mentioned merchants are taking every day our natives, sons of the land and the sons of our noblemen and vassals and our relatives, because the thieves and men of bad conscience grab them wishing to have the things and wares of this Kingdom which they are ambitious of; they grab them and get them to be sold; and so great, Sir, is the corruption and licentiousness that our country is being completely depopulated, and Your Highness should not agree with this nor accept it as in your service. And to avoid it we need from those [your] Kingdoms no more than some priests and a few people to teach in schools, and no other goods except wine

These extracts are translated from the original texts in Visconde de Paiva-Manso, *Historia do Congo (Documentos)* (Lisbon: 1877), which has 22 of King Affonso's letters, the other two that are known being in A. de A. Felner, *Angola* (Coimbra: 1933).

and flour for the holy sacrament. That is why we beg of Your Highness to help and assist us in this matter, commanding your factors that they should not send here either merchants or wares, because it is *our will that in these Kingdoms there should not be any trade of slaves nor outlet for them.** Concerning what is referred above, again we beg of Your Highness to agree with it, since otherwise we cannot remedy such an obvious damage. Pray Our Lord in His mercy to have Your Highness under His guard and let you do for ever the things of His service. I kiss your hands many times.

At our town of Congo, written on the sixth day of July.

João Teixeira † did it in 1526.

The King. Dom Affonso.

[On the back of this letter the following can be read:

To the most powerful and excellent prince Dom João, King our Brother.]

The Origins of Slaving

[1526] Moreover, Sir, in our Kingdoms there is another great inconvenience which is of little service to God, and this is that many of our people [*naturaes*], keenly desirous as they are of the wares and things of your Kingdoms, which are brought here by your people, and in order to satisfy their voracious appetite, seize many of our people, freed and exempt men ‡; and very often it happens that they kidnap even noblemen and the sons of noblemen, and our relatives, and take them to be sold to the white men who are in our Kingdoms; and for this purpose they have concealed them; and others are brought during the night so that they might not be recognized.

And as soon as they are taken by the white men they are immediately ironed and branded with fire, and when they are carried to be embarked, if they are caught by our guards' men the whites allege that they have bought them but they cannot say from whom,

---

* Emphasis in the original.

† Probably, from the evidence, a Congolese secretary educated by Portuguese missionaries at Mbanza Congo (S. Salvador). See J. Cuvelier, *L'Ancien Royaume de Congo* (Brussels: 1946), p. 294.

‡ The temptations of the slave trade, in short, were already at work.

so that it is our duty to do justice and to restore to the freemen their freedom, but it cannot be done if your subjects feel offended, as they claim to be.

And to avoid such a great evil we passed a law so that any white man living in our Kingdoms and wanting to purchase goods in any way should first inform three of our noblemen and officials of our court whom we rely upon in this matter, and these are Dom Pedro Manipanza and Dom Manuel Manissaba, our chief usher, and Gonçalo Pires our chief freighter, who should investigate if the mentioned goods are captives or free men, and if cleared by them there will be no further doubt nor embargo for them to be taken and embarked. But if the white men do not comply with it they will lose the aforementioned goods. And if we do them this favor and concession it is for the part Your Highness has in it, since we know that it is in your service too that these goods are taken from our Kingdom, otherwise we should not consent to this . . .

A Call for Aid

[1526] Sir, Your Highness has been kind enough to write to us saying that we should ask in our letters for anything we need, and that we shall be provided with everything, and as the peace and the health of our Kingdom depend on us, and as there are among us old folks and people who have lived for many days, it happens that we have continuously many and different diseases which put us very often in such a weakness that we reach almost the last extreme; and the same happens to our children, relatives and natives owing to the lack in this country of physicians and surgeons who might know how to cure properly such diseases. And as we have got neither dispensaries nor drugs which might help us in this forlornness, many of those who had been already confirmed and instructed in the holy faith of Our Lord Jesus Christ perish and die; and the rest of the people in their majority cure themselves with herbs and breads and other ancient methods, so that they put all their faith in the mentioned herbs and ceremonies if they live, and believe that they are saved if they die; and this is not much in the service of God.

And to avoid such a great error and inconvenience, since it is from God in the first place and then from your Kingdoms and from Your Highness that all the good and drugs and medicines have come to save us, we beg of you to be agreeable and kind enough to send us two physicians and two apothecaries and one surgeon, so that they may come with their drug-stores and all the necessary things to stay in our kingdoms, because we are in extreme need of them all and each of them. We shall do them all good and shall benefit them by all means, since they are sent by Your Highness, whom we thank for your work in their coming. We beg of Your Highness as a great favor to do this for us, because besides being good in itself it is in the service of God as we have said above.

[Extracts from letter of King Affonso to King of Portugal dated Oct. 18, 1526. By hand of Dom João Teixeira.]

ABREU DE BRITO

Angolan Currency

[1592] And this *zimbo* [cowrie] has such great value in this Kingdom, that, when I was in the village of Loanda, a huge amount of gold coins was sent to Congo for ransoming a number of slaves, but they were rejected by the sellers, who said that the true money and gold was the *zimbo* of Loanda, which made them rich, and the Portuguese should take back that sort of money in gold, which was useless for them; and many other things happen in this matter, for instance, that one *lifuco* [*lufuku:* a numerical measure of value] of *zimbos* is worth two of goods, so that it is clearly seen that the wealth is doubled . . .

From Visconde de Paiva-Manso, *Historia do Congo (Documentos)* (Lisbon: 1877), p. 137. Translated from a report by Domingos d'Abreu de Brito on the Kingdom of Angola, dated 1592, offered to King Philip of Spain.

JOHN LANDYE
Guinea Cargoes

Landye's is the second recorded voyage of the English to West Africa, the first being that of William Hawkins ten years earlier.

[February 24, 1540] A ship called the Pawle of Plymouth, whereof John Landye is master, left on the same day.

From William Hawkins, denizen:

for 940 hachettes, 940 comes and 375 sarpes
(knives), weighing 30 cwt. of iron ————
value 75s.   Subsidy 3s. 9d.
for 5 cwt. of copper (100s.) and 5 cwt. of lead
(20s.) in manelios ———————— value £6.   Subsidy 6s.
for 3 lengths of woolen cloth without grain —   Customs 3s. 6d.
for 19 dozen night cappes (40s.), 10 cwt. of
copper (£10) and 10 cwt. of lead (40s.) —
value £14.   Subsidy 14s.

[October 20, 1540] A ship called le Paule of Plymouth, whereof John Landye is master, entered on October 20.

From Wm. Hawkyns, denizen:

for 92 tons of brasyll — value £613. 6s. 8d.
                    subsidy £30. 13s. 4d.
1 dozen elephants' teeth
weighing 1 cwt. ———— value 30s.   Subsidy 18d.

From Plymouth Customs Accounts, PRO, E122, 116/13. Translation in J. W. Blake, *Europeans in West Africa* (2 vols., Hakluyt Society: 1942), vol. 2, p. 300, from text in J. A. Williamson, *Sir John Hawkins* (1927), p. 13. The *Paul* went to Brazil as well as Guinea.

RICHARD EDEN

English at Benin

[1553] But of force and not of will brought he the ships before the river of Benin, where riding at an Anker, they sent their pinnas up into the river 50 or 60 leagues, from whence certaine of the marchants with captaine Pinteado, Francisco a Portugale, Nicholas Lambart gentleman, and other marchants were conducted to the court where the king remained, ten leagues from the river side, whither when they came, they were brought with a great company to the presence of the king, who being a blacke Moore (although not so blacke as the rest) sate in a great huge hall, long and wide, the wals made of earth without windowes, the roofe of thin boords, open in sundry places, like unto lovers [louvres: ventilators] to let in the aire.

And here to speake of the great reverence they give to their king, it is such, that if we would give as much to our Savior Christ, we should remoove from our heads many plagues which we daily deserve for our contempt and impietie.

So it is therfore, that when his noble men are in his presence, they never looke him in the face, but sit cowring, as we upon our knees, so they upon their buttocks, with their elbowes upon their knees, and their hands before their faces, not looking up until the king command them. And when they are comming toward the king, as far as they do see him, they do shew such reverance, sitting on the ground with their faces covered as before. Likewise when they depart from him, they turn not their backs toward him, but goe creeping backward with like reverance.

The first extract is from Richard Eden's memoir of Thomas Windham's voyage to Guinea and Benin, 1553, in Richard Hakluyt, *The Principal Navigations, Voyages, Traffiques and Discoveries of the English Nation* (1598-1600), VI, p. 145. The second is from Richard Eden's memoir of John Lok's voyage to Guinea in 1554-1555, in Hakluyt, VI, p. 154.

And now to speake somewhat of the communication that was between the king and our men, you shall first understand that he himselfe could speake the Portugall tongue, which he had learned of a child. Therefore after he had commanded our men to stand up, and demanded of them the cause of their comming into that countrey, they answered by Pinteado, that they were marchants traveiling into those partes for the commodities of his countrey, for exchange of wares which they had brought from their countries, being such as should be no lesse commodious for him and his people. The king then having of old lying in a certaine store-house 30 or 40 kintals of Pepper (every kintall being an hundred weight) willed them to looke upon the same, and againe to bring him a sight of such merchandizes as they had brought with them. And thereupon sent with the captaine and the marchants certaine of his men to conduct them to the waters side, with other to bring the ware from the pinnas to the court. Who when they were returned and the wares seen, the king grew to this ende with the merchants to provide in 30 dayes the lading of al their ships with pepper. And in case their merchandizes would not extend to the value of so much pepper, he promised to credite them to their next returne, and thereupon sent the country round about to gather pepper, causing the same to be brought to the court: so that within the space of 30 dayes they had gathered fourescore tunne of pepper.

Gold and Ivory

They brought from thence at the last voiage [1554-1555] foure hundred pound weight and odde of gold, of two and twentie carrats and one graine of finenesse; also sixe and thirtie buts of graines, & about two hundred and fifty elephants' teeth of all quantities. Of these I saw & measured some of nine spans in length, as they were crooked. Some of them were as bigge as a man's thigh above the knee, and weyed about foure-score and ten pound weight a peece . . .

They are very wary people in their bargaining, and will not lose one sparke of golde of any value. They use weights and measures, and are very circumspect in occupying the same. They that shall have to doe with them, must use them gently; for they will not trafique or bring in any wares, if they be evill used. At the first voyage, that our men had into these parties, it so chanced that, at their departure from the first place where they did trafick, one of them either stole a muske-cat, or tooke her away by force, not mistrusting that that should have hindered their bargaining in another place whither they intended to goe. But for all the haste they coulde make with full sailes, the fame of their misusage so prevented them that the people of that place also, offended thereby, would bring in no wares; insomuch that they were inforced either to restore the cat, or pay for her at their price, before they could trafique there.

WILLIAM TOWERSON
Metal Goods

All their cloth, cordes, girdles, fishing lines, and all such like things, which they have, they make of the bark of certaine trees, and thereof they can worke things very pretily, and yron worke they can make very fine, and all such things as they doe occupy, as darts, fishhookes, hooking yrons, yron heads, and great daggers, some of them as long as a woodknife, which be on both sides exceeding sharpe, and bended after the maner of Turkie blades, and the most part of them have hanging at their left side one of those great daggers.

From the memoir of William Towerson's first voyage to Guinea, 1555-1556, in Richard Hakluyt, *The Principal Navigations, Voyages, etc.* (1598-1600), VI, p. 177.

JOHN HAWKINS
Towards the Slave Trade

The following is from a remarkable document, running to about twenty-two thousand words, which provides a detailed and graphic account of Hawkins's slaving voyage of 1562, and was very possibly written in the *Jesus*, Hawkins's ship, during that adventure. Its great interest for African history lies in its illustration of the way in which early European traders and raiders on the Guinea Coast — in this case what is now Sierra Leone — found it possible to make common cause with African potentates who were otherwise far too strong to be challenged; and of how this military partnership led on to the slave trade.

There came two ambassadors with one message (to our general . . . One) of them from where the King of Serra Lion (had his town, and) the other from Yhoma, King of the Castros, (to ask his aid) against Zacina and Zetecama, two kinges which (fought with them in the w)arres. These two kinges desired oure ge(nerall, as they ha)d besieged the other[kings] in a towne called Conga, . . . that our generall wolde . . . (assault) it by the river and batter it, and for his m(erit they would) help him to negros.

This towne was b(uilt after the) use of that cowntreye verye warlike, and was wal(led round with) mighty trees bownd together with greate wythes (and had) in it soldiers that had come thether 150 leagues. The (kings within) it had in it of principall soldiers negros 6000, bes(ide thereo)f innumerable sight of other menne, women and ch(ildren. Our) generall, thowe it was a harde enterprise, yet by(cawse) he must have departed to the Indias with the negros (above) mencioned, grawnted that he wolde ayde the said kinges, (and) with this awnswere the embassadors,

From Cotton MS, in J. A. Williamson, *Sir John Hawkins*, 1927.

whoe afterward gave oure generall gages for sauf goyng and com-
yng of oure menne and alsoe took gages of us, and the tyme appoincted that oure generall showlde send his ayde, who showld
doe their parte by the river to anoye and enter the towns, and
the two kinges oure frendes likewise by londe with their
campe . . .

. . . The (next) daye after oure generall came thether [to the
approaches of the town with his troops], somewhat (before) the
tyme of assault appoincted, the beseiged (negr)os beganne to
treat of peace with the negro kings oure friends by imbassadors,
but they were sente aweye withowte doung any thing. In the after
noone, as the generall had appoincted, he comaunded to sownde
the trompette and, having all thinges readye, beganne to sett
menne ashore and put in order, gave assaulte by that parte of the
towne which ajoyned to the river. The negros had many engines,
as false diches covered with light sticks, leaves and suche trompery,
to overthrowe oure menne in, and with theire invenimed arrowes
and dartes so defended the walles, having made loopes in everye
place to shote owte at for their savetye . . .

[After a stiff battle the town was taken by setting fire to it]
. . . The kinges Sacina and Setecama escaped, (but there we)re
slaine a greate nomber of menne of name (who had come) in
soccor of the towne, as the Kinge of Cesta . . . (Our) menne
here saw the negros our frendes eate (the prisoners whom) they
slewe everye daye in the camp . . . And oure generall came
downe to his ships and browghte with him abowte 260 negros that
he had taken in the towne. When he was come downe he sente to
the Castros, where with the negros the kinges sent and them the
generall took and others that he had in the rivers by trafique, we
had nowe abowt 470 negros in all . . . (Thus we set our) sayles
and directed oure cowrse over with the (West or Spanish) India
named America or the Newe Worlde the(re to trade with the
sa)id wares . . .

RICHARD JOBSON
Mandingo Towns

Written early in the seventeenth century, Jobson's is the first English account of West Africa that goes much beyond personal gossip, and makes a link with the much more solid reports of Dapper (see pp. 179-180) and of the best writers of the eighteenth century. He is writing of the Gambia Coast and neighborhood.

They have likewise Townes of force, according unto the manner of warre they use amongst them, fortified, and trencht in, after a strong and defencible nature; whereof (they say) the countrey within is full, especially where the Kings are seated, the maner whereof wee have seene in some two or three places, whereof I will instance onely one: which is the towne of Cassan, against which (as I sayd before) the shippe which was betrayed did ride, and we in our last voyage, did make it our highest port for our bigger shippe. This Towne is the Kings seate, and by the name of the Towne hee holdes his title, King of Cassan. It is seated upon the Rivers side, and inclosed round, neare to the houses, with hurdles, such as our shepheards use, but they are above ten foot high, and fastened to strong and able poles, the toppes whereof remaine above the hurdle; on the inside in divers places, they have rooms, and buildings, made up like Turrets, from whence they within may shoot their arrowes, and throw their darts over the wall, against their approaching enemies; on the outside likewise, round the wall, they have cast a ditch or trench, of a great breadth, & beyond that againe a pretty distance, the whole Towne is circled with posts and peeces of trees, set close and fast into the ground, some five foot high, so thicke, that except in stiles, or places made of purpose, a single man cannot get through, and in the like man-

From Richard Jobson, *The Golden Trade*, London, 1623.

ner, a small distance off againe, the like defence, and this is as they do signifie unto us, to keepe off the force of horse, to which purpose, it seemes to be very strong and availeable: considering what armes and Weapons they have in use, which in this place is necessary to be knowne.

Lords and Vassals

I saw and did eate and drinke with sixe of their Kings or Mansas, which have reference to greater Kings living further [inland]; all the South-side of the River as wee went, beeing subject to the King of Cantore, of the North-side halfe subject to the King of Bursale, the rest to the King of Woolley. These wee saw not, and they say, that they shew not themselves abroad but in pompe, hunting with great numbers of Horse, as our men saw the King of Bursall (when they passed to Cape Verde) and there are warres betwixt one side of the River and the other, which were it not, Bursale would soone with his Horse subdue a great part of the Countrey, or if he had meanes of transportation.

Gambia Craftsmanship

There are amongst them three principall Trades, the Smith which of Iron brought to them (for else they have none) makes their Swords, Assegay heads, Darts and Arrow heads barbed; and Instruments of Husbandry, without which they could not live. Hee hath his Bellowes, small Anvill, and Cole of a red wood, which alone will give the true heat to our Iron; who thus cut out Iron for us, eight inches going above as well as twelve inches below, at ten for one gaine. The Smith if he be not looked too, will steale.

The next Trade is the Sepatero, or Gregorie maker, made artificially in all shapes, round and square and triangle, so as Our men would acknowledge Art. They make also Bridles and Saddles, of which I have seene some very neat, hardly to be bettered heere: whereby it seemes they have skill to dress and dye their Deeres skins and Goats skins.

A third Profession is of those which temper the Earth for their wals and pots in which they boyle meats, using for other services the gourd. Their Tabacco Pipes also (without which few or none, either men or women walke, and cannot of all things want) have their bowles and neckes about two inches long of Earth, neatly glased, able commonly to hold halfe an ounce of Tabacco: they put a cane about a yard long into the necke, and so draw the smoake. These are peculiar Trades; other things are common to all, Mats to eate, sit, sleepe on, are their Staple commoditie, as at Mamgegar Market, we saw things bought and sold, without nominating any other price but Mats (How many Mats shall I give you?) for Coyne they have none.

But the generall Trade from which none but the Kings and principall persons are exempted, is Husbandry whereto . . . the people of all sizes after their abilitie are subject: God having not given them wisedome to serve themselves of the beasts to that purpose. They make furrowes as decently as we doe, but with handie labour, having a short sticke about a yard long, on the end of which is a broad Iron like to that of our Paddle-staves; with which Iron set into the ground, one leades the way cutting the Earth before him, others following in the same tract with their severall Irons, so many as will make a sufficient furrow thorow the length of a spacious field: and when they are at the end, they begin againe, many hands making lighter riddance.

OLIVEIRA CADORNEGA
A Million Slaves

[1680] And the fabulous amount of people inhabiting these kingdoms can be estimated if we say that the conquest of these kingdoms began about a hundred years ago, and since every second year have been dispatched from this port about eight to ten thousand units of slaves, which sum up almost to a million of souls.

From partial text of Antonio de Oliveira Cadornega, *Descripçam do Reino de Congo, etc.*, 1680-1681, in Visconde de Paiva-Manso, *Historia do Congo (Documentos)* (Lisbon: 1877), p. 265.

The Eighteenth Century

"GOD HAS DRAWN TO THIS FORTUNATE CITY A CERTAIN NUMBER OF learned and of pious men, strangers to the country, who have come to live here." Thus wrote the author of the *Tarikh es-Sudan* about the city of Djenné on the Middle Niger towards the middle of the seventeenth century. Fifty years later, round the turn of the eighteenth century, the cities of the Western Sudan were still respected as centers of Muslim learning (indeed, some of them have never ceased to be so), yet their confidence and breadth of contact with the wider world of Islam were sadly cut down. For this their sheikhs and mallams were not responsible. The grand Islamic system of political enterprise and speculative thought was now in far retreat and disarray before the eruptive vigor and violence of Christian Europe. The trans-Saharan routes continued to bear their patient many-cameled caravans. The merchants, now as before, toiled back and forth across the wilderness of sand and polished mountain. But they had lost their monopoly of West African trade with the north. Increasingly, this trade went by ship from the ports of Guinea. Commerce shifted more and more to the southward: commerce, and therefore the means of power.

Along the curving seaboard, now a gateway to livelihood and wealth as never before, new African states crystallized from small clans and scattered peoples. These began to form a girdle of political and economic self-defense — a new monopoly — against the sea-traders on one side and the inland-traders on the other. As time went by, this girdle became impenetrable. From a mere skin of "middlemen" chiefs and groups along the seashore, it broadened to include stronger peoples further into the countryside. By the middle of the eighteenth century, coastal monopoly and "protectionism" became at certain points as thick as two or three hundred miles from south to north. Its dominant powers counted new political and economic systems such as Ashanti and Dahomey.

Along the East Coast, from Zanzibar northwards, there occurred a new and memorable surge of Swahili civilization. Here the Portuguese had never won the suffocating grip by which they ruined the shoreward towns of Tanganyika and Mozambique. Zanzibar and Pemba, Malindi, Mombasa and other centers of this highly distinctive variant of Islamic African culture, passed into a period of renaissance. Was this a creative reaction to Portuguese assault and battery, or the product of more sheltered buds of intellectual growth? The question remains open. Whatever their causes, the effects were impressive. Swahili literature began in earnest, some of it "as grand in manner and diction," in Freeman-Grenville's view, "as Dante or Milton." Its beginning can be placed in 1728 (see also page 23) with the *Utendi wa Tambuka*, an epic written for the contemporary ruler of Pate (and now in the Library of the Seminar für Afrikanischen Sprachen at Hamburg) — until or unless, that is, earlier manuscripts should come to light. There was new building and civic growth. Even to the south of Zanzibar, a measure of recovery occurred at Kilwa, where the sultan and richer merchants built new mosques and spacious dwellings, though all in a style and ornamental taste that were much debased and coarsened in comparison with earlier times. A new town appeared at Kua on Juani Island in the Mafia Group: successor to the much older town at Mafia Kisimani, Kua shows in its ruins the same decline of taste but also the same density of new building as eighteenth-century Kilwa.

Far inside the continent, meanwhile, the steady growth of Iron Age feudalism within its specifically African framework and appearance continued to buttress old centers of authority and, at the same time, to challenge these by the ambitious hand of "royal heirs and barons." This is the period of supreme Karanga power on the plateau lands west of Mozambique; westward again, in Angola, it is also the period of new dynastic and "national" wars of rivalry for power. In the geographical heart of Africa it is the time of

Kuba stability and Lunda expansion, and of a crystallization of new kingdoms in the region of the Great Lakes. In the distant southeast it is likewise the time of a political gestation which was to give birth, less than a century later, to the military initiatives of the Nguni: a prelude to the northward-striking recoil from advancing European settlement, to the rise of the Zulu nation, the destructive migrations of the Matebele (Ndebele), and the founding of Basutoland. The eighteenth century can be regarded as a prolonged phase of Iron Age maturity among those Bantu-speaking peoples who had long commanded central-southern Africa, a culmination that was also the last slow epoch of inner-African isolation from the main currents that moved the world.

But for Europe and North America, if not for Asia, this was a time of tremendous change. Industrialism arrived. Science thrust superstition increasingly aside. The "cultural gap" between Europe and Africa widened so far in the eighteenth century that Europe's conquest of Africa in the nineteenth was to seem, for most Europeans, right and even necessary. We can mark the changing temper of European thought in records which increasingly recast the old trading partnership into new terms of "natural master" and "inevitable servant." This was largely the work of the slave trade; slaving must therefore have a place, and even a large one, in any selection of characteristic documents. We can also mark, as I have mentioned earlier, the emergence of a quasi-scientific note of impartial inquiry into the nature of peoples and their institutions. But there is little of this until the last years of the century. Ignorance of all but the coastal states remains omnipresent and opaque. The maps become less fantastic, yet even the better geographers are still inserting "elephants for want of towns."

There is little progress in discovery. The vaguely apprehended presence of a vast continent within the coastline nags continually at the minds of those educated Europeans who are now reaching the shores of Africa in less meager numbers than before. But there seems no way of penetrating to that inland country, and the few expeditions which make the attempt, and manage to return, fail to solve any of the obvious geographical problems. Bruce reaches the source of the Blue Nile, but everyone still guesses wildly at the source of the White. The Niger is still thought to flow westward, probably into the Senegal, and the springs of the Congo are confounded cartographically with those of the Nile. Only the seaboard of the continent is clearly understood.

Europe's first African colony was enlarged and confirmed in this century. Much earlier, of course, the Portuguese had settled themselves in forts and trading stations along the maritime fringe of Mozambique and Angola as well as far up the Zambezi, and other Europeans had done the same along parts of the Guinea littoral. But these were little more than points of strength from which to promote and monopolize trade with African partners who were generally too strong to be seriously challenged. The Dutch settlement at the Cape of Good Hope was different. Almost from the first it took a colonial shape. "Twenty-five years after the landing of van Riebeeck [in 1652], a cattle and hunting frontier had already come into existence. The sons of the first generation of free burghers became, some of them, genuine frontiersmen . . . Their guns gave them self-reliance, their wagons freedom of movement, and their cattle economic independence . . . From the beginning of the eighteenth century there was always a fringe of settlement that was not wholly within the official limits of the Colony . . . In 1702 a party had wandered far enough afield to brush against some Ama-Xosa tribesmen. It was the first clash between Boer and Bantu. In 1760 Jacobus Coetzee, an elephant hunter, crossed the Orange River." *

This colony stamped the brand of racial segregation and contempt on all the land it took. The first to suffer were the Hottentots. Van Riebeeck had called them "black stinking dogs." His successors destroyed them. "In the beginning the administration strove desperately to keep whites and Hottentots apart. It even thought at one moment fantastically of digging a canal or growing a hedge across the Cape peninsular . . . The Hottentots broke down simply and undramatically . . . Before the pressure of the colonists upon them their institutions failed them, and their loose tribal structure collapsed entirely." The colonists took it as a divine gift to their superior humanity. "According to their belief it was

* C. W. de Kiewiet, *A History of South Africa* (Oxford: 1950), p. 10.

more than their arms that made them prevail over the natives, and their superiority depended upon more than their intelligence or their institutions. Their superiority was born of race and faith, a quality divinely given which could not be transmitted to other races or acquired by them." * Their economy became, by the same token, a slave economy. It has remained one.

The early writings of Boer authors are occasionally useful for the light they throw on the Hottentots and the Bushmen, but generally they are little more than studies in a peculiar cast of Christian prejudice. I have accordingly ended this section with some Cape Province memoirs of a Swedish traveler.

* C. W. de Kiewiet, *A History of South Africa* (Oxford: 1950), p. 20.

JOHN BARBOT
The Trade in Captives

Although Barbot belongs to the seventeenth century — an agent of the French African companies, he made at least two West African voyages in 1678-1682 — he sets the scene better than any other writer for that baleful period of oversea slaving which entirely overwhelmed the whole European-African connection in the eighteenth and early nineteenth centuries. (An inquiry into how this came about, and why and under what conditions some African peoples sold other African peoples, will be found in my *Black Mother*, 1961.)

The trade of slaves is in a more peculiar manner the business of kings, rich men, and prime merchants, exclusive of the inferior sort of blacks . . .

The Gold Coast, in times of war between the inland nations, and those nearer the sea, will furnish great numbers of slaves of all

From John Barbot, *A Description of the Coasts of North and South Guinea, etc.*, first published in 1732 in A. and J. Churchill's *Collections of Voyages and Travels*, 5, p. 420.

sexes and ages; sometimes at one place, and sometimes at another, as has been already observed, according to the nature of the war, and the situation of the countries between which it is waged. I remember, to this purpose, that in the year 1681, an English interloper at Commendo got three hundred good slaves, almost for nothing besides the trouble of receiving them at the beach in his boats, as the Commendo men brought them from the field of battle, having obtained a victory over a neighbouring nation, and taken a great number of prisoners.

At other times slaves are so scarce there, that in 1682 I could get but eight from one end of the coast to the other; not only because we were a great number of trading ships on the coast at the same time, but by reason the natives were everywhere at peace. At another time, I had two hundred slaves at Accra only, in a fortnight or three weeks time; and the upper coast men, understanding I had those slaves aboard, came down to redeem them, giving me two for one, of such as I understood were their near relations, who had been stolen away by inland blacks, brought down to Accra, and sold to us . . .

As to the different sorts of goods the Europeans generally carry thither for trade; each nation commonly supplies the coast, as much as is convenient, with such as their respective countries afford; and what they want at home for well assorting their cargo, they buy in other parts of Europe.

For instance, the French commonly carry more brandy, wine, iron, paper, firelocks, etc., than the English and Dutch can do, those commodities being cheaper in France; as, on the other hand, they supply the Guinea trade with greater quantities of linen cloth, bugles, copper basons, and kettles, wrought pewter, gunpowder, says, perpetuanas, chints, cawris, old sheets, etc., than the French; because they must get these wares from England or Holland.

The French commonly compose their cargo for the Gold Coast trade, to purchase slaves and gold dust; of brandy mostly, white and red wine, ros solis, firelocks, muskets, flints, iron in bars, white and black contecarbe, red frize, looking glasses, fine coral, sarsaparilla, bugles of sundry sorts and colours, and glass beads, powder, sheets, tobacco, taffeties, and many other sorts of silks wrought, as brocardels, velvets, etc., shirts, black-hats, linen, paper, laces of many sorts, beads, shot, lead, musket-balls, flints, callicoes, serges, stuffs, etc., besides the others goods for a true assortment, which they have commonly from Holland.

The Dutch have Coesveld linen, sleysiger lywat, old sheets, Leyden serges, dyed indigo-blue, perpetuanas, green, blue and purple: Konings-Kleederen, annabas, large and narrow, made at Haerlem, Cyprus and Turkey stuffs, Turkey carpets, red, blue, and yellow cloths, green, red and white Leyden rugs, silk stuffs, blue and white; brass kettles of all sizes; copper basons, Scotch pans, barbers basons, some wrought, others hammered; copper pots, brass locks, brass trumpets, pewter, brass and iron rings, hair trunks, pewter dishes, and plates (of a narrow brim); deep porringers, all sorts and sizes of fishing-hooks, and lines, lead in sheets, and in pipes, three sorts of Dutch knives; Venice bugles, and glass beads, of sundry colours and sizes; Sheepskins, iron bars, brass pins, long and short; brass bells, iron hammers, powder, muskets, cutlasses, cawris, chints, lead balls, and shot, of sundry sorts; brass cups, with handles, cloths of Cabo-Verdo, Quaqua, Ardra, and of Rio-Forcado; blue coral, alias akory, from Benin; strong waters, and abundance of other wares, being near a hundred and fifty sorts, as a Dutchman told me.

The English, besides many of the same goods above-mentioned, have tapseils broad and narrow, nicanees fine and coarse; many sorts of chints, or Indian callicoes printed, tallow, red painting colours; Canary wine, sayes, perpetuanas, inferior to the Dutch, and sack'd up in painted tillets, with the English arms: many sorts of white callicoes; blue and white linen, China sattins, Barbadoes rum, or aqua-vitae, made from sugar, other strong waters, and spirits, beads of all sorts, buckshaws, Welsh plain, boysades, romberges, clouts, gingarus taffeties, amber, brandy, flower, Hamburgh brawls, and white, blue and white, and red chequer'd linen, narrow Guinea stuffs chequer'd, ditto broad, old hats, purple beads.

JOHN CASSENEUVE
Docile Slaves?

The records of the oversea slave trade bear marginally, but at certain points significantly, on African history. It would become part of the "myth of the Negro past," in later years, to consider that Africans were in some way peculiarly fitted for enslavement, since they submitted to it "with docility." The slaving captains, as the two following extracts show, knew otherwise.

[1700] About one in the afternoon, after dinner, we according to custom [on board the *Don Carlos*] caused them, one by one, to go down between decks, to have each his pint of water; most of them were yet above deck, many of them provided with knives, which we had indiscreetly given them two or three days before, as not suspecting the least attempt of this nature from them; others had pieces of iron they had torn off our forecastle door, as having premeditated a revolt, and seeing all the ship's company, at best but weak and many quite sick, they had also broken off the shackles from several of their companions feet, which served them, as well as billets they had provided themselves with, and all other things they could lay hands on, which they imagin'd might be of use for their enterprise.

Thus arm'd, they fell in crouds and parcels on our men, upon the deck unawares, and stabb'd one of the stoutest of us all, who receiv'd fourteen or fifteen wounds of their knives, and so expir'd. Next they assaulted our boatswain, and cut one of his legs so round the bone, that he could not move, the nerves being cut through;

From James Barbot and John Casseneuve, *An Abstract of a Voyage to Congo River . . . in the Year* 1700, in A. and J. Churchill, *Collections of Voyages and Travels* (1732), 5, pp. 497-522. This Barbot, a nephew of John, was supercargo of the *Don Carlos*, London, and Casseneuve its first mate.

others cut our cook's throat to the pipe, and others wounded three of the sailors, and threw one of them overboard in that condition, from the forecastle into the sea; who, however, by good providence, got hold of the bowlin of the foresail, and sav'd himself, along the lower wale of the quarterdeck, where, [says Casseneuve] we stood in arms, firing on the revolted slaves, of whom we kill'd some, and wounded many: which so terrify'd the rest, that they gave way, dispersing themselves some one way and some another between decks, and under the forecastle; and many of the most mutinous, leapt over board, and drown'd themselves in the ocean with much resolution, shewing no manner of concern for life. Thus we lost twenty-seven or twenty-eight slaves, either kill'd by us, or drown'd; and having master'd them, caused all to go betwixt decks, giving them good words.

"BOSTON POST BOY"
Revolt at Sea

By a Vessel lately arrived here from the West-Indies, we have Advice, that a Ship belonging to Liverpool coming from the Coast of Africa, with about 350 Slaves on board, and when in Sight of the Island Guardaloupe, the Slaves, as 'tis supposed, being admitted to come upon Deck to air themselves, took an Opportunity on the 28th of May . . . and kill'd the Master and Mate of the Ship, and threw fifteen of the Men overboard, after which they sent the Boat with two white Lads and three or four others to discover what Land it was, meanwhile the Ship drove to the Leeward, which gave the Lads an Opportunity to discover the Affair to the Commandant of that Quarter of the Island, who immediately raised about 100 Men, and put them on board a Sloop, who went

From a report in the *Boston Post Boy*, June 25, 1750, in E. Donnan, *Documents Illustrative of the History of the Slave Trade to America* (Carnegie Institution, Washington, D.C.: 1931), vol. 2, p. 485.

in Pursuit of the Ship, and in a few Hours took her and carried her into Port Louis.

JAMES BARBOT
Slaving Manners

[1700] As it is the usual custom among Europeans that buy slaves in Africa, to examine each limb, to know whether sound or not; the king of Zair [Congo estuary] observing Casseneuve [first mate of the *Don Carlos* slaver of London] thus trying the four slaves he had sold him, burst out a-laughing, as did likewise the great men that were about him. He asked the interpreter what was the occasion of their laughter?, and was answered, it proceeded from his so nicely viewing the poor slaves; but that, however, the king and his attendants were so much asham'd of it, that he requir'd him, for decency sake, to do it in a private place: which shews these Blacks are very modest.

The System in Angola

The chiefest trade of the Portuguese and other whites [in Congo and Angola] consists in slaves . . . It is affirm'd that when the Spaniards were masters of Portugal, they transported every year fifteen thousand slaves out of Angola into the new world. And the Portuguese still [1701] transport a very great number.

All those slaves the Portuguese cause to be bought, by their pomberroes [*pombeiros:* Afro-Portuguese subtraders], a hundred and fifty or two hundred leagues up the country, whence they bring them down to the seacoasts . . .

These slaves, called *Pombeiros*, have other slaves under them, sometimes a hundred, or a hundred and fifty, who carry the commodities on their heads up into the country [to buy captives] . . .

From James Barbot in A. and J. Churchill, *Collections of Voyages and Travels* (1732), 5, pp. 497-522.

Sometimes these *Pombeiros* stay out a whole year, and then
bring back with them four, five and six hundred new slaves. Some
of the faithfullest remain often there, sending what slaves they buy
to their masters, who return them other commodities to trade with
a-new.

An Angolan "Zimbabwe"

The king of Angola, or Dongo, resides a little above the city
Massingan, on a stony mountain seven leagues in compass, in
which are many rich pastures, fields, and meadows, yielding a
plentiful provision for all his retinue; into which there is but one
single passage, and that according to their method well fortified; so
that he needs fear no enemies . . .

WILLIAM BOSMAN
A Report on Gold

Chief factor for the Dutch West India Company of what was then
their main trading station at Elmina Castle, William Bosman's description consists of twenty letters to a friend in Holland, the first of which
is dated September 1, 1700.

There is no small number of Men in Europe who believe that the
Gold Mines are in our Power; that we, like the Spaniards in the
West-Indies, have no more to do but to work them by our Slaves:
Though you perfectly know we have no manner of access to these
Treasures; nor do I believe that any of our People have ever seen
one of them: Which you will easily credit, when you are informed
that the Negroes esteem them Sacred, and consequently take all
possible care to keep us from them. But to come nearer the Sub-

From William Bosman, *A New and Accurate Description of Guinea, etc.,*
translated, London, 1705.

ject: This Illustrious Metal is generally found in three sorts of places: First, the best is found in or betwixt particular Hills; and the Negroes apprehending where the Gold is, dig Pits; and separate it from the Earth which comes out with it.

The second place is in, at, and about some Rivers and Waterfalls; whose violence washeth down great Quantities of Earth, which carry the Gold with it.

The third is on the Sea-shore; where (as at Elmina and Axim) there are little Branches or Rivulets into which the Gold is driven from Mountainous Places, as well as to the Rivers; and after violent Showers of Rain in the Night, next Morning these places are sure to be visited by hundreds of Negroe-Women naked, except a Cloth wrapped about them to hide what Modesty obligeth. Each of these Women is furnished with large and small Troughs or Tray, which they first fill full of Earth and Sand, which they wash with repeated fresh Water, till they have cleansed it from all its Earth; and if there be any Gold, its Ponderosity forces it to the bottom of the Trough; which if they find, it is thrown into the small Tray, and so they go to washing it again: which Operation generally holds them till Noon: Some of them not getting above the value of Sixpence; some of them find pieces of six or seven Shillings, though not frequently; and often they intirely loose their labour. Thus the digging of Pits, the gathering it, at or about the Rivers, and this last mentioned manner, are all the ways they know to come at Gold.

The Guinea Partnership

The first business of one of our Factors when he comes to Fida [Ouidah or Whydah on what was soon to become one Dahomey Coast], is to satisfie the Customs of the King and the great Men, which amount to about 100 Pounds in Guinea value, as the Goods must yield there. After which we have free Licence to Trade, which is published throughout the whole land by the Cryer.

But yet before we can deal with any Person, we are obliged to buy the King's whole stock of Slaves at a set price; which is commonly one third or one fourth higher than ordinary: After which we obtain free leave to deal with all his Subjects of what Rank soever. But if there happen to be no stock of Slaves, the Factor must then resolve to run the Risque of trusting the Inhabitants with Goods to the value of one or two hundred Slaves; which Commodities they send into the In-land Country, in order to buy with them Slaves at all markets, and that sometimes two hundred Miles deep in the Country: For you ought to be informed that Markets of Men are here kept in the same manner as those of Beasts with us.

Not a few in our Country fondly imagine that Parents here sell their Children, Men their Wives, and one Brother the other: But those who think so deceive themselves; for this never happens on any other account but that of Necessity, or some great Crime: But most of the Slaves that are offered to us are Prisoners of War, which are sold by the Victors as their Booty.

When these Slaves come to Fida, they are put in Prison all together, and when we treat concerning buying them, they are all brought out together in a large Plain; where, by our Chirurgeons, whose Province it is, they are throughly examined, even to the smallest Member, and that naked too both Men and Women, without the least Distinction or Modesty. Those which are approved as good are set on one side; and the lame or faulty are set by as Invalides, which are here called Mackrons. These are such as are above five and thirty Years old, or are maimed in the Arms, Legs, Hands or Feet, have lost a Tooth, are grey-haired, or have Films over their Eyes; as well as all those which are affected with any Veneral Distemper, or with several other Diseases.

The Invalides and the Maimed being thrown out, as I have told you, the remainder are numbred, and it is entred who delivered them. In the mean while a burning Iron, with the Arms or Name of the Companies, lyes in the Fire; with which ours are marked on the Breast.

This is done that we may distinguish them from the Slaves of the English, French or others; (which are also marked with their Mark) and to prevent the Negroes exchanging them for worse, at which they have a good Hand.

I doubt not but this Trade seems very barbarous to you, but since it is followed by meer necessity it must go on; but we yet take all possible care that they are not burned too hard, especially the Women, who are more tender than the Men.

We are seldom long detained in the buying of these Slaves, because their price is established, the Women being one fourth or fifth part cheaper than the Men. The Disputes which we generally have with the Owners of these Slaves are, that we will not give them such Goods as they ask for them, especially the Boesies* (as I have told you, the Money of this Country) of which they are very fond, though we generally make a Division on this Head in order to make one sort of Goods help off another, because those Slaves which are paid for in Boesies cost the Company one half more than those bought with other Goods . . .

When we have agreed with the Owners of the Slaves, they are returned to their Prison; where from that time forwards they are kept at our charge, cost us two pence a day a Slave; which serves to subsist them, like our Criminals, on Bread and Water: So that to save Charges we send them on Board our Ships with the very first Opportunity; before which their Masters strip them of all they have on their Backs; so that they come Aboard stark-naked as well Women as Men: In which condition they are obliged to continue, if the Master of the Ship is not so Charitable (which he commonly is) as to bestow something on them to cover their Nakedness.

Guns for Africa

The chief of [the coastal Africans' military arms] are Musquets or Carabins, in the management of which they are wonderful dextrous. 'Tis not unpleasant to see them exercise their Army; they handle their Arms so cleverly, discharging them several ways, one sitting, the second creeping, or lying & etc. that 'tis really to be admired they never hurt one another. Perhaps you wonder how the *Negroes* come to be furnished with Fire-Arms, but you will have no Reason when you know we sell them incredible quantities, thereby obliging them with a Knife to cut our own Throats. But we are forced to it; for if we would not, they might be sufficiently stored with that Commodity by the *English, Danes,* and *Branden-*

* Cowries.

burghers; and could we all agree together not to sell them any, the *English* and *Zeeland* Interlopers [i.e., private traders] would abundantly furnish them: And since that and Gunpowder for some time hath been the chief vendible Merchandise here [i.e., on the Gold Coast], we should have found but an indifferent Trade without our share in it . . .

MICHEL ADANSON

A *Scientific Traveler*

Scientific inquiry appears in the eighteenth century. Michel Adanson, a French botanist, is one of its earliest exponents.

[1720] As the island of Senegal is within the dependence of the kingdom of Oualo [Wolof], the negroes who live there, especially those who are free, are of that nation. They are, generally speaking, very good-natured, sociable and obliging. Those whom the company entertained in my service, were Oualofes, as they call themselves, or by corruption Jallofs.

Immediately after my arrival, I employed some months, not only in studying the manners and character of the inhabitants, but likewise in learning the Oualof language which obtained most generally in that country: for I was sensible that it would be of great service to me, and even indispensably necessary in regard to the researches I purposed to make. With this view I frequented their company, and was among them as much as possible. At length when I looked upon myself as sufficiently acquainted with their usages and manners, and able to judge how to conduct myself in a country which had long been the object of my most ardent wishes, I determined to set out upon a ramble . . .

From Michel Adanson, *Voyage au Sénégal:* translated in J. Pinkerton, **A General Collection of the Best Voyages, etc.** (London: 1814).

After . . . a passage through thorns, rivers and burning sands, where I coursed and herborized all the way, I arrived at the village of Sor. There I found the governor, whom the negroes distinguished by the name of *Borom-dek*, that is, master of the village. He was a venerable old man, about fifty`. . . whose physiognomy bespoke him a person of gentle manners and great good nature. His name was Baba-Sec: he was sitting on the sand, under the shade of a jujube, planted before his hut, where he was smoking and conversing with a few friends. As soon as he saw me, he rose up, presented his hand to me thrice, then laid it upon his forehead, and afterwards upon his breast, asking me each time, in his language, how I did. I performed the same ceremony myself at the same time, because I understood that such was the manner of saluting in this country . . . It was near their dinner time, and Baba-Sec counted upon my staying . . . He made me sit down by him; then he began to fall to, and thrusting his hand into the dish, he took a handful of couscous, which he rolled about with his fingers, for want of a fork and spoon, a conveniency they have not yet learnt. He invited me afterwards to do the same. I did not let him press me hard, but followed his example: for I never departed from this principle, that nothing contributes more to gain the confidence and friendship of strangers among whom you reside, than to conform to their customs and manner of living . . .

JOHN ATKINS
Ouidah in 1721

Whydah [Ouidah or Fida] is the greatest trading Place on the Coast of Guinea, selling off as many Slaves, I believe, as all the rest together; 40 or 50 Sail (French, English, Portuguese, and

From John Atkins, Surgeon in the Royal Navy, A *Voyage to Guinea, etc.* (London: 1735), p. 168. Ouidah was one of the most important middleman trading-stations of the Slave Coast (Dahomey in later years).

Dutch) freighting there every year. The King is absolute as a Boar; making sometimes fair Agreements with his Country Neighbours, it being often the Interest of Traders to be honest (perhaps the only reason that makes them so) but if he cannot obtain a sufficient number of Slaves that way, he marches an Army, and depopulates. He, and the King of Ardra adjoining, commit great Depredations inland.

On the Ships he lays these Impositions, and to prove his Folly, does it mostly for the benefit of those that rule him: First, of having the refusal of all Goods; Secondly, the Value of twenty Slaves from every Ship, small or great, as a Duty; and thirdly, forces his own upon them at an advanced Price . . .

The French, the Dutch, and English, have each a House, or mud Fort about three miles from the Sea, keeping Tents on the Beach for the convenient receiving and securing their Cargoes as it comes from the Ship, and transmitting the Returns; which, by a dangerous double Barr upon the Coast, is rendred impassable sometimes (by the alteration of the Winds) for a fortnight together; the Negroes only know how to paddle thro' it, and when they think it safe, a Signal is made to the Ships, from those Tents, by hoisting their Flags.

The Chief of either Factory that gets first on board any Ship coming into the Road, has a right to serve her with Boats and Servants, and has a Due of seven Slaves for it.

The Commanders, with their Surgeons, (as skilled in the Choice of Slaves) attend the whole time on shore, where they purchase, in what they call a fair open Market.

The Mates reside on board, receiving from time to time their Master's Directions as to the Goods wanted, and to prepare the Ship for the Reception and Security of the Slaves sent him; where this is a Rule always observed, to keep the Males apart from the Women and Children, to handcuff the former . . .

WILLIAM SMITH
The Palace of Benin

The master of the *Bonetta* was on the Coast in 1726-1727. Although the account that follows is mainly at second hand, it is useful in showing how greatly Benin had impressed Europeans.

The King's Court is situated in a very large Plain. The first Place we come into, is, a very long Gallery which is sustained by fifty-eight strong Planks, which are only hack'd out rough. At the End of which we come to the Mudwall with three Gates, at each Corner one, and another in the Middle. At the Top of all is fix'd a large Copper Snake, which is well cast and carved. Entring one of these Gates we next come into a Plain, which is about a Quarter of a Mile Square, and encompass'd with a low Mud-wall; then we come to another Gallery, which has a Gate leading to the third Gallery, which is supported by Human Figures. Going through a Gate we come to the fourth Gallery, beyond which is the King's House. Here is another Snake. In his Anti-chamber his three Great Lords attend, who acquaint the King with the Desires of his Subjects and report his Answers, for no other Person dare to come nearer to him than the Distance of Thirty Paces.

The King appears publickly but once a Year, and that is at the CORAL-FEAST, as they call it, when he comes to the Plain most magnificently dress'd attended by his Wives, Prime Ministers of State, and all the Gentry, or Viceroys, where His Majesty sacrifices to his Gods in the open Air, which begins the Feast; the Nobles and Gentry follow his Example, and the Day proceeds with all Manner of Drinking, etc. and concludes with great Mirth and Gladness. It is call'd the Coral-Feast, because at this Time the

From William Smith, *A New Voyage to Guinea* (London: 1744), p. 236.

King bestows the Strings of Coral on those, whom he advances to any Preferment, or Post of Honour, which he never does, but on this Festival, unless a particular Urgency of State requires it.

RICHARD BREW
A *Dearth of Victims*

Such was now the demand for slave labor that Europeans were paying in gold for captives — even on its Gold Coast.

———

[1771] . . . there remains only to tell you that gold commands the trade; there is no buying a slave without one ounce of gold at least on it, and the windward Coast has been so ransacked, that there is no such thing as getting gold, even though you sell your goods from forty to fifty per cent. under prime cost . . .

A most pernicious practice has of late crept into the trade of the Gold Coast, which is the giving gold upon slaves; and it is greatly to be wished that some methods may be fallen upon to put a timely stop to it, otherwise it will be impossible for any man to continue to trade here with any prospect of success; Appolonia, the only place from which the shipping used to be supplied with gold, you are effectually shut out from; that fort, Dixcove, Succondee, and Commenda being factories to the governor of Cape Coast, who is so plentifully supplied with gold from these places, that he carries everything before him; for the truth of which I appeal to all the Liverpool and Bristol captains that have been here this year.

Formerly owners of ships used to send out double cargoes of

From three letters by Richard Brew in A *Treatise upon the Slave Trade*, written in 1771-1772 from the Gold Coast. In E. Donnan, *Documents Illustrative of the Slave Trade to America* (Carnegie Institution, Washington, D.C.: 1931), vol. 2, p. 536.

goods, one for slaves, the other for gold; if slaves happened to be dearer than usual, the cargoe for gold was thrown into the slave cargoe in order to fill the ship; on the other hand, if slaves were reasonable the gold cargoe was disposed of for gold and ivory, at a profit of thirty, forty, or fifty per cent. which went a great way towards paying the portlidge bill in the West Indies; as I have frequently known from five to fifteen hundred pounds sterling in gold and ivory carried off from this coast, over and above a compleat cargoe of slaves. How strangely things are reversed now, you have experienced; we scarce see a ship go off with her complement of slaves, notwithstanding her cargoe is laid in from eighteen to twenty pounds sterling per head on an average, reckoning goods at prime cost, without a shilling charges on them; a great part of which they are obliged to sell where they can for gold, greatly under prime cost, or lie here till their provisions are all expended, and their bottoms eat out with the worms . . .

There is no buying slaves now [1772] without you give two ounces of gold on each; to procure which, you must sell your goods 20 per cent. under prime cost, and you may think yourself happy to get it even at that rate.

CAPTAIN HEATLEY

The Reverence of Kings

[1789] When a Ship arrives in the River Gambia she comes to an Anchor at Gillofree Port, in the Kingdom of Barra, opposite James Fort on James's Island, Nine or Ten Leagues from the Entrance. You send your Boat on Shore to acquaint the Alkaide or Mayor of the Town of your Arrival; he in common returns with the Boat, and receives from you Anchorage-money, Ten Gallons of

From evidence before the 1789 Committee of the Privy Council for Inquiry into the Slave Trade. In E. Donnan, *Documents Illustrative of the History of the Slave Trade to America* (Carnegie Institution, Washington, D.C.: 1931), vol. 2, p. 593.

Liquor for the King, Value 30 s. and Two Iron Bars for himself, Value 7s. and perhaps Presents, a few Bottles of Wine, Beer, Cyder, etc. He immediately dispatches Messengers with the Liquor as above to the King, informing that such Vessel is arrived, and only waits to pay his Customs, intending to proceed up the River. The King consults his Councillors for a proper Day to receive the same, and sends Word to the Alcaide accordingly. After a Detention of Four, Five, Six, and Seven Days, he sends his People to receive his Custom, 140 Bars in Merchandize, Amount Sterling on an Average £16. An English Ship seldom or ever meets with Trade here; the French (who have their King's Residence at Albreda, a Town in the Kingdom of Barra, about 17 Miles West of Gillofree) engross most or all of the Trade of the lower Parts of this River.

JAMES PENNY

The Business of Kings

[1789] At Bonny Slaves are purchased of the King, who is the principal Trader, and of other Traders; at New Calabar, of the before-mentioned Amachree, and of other Traders. These Traders go up into the Country to purchase Slaves. They go up the Rivers to the Distance of about Eighty Miles from Bonny, and the same from New Calabar, in large Canoes with Two or Three principal Persons, and about Forty Men in each. The Canoes go in a Body

From evidence before the 1789 Committee of the Privy Council. In E. Donnan, *Documents Illustrative of the History of the Slave Trade to America* (Carnegie Institution, Washington, D.C.: 1931), vol. 2, p. 537. Penny was a Liverpool man who had made eleven voyages to West Africa. He told the Privy Council that fourteen thousand slaves were annually exported from the region of Bonny and Calabar in the Niger delta, eleven thousand of these being purchased by the English. His estimate for Congo-Angola annual exports of slaves at this time was thirteen to fourteen thousand, while as many as twenty-five thousand, he thought, were taken every year from the Windward Coast (central and western seaboard).

all together to defend themselves if attacked. At the Head of these Two Rivers there is a Mart for Trade, where the Black Traders purchase these Slaves of other Black Traders, who bring them from the interior Country.

COMPANY DIRECTORS
Abuses of the Trade

[1795] The slave trade is decreasing very much at Sierra Leona, the price of slaves having risen to £25 or £30 sterling each; and not above 1000 are now annually exported from this river. They are chiefly brought down through a chain of factories, but not through the company's ground, and a great many are children. The kings and chiefs trade in slaves; but the principal traders are the French and English factors.

It is customary to credit the black factors who either travel themselves, or deal with other factors still farther up, with European goods (chiefly gunpowder and spirits) and, if they fail in bringing the stipulated slaves, they are made slaves themselves; or, if they do not return in a certain time, any one of their families are taken. King Naimbanna, in his letter to Mr. Sharp,* after mentioning "the horrid depredations committed here by all the countries that come here to trade," says, "There are three distant relations of mine now in the West Indies, carried away by one Capt. Cox, captain of a Danish ship. Their names are Corpro, Banna and Morbour. These were taken out of my river Sierra Leona. I know not how to get them back. I never hurt or deprived any person of their right or property, or withheld from them what is their

From a report of 1795 by the Directors of the Sierra Leone Company. In E. Donnan, *Documents Illustrative of the History of the Slave Trade to America* (Carnegie Institution, Washington, D.C.: 1931), vol. 2, p. 618.

* Granville Sharp, a leader of the British antislavery movement.

due. So I only let you know of these lads, that there will be an account taken of them, one day or another."

King Naimbanna's son relates, that a cousin of his father's, named Jack Rodney, was asked to pilot a slave-ship down from Bance Island. He begged to be put on shore at Robanna; but the captain refused, saying he would land him at the river's mouth, instead of which he carried him to Jamaica. As he spoke good English, he obtained several interviews with the governor of that island, and was recovered by a ship which brought a letter concerning him from Sierra Leona . . .

An American ship arriving in Sierra Leona river, the supercargo, who seems to have known little of the Company's principles, went hastily to the governor and council and offered them his cargo, for a cargo of slaves, saying he would take no other articles, and hoped they would soon favour him with the slaves he wanted. A counselor asked him how the American laws stood, respecting this trade. He said that, where he came from, it was prohibited, under forfeiture of the ship and £1000 penalty on the captain. "But," added he, "nobody will inform."

Indeed Sir, replied the counselor, I myself shall inform, if none else will. I hope, Sir, you will not do so unfriendly a thing. I would rather prevent evil than punish it, (said the counselor) and I warn you, that if you carry a single slave from this coast, you shall find an information lodged against you in America. The supercargo then said, he was not in earnest, and that he really abhorred the slave trade.

JOHN JOHNSTON
The Price of Slaves

Slave Trade at Quashies Town, August 1789:

			Oz.	Ac.	Oz.	Ac.
Aug. 18th.	No. 1 a Prime Man slave for					
	4 Dane Guns		1	8		
	2 Half Barrells powder		2			
	2 fine Chintss		1	4		
	2 Patna Do		1			
	4 Bajudepants		2	8		
	2 Necanees		1			
	6 Romauls		2	4		
	3 Hlf Cottons			12		
	3 Two Blues			12		
	1 Half Taffaty			10		
	4 Lead Barrs			2		
	2 Small Brass panns			2	13	14
Aug. 19th.	No. 2 A Man Slave for					
	4 Dane guns 2½ Barrells powder	4				
	2 fine Chintz		1	4		
	2 Patna Do		1			
	2 Nicanees		1			
	6 Romauls		2	4		
	2 Half Cottons			8		
	3 Two Blues			12	10	12
	Carried Forward				24	10

From a "Manuscript Book kept by one John Johnston, while on a Slaving Expedition in Africa, in 1792, 84 pages, 1792." From *Proceedings* of the American Antiquarian Society, vol. 39, pp. 379-465. In E. Donnan, *Documents Illustrative of the History of the Slave Trade to America* (Carnegie Institution, Washington, D.C.: 1931), vol. 2, p. 612.

		Oz.	Ac.	Oz.	Ac.
Brought Forward				24	10
4	Bajudepants	2	8		
1	Half Taffaty		10		
2	Brass panns		2	3	4

August 21st.   No. 3 a Stout Man for Vizt

5	Half Barrells powder	5			
6	Guns	2	4		
2	Bajudepants	1	4		
2	Necanees	1			
2	Green Ells	1			
2	Romauls		12		
1	Two Blue and 1 Half Cotton		8		
1	Patch 3 Kegs Tallow		14		
3	lbs Pewter Basons		2	12	12
				40	10

C. B. WADSTRÖM
An Enlightened Ruler

Returning from Africa with his fellow-scientist Sparrman, the Swedish traveler Wadström was in time to give evidence against the slave trade to the Privy Council Committee of 1789. His account gives a fair picture of the political chaos in which the trade had by now involved large regions of West Africa.

The Wars which the inhabitants of the interior parts of the country, beyond Senegal, Gambia, and Sierra Leona, carry on with each other, are chiefly of a predatory nature, and owe their origin to the yearly number of slaves, which the Mandingoes, or

From C. B. Wadström, *Observations on the Slave Trade . . . made in 1787 and 1788 in Company with D'A. Sparrman and Captain Arrhenius* (London: 1789).

the inland traders suppose will be wanted by the vessels that will arrive on the coast. Indeed these predatory incursions depend so much on the demand for slaves, that if in any one year there be a greater concourse of European ships than usual, it is observed that a much greater number of captives from the interior parts of the country is brought to market the next.

The Moors, who inhabit the countries on the north of the River Senegal, are particularly infamous for their predatory Wars. They cross the river, and attacking the negroes, bring many of them off. There are not a few who subsist by means of these unprovoked excursions. The French, to encourage them in it, make annual presents to the Moorish kings. These are given them under certain conditions, first, that their subjects shall not carry any of their gum to the English at Portendic; and, secondly, that they shall be ready on all occasions, to furnish slaves. To enable them to fulfill this last article, they never fail to supply them with ammunition, guns, and other instruments of War.

To confirm what I have now said, I shall put down the following example:

The King of Almammy had, in the year 1787, very much to his honour, enacted a law, that no slave whatever should be marched through his territories. At this time several French vessels lay at anchor in the Senegal, waiting for slaves. The route of the black traders in consequence of this edict of the king, was stopped, and the slaves carried to other parts. The French, unable on this account to complete their cargoes, remonstrated with the king. He was, however, very unpropitious to their representations, for he returned the presents which had been sent him by the Senegal company, of which I myself was a witness; declaring, at the same time, that all the riches of that company should not divert him from his design. In this situation of affairs, the French were obliged to have recourse to their old friends, the Moors. These, who had before shewn themselves so ready on such occasions, were no less ready and active on this. They set off in parties to surprise the unoffending negroes, and to carry among them all the calamities of War. Many unfortunate prisoners were sent, and for some time continued to be sent in. I was once curious enough to wish to see some of those that had just arrived. I applied to the Director of the company, who conducted me to the slave-prisons. I there saw the unfortunate captives, chained two and two together, by the foot.

A second source, from whence the Europeans are supplied with slaves on the coast of Africa, is Pillage, which is of two kinds; publick and private. It is publick, when practiced by the direction of the king, private when practiced by individuals. I must also make a further distinction, namely, as it is practiced by the blacks and the whites. This last I call Robbery, which will be the subject of the next article.

The publick Pillage is, of all others, the most plentiful source, from which the slave trade derives its continuance and support. The kings of Africa (I mean in that part of the country which I have visited) incited by the merchandise shewn them, which consists principally of strong liquors, give orders to their military to attack their own villages in the night . . .

I have been hitherto describing the Pillage, as it is either publick or private. I have also considered it as practiced by the blacks upon one another. I come now to speak of it, as it is practiced upon these by the whites; and this I call Robbery . . .

When I was at Goree,* in the year 1787, accounts came down by some French merchantmen from the Gambia of the following particulars.

The captain of an English ship, which had been some time in that river, had enticed several of the natives on board, and, finding a favourable opportunity, sailed away with them. His vessel however was, by the direction of Providence, driven back to the coast from whence it had set sail, and was obliged to cast anchor on the very spot where this act of treachery had been committed. At this time two other English vessels were lying in the same river. The natives, ever since the transaction, had determined to retaliate. They happened, at this juncture, to be prepared. They accordingly boarded the three vessels, and, having made themselves masters of them, they killed most of their crews. The few who escaped to tell the tale, were obliged to take refuge in a neighbouring French fac-

* An island off Dakar on the Senegal Coast, much used as a slaving base.

tory. Thus did the innocent suffer the same punishment as the guilty; for it did not appear that the crews of the other two vessels had been at all concerned in this villainous measure.

ARCHIBALD DALZELL
Rise of Dahomey

Forced to defend themselves against slaving raids and eager to break the coastal monopoly on the import of European goods, notably fire-arms, the Fon people of Dahomey broke through to the sea in 1724. They became a power with whom the Europeans had to reckon and soon learned to respect.

Dalzell was governor of the English trading station and castle at Cape Coast, and also spent four years at Ouidah where he came into personal contact with the new-risen state of Dahomey.

The Dahomans were formerly called Foys [Fons], and inhab-ited a small territory, on the northeast part of their present king-dom, whose capital, Dawhee, lay between the towns of Calmina and Abomey, at about 90 miles from the seacoast . . .

The conquest of Abomey happened about the year 1625; after which, Tacoodonou fixed his residence in that town, assuming the title of King of Dahomy . . .

It is not till the reign of Guadja Trudo [Agaja], who succeeded Weebaigah in 1708, that any thing is precisely known about this extraordinary people. All before this time stands on the ground of tradition . . . But when the active spirit of Trudo began to threaten the maritime states [i.e., the coastal city-states of Ardra, Ouidah and the like], his neighbours, it quickly attracted the atten-tion of the Europeans, whom commerce have brought and settled amongst them . . .

A very little experience must have taught such a mind as that of

From Archibald Dalzell, *History of Dahomey* (London: 1793), p. 60.

Around 1477 B.C. Queen Hatshepsut of Egypt sent trading ships to the land of Punt, on the Red Sea coast of Ethiopia or northern Somalia. Later, at Deir el-Bahri, her artists made a record of that fruitful expedition. In this superb relief, a fragment recovered from oblivion by the American Research Center in Egypt, three men of Punt attend their king in a welcome to Egypt's mariners. Branches of a "myrrh tree," the incense wood for which Punt was renowned in ancient times, appear at the lower left edge. The descriptive records of inner Africa really begin with this remarkable picture. (*The American Research Center in Egypt*)

The writing shown here offers one of ancient Africa's great unsolved problems. Towards the third century B.C. the priests and merchants of the inner-African state of Meroë invented an alphabet of their own. They used it extensively, but little of it can yet be read. This particular inscription, from a cemetery on the Middle Nile, is late Meroitic and may date from the third century. It appears to commemorate someone called Mli-wês, the kinswoman of a Meroitic envoy to the Romans. (*The Pennsylvania-Yale Expedition to Egypt and the Yale Peabody Museum*)

This little statue in schist comes from Professor Jean Leclant's excavations at Melazo near the ancient Ethiopian capital of Axum, and bears a dedication to Almaqah, the moon-god, in old Ethiopian script. (*Professor J. Leclant*)

Axumite funerary inscription from Melazo. It was from this handsome script that modern Ethiopian writing has developed. (Professor J. Leclant)

This page from the Imperial Ethiopian Library's oldest manuscript in
Ge'ez, the Guebre Hemamat (a prayer book for Lent), was written
about six hundred years ago. (*The National Library of Ethiopia and
Professor Richard Pankhurst*)

An Ethiopian illuminated manuscript of the reign of Dawit II (1508-1540), showing Hanna delivering the three-day-old Mary to the High Priest. The original is in the Church of Bethlehem near Debra Tabor. (*The Ethiopian Observer*)

The legend of King Solomon and the Queen of Sheba — of Ethiopia — is still vividly alive in folklore, as may be seen by this traditional though modern wall hanging from the Ethiopian countryside. In the top two registers the people sacrifice to the serpent-king; the Queen's father dies and the Queen succeeds him; and she, hearing tales of wonder from Jerusalem, decides to visit Solomon. Dazzled by her beauty, Solomon then desires a son by her, tricks her into lying with him, and in due course she gives birth to Menelik, father of the line of the Lion of Judah. (Mrs. F. Elwyn Jones)

Linha equin

Motes lune

Biblioteca Estense – Modena.
"Carta del Cantino,, sec. XVI" (C.G.A.2).

This remarkable map of western Africa shows how well the mariners of Portugal had scanned the whole long coastline by as early as 1507, when the map was made, only nine years after Vasco da Gama had sailed into the Indian Ocean. They understood little of the interior as yet — the Mountains of the Moon appear in Angola instead of in East Africa — but were well aware of the strength and reputation of the kingdoms of Guinea and the Western Sudan, as the drawings along the top of the picture clearly indicate. (*Portuguese Secretary of State for Information, Lisbon, and the Extense Library, Modena, C. G., A. 2*)

One of many interesting documents to have survived from the history of the Western Sudan, a letter written by the renowned Sultan Bello of Sokoto to his vassal, the Emir of Bauchi. Part of the translation is on pages 326-327. (Dr. A. D. H. Bivar and the Bulletin of the School of Oriental and African Studies)

الحمد لله والصلاة والسلام على رسول الله

من عبد الله تعالى عمر بن محمد الامير للكانمي
المحضرة الاجل الاحضرة الاعز الاكرم الا كملت امير
قومه ٠٠ ومالك زمام ارضه٠ محبنا السلطان معاذ
ابو التفر محمد بلتوا المرحوم السلام التام ورحمة
الله تعالى وبركاته اما بعد جاء اوصل اليك
كتابنا هذا فبالذ نعلمك به ان ابننا ابابكر
فداعلمنا بانقطاع التنازع بينه وبين وزيرك
صاحب كتم في شار البدود التي بيننا
وبينكم جارتبنت علم ما تواقف عليه ورضيت
به٠٠ وقد استقام الامر ورجع السير المراصله٠٠
ولايكون من جهتنا ان شاء الله تعالى الا التيم
وتاكيد العهد والامانة على الوجه السابق
هذا اما اعلمنك به ووقفنا الله وايا كم على
رعاية العهد والميثاق المريوم السفر. والتلاوت٠٠
بجاه افضل النبي على الاطلاوت٠ سيد نامحمد
عليه صلاة الملك التلاوت٠ اميرت والسلام

Chief Moshesh of the Basuto in 1833. *(Les Bassoutos, by E. Casalis)*

King Kazembe, as Gamitto found him in 1831. *(O Muata Kazembe, by A.C.P. Gamitto, translated as King Kazembe by Ian Cunnison)*

Exploring the Western Sudan. An illustration from Petermann's Royal Folio of 1854, showing Heinrich Barth in the bottom left-hand corner, together with his three fellow-explorers, Richardson, Overweg and Vogel. (*The Clarendon Press and Mr. A. H. M. Kirk-Green*)

Trudo, how much more effective in war were the European weapons, than those used by the inland people of Africa; and this must have suggested to him the advantage of a seacoast, where only those weapons were to be obtained. For, as to the supply, that might be procured through the hands of the maritime nations [Ardra and its like], it was at best precarious. Their jealousy might wish to keep from others the means of becoming as formidable as they supposed themselves to be; and so they might either refuse to furnish him at all, or they might set so high a price upon them, as would amount to a prohibition.

This made him determine to possess himself of a part of the coast; but, previous to this undertaking, the event of which was uncertain, he endeavoured to obtain his principal end by negotiation. He sent ambassadors to Ardra and Ouidah, to whose very borders he had already extended his conquests, requesting an open traffic to the seaside, offering at the same time to pay the customary duties. This, as he probably expected, was peremptorily refused; which furnished him with a pretense for obtaining his desire by force, when he should find an opportunity. Nor was it long before such an opportunity offered . . . [Dahomey conquered the coastal city-state of Jacquin in 1724 and of Ouidah — Whydah or Fida — in 1727. Some ten years later Dahomey was in turn invaded by the neighbouring Yoruba empire of Oyo, then very powerful.]

ROBERT NORRIS

Oyo and Dahomey

. . . To the northeast of Dahomy lies a fine, fertile, and extensive country, inhabited by a great and warlike people, called the

From Robert Norris, *Memoirs of the Reign of Bossa Ahadee, King of Dahomy* (London: 1789), p. 11. Norris wrote in 1773. The Bossa Ahadee in question was King Tegbesu, who reigned between about 1727 to 1775.

Eyoes [Oyos]; the scourge and terror of all their neighbours . . .

The Dahomans, to give an idea of the strength of an Eyoe army, assert, that when they go to war, the general spreads the hide of a buffaloe before the door of his tent, and pitches a spear in the ground, on each side of it; between which the soldiers march, until the multitude, which pass over the hide, have worn an hole through it; as soon as this happens, he presumes that his forces are numerous enough to take the field. The Dahomans may possibly exaggerate, but the Eyoes are certainly a very populous, warlike and powerful nation.

They invaded Dahomy in 1738 with an irresistible army, and laid the country waste with fire and sword to the gates of Abomey; here, the Foys [Fons, Dahomans] had collected their whole strength, and waited the arrival of the enemy, who were advancing with an incredible multitude.

The Foys though inferior in numbers, were not intimidated; they had seen service under Trudo [King Agaja, 1708-1727], but never was their valour called forth upon a more trying occasion . . . The enemy attacked them in the morning; they acted wonders on that day; twice they repulsed the Eyoes, and had nearly given them a total defeat; but fresh supplies of the enemy continually pouring in, to replace those who fell, the Foys, worn out with fatigue, were obliged to yield at last and retreated, under cover of the night, into Abomey . . .

Abomey is a very large town, surrounded with a deep moat, but has no wall nor breastwork to defend the besieged; nor are there any springs of water in it; consequently it could not be tenable. The first care of the Dahomans on the night after the battle, whilst the Eyoes were too much fatigued to interrupt them, was to send away the wounded, and the women and children, to Zassa, a town about twenty-five miles off, where the king then was; who, when he learned the unfortunate issue of the day, was immediately conveyed, with his women and treasures, to an inaccessible retreat . . .

Agaow, the king's general at Abomey, continued to defend the place, and amuse the enemy, until he learned that the king was safe and Zassa evacuated; he then took advantage of the dark night, conducted the remains of his army safe, passed the enemy, and fled; leaving the town to the mercy of the Eyoes, who afterwards plundered and burnt it, as they also did Calonina and Zassa . . .

The Eyoes continued for several years to harass Dahomy with an annual visit; the Foys never thought it prudent to engage them afterwards; but when apprized of their coming, used to evacuate their towns, divide into small parties, and shelter themselves as well as they could in their fastnesses and woods. The king used all his efforts to obtain an accommodation, and offered them any reasonable compensation to refrain from hostilities; but it was difficult to satisfy their demands. They claimed, in consequence of an old treaty, an annual tribute; the payment of which had been omitted in the prosperous days of Trudo [King Agaja]. These arrears were considerable; and fresh demands were also added, on account of the conquest of Whydah, which the Eyoes looked upon as an inexhaustible source of wealth to the king . . . In the year 1747, however, the Eyoes consented to an accommodation, and compromised the matter for a tribute, which is paid them annually at Calonina, in the month of November. [In the nineteenth century Dahomy in turn invaded Oyo, then in decline.]

ABBÉ PROYART

Congo Government

The Abbé Proyart was a French missionary in the states to the immediate north of the Congo estuary. His account refers to the early part of the second half of the eighteenth century, and is useful if read with due allowance for prejudice. It may be compared with the earlier

From the Abbé Proyart, *History of Loango, Kakongo, etc.* (Paris: 1776), translated in J. Pinkerton, *A General Collection of the Best and Most Interesting Voyages and Travels, etc.* (London: 1814), vol. 16, p. 568.

writings on this subject by Father Cavazzi and other missionaries (see pp. 177-178).

Though the kings do not employ the most proper means for promoting the welfare of their subjects, they hold this as a principle, that it is their interest as well as their duty, to occupy themselves with the care of rendering them happy, and maintaining peace and justice among them. Every day they pass several hours in deciding the processes of those who have appealed to them to their tribunals; they hold frequent councils; but it is rare that they have a real friend and a disinterested man among those they invite thither. The ministers stand charged with the execution of whatever has been determined in the king's council; but as this prince blindly defers to them, it frequently happens that while occupied with the details of justice he pacifies the differences of a few families, one of his ministers, in his name though without his knowledge, spreads trouble and desolation over a whole province.

The principal ministers are the *ma-ngovo*, the *ma-npontu*, the *ma-kaka*, the *m-fuka*, and the *ma-kimba*. The *ma-ngovo*, whom we call *mangove*, is the minister for foreign affairs, and the introducer of foreigners at court. The *ma-npontu* is associated to the department of the *mangove*, and represents him when absent. The *ma-kaka* is minister of war, and even generalissimo of the armies. It is he who causes the troops to be mustered in time of war, who appoints their officers, reviews them, and also leads them to battle. The *m-fuka*, whom the French call *mfouque*, is minister of commerce. He makes frequent voyages on the sea coasts, where are the warehouses and factories [trade-stations] of the Europeans. He is obliged, by the nature of his office, to make frequent representations of the state of the exchanges which are made between the Europeans and the Africans, and to take care that no frauds are committed on either side. He also presides over the recovery of the taxes which the king exacts from strangers who trade in his states; and he is charged with the general police of the markets. The *ma-kimba* is grand master of the waters and forests. It is he who has the inspection of all the boatmen, fishermen and hunters; and it is to him that the fish and game intended for the king are directed . . .

These ministers have no offices or houses of business as ours have; they even know not how either to read or write: with the exception of a small number of important affairs, they dispatch all others on the spot and as soon as they present themselves, in order not to run the risk of forgetting them. Their clerks are diligent slaves whom they send into the towns and provinces, to signify to private individuals, as well as persons in place, the king's intentions. In all the provinces and in all the towns, there is a governor for the king. The chiefs of the villages are also king's officers; they administer justice in his name . . .

The crown among these people is not hereditary, as several authors aver . . . There is in each kingdom a family, or if you please a class of princes . . . It is sufficient to be a prince in order to have the right of pretending to the crown; and it must necessarily be so, in order to possess certain noble fiefs which are held more immediately on that tenure.

No nobles are known in these countries, except the princes, and nobility does not descend except by the females, so that all the children of a princess-mother are princes or princesses, though begotten by a plebian father; as, on the other hand, the children of a prince or even those of a king are not nobles, unless their father has married a princess . . .

On the death of every king, there is always an interregnum, during which are celebrated the obsequies of the defunct, who is commonly interred after the lapse of some years. The kingdom is then governed by a regent who takes the name of *ma-boman*, that is to say, *lord of terror*, because he has the right to make himself feared throughout the whole kingdom . . . It is during this interregnum that the pretender to the crown, from their canvass, and by means of presents and promises, try to render the electors favourable to themselves. These electors are the princes, the ministers, and the regent. The present king of Loango [to the north of the Congo estuary] was not elected till after an interregnum of seven years . . .

When anyone is accused of a crime of which they cannot convict him, they permit him to justify himself by drinking the *kassa*. The *kassa* is prepared by infusing in water a bit of wood so called. This potion is a true poison to weak stomachs, which have not the strength to throw it up immediately. He who stands the proof is declared innocent, and his accuser is condemned as a slanderer. If the fault of which the pretended culprit is accused does not deserve death, as soon as they perceive him ready to expire they make him take an antidote, which excites vomiting, and brings him back to life; but they condemn him as a culprit to the penalty fixed by law.

The inhabitants of the country have the greatest faith in this cordial. The princes and lords sometimes cause *kassa* to be taken in order to clear up their suspicions, but they must first obtain the king's permission to do so, which is not difficult when the suspicions are of weighty concern . . .

In these countries where the crown is elective, the death of the kings . . . is as it were the signal of a civil war. A prince who, ambitious enough to direct his views to the throne, has no reason to count on the favour of the electors, makes his vassals take up arms to force their suffrages, or to dispute the crown with him whom they may have preferred. If he fears that his party may not be the strongest, he addresses himself to a foreign prince, who, for a few pieces of European stuffs, or vessels of silver, sends him a whole army . . .

The sovereigns of these countries maintain no regular troops. When a king has determined on war, his *ma-kaka*, minister of war and generalissimo of his armies, transmits orders to the princes and governors of provinces, to levy troops; the latter never fail to lead to the rendezvous the quota demanded of them . . .

The armies in general do not make long campaigns; a war is sometimes over in less than eight days. When the soldiers have eaten the provisions they brought with them, and find none in the hostile country, or when they want powder and lead, nothing can hold them; all, without asking leave, take the road home . . .

OLAUDAH EQUIANO

In Iboland

Olaudah Equiano's memoirs are perhaps the best of all the books written by Africans who were taken into European slavery and won their freedom. Appearing very appropriately in the momentous year of 1789, it argued the case for regarding traditional African society with a new interest, tolerance and understanding; and it did this with a tactful grace which nonetheless contained a powerful note of confidence and determination.

Born in about 1745, Equiano was kidnapped for enslavement in about 1756, sold to Virginia and thence to England. He purchased his freedom in 1777 and made his living as a deep-sea sailor, later became active in the antislavery movement, and married the daughter of James and Ann Cullen of Cambridge in 1792.

This kingdom [of Benin] is divided into many provinces or districts: in one of the most remote and fertile of which I was born . . . The distance of this province from the capital of Benin and the sea coast must be very considerable, for I had never heard of white men or Europeans, nor of the sea; and our subjection to the king of Benin was little more than nominal . . . As our manners [in that country] are simple, our luxuries are few. The dress of both sexes are nearly the same. It generally consists of a long piece of calico, or muslin, wrapped loosely round the body . . . This is usually dyed blue, which is our favourite colour. It is extracted from a berry, and is brighter and richer than any I have seen in Europe . . . Our manner of living is entirely plain . . . bullocks, goats, and poultry supply the greatest part of their food. These

From *The Interesting Narrative of the Life of Olaudah Equiano, or Gustavus Vassa, the African*, written by himself (London: 1789). A much longer extract is in Thomas Hodgkin, *Nigerian Perspectives* (Oxford: 1960).

constitute likewise the principal wealth of the country, and the chief articles of commerce . . . In our buildings we study convenience rather than ornament. Each master of a family has a large square piece of ground, surrounded with a moat or fence, or enclosed with a wall made of red earth tempered, which, when dry, is as hard as brick. Within this are his houses to accommodate his family and slaves; which, if numerous, frequently present the appearance of a village . . . These houses never exceed one story in height; they are always built of wood, of stakes driven into the ground, crossed with wattles, and neatly plastered within and without. The roof is thatched with reeds . . . Houses so constructed and furnished require but little skill to erect them. Every man is a sufficient architect for the purpose. The whole neighbourhood afford their unanimous assistance in building them, and in return receive and expect no other recompense than a feast.

As we live in a country where nature is prodigal of her favours, our wants are few, and easily supplied; of course we have few manufactures. They consist for the most part of calicoes, earthenware, ornaments, and instruments of war and husbandry . . . We have also markets . . . These are sometimes visited by stout mahogany-coloured men from the southwest of us: we call them *Oye-Eboe*, which term signifies red men living at a distance. They generally bring us firearms, gunpowder, hats, beads, and dried fish . . . They always carry slaves through our land; but the strictest account is exacted of their manner of procuring them before they are suffered to pass. Sometimes indeed we sold slaves to them, but they were only prisoners of war, or such among us as had been convicted of kidnapping, or adultery, and some other crimes, which we esteemed heinous. This practice of kidnapping induces me to think, that, notwithstanding all our strictness, their principal business among us was to trepan our people . . .

[Equiano then speaks of warfare among the peoples of Iboland.] From what I can recollect of these battles, they appear to have been irruptions of one little state or district on the other, to obtain prisoners or booty. Perhaps they were incited to this by those traders who brought the European goods mentioned amongst us . . . When a trader wants slaves, he applies to a chief for them, and tempts him with his wares . . .

[Being kidnapped himself, he was taken with others to the Niger Delta port of sale and embarkation. Seeing "white men with horrible looks, red faces, and long hair," he greatly feared that he was to be eaten — this being, indeed, the common fear of many such captives from the interior.] When I looked round the ship, and saw a large furnace or copper boiling, and a multitude of black people of every description chained together, every one of their countenances expressing dejection and sorrow, I no longer doubted of my fate . . .

THOMAS WINTERBOTTOM
A Wider Picture

Physician to the colony of Sierra Leone, Thomas Winterbottom was one of the forerunners, perhaps the best, of scientific reporting on African life and customs. He first visited the Coast in 1796. His admirable book was published in two volumes seven years later.

The division of labor and separation of trades is almost unknown, or at least not practiced among the people who inhabit the sea coast; the most ingenious man in the village is usually the blacksmith, joiner, architect, and weaver, the chief trades which they require or exercise . . . Among the Foolas [Fulani], however, and other nations beyond them, some progress has been made in forming distinct occupations or trades. One set of men, called *garrankees* or shoemakers, are exclusively employed in manufacturing leather, and converting it into useful articles, as

From Thomas Winterbottom, *An Account of the Native Africans, etc.* (2 vols., London: 1803).

sandals, quivers for arrows, bridles, saddles & etc. . . . Another class of men are equally celebrated as blacksmiths: besides making every kind of necessary utensil, they inlay the handles and chase the blades of swords & etc., with great neatness, and they make a variety of elegant fancy ornaments for the women out of pieces of gold and silver dollars. A considerable degree of ingenuity in the arts with which they are acquainted must be allowed to all these nations, and is evident in the construction of their houses, and the formation of a variety of domestic and agricultural utensils with the rudest instruments. They form canoes, from a single tree, capable of carrying eight or ten tons. Their mats show much neatness and ingenuity; they are composed of split bamboo or grass, and wove into a great variety of patterns, and are stained with very beautiful and indelible colors . . .

They have various substitutes for hemp and flax, of which they make fishing lines and nets equal in strength and durability to those of Europeans . . . Although they are ignorant of the use of the potter's wheel, they make earthen pots fit for every domestic use . . . Upon the Gold Coast, the accuracy and dexterity of the people called *Goldtakers*, employed by Europeans to detect false gold, is wonderful. They also fuse the gold dust, and work it into buckles, buttons, and a great variety of trinkets . . . They raise upon most parts of the coast a sufficient quantity of cotton for their own use . . . They spin the cotton in a very tedious manner, by twirling a spindle, one end of which is loaded with clay, in a large shell or wooden dish, passing the thread between the finger and thumb of one hand. They dye the threads, which are very fine and even, several colors, which are both vivid and permanent, especially blue, of a kind equal or superior to the finest blues of Europe. Upon the Gold Coast, this blue dye is obtained by infusing the leaves of a species of bignonia, and the root of a species of tabernamontana, in a solution of the ashes of the palm nut in water . . . The looms resemble those used in England to weave shalloons, except in being much narrower . . . The men are the weavers, and as the cloth is wove so very narrow, not more than six inches in breadth, seven such pieces, between four and five feet in length, must be joined to form a cloth for a woman; but they are so exact in the pattern, that at a small distance the junctures cannot be easily discovered . . .

Nicotine and Kola

The Mahommedan nations very religiously abstain from the use of spirits and fermented liquors of every kind; but they, as well as the other Africans, are universally enslaved by the charms of tobacco . . . Tobacco is chiefly used in the form of snuff . . . The Foolas [Fulani] have no idea of using it in any other way than snuff, and often use it as a dentifrice in this form; but those who live upon the coast frequently smoke this herb, a custom which they have probably copied from the Europeans.

A more innocent luxury in which they indulge, and which ranks in their esteem next to tobacco, is the chewing of kola. This is the fruit of a large and beautiful tree, which grows in abundance upon the coast, and is in as high esteem, and as much used by the natives of this part of Africa, as is the areca nut in the East Indies. The kola, seven or eight kernels of which, of the size and shape of a chestnut, are included in a thick green capsule, is a very pleasant bitter and astringent. It is much esteemed for its stomachic powers, and is generally washed down with a draught of cold water, to which it imparts a remarkably pleasant sweetish taste . . .

Kola is always presented to the guests, in visits of ceremony or of friendship, and is looked upon as a mark of great politeness. It generally forms a part of every considerable present, and at public meetings, or palavers between different nations, it is a substitute for the olive branch. Two *white* kolas presented by one party to the other betoken peace and a continuance of friendship, while two *red* ones are considered as an indication of war.

JAMES BRUCE
Ethiopian Encounters

If his vivid writings were better known or eighteenth-century reports on Ethiopia less rare, James Bruce might deserve a lesser place than he here receives. As it is, he seems to merit a large place, not because he was the first European to reach the source of the Blue Nile, although that was much to his credit, but because he offers a personal and political description of Ethiopia that is unique and full of illuminating detail, besides being highly readable. A good deal of what he told on his return was disbelieved in England, and some of the incidents may have been embellished to the man's own advantage; but there is no doubting the veracity of the picture as a whole.

Of considerable education — because of, or perhaps in spite of, Harrow School — Bruce had the dash and courage of a Scottish laird, the physique of a giant (standing six feet four inches tall, and sturdy all the way), and the curiosity of a good journalist. There is no one else quite like him in the annals of European exploration of Africa.

He prepared himself well for his great adventure, serving as British Consul in Algiers, there and elsewhere in North Africa studying antiquities and Arabic, and living for a time in Egypt where his skill in medicine helped to win him influential friends. Some of these gave him valuable letters of introduction to Muslim and Christian leaders further south. More remarkable still, he set himself seriously to learning Amharic before departure on his journey. He reached Gondar, then the Ethiopian capital, in 1770 and stayed until 1772.

In the first passage below we find him in a desperate brush with a swashbuckling nobleman called Guebra Mascal. Later he goes with the emperor's army in its battles against a rebel army, and writes a vigorous

From James Bruce, *Travels to Discover the Source of the Blue Nile*, 1768-1773 (5 vols., London: 1790). The first extract is from vol. 3, p. 233; the second from vol. 4, p. 116 and p. 194; the third from vol. 4, p. 437; and the fourth from vol. 4, p. 538.

description of those feudal wars. He returns by way of the Middle Nile, and guesses rightly that he has seen the ruins of Meroë.

Adventure at Gondar

We went all to Authule's house to supper in violent rage, such anger as is usual with hungry men. We brought with us from the palace three of my brother Baalomaals, and one who had stood to make up the number, though he was not in office; his name was Guebra Mascal; he was a sister's son of the Ras,* and commanded one-third of the troops of Tigre, which carried firearms, that is, about two thousand men. He was reputed the best officer of that kind that the Ras had, and was a man about thirty years of age, short, square, and well made, with a very unpromising countenance; flat nose, wide mouth, of a very yellow complexion, and much pitted with the smallpox; he had a most uncommon presumption upon the merit of past services, and had the greatest opinion of his own knowledge in the use of firearms, to which he did not scruple to say Ras Michael owed all his victories. Indeed it was to the good opinion that the Ras had of him as a soldier that he owed his being suffered to continue at Gondar; for he was suspected to have been familiar with one of his uncle's wives in Tigre, by whom it was thought he had a child; at least the Ras put away his wife, and never owned the child to be his.

This man supped with us that night, and thence began one of the most serious affairs I ever had in Abyssinia. Guebra Mascal, as usual, vaunted incessantly his skill in firearms, the wonderful gun that he had, and feats he had done with it. Petros said, laughing, to him, "You have a genius for shooting, but you have had no opportunity to learn. Now Yagoube [i.e., Bruce] is come, he will teach you something worth talking of." They had all drank abundantly, and Guebra Mascal had uttered words that I thought were in contempt of me. "I believe," replied I, peevishly enough, "Guebra Mascal, I should suspect from your discourse, you neither knew men nor guns; every gun of mine in the hands of my serv-

* The redoubtable Ras Michael of Tigre.

ants shall kill twice as far as yours; for my own, it is not worth my while to put a ball in it. When I compare with you, the end of a tallow-candle in my gun shall do more execution than an iron ball in the best of yours, with all the skill and experience you pretend to."

He said I was a Frank, and a liar, and, upon my immediately rising up, he gave me a kick with his foot. I was quite blind with passion, seized him by the throat and threw him on the ground, stout as he was. The Abyssinians know nothing either of wrestling or boxing. He drew his knife as he was falling, attempting to cut me in the face; but his arm not being at freedom, all he could do was to give me a very trifling stab, or wound, near the crown of the head, so that the blood trickled down over my face. I had tript him up, but till then had never struck him. I now wrested the knife from him with a full intention to kill him; but Providence directed better. Instead of the point, I struck so violently with the handle upon his face as to leave scars, which would be distinguished even among the deep marks of the smallpox. An adventure so new, and so unexpected, presently overcame the effects of the wine. It was too late to disturb anybody either in the palace or at the house of the Ras. A hundred opinions were immediately started; some were for sending us up to the king, as we were actually in the precincts of the palace, where lifting a hand is death. Ayto Heikel advised that I should go, late as it was, to Koscam, and Petros, that I should repair immediately to the house of Ayto Aylo, while the Baalomaals were for taking me to sleep in the palace. Authule, in whose house I was, and who was therefore most shocked at the outrage, wished me to stay in his house, where I was, from a supposition that I was seriously wounded, which all of them, seeing the blood fall over my eyes, seemed to think was the case; and he, in the morning, at the king's rising, was to state the matter as it happened. All these advices appeared good when they were proposed; for my part, I thought they were only tended to make bad worse, and bore the appearance of guilt, of which I was not conscious.

I now determined to go home, and to bed in my own house. With that intention, I washed my face and wound with vinegar, and found the blood to be already staunched. I then wrapt myself up in my cloak and returned home without accident, and went to bed. But this would neither satisfy Ayto Heikel nor Petros, who went to the house of Ayto Aylo, then past midnight, so that early in the morning when scarce light, I saw him come into my chamber. Guebra Mascal had fled to the house of Kefla Yasous his relation; and the first news we heard in the morning after Ayto Aylo arrived, were, that Guebra Mascal was in irons at the Ras's house.

Every person that came afterward brought up some new account; the whole people present had been examined and had given, without variation, the true particulars of my forbearance, and his insolent behaviour. Everybody trembled for some violent resolution the Ras was to take on my first complaint. The town was full of Tigre soldiers, and nobody saw clearer than I did, however favourable a turn this had taken for me in the beginning, it might be my destruction in the end.

I asked Ayto Aylo his opinion. He seemed at a loss to give it to me; but said, in an uncertain tone of voice, he could wish that I would not complain of Guebra Mascal while I was angry, or while the Ras was so inveterate against him, till some of his friends had spoken, and appeased, at least, his first resentment. I answered, "That I was of a contrary opinion, and that no time was to be lost: remember the letter of Mahomet Gibberti; remember his confidence yesterday of my being safe where he was; remember the influence of Ozoro Esther,* and do not let us lose a moment."

"What," says Aylo to me in great surprise, "are you mad? Would you have him cut to pieces in the midst of twenty thousand of his countrymen? Would you be *dimmenia*, that is guilty of the blood of all the province of Tigre, through which you must go in your way home?"

"Just the contrary," said I; "nobody has so great a right over the Ras's anger as I have, being the person injured; and, as you and I can get access to Ozoro Esther when we please, let us go immediately thither, and stop the progress of this affair while it is not yet generally known. People that talk of my being wounded expect to

* Ras Michael's young and beautiful wife, who befriended Bruce after he had helped to cure her son of smallpox.

see me, I suppose, without a leg or an arm. When they see me so early riding in the street, all will pass for a story as it should do. Would you wish to pardon him entirely?"

"That goes against my heart, too," says Aylo: "he is a bad man."

"My good friend," said I, "be in this guided by me; I know we both think the same thing. If he is a bad man, he was a bad man before I knew him. You know what you told me yourself of the Ras's jealousy of him. What if he was to revenge his own wrongs, under pretense of giving me satisfaction for mine? Come, lose no time, get upon your mule, go with me to Ozoro Esther, I will answer for the consequences."

We arrived there; the Ras was not sitting in judgment; he had drank hard the night before, on occasion of Powussen's marriage, and was not in bed when the story of the fray reached him. We found Ozoro Esther in a violent anger and agitation, which was much alleviated by my laughing. On her asking me about my wound, which had been represented to her as dangerous, "I am afraid," said I, "poor Guebra Mascal is worse wounded than I." "Is he wounded too?" says she; "I hope it is in his heart." "Indeed," replied I, "madam, there are no wounds on either side. He was very drunk, and I gave him several blows upon the face as he deserved, and he has already got all the chastisement he ought to have; it was all a piece of folly." "Prodigious!" says she, "is this so?" "It is so," says Aylo, "and you shall hear it all by-and-by; only let us stop the propagation of this foolish story."

The Ras in the instant sent for us. He was naked, sitting on a stool, and a slave swathing up his lame leg with a broad belt or bandage. I asked him, calmly and pleasantly, if I could be of any service to him. He looked at me with a grin, the most ghastly I ever saw, as half displeased.

"What," says he, "are you all mad? Aylo, what is the matter between him and that miscreant Guebra Mascal?"

"Why," said I, "I am come to tell you that myself; why do you ask Ayto Aylo? Guebra Mascal got drunk, was insolent, and struck me. I was sober and beat him, as you will see by his face; and I have not come to you to say I am sorry that I lifted my hand against your nephew; but he was in the wrong, and drunk; and I thought it was better to chastise him on the spot, than trust him to you, who perhaps might take the affair to heart; for we all know your justice, and that being your relation is no excuse when you judge between man and man."

"I order you, Aylo," says Michael, "as you esteem my friendship to tell me the truth, really as it was, and without disguise or concealment."

Aylo began accordingly to relate the whole history, when a servant called me out to Ozoro Esther. I found with her another nephew of the Ras, a much better man, called Welleta Selasse, who came from Kefla Yasous, and Guebra Mascal himself, desiring I would forgive and intercede for him, for it was a drunken quarrel without malice. Ozoro Esther had told him part. "Come in with me," said I, "and you shall see I never will leave the Ras till he forgive him." "Let him punish him," says Welleta Selasse; "he is a bad man, but don't let the Ras either kill or maim him." "Come," said I, "let us go to the Ras, and he shall neither kill, maim, nor punish him if I can help it. It is my first request; if he refuses me, I will return to Jidda; come and hear."

Aylo had urged the thing home to the Ras in the proper light — that of my safety. "You are a wise man," says Michael, now perfectly cool, as soon as he saw me and Welleta Selasse. "It is a man like you that goes far in safety, which is the end we all aim at. I feel the affront offered you more than you do, but will not have the punishment attributed to you; this affair shall turn to your honour and security, and in that light only I can pass over his insolence."

"Welleta Selasse," says he, falling into a violent passion in an instant, "what sort of behaviour is this my men have adopted with strangers; and my stranger, too, and in the king's palace, and the king's servant? What! am I dead? or become incapable of governing longer?" Welleta Selasse bowed, but was afraid to speak, and indeed the Ras looked like a fiend.

"Come," says the Ras, "let me see your head." I shewed him where the blood was already hardened, and said it was a very slight cut. "A cut," continued Michael, "over that part, with one of our knives, is mortal."

"You see, sir," said I, "I have not even clipt the hair about the wound; it is nothing. Now give me your promise you will set Guebra Mascal at liberty; and not only that, but you are not to reproach him with the affair further than that he was drunk, not a crime in this country."

"No, truly," says he, "it is not, but that is, because it is very rare that people fight with knives when they are drunk. I scarce ever heard of it, even in the camp."

"I fancy," said I, endeavouring to give a light turn to the conversation, "they have not often wherewithal to get drunk in your camp." "Not this last year," says he, laughing, "there were no houses in the country." "But let me only merit," said I, "Welleta Selasse's friendship, by making him the messenger of good news to Guebra Mascal, that he is at liberty, and you have forgiven him." "At liberty!" says he, "where is he?" "In your house," said I, "somewhere, in irons." "That is Esther's intelligence," continued the Ras; "these women tell you all their secrets, but when I remember your behaviour to them, I do not wonder at it; and that consideration likewise obliges me to grant what you ask. Go, Welleta Selasse, and free that dog from his collar, and direct him to go to Welleta Michael, who will give him his orders to levy the meery in Woggora; let him not see my face till he returns."

The Civil Wars

The king's army halted upon the same ground they had done on their return to Gondar. They were then supposed to be near twenty thousand foot, belonging to Tigre and its dependencies, incomparably the best troops of the empire, six thousand of which were armed with muskets, six times the number that all the rest of Abyssinia could furnish, and, considering they were all matchlocks, very expert in the management of them. The rest of the foot which joined them since he passed the Tacazze [Atbara] were about ten thousand, besides two thousand of the king's household, five hundred of which were horsemen; of these, few short of two hundred were his black servants, armed with coats of mail, the horses with plates of brass on their cheeks and faces, with a sharp iron spike of about five inches in length, which stuck out in the middle of their forehead, a very troublesome, useless piece of their armour; their bridles were iron chains; the body of the horse covered with a kind of thin quilt stuffed with cotton, with two openings made above the flaps of the saddle, into which the horseman put his thighs and legs, and which covered him from his hip (where his shirt of mail ended) down to a little above his ancle: his feet were covered with slippers of thin leather, without heels, and his stirrups were of the Turkish or Moorish form, into which his whole foot entered, and, being hung very short, he could raise himself, and stand as firmly as if he was upon plain ground.

The saddles were in the Moorish form likewise, high before and behind; a strong lace made fast to the coat of mail by the one end, the other passed through a small hole in the back of the saddle, kept it close down, so that the back was never exposed by the coat of mail rising over the hinder part of the saddle. Each had a small ax in the furcingle of his saddle, and a pike about fourteen feet long, the weapon with which he charged; it was made of very light wood, brought from the banks of the Nile, with a small four-edged head, and the butt end balanced by a long spike of iron; this entered a leather case fastened by a thong to the saddle, and was rested sometimes below the thigh, and sometimes above, and guided by the right hand at the height the point was intended to strike at. The horseman's head was covered with a helmet of copper, or block tin, much like those of our light horse, with large crests of black horse tail.

The officers were distinguished from the soldiers by locks of hair dyed yellow, interspersed with the black. Upon the front of each helmet was a silver star, at least a white-metal one, and before the face, down to the top of the nose, a flap of iron chain, made in the same manner as the coat of mail, but only lighter, which served as a vizier. This was the most troublesome part of the whole, it was hot and heavy and constantly fretted the cheek and the nose, when either the man or the horse were in motion; and therefore I always substituted a black silk net, which concealed my colour better, and for the rest of my face I committed it to the care of Providence . . .

The horsemen of the king's army were about seven thousand, mostly very indifferent troops; so that his whole muster was nearly seven thousand musqueteers, twenty-five thousand foot, armed with lances and shields, and about seventy-five hundred horsemen; in round numbers about forty thousand men. It is not possible, I believe, to know, with greater precision, the number, such is the confusion of barbarous armies on these occasions, and such the inclination of their leaders to magnify and increase their quotas. Besides these, Ayto Confu and Sanuda were left with about six hundred men each, to protect Gondar from flying, pillaging parties, and to keep the communication open between the army and the capital, from whence the provisions were to be supplied.

This army was furnished with a number of excellent officers, veterans of noble families, who had spent their whole life in war, which we may say, for these last four hundred years, has never ceased to lay desolate this unhappy country; the principal were Ras Michael, who, arrived at the age of seventy-four, had passed the last fifty years of his life in a course of continued victories . . .

[Several battles are now fought between the king's army and the rebel army.]

The fire increasing on the hill, and several musquets having been heard, it was plain the enemy, in all the camps, were alarmed, and our further stay became every moment more dangerous. Kefla Yafous now beat a retreat, and sent the horsemen all round to force the foot to make the best of their way back, ordering also all mules taken to be hamstringed and left, not to retard our return. Trumpets and drums were heard from our camp, to warn us not to stay, as it was not doubted but mischief would follow, and accordingly we were scarce arrived within the limits of our camp when we heard the sound of horse in the valley.

Michael, always watchful upon every accident, no sooner saw the fires lighted on the hill, than he ordered Guebra Mascal to place a good body of musqueteers about half way down the hill, as near as possible to the ford of Mariam, thinking it probable that the enemy would enter at both ends of the long hill, in order to surround those who were destroying their camp, which they accordingly did, whilst those of our people, who had taken to drinking, fell into the hands of the troops that came by the lower road, and were all put to death. Those that reached the upper ford served to afford us a severe revenge, for Guebra Mascal, after having seen them pass between him and the river, though it was a dark and very windy night, guessed very luckily their position, and gave them so happy a fire, that most of those who were not slain returned back without seeing Ayto Tesfos's camp, being afraid that some other trap might still be in their way . . .

Provisions were now become scarce in the camp, and there was a prospect that they would be every day scarcer; and, what was still worse, Deg-Ohha, which long had stood in pools, was now almost dry, and, from the frequent use made of it by the number of beasts, began to have both an offensive smell and taste; whilst, every time we attempted to water at the Mariam river, a battle was to be fought with Tesfos's horse in the valley. On the other hand, an epidemical fever raged in the rebels camp on the plain, especially in that of Gufho and Ayabdar. The rain, moreover, was now coming on daily, and something decisive became necessary for all parties . . .

The hill of Serbraxos, when we first took post on it, was rugged and uneven, full of acacia and other ill-thriving trees, and various stumps of these had been broken by the wind, or undermined by the torrents. The great need the soldiers had of fuel to roast the miserable pittance of barley (which was all their food), had cleared away these encumbrances from the side of the hill, and the constant resort of men going up and down, had rendered the surface perfectly smooth and slippery; so that our camp did not appear as placed so high, nor nearly so inaccessible as it was at first. For this reason, Ras Michael had ordered the soldiers to gather all the stones on the hill, and range them in small walls, at proper places, in a kind of zigzag, under which the soldiers lay concealed, and with their firearms protected the mules which went down to drink. Michael had lined all these little fortifications with musquetry, from the bottom of the hill to the door of his tent and the king's.

About noon the hill was assaulted on all sides that were accessible, and the ancient spirit of the troops seemed to revive upon seeing the enemy were the aggressors. Without any aid of musquetry, the king's foot repulsed Coque Abou Barea, and drove him from the hill into the plain, without any considerable stand on his part: the same success followed against Mammo and Heraclius; they were chased down the hill, and several of their men pursued and slain on the plain; but a large reinforcement coming from the camp, the king's troops were driven up the hill again, and Tesfos, with his musquetry, had made a lodgment in a pit on the low side of one of these stone walls Ras Michael had built for his own defense, from which he fired with great effect, and the king's troops were obliged to fall back to the brow of the hill immediately below the tent, and that of the Ras. In a moment appeared Woodage Asahel, with a large body of horse, supported likewise with a considerable number of foot. This was the most accessible part of the hill, and under the cover of Tesfos's continued fire: they mounted it with great gallantry . . .

Woodage Asahel had now advanced within about thirty yards of the musquetry that were expecting him, when unluckily the hill became more steep, and Ayto Tesfos (for some reason not then known) ceased firing. The king was now close to the very brow of the hill, nor could any one persuade him to keep at a greater distance. I was not far from him, and had no sort of doubt but that I should presently see the whole body of the enemy destroyed by the fire awaiting them, and blown into the air. Woodage Asahel was very conspicuous by a red fillet, or bandage, wrapt about his head, the two ends hanging over his ears, whilst he was waving with his hands for the troops below to follow briskly, and support those near him, who were impeded by the roughness and mossy quality of the ground. At this instant the king's troops fired, and I expected to see the enemy strewed dead along the face of the hill. Indeed we saw them speedily disappear, but like living men, riding and running down the declivity so as even to excite laughter. Woodage Asahel, with two men only, bravely gained the top of the mountain, and, as he passed the king's tent, pulled off his red fillet, making a sign as of saluting it, and then galloped through the middle of the camp.

He was now descending unhurt upon the left, where Abou Barea had been engaged and beaten, when Sebastos, a Greek, the king's cook, seventy-five years of age, of whom I have already spoken in the campaign of Maitfha, lying behind a stone, with his gun in his hand, seeing the troops engaged below, fired at him as he passed: the ball took place in the left side of his belly. He was seen stooping forward upon the tore of his saddle, with some men supporting him on each side, in his way to his tent, where he died in the evening, having, by his behaviour that day, deserved a better fate. Sebastos reported this feat of his to the king, but it was not believed, till a confirmation of the fact came in the evening, when Sebastos was cloathed, and received a reward from the king.

[Bruce leaves Ethiopia and returns home by way of the Blue Nile. He tarries at Sennar, and visits one of the rulers of the Fung Confederacy founded two centuries earlier.]

Cavalry of Sennar

It was not till the eighth of May I had my audience of Sheikh Adelan at Aira, which is three miles and a half from Sennaar; we walked out early in the morning, for the greatest part of the way along the side of the Nile, which had no beauty, being totally divested of trees, the bottom foul and muddy, and the edges of the water white with small concretions of calcarious earth, which, with the bright sun upon them, dazzled and affected our eyes very much.

We then struck across a large sandy plain without trees or bushes, and came to Adelan's habitation; two or three, very considerable houses of one story occupied the middle of a large square, each of whose sides was at least half of an English mile. Instead of a wall to inclose this square, was a high fence or impalement of strong reeds, canes, or stalks of dora, (I do not know which) in fascines strongly joined together by stakes and cords.

On the outside of the gate, on each hand, were six houses of a slighter construction than the rest; close upon the fence were sheds where the soldiers lay, the horses picqueted before them with their heads turned towards the sheds, and their food laid before them on the ground; above each soldier's sleeping-place, covered only on the top and open in the sides, were hung a lance, a small oval shield, and a large broadsword. These, I understood, were chiefly quarters for couriers, who, being Arabs, were not taken into the court or square, but shut out at night.

Within the gate was a number of horses, with the soldiers' barracks behind them; they were all picqueted in ranks, their faces to their masters' barracks. It was one of the finest sights I ever saw of the kind. They were all above sixteen hands high, of the breed of the old Saracen horses, all finely made, and as strong as our coach-horses, but exceedingly nimble in their motion; rather thick and short in the forehand, but with the most beautiful eyes, ears, and heads in the world; they were mostly black, some of them black and white, some of them milk-white foaled, so not white by age, with white eyes and white hoofs, not perhaps a great recommendation.

A steel shirt of mail hung upon each man's quarters opposite to his horse, and by it an antelope's skin made soft like shamoy, with which it was covered from the dew of the night. A headpiece of copper, without crest or plumage, was suspended by a lace above the shirt of mail, and was the most picturesque part of the trophy. To these was added an enormous broadsword in a red leather scabbard; and upon the pummel hung two thick gloves, their fingers in one poke. They told me, that, within that inclosure at Aira, there were four hundred horses, which, with the riders, and armour complete for each of them, were all the property of Sheikh Adelan, every horseman being his slave, and bought with his money . . .

Ruins of Meroë

[Beyond Shendi, about one hundred miles north of modern Khartoum, we saw] heaps of broken pedestals, like those of Axum, all plainly designed for the statues of the dog; some pieces of obelisk, likewise, with hieroglyphics, almost totally obliterated. The Arabs told us these ruins were very extensive; and that many pieces of statues, both of men and animals, had been dug up there; the statues of the men were mostly of black stone. It is impossible to avoid risking a guess that this is the ancient city of Meroë . . .

ANDREW   SPARRMAN

The Hottentots

A Swede who had studied medicine at Uppsala, Andrew Sparrman sailed to the Antarctic as assistant naturalist on board the *Resolution* with Captain James Cook, and afterwards (1772-1776) saw much of life in what is now the Cape Province of South Africa.

The Hottentots who live in these parts, or within the boundaries of the Dutch colonies, seldom make use of any weapons. Here and there, indeed, a man will furnish himself with a javelin, by way of defense against the wolves: this is called a hassagai.

Their habitations are as simple as their dress, and equally adapted to the wandering pastoral life they lead in those parts. In fact, they scarcely merit any other name than that of huts; though not, perhaps, as spacious and eligible as the tents and dwelling-places of the patriarchs, at least they are sufficient for the Hottentot's wants and desires; who may therefore be considered as a happy man, in being able in this point likewise so easily to satisfy them. The great simplicity of them is, perhaps, the reason, why in a Hottentot's craal, or village, the huts are all built exactly alike; and that one meets there with a species of architecture, that does not a little contribute to keep envy from insinuating itself under their roofs. The equality of fortune and happiness in some measure

From Andrew Sparrman, *A Voyage to the Cape of Good Hope, etc.*, 1772-1776 (London: 1785), vol. 1, For earlier — seventeenth century — accounts of the Hottentots, see *The Early Cape Hottentots*, ed. I. Schapera and B. Farrington (1933), which prints selections from Dapper (1668), Willem ten Rhyne (1686), and Johannes de Grevenbrock (1695).

enjoyed by these people, cannot but have a singular effect in preventing their breasts from being disturbed by this baneful passion.

Every hut is disposed in the following manner. Some of them are of a circular, and others of an oblong shape, resembling a round beehive or a vault. The ground-plot is from eighteen to twenty-four feet in diameter. The highest of them are so low, that even in the center of the arch, it is scarcely ever possible for a middle-sized man to stand upright. But neither the lowness thereof, nor that of the door, which is but just three feet high, can perhaps be considered evidence as any inconvenience to a Hottentot, who finds no difficulty in stooping and crawling on all fours, and who is at any time more inclined to lie down than stand.

The fireplace is in the middle of each hut, by which means the walls are not so much exposed to danger from fire. From this situation of their fireplace, the Hottentots likewise have this additional advantage, that when they sit or lie in a circle round the fire, the whole company equally enjoys benefit of its warmth.

The door, low as it is, is the only place that lets in the daylight; and at the same time, the only outlet that is left for the smoke. The Hottentot, inured to it from his infancy, sees it hover round him, without feeling the least inconvenience arising from it to his eyes; while lying at the bottom of his hut in the midst of the cloud rolled up like a hedgehog, and wrapped up snug in his sheepskin, he is now and then obliged to peep out from beneath it in order to stir the fire, or perhaps light his pipe, or else sometimes to turn the steak he is broiling over the coals.

The materials for these huts are by no means difficult to be procured; and the manner of putting them together being both neat and inartificial, merits commendation in a Hottentot, and is very suitable to his character. The frame of this arched roof, as I have described it above, is composed of slender rods or sprays of trees. These rods, being previously bent into a proper form, are laid, either whole or pierced, some parallel with each other, others crosswise; they are then strengthened, by binding others round them in a circular form with withies. These withies, as well as the rods themselves, are taken, as well as I can recollect, chiefly from the *cliffortia conoides,* which grows plentifully in this country near the rivers. Large mats are then placed very neatly over this lattice-work, so as perfectly to cover the whole. The aperture which is left for the door is closed, whenever there is occasion for it, with a skin fitted to it, or a piece of matting. These mats are made of a kind of cane or reed. These reeds, being laid parallel to each other, are fastened together with sinews or catgut, or else some kind of packthread, such as they have had an opportunity of getting from the Europeans. They have it therefore, in their power, to make their mats as long as they chuse, and at the same time as broad as the length of the rush will admit of, viz., from six to ten feet. This same kind of matting is now made use of likewise by the colonists, next to the tilts of their wagons, by way of preventing the sail-cloth from being rubbed and worn by them, as well as by helping to keep out the rain.

When a Hottentot has a mind to take his house down and remove his dwelling, he lays all his mats, skins, and sprays on the back of his cattle, which to a stranger makes a monstrous, un-wieldy, and, indeed, ridiculous appearance . . .

The Bushmen

There is another species of Hottentots, who have got the name of boshies-men, from dwelling in woody or mountainous places. These, particularly such as live round about the Camdebo and Sneeberg, are sworn enemies to the pastoral life. Some of their maxims are, to live on hunting and plunder, and never to keep any animal alive for the space of one night. By this means they render themselves odious to the rest of mankind, and are pursued and exterminated like the wild beasts, whose manners they have assumed. Others of them again are kept alive, and made slaves of. Their weapons are poison arrows, which, shot out of a small bow, will fly to the distance of two hundred paces; and will hit a mark with a tolerable degree of certainty, at the distance of fifty, or even a hundred paces. From this distance they can by stealth, as it were, convey death to the game they hunt for food, as well as to their foes, and even to so large and tremendous a beast as the lion: this noble animal thus falling by a weapon which, perhaps, it despised, or even did not take notice of. The Hottentot, in the meantime, concealed and safe in his ambush, is absolutely certain of the operation of his poison, which he always culls of the most virulent kind; and it is said, he has only to wait a few minutes, in order to see the wild beast languish and die.

I mentioned that their bows were small; they are, in fact, hardly a yard long, being at the same time scarcely of the thickness of an inch in the middle, and very much pointed at both ends. What kind of wood they are made of I cannot say, but it does not seem to be of a remarkably elastic nature. The strings of the bows that I saw were made some of them of sinews, others of a kind of hemp, or the inner bark of some vegetable, and most of them are made in a very slovenly manner; which shows, that these archers depend more on the poison of their weapons, than on any exactness in the formation of them or in other perfection in them.

Their arrows are a foot and a half long, and of the same thickness. They are made of a reed one foot in length, which, at the base, or the end that receives the bowstring, has a notch of a proper size to fit it. Just above this notch there is a joint in the reed, about which strings made of sinews are wound, in order to strengthen it. The other end of the reed is armed with a highly polished bone, five or six inches long. At the distance of an inch or two from the tip of this bone, a piece of a quill is bound on very fast with sinews. This is done, in order that the arrow shall not be easily drawn out of the flesh; and thus there may be so much longer time for the poison, which is spread on of a thick consistence like that of an extract, to be dissolved, and infect the wound . . .

The capture of slaves from among this race of men is by no means difficult, and is effected in the following manner. Several farmers, that are in want of servants, join together, and take a journey to that part of the country where the Boshies-men live. They themselves, as well as their Lego-Hottentots, or else such Boshies-men as have been caught some time before, and have been trained up in fidelity in their service, endeavor to spy out where the wild Boshies-men have their haunts. This is best discovered by the smoke of their fires. They are found in societies from ten to fifty and a hundred, reckoning great and small together. Notwithstanding this, the farmers will venture on a dark night to set upon them with six or eight people, which they contrive to do, by previously stationing themselves at some distance round about the craal. They then give the alarm by firing a gun or two. By this means there is such a consternation spread over the whole body of these savages, that it is only the most bold and intelligent among them, that have the courage to break through the circle and steal off . . .

The Nineteenth Century

*T*HE CONCEPT OF AFRICAN HISTORY IN THE NINETEENTH CENTURY, as distinct from the eighteenth, can be justified by more than mere convenience. Three large grounds of evidence may be called in witness, each of them the scene of crucial change: the first is the Western Sudan, the second is Southern Africa, and the third is the widening range of European presence which finally gathered into the race for imperialist partition. All these support a story of enormous scope and drama; and it is one to which the records give voluminous and pointful meaning. My own small selection is designed merely to project the general shape and outline of these vast events.

To the Western Sudan, as a British Islamic scholar, H. F. C. Smith, has written, the nineteenth century brought "political revolution on a remarkable scale." * Into the "power vacuum" left by the collapse of the Songhay imperial system, by the challenge to Muslim orthodoxy of new and subversive schools of Islamic thought, and by the general chaos that remained in many regions after the disruptive pressures of the oversea slave trade (the overland slave trade being never a dominant factor), there plunged visionaries and reformers, adventurers and statesmen, soldiers and captains with devout armies at their backs or raised at their inspiring call: Uthman dan Fodio and his memorable son Muhammad Bello, al Hajj Umar, Ahmadu, Samory Touré, Rabeh and others of their kind whose names and titles, better understood

* H. F. C. Smith, "A Neglected Theme of West African History: The Islamic Revolutions of the 19th Century," in *Journal* of the Historical Society of Nigeria, 2 of 2, 1961, p. 169.

today, drum like a roster of pioneers who spoke and acted, whether for better or for worse, in the name of idealized faith and practical ambition. This ambition, as we can begin to apprehend it now, was nothing less than to settle the "problem of power" in broad grassland regions of the Sudan after the ravaging decades of the previous two centuries. Their efforts to resolve this problem make a vital part of the documentary record; and it is a part, most happily, that may be read quite often in their own writings.

This was a phase of rebirth and new directions. Historians have passed over it, even ignored it altogether. For this the fault has lain with the lack of balance in imperialist attitudes. Painfully detailed attention has been given to the "subjects" of colonial conquest and reorganization, to the Faidherbes and Rhodeses and Lugards, while the "objects" of this sprawling enterprise have suffered a corresponding diminishment or eclipse. Men like al Hajj Umar appear in the European story as nothing more than wild fanatics or frantic nuisances; leaders like Samory as bloodthirsty bandits or mere adventurers. In truth, these men responded, as outstanding leaders always will, to the most profound movements of social need and thought of their time. They followed an impulse that came from revolutionary trends within Islamic thought, particularly through the *tariqa* or discipleship of the Tijaniyya brotherhood.

The Tijaniyya may be likened without great distortion to the Puritan movement in seventeenth-century England, or, within a narrower and perhaps more accurate comparison, to England's later "low church" revolt against the upper-class establishment of Church of England conformity. For while the older brotherhoods of the Sudan had settled into stratified orders of privilege and grace, "the Tijaniyya broke through these barriers and established direct contact between simple folk and the Caliph, opening to everyone, by courage or by learning, the road to the highest destinies . . . It is this that accounts for the prodigious success of al Hajj Umar, as well as for the respect and even fear that he inspired among men of power." * This Tijaniyya brotherhood, of which al Hajj Umar became Caliph, was "something new and

* J. Suret-Canale, *Afrique Noire* (2nd ed., Paris: 1961), p. 191.

sensational. Sheikh Ahmad al-Tijani (1737-1815) taught a complete break with the old orders, and a new way of spiritual salvation through strict moral discipline . . ." *

Yet Umar was no isolated figure. Before embarking on his own holy war of religious and political reconstruction in the westerly regions of the Western Sudan, he had passed twelve years at the Fulani court of Sultan Bello in the easterly regions. There he had written an important book, the *Suyuf al-Said*; and "it is clear that he collected many followers in the Hausa country, some of whom occupied prominent positions in his organization." † Like his great contemporaries, Umar was concerned with the reframing of social life throughout the Sudan: he stepped, as they did, far across the boundaries of narrow ethnic loyalty, considering, no differently from the leaders of much older states in these grasslands, that this was a cause which could and should unite every Muslim people. He failed a long way short of that mark. But it was not for want of trying.

None of this had anything to do with Europe except by pressure from the distant coastland. It was more than twenty years after the Fulani reorganization of Hausaland that the first European travelers reached Sultan Bello and found him, as Clapperton afterwards recalled, considering Euclid. Barth, thirty years later, began to sketch what may reasonably be called the grand design of all that effort. But not until the 1870s, with Edward Blyden, do we come upon a clear external recognition of what it meant or was intended to mean. Speaking in a London suburb on the anniversary of Liberian independence, Blyden had this to say in 1874 of the Muslim leaders and states of the Sudan‡:

They read constantly the same books, and from this they derive that community of ideas and that understanding of each other . . . which gives them the power of ready organization and effective action . . . Without the aid or hindrance of foreigners, then, they are growing up gradually and normally to take their place in the great family of na-

* H. F. C. Smith, *loc. cit.*
† *Ibid.*
‡ E. W. Blyden, *The Prospects of the African* (London: 1874), quoted by J. F. Ade Ajayi in *Journal of Negro Education*, 3, 1961, p. 206.

tions, a distinct but integral part of the great human body, who will neither be spurious Europeans, bastard Americans, nor savage Africans, but men developed upon the basis of their own idiosyncracies and according to the exigencies of the climate and country.

It was of course to this complex of ideas and beliefs that the Mahdi of the Eastern (Anglo-Egyptian) Sudan adhered, a vivid figure in the story to whom, for lack of space, no justice can be done here.

Switching to Southern Africa, we can see that the quenching of Rozwi-Karanga power in the plateau lands between the Limpopo and Zambezi also had its origin in European penetration only by remote effect. These social structures were thrown down by African invaders from the far southeast. No doubt it may be true that those regiments had been set in motion by the shock of European arrival from the Cape of Good Hope; none of that was clear at the time. In this respect the nineteenth-century records are of little help. Nor do we know why the Karanga state collapsed so easily; we can only suppose that long security and prosperity had disarmed it beyond any chance of real resistance to invading bands whose ferocity was savage.

About European motives and actions, however, the records are copious. And with reason. The eighteenth century had opened the way for the men of property; in the nineteenth they set forth and followed it. They journeyed along it to such purpose that by 1900 there was hardly any part of Africa which had yet to feel the impact of Europe's spirit of possession. They strode into an epoch of ownership considered as the *summum bonum*, as the touchstone of happiness, as the token of a money-gathering obsession so compelling that even now, in the wake of two tremendous wars, the world is still dazed and dazzled by it. The records are enormously concerned with the question of possession.

Conquest followed hard on geographical discovery. This is not to say that the second must in any case have led to the first, not even that the explorers always had conquest in mind (though most of the later ones did); but it is to say that the geographical enterprises of the period were part and parcel of an expansive movement which already nourished ambitions of African empire. One school of British historians, pointing to the well-known reluctance of most British governments in the nineteenth century to accept a policy of imperial annexation, have lately argued that "the scramble for Africa" should be explained merely by diplomatic and strategic motives.* These motives certainly existed, especially in relation to England's command of Egypt and therefore of the Isthmus of Suez, but they could have counted for little in promoting the colonial partition of Africa had it not been for other pressures, economic and commercial, which formed part of all that vast combination of capital investment and accumulation which now gave world leadership to Western Europe. The motives and the men who really moved "the scramble" were those who were represented, at the point of parliamentary and city politics, by what Mary Kingsley was to call "our great solid understuff — the Merchant Adventurers."

To all this, national pride now added a new frenzy. This bore down all barriers of discretion. Discussing partition west of the Niger in 1883, a senior official of the British Foreign Office wrote that "protectorates are unwelcome burdens, but in this case it is . . . a question between British protectorates, which would be unwelcome, and French protectorates, which would be fatal." Commenting on a similar attitude in France, an elderly economist remarked more in sorrow than in anger that the French no longer calculated their steps in Africa nor thought about them without passion. "We want annexations, and we care only for their size, not troubling about their quality." Such was the mental background against which most of the later writers of the nineteenth century composed their memoirs of Africa. It explains a great deal of their contempt for weaker men.

But the "scramble" was still far ahead when the century opened. The great questions then were the ending of the oversea slave trade and, imminently, the discovery of what lay behind the

---

* See R. Robinson, J. Gallagher, A. Denny: *Africa and the Victorians* (New York: Macmillan, 1961); and, for an opposing and to me convincing view, J. Stengers, "L'Impérialisme Colonial, etc.," in *Journal of African History*, 3, 1962, p. 469.

coastal barriers erected by slave-dealing kings and middleman chiefs. The year 1807 brought the end of the slave trade in British ships (and they, during the previous century, had carried more captives to the Americas than the ships of any other nation); but the work of discovery had already begun. We can divide it for brevity's sake into parts concerning west, east, and central-south Africa.

Mungo Park, a young Scots surgeon, settled the main problem of the Niger river — whether it flowed westward or eastward — in two great journeys from the Gambia in 1795-1797 and 1805-1806; if I have given him what may appear an undue share of space, it is because his moral qualities were such that no anthology of African discovery could be complete without the note they strike so clearly and so bravely. Then in eight epoch-making years, between 1823 and 1830, the inland country of West Africa was widely opened by six notable men, one French and five English: Dixon Denham, Hugh Clapperton, Dr. Walter Oudney, René Caillié and Richard and John Lander.* The Englishmen explored the lower course of the Niger, established its true direction and outflow, and encountered many rulers and peoples; little is said of them here because their books have been much anthologized and their discoveries were mainly geographical. Caillié's contribution was a remarkable feat of patient endurance in Muslim disguise: entering West Africa from the far southwest he emerged at last in Tangier, the first European of modern times to reach Timbuktu, where he was disappointed in its golden legend by finding only "a mass of ill-looking houses, built of earth."

Like the others, Caillié was nonetheless impressed by the many-sided quality of Western Sudanese civilization, mingling at Djenné with "a concourse of strangers from all parts of the Sudan." Den-

---

* For the first three see *Narrative of Travels and Discoveries in Northern and Central Africa* (London: 1826); Clapperton's *Journal of a Second Expedition into the Interior of Africa* (London: 1829); R. and J. Lander, *Journal of an Expedition to . . . the Niger* (London: 1832).

For Caillié in English translation see *Travels through Central Africa to Timbuctoo* (London: 1830).

Valuable extracts from all these, and others, will be found in *West African Explorers*, ed. C. Howard with introduction by J. H. Plumb (Oxford: 1951).

ham, a few years earlier, had noted of Bornu (northeastern Nigeria) that there "are many hajjis, who have made the pilgrimage to Mecca, and excel in writing Arabic characters, as well as teaching the art to others"; while Clapperton, introduced to Sultan Bello at Sokoto in 1824, was at once asked "a great many questions about Europe" and found himself plunged into an erudite discussion on Christianity. The Sultan "continued to ask several other theological questions, until I was obliged to confess myself not sufficiently versed in religious subtleties to resolve these knotty points . . ." Only in 1849, with the arrival of a remarkable German traveler, Heinrich Barth, was there to be a European in these countries with an intellectual formation adequate to the task of political, social and economic analysis that Europe now required.

After the travels of Bruce in Ethiopia and along the Middle Nile, the exploring of East Africa really begins with two German missionaries, Johann Krapf and Johannes Rebmann, in the 1840s, notably with Rebmann's journey to the Chagga of Kilimanjaro and Krapf's to Usumbura. Their journals are well worth reading. Then the 1850s and 1860s did for the inland country of East Africa what the 1820s had accomplished in the west. Richard Burton walked to Lake Tanganyika in 1857; John Hanning Speke went on to the southern shores of Lake Victoria, and, with James Grant a few years later, pushed northward to the White Nile while Samuel Baker, coming south from Egypt at the same time, continued into what is now Western Uganda.*

Meanwhile other men were riding or walking up from the Cape

* For Krapf and Rebmann in English translation see *Travels, Researches and Missionary Labours* (London: 1860).

For Burton, *First Footsteps in East Africa* (London: 1856; reprinted in Everyman Ed., London, 1910); *The Lake Regions of Equatorial Africa* (London: 1860, reprinted 1961).

For Speke, *What Led to the Discovery of the Source of the Nile?* (London: 1864).

For Grant, *A Walk Across Africa* (London: 1864).

See also G. Schweinfurth, *Im Herzen von Afrika* (Leipzig: 1874); English translation, *The Heart of Africa* (London: 1873). Selections from the books of eighteen of these travelers are in *East African Explorers*, C. Richards and J. Place (Oxford: 1960).

Province of South Africa, hunters and prospectors who have left us little of their stories, and missionaries who have left us much. Fifteen years of pioneer travel took David Livingstone, between 1841 and 1856, from Kuruman in Bechuanaland north to the Zambezi, west through Angola to its capital city of Luanda on the Atlantic coast, and thence back again eastward to the lower course of the Zambezi. Eager to open a route from the eastern seaboard, he set out once more in 1858 and a third time in 1866, coming now up the course of the Ruvuma river to Lake Nyasa and onward to the upper waters of the Congo.* Henry Stanley went to find him and succeeded; but Stanley's real achievement came during 1874-1877 when he crossed the whole Congo basin in a thousand quelling days from Bagamoyo on the coast of Tanganyika to Boma at the mouth of the Congo. His long book about this journey, *Through the Dark Continent*, may still be read with perseverance if not with much enjoyment, for his prose was awkward and pretentious; those who want to know more of the man and what he did will probably do better with his much shorter and unvarnished *Exploration Diaries*, lately discovered by his grandson in a box-file containing "four closely written reporter's pads." †

How much, in the light of what we know today, may it be said that these men understood of what they saw and found? They varied as greatly in their capacity as in their morality. Faced by systems and situations more or less strange to the Europe from which they came, they reacted according to their individual formation without having much chance to correct its shortcomings, or even of knowing that it should be corrected. Some made a

---

* For Livingstone, see especially *Missionary Travels, etc.* (London: 1857; *Private Journals 1851-1853*, ed. I. Schapera (London: 1960); and *Missionary Correspondence 1841-1856*, ed. I. Schapera (London: 1961).

† *The Exploration Diaries of H. M. Stanley*, ed. R. Stanley and A. Neame (London: 1961).

See also V. L. Cameron, *Across Africa* (1877); and, for a most useful selection from Southern African explorers' books, *South African Explorers*, ed. E. Axelson (Oxford: 1964).

For early times in Southern Rhodesia (Matabeleland and Mashonaland) the reader will enjoy F. C. Selous, *Travel and Adventure in South-east Africa* (London: 1893).

tremendous and successful effort to come to grips with this peculiar reality; Barth and Livingstone stand at the head of these. Others
made little or none, and the books they wrote are practically un-
readable today. Others again made an effort, but were unable to
escape the mold of their own preconceptions: few exerted themselves more than Burton, for example, yet Burton could seldom
bring himself into any constructive sympathy with Africans who
were so clearly different from English gentlemen. Consequently,
as Henry Nevinson wrote of him in 1910, Burton "saw everything
clearly, but everything on the flat." Few risked more than Stanley,
but Stanley was already involved in dreams of commercial enterprise which could be no different from imperial conquest: he
traveled much, but thought little. Few covered more ground than
Baker, yet Baker was nothing if not a product of England's Vic-
torian Age, confident from sheer technical superiority that Africans
were "Nature's children" and, as such, doomed to no good if
left in charge of themselves.

Besides, as we have seen at another point in this book, they
entered a continent in crisis. They met with situations of large
instability and, often enough, ferocious chaos. Throughout much
of East Africa the advent of a massive Arab-Swahili slave trade in
the 1830s had thrown whole regions and peoples into violent collision and political disruption, forming the main reason why
Stanley had to fight his way down the Congo. Each people had
come to fear the intended evil of its neighbors. That was not yet
true a little to the southward, along the course of the Middle
Zambezi, where Livingstone found an agreeable security of life.
But southward again, on the plateau lands of what was to become
Southern Rhodesia, the same disruption had followed on the
recent incursion of African invaders from Natal in the far southeast. The more intelligent explorers were aware that much of this
confusion and fear formed relatively new factors in African life,
but — understandably — they could not see back beyond it, and
they tended to assume that life had "always been like this." The
colonial period, which now followed, was born under the philan-
thropic banner of "trusteeship"; the poor savages, unable to help
themselves, should be taken in hand by their betters, and shown

the way they should go. Reaching out for his share of the "magnificent cake," Leopold of Belgium blew loud trumpet voluntaries to the cause of charity and good will; and others did the same.

Formally, the colonial period may be thought to have begun with the international "share-out" conference of 1884-1885 in Berlin. From around this time, in any case, books and memoirs about Africa become so abundant that a lifetime's reading would scarcely avail to know them all. Spurred by the desire for possession, jostled by their rivals, driven by the furies of an extreme patriotism, each of the imperialist powers strove to outdo its rivals. The newspapers of the period show that any argument, true or false, was pressed into the service of this colossal adventure.

All that makes sad reading today. Fortunately, with the colonial period over and done with, rather little of this ocean of words need be navigated by those who wish to understand African as distinct from European history. So I make no excuse for mentioning only a few of the books of the late nineteenth century, and I conclude this section with some passages from the work of Mary Kingsley because, as Hodgkin has rightly said, she was the last great European traveler-reporter "who could go where her genius led her, accepting Africans and accepted by them as a person among persons, without the privileges and embarrassments associated with membership of an imperial nation, and with a total disregard of what a European administration might think of her way of life";* and, finally, with a comment from one of those Africans who faced the colonial onslaught but could not see — as who could have seen? — how it all would end.

---

* For a wide selection of late nineteenth-century extracts for various regions, see Thomas Hodgkin, *Nigerian Perspectives* (Oxford: 1960); F. Wolfson, *Pageant of Ghana* (Oxford: 1958). See also Howard, ed., *West African Explorers*; Richards and Place, eds., *East African Explorers*; and Axelson, ed., *South African Explorers*, cited in footnotes above. For "French West Africa" see especially L. G. Binger, *Du Niger au Golfe de Guinée* (2 vols., Paris: 1892).

FRÉDÉRIC CAILLAUD
Rediscovering Kush

Since this was the century of Europe's discovery of the African interior, it seems appropriate to begin with Meroë, although it would still be many years before Kushite civilization was to be recognized in its broader African context. Bruce had glimpsed the ruins of Meroë in 1772, but the first clear descriptions are the work of two French explorers, Linant de Bellefonds and Frédéric Caillaud. They extended to the southward that great field of research in the Nile Valley which French scholars had opened two decades earlier as a happy byproduct of Napoleon's invasion of Egypt. Just as Vivant Denon and others had then given Europe its first effective view of the civilization of ancient Egypt, so now his fellow-countrymen surveyed the physical remains of Kush.

[1822: On first crossing the Nile from the western bank, he failed to see any ruins and came to the conclusion that he was "chasing a chimera." But the next day went better:] Imagine my joy when I saw the tops of a crowd of pyramids raised a little on the horizon, and tipped by the rays of the sun . . . I climbed to the summit of the highest of them and there, wishing to pay my small tribute to the illustrious geographer whose genius had guided me to this place, I carved the name of d'Anville in the stone [this great eighteenth-century French geographer had made a near guess at Meroë's true position]. Looking round, I saw a second group of pyramids to the west, and, not far from the river, a huge field of ruins and remains indicating the site of an ancient city . . .

From Frédéric Caillaud, *Voyage à Meroé, etc.,* 1819-1822 (2 vols. Paris), vol. 2, p. 142. Translated here by B. Davidson.

JOHN BARROW
Beyond the Orange River

As Mungo Park was discovering the Niger, others, far away in the south, came pushing northward into the lands beyond the Orange. The following account of the Bechuana and other peoples was set down at second hand by John Barrow, who had gone to South Africa as secretary to the governor, and who was afterwards one of the founders of Britain's Royal Geographical Society.

[1801] The town of Leetakoo, according to the direction and the distance traveled by the expedition from the Roggeveld, is situated in latitude 26° 30′ south, and longitude 27° east. A river, which from the width of the channel must occasionally be of considerable size, runs through the midst of it. The town, in its circumference, was estimated to be fully as large as Cape Town, including all the gardens of Table Valley; but from the irregularity of the streets, and the lowness of the buildings, it was impossible to ascertain, with any degree of accuracy, the number of houses; it was concluded, however, that they could not be less than two nor more than three thousand, all nearly of the same size and construction, and differing in nothing from that of the chief except that his was a little larger than the others. The whole population, including men, women and children, they considered to be from ten to fifteen thousand persons. Round numbers are rarely exact. The two commissioners, it seems, at the end of fifteen days, on comparing notes, found that the estimate of one was ten, of the other fifteen thousand. The truth may probably lie in the middle.

From John Barrow, *Voyage to Cochinchina, etc.* (London: 1806). To this volume Barrow added an account of travels beyond the Orange River by his father-in-law, Pieter Trater, and a surgeon called William Sullivan, in 1801-1802.

The ground plan of every house was a complete circle, from twelve to fifteen feet in diameter; the floor of hard beaten clay, raised about four inches above the general surface of the enclosure. About one fourth part of the circle, which was the front of the house and observed generally to face the east, was entirely open; the other three fourths were walled up with clay and stones, to the height of about five feet . . .

The dwelling of a Booshuana is not ill calculated for the climate. In elegance and solidity it may probably be as good as the *Casae* or first houses that were built in imperial Rome, and may be considered in every respect superior in its construction and in comfort to most of the Irish cabins, into which the miserable peasantry are ofttimes obliged to crawl through puddles of water. The hut of a Booshuana is not only raised upon an elevated clay flooring, but the ground of the whole enclosure is so prepared that the water may run off through the gateway; and the whole of their cookery being carried on in this open area, the inside of the dwelling is free from smoke and soot. So well is he acquainted with the comfort and convenience of shade, that his hut is usually built under the branches of a spreading mimosa, every twig of which is preserved with a religious care, and not a bough suffered to be broken off on any emergency, though the article of fuel must sometimes be sought at a very considerable distance.

So large a population collected together on one spot, surrounded by barren deserts occasionally inhabited by a few savages, and cut off from all communication with other civilized societies, necessarily implies the adequate means of subsistence within themselves. One great source from which they draw their support is their cattle, whose flesh, however, they eat but very sparingly; milk is mostly used in a curdled state, which they keep not in grass baskets, like the Eastern Kaffers, but in leathern bags and clay pots . . .

The grain chiefly cultivated, as appeared by the samples brought back by the commissioners, consisted of the holcus sorghum, a small species of the same genus which from the reddish colored seed appeared to be the Saccharatus, a Dolichos not unlike the cadjan, and a small spotted Phaseolus or kidney bean. These different kinds of grain and pulse appear to be sown promiscuously and, when reaped, to be thrown indiscriminately into their earthern granaries; from whence they are taken and used without selection, sometimes by broiling, but more generally boiling in milk. It will readily be supposed that the art of agriculture among this people is yet in its lowest stage. In fact, the only labor bestowed on the ground is performed by the women, and with a rude instrument, something like the hoe. It is a flat piece of iron fixed into the knob of the Kaffer *keerie*. When its horizontal edge is so fitted that it stands at right angles with the handle, it serves as a hoe; when turned round so as to be parallel with the handle, it is then a hatchet.

But the Booshuanas are arrived at that stage of civilization which is not satisfied with the mere necessaries of life supplied to them abundantly from the three sources of agriculture, grazing, and hunting; they are by no means insensible of its conveniences and its luxuries. Their skin cloaks for the winter are pliant, soft and warm, being frequently lined with the fur-skins of tyger-cats, viverras and other small animals; and when in summer they go without clothing, they rarely expose their bodies to the rays of the sun, but carry umbrellas made of the broad feathers of the ostrich fixed to the end of a stick. They vary their mode of dressing both animal food and grain, occasionally boiling, broiling, or roasting the former, and simply broiling the latter, or bruising it into flour and boiling it up with milk. Among the luxuries of the appetite tobacco seems to hold the highest estimation . . .

Every man had a knife slung about the neck by a leather thong, and fitted into a scabbard. The blade is generally about six inches long, an inch broad, rounded at the end, and brought to an edge on each side; the handle sometimes of wood, and sometimes of ivory; in the latter case, it is usually carved into the shape of the elephant's proboscis. The party had with them a quantity of common knives intended for barter, but the Booshuanas held them very cheap, observing that their own were at least twice as good, because they were made to cut with two edges, whereas those of the white people only cut with one. The knife, in fact, is so useful an instrument to such as live by the chase and on roots, that it may almost be considered as an article of the first necessity, and is valued accordingly. A Booshuana is accounted wealthy according to the number of cattle, knives and beads he may possess: these are the money and the currency of Leetakoo . . .

The system on which their government is founded appears to be completely patriarchal, and the chief must of course be a man idolized by the people; and the consequence is, that he has the nomination of his successor. From the elders of the society he is informed of the general sentiments of the people; and with their advice such rules and regulations are framed or altered as are best calculated to give general satisfaction, and consequently to make himself popular. No young man can be admitted into the king's council, which is established on the principles of true primitive simplicity, when, in almost every nation and language, age and authority were synonymous terms. If any man in the society feels himself aggrieved, and is not satisfied with the decision of the council, he is at full liberty to settle his affairs and leave the horde with his whole property.

HENRY FYNN
Shaka the Zulu

A surgeon's assistant who went to South Africa in 1818, Henry Fynn six years later visited the famous chief who had formed and militarized the Zulu nation.

[1824] On the following morning we were requested to mount our horses and ride to the king's kraal. On our arrival we found him sitting under a tree, in the act of decorating himself. He was

From an account of Henry Fynn's travels in J. Bird, *Annals of Natal* (Pietermaritzburg: 1888). For Zulu history see A. T. Bryant, *Olden Times in Zululand and Natal* (London: 1929); and E. A. Ritter, *Shaka Zulu* (London: 1955).

surrounded by about two hundred people, a servant standing at his side, and holding a shield over him to keep the glare of the sun from him. Round his forehead he wore a turban of otter-skin, with a feather of a crane erect in front, full two feet long. Earrings of dried sugar cane, carved round the edge, with white ends, and an inch in diameter, were let into the lobes of the ears, which had been cut to admit them. From shoulder to shoulder he wore bunches, three inches in length, of the skins of monkeys and genets, twisted like the tails of these animals, and hanging half down the body.

Round the ring on the head . . . were a dozen bunches of the red feathers of the loorie, tastefully tied to thorns which were stuck into the hair. Round his arms were white ox-tails, cut down the middle so as to allow the hairs to hang about the arm, to the number of four for each. Round the waist a petticoat, resembling the Highland plaid, made of skins of monkeys and genets, and twisted as before described, having small tassels round the top, the petticoat reaching to the knees, below which were white ox-tails to fit round the legs, so as to hang to the ankles. He had a white shield with a single black spot, and an assagai. While he was thus dressing himself, the natives proceeded, as on the day before, to show droves of cattle, which were still flocking in, and repeatedly varying the scene by dancing and singing. Meanwhile it became known to us that Shaka had ordered that a man standing near us should be put to death, for what crime we could not learn: but we soon found it to be one of the common occurrences in the course of the day . . .

EDOUARD CASALIS
In the Wake of Many Wars

Of Shaka's great and very different contemporary, Moshesh of the Basuto, we are fortunate in having an early firsthand account by Casalis, who was a member of the Paris Evangelical Missionary Society. Casalis arrived in the wake of what the Basuto traditionally call the *Lifaqane,* the terrible "wars of wandering" set in motion throughout southeast Africa by the Zulus around 1822.

[1833] Six months after leaving Paris we entered the country of the Basuto two hundred leagues from the Cape, and saw with astonishment the majestic chain of the Maluti [mountains] which separate Bechuanasie [i.e., later Orange Free State] from the land of Natal . . . Up to forty or fifty kilometers from this chain our wagon had encountered no serious obstacle. Pulled by twelve oxen driven by a patient native of the country, it advanced a few leagues every day across interminable plains while we amused ourselves in pursuit of multitudes of gazelles, elands and zebras. But when we were only two days' travel from our destination, everything changed. Isolated hills five or six hundred meters high stood across our passage . . .

Arriving here, what struck us most was the solitary and desolate aspect of the country. We looked in vain for hamlets, for those groups of cultivators whose presence we associated with a fertile and varied soil. On every side we saw human bones whitening in the sun and rain, and more than once we had to turn our wagon out of its course so as to avoid passing over these sad remains.

From Edouard Casalis, *Les Bassoutos, etc.* (Paris: 1859). Translated by B. Davidson. For Basuto history, see also D. F. Ellenberger, *History of the Basuto* (London: 1912); and G. Lagden, *The Basutos,* 2 vols. (London and New York: 1910).

When we asked our guides where the owners of the country lived
they pointed a finger towards a few wretched huts on the top of
the steepest hills. And whenever we chanced to meet a hunter, the
unfortunate man no sooner saw our caravan than he threw himself to the ground so as to hide in the grass.

Yet as we came nearer to the residence of the chief [Moshesh],
appearances changed encouragingly. We began to meet fairly big
herds pasturing under the care of well-armed herdsmen. We saw
fields in what looked like careful cultivation . . .

Moshesh of the Basuto

We found that it was not without reason that the king of the
Basuto was known as the *chief of the mountain*. His main town
was and still is placed on the plateau of Thaba Bosiu, a pentagon-
shaped hill which is perfectly fortified by nature. We were received
with the greatest expressions of joy. The first days [after our ar-
rival] were taken up in explaining to our new acquaintances the
object we had in view. It was no easy thing to do . . . But when
God wills a thing, all obstacles are overcome. He inspired in the
Basuto and their chief a deep confidence in our good intentions.
This population had passed through many evil years. There was
a gleam of hope in their eyes; they received us eagerly . . .

Moshesh has a pleasant and intelligent appearance. His bearing
is noble and assured. One can see in his face the habit of thought
and of command, but this does not prevent him from having a
smile of great good will. At the time of his birth,* the country of
the Basutos was densely populated. In miniature form the tribe
presented the aspect of our own country [France] in feudal
times. In principle the supremacy of the house of Monahing was
recognized, Moshesh being one of its representatives; but each
chief tried to win as much independence as possible. There were
quarrels at one time or another between the various communities,
but generally little blood was spilt, and the whole affair usually
came down to the raiding of a few herds.

This state of things lasted until 1820. Moshesh was then living

* In about 1790, according to G. Lagden, *The Basutos* (New York: 1910),
vol. 2, p. 463.

in his native country two days towards the north from Thaba Bosiu. The national songs still celebrate the green pastures of Butabute and the steep hills where the son of Mokachane and his companions hunted the eland and the wild boar. In a moment least expected, disastrous invasion put an end to these pastimes. It came from Natal, whence we have already seen the emergence of the terrible Moselekatse. An iron yoke weighed on the peoples of that country. Shaka, a chief as clever as he was cruel, had subjugated them and kept them in obedience . . . One of his strongest vassals, Matewane, tired of that regime, secretly left the country with several thousand warriors faithful to himself. On his way he met Pakalita, chief of the Fingos, and drove him into flight after several battles. Hotly pursued, Pakalita crossed the Maluti mountains and turned towards the Mantatees . . . and these people, helped by their knowledge of the country, pushed into the gorges of the mountains and moved rapidly towards the south, carrying desolation into the heart of the peaceful valleys of Lesuto (the name that the Basutos give their country). After that this land became the scene of continual massacres. Matewane, believing himself safe at last from Shaka, settled on the banks of the Caledon River. Pakalita did the same. The two peoples continued to harass one another; and the Mantatees and Basutos, always involved, felt the terrible effects of their presence. This state of things continued for years. Fields lay fallow and famine piled fresh horrors on those of war. Whole populations succumbed . . .

Moshesh resisted. Gifted with remarkable powers of observation, with much subtlety, with great force of character, he knew how to resist or give way at the right moment, how to win allies even among the invaders of his territory, how to set his enemies at odds with one another, and, by acts of good will, how to gain the respect even of those who had sworn his ruin . . .

ROBERT MOFFAT
Chief Moselekatse

To complete the triptych, here is Robert Moffat's famous description of the warrior chief of those predatory Matebele who, breaking away from their Zulu fellow-tribesmen and then finding themselves in conflict with Boer settlers, swept northward in 1837 across the Limpopo, where they finished off the ruin of the Karanga, finding a new home for themselves but terrorizing the country far and wide. Moffat finds them before they embarked on that enterprise, another of the destructive consequences of the "war of wandering" which ravaged southern Africa at this time.

[1829] At Sitlagole River, about 160 miles from the Kuruman, we halted in the afternoon, and allowed our oxen to graze on a rising bank opposite our wagons, and somewhat farther than a gunshot from them. Having but just halted, and not having loosened a gun, we were taken by surprise by two lions rushing out from the neighbouring thicket. The oldest one, of enormous size, approached within ten yards of the oxen, and bounding on one of my best, killed him in a moment, by sending his great teeth through the vertebrae of the neck. The younger lion couched at a distance, while the elder licked his prey, turning his head occasionally towards the other oxen, which had caught his scent and scampered off; then, with his forefeet upon the carcass, he looked and roared at us, who were all in a scuffle to loosen our guns, and attack his majesty. Two of our number, more eager to frighten than to kill, discharged their muskets; and, probably, a ball whistling past his ear, induced him to retire to the thicket

From Robert Moffat, *Missionary Labours and Scenes in South Africa* (London: 1842).

whence he had come, leaving us in quiet possession of the meat. At Meritsane, the bed of another dry river, we had a serenade of desert music, composed of the treble, counter, and bass voices of jackals, hyenas, and lions . . .

Having traveled one hundred miles, five days after leaving Mosega we came to the first cattle outposts of the Matebele, when we halted by a fine rivulet . . .

We now traveled along a range of mountains running near east-southeast [the Magaliesberg], while the country to the north and east became more level, but beautifully studded with ranges of little hills, many isolated, of a conical form, along the bases of which lay the ruins of innumerable towns, some of which were of amazing extent. The soil of the valleys and extended plains was of the richest description. The torrents from the adjacent heights had, from year to year, carried away immense masses, in some places laying bare the substratum of granite rocks, exhibiting a mass of rich soil from ten to twenty feet deep, where it was evident native grain had formerly waved; and watermelons, pumpkins, kidney beans, and sweet reed had once flourished.

The ruins of many towns showed signs of immense labour and perseverance; stone fences, averaging from four to seven feet high, raised apparently without mortar, hammer, or line. Everything was circular, from the inner walls which surrounded each dwelling or family residence, to those which encircled a town. In traversing these ruins, I found the remains of some houses which had escaped the flames of the marauders. These were large, and displayed a far superior style to anything I had witnessed among the aboriginal tribes of Southern Africa. The circular walls were generally composed of hard clay, with a small mixture of cow-dung, so well plastered and polished, a refined portion of the former mixed with a kind of ore, that the interior of the house had the appearance of being varnished. The walls and doorways were also neatly ornamented with a kind of architraves and cornices. The pillars supporting the roof in the form of pilasters, projecting from the walls, and adorned with flutings and other designs, showed much taste in the architectresses. This taste, however, was exercised on fragile, materials, for there was nothing in the building like stone, except the foundations. The houses, like all others in the interior, were round, with conical roofs, extending beyond the walls, so as to afford considerable shade, or what might be called a verandah. The raising of the stone fences must have been a work of immense labour, for the materials had all to be brought on the shoulders of men, and the quarries where these materials were probably obtained, were at a considerable distance. The neighbouring hills also gave ample demonstration of human perseverance, with instruments of the most paltry description. . . .

Nothing now remained but dilapidated walls, heaps of stones, and rubbish, mingled with human skulls, which, to a contemplative mind, told their ghastly tale. These are now the abodes of reptiles and beasts of prey. Occasionally a large stone-fold might be seen occupied by the cattle of the Matebele, who had caused the land thus to mourn. Having Matebele with me, I found it extremely difficult to elicit local information from the dejected and scattered aborigines who occasionally came in our way. These trembled before the nobles, who ruled them with a rod of iron.

It was soon evident that the usurpers were anxious to keep me in the dark about the devastations which everywhere met our eyes, and they always endeavoured to be present when I came in contact with the aborigines of the country, but as I could speak the language some opportunities were afforded. One of the three servants who accompanied the two ambassadors to the Kuruman was a captive among the Mantatees, who had been defeated at Old Lithako. He, as well as his fellow-servants, felt a pleasure in speaking with us in Sechuana, their native language. He, and many hundreds more of that people, were, on their return from the defeat, taken prisoners by Moselekatse. This individual, though an athletic and stern-looking being, was also a shrewd observer of character, and possessed a noble mind, which revolted at the tyranny of his new masters. He was a native of the regions through which we were now passing, and would sometimes whisper to me events connected with the desolations of his fatherland.

These nations he described as being once numerous as the locusts, rich in cattle, and traffickers, to a great extent, with the distant tribes of the north. My informant, with his fellow Bakones, had witnessed the desolation of many of the towns around us — the sweeping away of the cattle and valuables — the butchering of the inhabitants, and their being enveloped in smoke and flames. Commandos of Shaka, the once bloody monarch of the Zoolus, had made frightful havoc; but all these were nothing to the final overthrow of the Bakone tribes by the arms of Moselekatse. The former inhabitants of these luxuriant hills and fertile plains had, from peace and plenty, become effeminate — while the Matebele, under the barbarous reign of the monster Shaka, from whose iron grasp they had made their escape, like an overwhelming torrent, rushed onward to the north, marking their course with blood and carnage . . .

[Arriving at their destination, they] proceeded directly to the town, and on riding into the centre of the large fold, which was capable of holding ten thousand head of cattle, we were rather taken by surprise to find it lined by eight hundred warriors, besides two hundred who were concealed in each side of the entrance, as if in ambush. We were beckoned to dismount, which we did, holding our horses' bridles in our hands. The warriors at the gate instantly rushed in with hideous yells, and leaping from the earth with a kind of kilt around their bodies, hanging like loose tails, and their large shields, frightened our horses. They then joined the circle, falling into rank with as much order as if they had been accustomed to European tactics. Here we stood surrounded by warriors, whose kilts were of ape skins, and their legs and arms adorned with the hair and tails of oxen, their shields reaching to their chins, and their heads adorned with feathers.

Although in the centre of a town, all was silent as the midnight hour, while the men were motionless as statues. Eyes only were seen to move, and there was a rich display of fine white teeth. After some minutes of profound silence, which was only interrupted by the breathing of our horses, the war song burst forth. There was harmony, it is true, and they beat time with their feet, producing a sound like hollow thunder, but some parts of it was music befitting the nether regions, especially when they imitated the groanings of the dying on the field of battle, and the yells and hissings of the conquerors. Another simultaneous pause ensued, and still we wondered what was intended, till out marched the monarch from behind the lines, followed by a number of men bearing baskets and bowls of food. He came up to us, and having been instructed in our mode of salutation, gave each a clumsy but hearty shake of the hand. He then politely turned to the food, which was placed at our feet, and invited us to partake. By this time the wagons were seen in the distance, and having intimated our wish to be directed to a place where we might encamp in the outskirts of the town, he accompanied us, keeping fast hold of my right arm, though not in the most gracious manner, yet with perfect familiarity. "The land is before you; you are come to your son. You must sleep where you please." . . .

During one of my first interviews with Moselekatse, the following incident took place, which shows that, however degraded and cruel man may become, he is capable of being subdued by kindness. He drew near to the spot where I stood, with some attendants bearing dishes of food; the two chiefs who had been at the Kuruman were with me, but on the approach of their sovereign, they bowed and withdrew, shouting, as usual, "*Baaite 'nkhosi enkolu*," but were instantly desired to return. Moselekatse, placing his left hand on my shoulder, and his right on his breast, addressed me in the following language: "Machobane, I call you such because you have been my father. You have made my heart as white as milk; milk is not white today, my heart is white. I cease not to wonder at the love of a stranger. You never saw me before, but you love me more than my own people. You fed me when I was hungry; you clothed me when I was naked; you carried me in your bosom"; and, raising my right arm with his, added, "that arm shielded me from my enemies." On my replying, I was unconscious of having done him any such services, he instantly pointed to the two ambassadors who were sitting at my feet, saying, "These are great men; 'Umbate is my right hand. When I sent them from my presence to see the land of the white men, I sent my ears, my eyes, my mouth; what they heard I heard, what they saw I saw, and what they said, it was Moselekatse who said it. You fed them and clothed them, and when they were to be slain, you were their shield. You did it unto me. You did it unto Moselekatse, the son of Machobane."

ANTONIO GAMITTO
The Land of Kazembe

By the beginning of the century, the central regions of Africa had become organized into a number of important states and confederations, with those of the Marave (Malawi) and of the Western Lunda and Eastern Lunda prominent among them. The Western Lunda were ruled by a supreme chief whose title was the *Muata* Yamvo, while the Eastern Lunda owed allegiance to a vassal of the *Muata* Yamvo, whose title was the *Kazembe* and whose territory was in that of the modern Katanga.

These Central African states and rulers were possibly visited by a handful of Portuguese traders; and the first account of this broad belt of central African land comes with the notes and journals of two *pombeiros* — Afro-Portuguese traders — Pedro João Baptista and Amaro José, who crossed Africa from Angola to Mozambique between 1806 and 1811. Their notes and journals were published in London in 1873 in a translation by Richard Burton, and form an important if slim addition to the record. Obliged to live for four years at the court of the *Kazembe*, the two *pombeiros* found that country "supplied with provisions all the year round and every year: manioc flour, millet, maize, large haricot beans, small and round beans . . . bananas, sugar canes, yams, gourds . . . and much fish . . ."

Captain Antonio Gamitto visited the *Kazembe*, passing northwestward from Tete on the Zambezi through the country of the Marave (Malawi), in the year 1831-1832, as second-in-command of a Portuguese expedition headed by Major José Monteiro. Gamitto is among

From A. C. P. Gamitto, *O Muata Kazembe, etc.*, 1831-1832 (Lisbon: 1854), in the translation of Ian Cunnison, *King Kazembe, etc.* (2 vols., Lisbon: 1960). The first extract is from vol. 1, p. 50; the second from vol. 1, p. 55; the third from vol. 1, p. 109; and the fourth from vol. 2, p. 15.

the most satisfactory of nineteenth-century travelers: patient, curious, long-suffering, and gifted with strong powers of observation. A brief résumé of his book was made available in English in 1873; but an admirably produced full-scale translation by Ian Cunnison appeared in 1960.

Marave Bridges

The Luangwa-Pire or Luangwa-Jaua which we crossed today has very little water in this dry season but swells greatly in the rains, and such is the velocity of the current then that it does not afford passage even to canoes, for great stones and tree trunks are washed down with it; and the water reaches such a height that the Marave are forced to erect bridges, which they call Uraro, in the most frequented places.

They are constructed with bamboos laid parallel and tied together with bark (which they call Maruze), the first lengths at each end being fixed firmly to some tree already there. Other bamboos are tied athwart these, six spans in length, which is the width of the bridge, the top of them being the path one crosses by. The bridge dips to make an obtuse angle at the centre, being eighty spans high at this point, and it has no support except at the two banks. Crossing it produces such an extraordinary movement that it seems to be coming apart at every moment; but the Marave are very careful in securing them although they do not cross them unless it is absolutely essential. To disabuse myself I crossed one, although I would not have done it if they had not placed two bamboos high on it, which, although slender, served as a balustrade and support on each side. These are the only people whom I have seen to construct such a thing.

Metallurgy

João Pedro told me, and I do not doubt it, that he has nine hundred negro women mining gold, of which he gets 42 *pastas* a year. Many years ago this Bar had slaves of Tete citizens employed in mining, but few in number; Botelho extended the mining and made this the principal part of his establishment. Mining aside, he augments his income and furthers his interests by trading in ivory, for the road here is frequented by Bisa . . .

I gave him to understand that I wanted to see the African women at work mining, but he excused himself and said they did not work at this time. I learned later what I had not known, that there is a superstition that the work may be seen only by those who actually perform it, for otherwise the metal would be lost. The metals known here are gold, tin, which they do not care about, and iron: the latter is found in such quantities on the surface that they do not need to dig for it; they collect it and put it into a funnel built of clay, forty spans high and one in diameter; the lower part has a wood fire which they blow with goatskin bellows like those of our wandering tinkers. The iron comes out through holes in the bottom of the funnel; and with this simple operation they draw off the smelted metal, which they then use in their manufactures. These are principally hoes, axes, knives, arrows and spears. For this the tools used are: bellows of the same kind to make a forge on the ground, a stone serving as an anvil, another smaller one as a hammer, and two pieces of wood as pincers; and it is with this set of tools that they make all their work, which is as polished as if it were done by European instruments. The people making them are the Marave blacksmiths. Our blacksmiths of Tete work in our way with proper tools but not so well. When the iron is hot it is malleable like lead, and like it does not crack; but when cold it is hard as steel . . .

Botelho is said to have announced that he would behead any slave who sold gold to the expedition.

The slaves employed at the mine are divided into *Insakas* as usual, but each of these has six negresses, it being, as I have said, only women who mine. Each *Insaka* is under the charge of a Nyakoda who gives a weekly account of the work of her people. These weeks are of four days, and each woman has to account for six Tangas a week; this satisfied, the rest is hers. It often happens that a woman gets enough on the first day to pay the quota and in this case she is not required to turn up on the following days. Owners of Bars usually have imported cloths, beads, etc., at them to sell to their slaves at exorbitant prices; and so these slaves buy from any passing merchant, secretly, what they need; and this was why Botelho forbade the sale of gold to members of the expedition. In spite of this they kept selling it.

Devastation

In remote times, perhaps at the period of Portuguese conquests in this part of Africa, there existed two great *Mambos*, one of whom ruled the Marave, a people who inhabited the left or eastern bank of the Zambezi; and the other of whom dominated the Munhaes, who occupied its right or western margin.* The Mozungos, or Portuguese, caused these *Mambos* to lose all their ancient power; and today they exist in the form we have indicated, their decadence still continuing. Meanwhile the main cause of this is the devastation of the country, a result of the continual warfare in which they are engaged. In other times, there was great commerce in gold, ivory and cereals, but today there is hardly any, and this results from the same cause.

King Kazembe

[1831] All five Whites with the expedition have let their hair and beards grow; my hair, falling over my shoulders, comes down to the level of my thick beard, which reaches my chest. My uniform is a tunic of blue nankeen and white breeches; as a sash I have scarlet cords and tassels about my waist. On my head I have an otter-skin cap, and from my side hangs a fine sword, whose metal sheath the climate has turned the colour of the local inhabitants. Dressed in this array and mounted on a donkey as I have described, I made solemn entry into what is perhaps the greatest town of Central Africa.

Continuing our march we entered, at some distance from the place we had stopped, a long street of enclosures made with posts fixed into the ground and interlaced with grass to a height of ten or twelve spans and which, by the regularity of their construction, looked like walls. On each side were small gates opening into a straight grass fence bordering the road, which would be about a mile long. At the end of this road was a small rectangular hut,

* A memory, of course, of the great period of the Monomotapa rulers.

open only on the part facing west, in the centre of which on a wooden base was a bust of a human figure made roughly of wood, about three spans high; and outside in front of the hut door was a heap of more than three hundred skulls . . .

This morning we were advised to present ourselves before the Mwata Kazembe, who was expecting the principal persons of the expedition. As we had previously been advised, we marched with all possible ceremony, each detachment going armed under the command of its respective leader; and each of us took something to offer the Mwata, so that he might know thereby how many and who were the persons with whom he had to deal. We each took a piece of cloth.

Arriving at the Musumba [the Mwata's residence] we found the great square filled with a throng of people, so arranged as to leave empty a small area in front of the eastern gate of the Chipango. This is the name given to a fence enclosing a dwelling; but when they speak of the Chipango, by itself, they are referring to the Mwata's residence; others they would specify by saying "the Chipango of so-and-so." The Mwata's is very big, and higher and better built than the others.

The warriors in the square were the Lunda army, which would comprise some five or six thousand men, all armed with bows and arrows, Mpok and spears. They were standing about without any appearance of military discipline. The Mwata was seated on the left side of the eastern gate of the Musumba; many leopard skins served him as a carpet, the tails pointing outwards to form a star; over these was an enormous lion skin, and on this a stool covered with a big green cloth. On this throne the Mwata was seated, in greater elegance and state than any other *Mambo* I have seen.

His head was ornamented with a kind of mitre, pyramidal in shape and two spans high, made of brilliant scarlet feathers; round his forehead was a dazzling diadem of beads of various kinds and colours. Behind his head a band of green cloth, supported by two small ivory needles, fanned out from the back of his neck. Neck and shoulders were covered with a kind of capuchin the upper part of which was covered with upturned cowries; there followed a band of pretty imitation jewels, made of glass, and the lower part had a string of alternately placed little round and square mirrors, in symmetry. This fell round his shoulders and over his chest, and when struck by the sun's rays it was too bright to look upon. Above each elbow was a band of blue feathers four inches wide, edged with what looked like a fringe, but which was in fact very fine strips of hide, the hair of which, four or five inches long, was black and white in colour. This ornament only Kazembe and his closest relatives may use, for it is a royal emblem. The arm from elbow to wrist was decorated with a string of bright blue beads . . .

From beside the Mwata's seat two curved lines went out and met some twenty paces in front of him. The left-hand line was indicated by a scratch on the ground, and the right-hand one by means of Mpemba, a kind of gypsum. In front of Kazembe were various figurines in two parallel files beginning from the ends of the curved lines. They formed wings about three spans wide. These figurines were attached to sticks thrust into the ground, they all had Kaffir features, and were adorned with animals' horns. In the centre of the wing, and at the end nearest Kazembe, was a cage in the shape of a barrel, and inside this was another figurine. Two negroes sat beside the two end figurines, facing them, and each had before him a small clay pot of embers into which he threw leaves which produced a thick aromatic smoke. All these figurines had their backs turned to Kazembe. From under the end one on the right, nearest the censer, a string extended to the Mwata's feet, but I do not know its purpose.

The gate of the Chipango was open, and seated in it were the two principal wives of Kazembe. The first was to the right, sitting on a stool and mantled in a large green cloth; her arms, neck and forehead were ornamented with differently coloured beads, while on her head was an ornament of scarlet feathers like Kazembe's only smaller. This first wife is called Mwadi-Ngombe. The second wife, who was to the left sitting on a lion skin on the ground, was simply dressed in a cloth, without ornament; she was called Ntemena. Behind them stood more than four hundred wives of various ages dressed in Nyandas, all of them being the wives of the Chipango, or harem, that being the meaning of the word. These women are divided among the four great wives as servants . . .

Mwata Kazembe looks fifty years old but we were told he is much older. He has a long beard, already turning gray. He is well built and tall, and has a robustness and agility which promises a long life; his look is agreeable and majestic, and his style splendid in its fashion. We certainly never expected to find so much ceremonial, pomp and ostentation in the potentate of a region so remote from the seacoast, and in a nation which appears so barbarous and savage.

DAVID LIVINGSTONE
Central Africa in the 1840s

There is no need to introduce David Livingstone except, in this context, to situate these extracts from his *Missionary Travels and Researches*. They refer to his labors and journeys in what is now the northern part of South Africa, Bechuanaland, and Southern Rhodesia.

The Roots of Apartheid

The word Boer simply means "farmer," and is not synonymous with our word boor. Indeed, to the Boers generally the latter term would be quite inappropriate, for they are a sober, industrious, and most hospitable body of peasantry. Those, however, who have fled from English law on various pretexts, and have been joined by English deserters and every other variety of bad character in their distant localities, are unfortunately of a very different stamp. The great objection many of the Boers had, and still have, to English law is that it makes no distinction between black men and white. They felt aggrieved by their supposed losses in the emancipation of their Hottentot slaves, and determined to erect themselves into

From David Livingstone, *Missionary Travels and Researches in South Africa* (London: 1857); extracts: pp. 29, 39, 184, 505, 630-650.

a republic, in which they might pursue without molestation the "proper treatment of the blacks." It is almost needless to add that the "proper treatment" has always contained in it the essential element of slavery, namely, compulsory unpaid labour.

One section of this body, under the late Mr. Hendrick Potgeiter, penetrated the interior as far as the Cashan Mountains, whence a Zulu or Caffre chief, named Moselekatse, had been expelled by the well-known Caffre Dingaan; and a glad welcome was given them by the Bechuana tribes, who had just escaped the hard sway of that cruel chieftain. They came with the prestige of white men and deliverers; but the Bechuanas soon found, as they expressed it, "that Moselekatse was cruel to his enemies, and kind to those he conquered; but that the Boers destroyed their enemies, and made slaves of their friends." The tribes who still retain the semblance of independence are forced to perform all the labour of the fields, such as manuring the land, weeding, reaping, building, making dams and canals, and at the same time to support themselves.

I have myself been an eyewitness of Boers coming to a village, and, according to their usual custom, demanding twenty or thirty women to weed their gardens, and have seen these women proceed to the scene of unrequited toil, carrying their own food on their heads, their children on their backs, and instruments of labour on their shoulders. Nor have the Boers any wish to conceal the meanness of thus employing unpaid labour; on the contrary, every one of them, from Mr. Potgeiter and Mr. Gert Krieger, the commandants, downwards, lauded his own humanity and justice in making such an equitable regulation. "We make the people work for us, in consideration of allowing them to live in our country."

Boer Policy

The Boers, four hundred in number, were sent by the late Mr. Pretorius to attack the Bakwains in 1852. Boasting that the English had given up all the blacks into their power, and had agreed to aid them in their subjugation by preventing all supplies of ammunition from coming into the Bechuana country, they assaulted the Bakwains, and, besides killing a considerable number of adults, carried off two hundred of our school children into slavery. The natives under Sechele defended themselves till the approach of night enabled them to flee to the mountains; and having in that defense killed a number of the enemy, the very first ever slain in this country by Bechuanas, I received the credit of having taught the tribe to kill Boers! *

My house, which had stood perfectly secure for years under the protection of the natives, was plundered in revenge. English gentlemen, who had come in the footsteps of Mr. Cumming to hunt in the country beyond, and had deposited large quantities of stores in the same keeping, and upwards of eighty head of cattle as relays for the return journeys, were robbed of all; and when they came back to Kolobeng found the skeletons of the guardians strewed all over the place. The books of a good library — my solace in our solitude — were not taken away, but handfuls of the leaves were torn out and scattered over the place. My stock of medicines was smashed; and all our furniture and clothing carried off and sold at public auction to pay the expenses of the foray.

African Justice

The complainant [in common cases] asks the man, against whom he means to lodge his complaint, to come with him to the chief. This is never refused. When both are in the *kotla*, the complainant stands up and states the whole case before the chief and the people usually assembled there. He stands a few seconds after he has done this, to recollect if he has forgotten anything. The witnesses to whom he has referred then rise up and tell all they themselves have seen or heard, but not anything that they have heard from others.

The defendant, after allowing some minutes to elapse so that he may not interrupt any of the opposite party, slowly rises, folds his cloak around him, and, in the most quiet, deliberate way he can assume — yawning, blowing his nose, etc. — begins to explain the affair, denying the charge or admitting it, as the case may be. Sometimes, when galled by his remarks, the complainant utters a sentence of dissent; the accused turns quietly to him, and says, "Be silent: I sat still while you were speaking; can't you do the same?

* Livingstone does not mean, however, that he did the killing himself.

Do you want to have it all to yourself?" And as the audience acquiesce in this bantering, and enforce silence, he goes on till he has finished all he wishes to say in his defense. If he has any witnesses to the truth of the facts of his defense, they give their evidence.

No oath is administered; but occasionally, when a statement is questioned, a man will say, "By my father," or "By the chief, it is so." Their truthfulness among each other is quite remarkable; but their system of government is such that Europeans are not in a position to realize it readily. A poor man will say, in his defense against a rich one, "I am astonished to hear a man so great as he make a false accusation"; as if the offense of falsehood were felt to be one against the society which the individual referred to had the greatest interest in upholding.

If the case is one of no importance, the chief decides it at once; if frivolous, he may give the complainant a scolding, and put a stop to the case in the middle of the complaint, or he may allow it to go on without paying any attention to it whatever. Family quarrels are often treated in this way, and then a man may be seen stating his case with great fluency, and not a soul listening to him. But if it is a case between influential men, or brought on by under-chiefs, then the greatest decorum prevails. If the chief does not see his way clearly to a decision, he remains silent; the elders then rise one by one and give their opinions, often in the way of advice rather than as decisions; and when the chief finds the general sentiment agreeing in one view, he delivers his judgment accordingly. He alone speaks sitting: all others stand.

No one refuses to acquiesce in the decision of the chief, as he has the power of life and death in his hands, and can enforce the law to that extent if he chooses; but grumbling is allowed, and, when marked favouritism is shown to any relative of the chief, the people generally are not so astonished at the partiality as we would be in England.

Security

I believe that the interior of this country presents a much more inviting field for the philanthropist than does the west coast . . .

But I am not to be understood as intimating that any of the numerous tribes are anxious for instruction: they are not the inquiring spirits we read of in other countries; they do not desire the gospel, because they know nothing about either it, or its benefits; but there is no impediment in the way of instruction. Every headman would be proud of a European visitor or resident in his territory, and there is perfect security for life and property all over the interior country. The great barriers which have kept Africa shut are the unhealthiness of the coast, and the exclusive, illiberal disposition of the border tribes.

Gold and Iron

The fort of Tete [on the middle Zambezi] has been the salvation of the Portuguese power in this quarter. It is a small square building, with a thatched apartment for the residence of the troops; and though there are but few guns, they are in a much better state than those of any fort in the interior of Angola. The cause of the decadence of the Portuguese power in this region is simply this. In former times considerable quantities of grain, as wheat, millet, and maize, were exported, also coffee, sugar, oil, and indigo, besides gold dust and ivory. The cultivation of grain was carried on by means of slaves, of whom the Portuguese possessed a large number. The gold dust was procured by washing at various points on the north, south, and west of Tete. A merchant took all his slaves with him to the washings, carrying as much calico and other goods as he could muster. On arriving at the washing-place he made a present to the chief, of the value of about a pound sterling. The slaves were then divided into parties, each headed by a confidential servant, who not only had the supervision of his squad while the washing went on, but bought dust from the inhabitants, and made a weekly return to his master.

When several masters united at one spot, it was called a "Bara," and they then erected a temporary church, in which a priest from one of the missions performed mass. Both chiefs and people were favourable to these visits, because the traders purchased grain for the sustenance of the slaves with the goods they had brought. They continued at this labour until the whole of the goods were expended, and by this means about 130 pounds of gold were annually produced. Probably more than this was actually obtained, but, as it was an article easily secreted, this alone was submitted to the authorities for taxation. At present the whole amount of gold obtained annually by the Portuguese is from eight to ten pounds only.

When the slave trade began, it seemed to many of the merchants a more speedy mode of becoming rich, to sell off the slaves, than to pursue the slow mode of gold-washing and agriculture, and they continued to export them, until they had neither hands to labour nor to fight for them. It was just the story of the goose and the golden egg. The coffee and sugar plantations and gold-washings were abandoned, because the labour had been exported to the Brazils. Many of the Portuguese then followed their slaves, and the Government was obliged to pass a law to prevent further emigration, which, had it gone on, would have depopulated the Portuguese possessions altogether . . .

The only other metal, besides gold, we have in abundance in this region, is iron, and that is of excellent quality. In some places it is obtained from what is called the specular iron ore, and also from black oxide. The latter has been well roasted in the operations of nature, and contains a large proportion of the metal. It occurs generally in tears or rounded lumps, and is but slightly magnetic. When found in the beds of rivers, the natives know of its existence by the quantity of oxide on the surface, and they find no difficulty in digging it with pointed sticks. They consider English iron as "rotten"; and I have seen, when a javelin of their own iron lighted on the cranium of a hippopotamus, it curled up like the proboscis of a butterfly, and the owner would prepare it for future use by straightening it cold with two stones. I brought home some of the hoes which Sekeletu gave me to purchase a canoe, also some others obtained in Kilimane, and they have been found of such good quality that a friend of mine in Birmingham has made an Enfield rifle of them.

JAMES PRIOR
Kilwa in Ruins

Although Kilwa still had a sultan, its wealth and power were long since gone. Anyone today who visits the island and its neighboring sites will have much the same impression as James Prior, surgeon of the *Nisus* frigate, and his commander Captain Beaver, although, thanks to the work of Neville Chittick, the modern visitor can refer as well to an excellent archeological guidebook.

[1812] Quitting the ship next morning with three boats and forty men, a variety of fresh obstacles were started by the old minister [of the sultan of Kilwa], while Captain B—— and I, during the interval, rambled through the greatest part of the village. It is larger than could be at first conjectured, extending from the shore inland, by winding footpaths, between enclosures of plantain, banana, tamarind, and cocoa-nut trees. The huts are generally unconnected, and formed of these convenient materials, combined with bamboo, twigs, and thatch; footpaths form the only streets, and abundant foliage gives it the appearance of a wood. We saw but two or three stone houses, one of which belongs to the sultan. It is a large irregular ill-built edifice, tolerably high, and partly surrounded with walls. I had penetrated through the courtyard to the outer door, when some females, looking carelessly out of a latticed window above, beckoned me not to enter . . .

The remains of the wall that formerly encircled the town are still partially visible, though overgrown with weeds. We traced it to some distance; it has been above two feet thick, and seems to have enclosed a very considerable space. Captain B—— justly re-

From James Prior, *Voyage along the Eastern Coast of Africa, etc.* (London: 1819).

marked, as we walked along, turning the grass to one side, in following the line of the foundation, that the older writers gave such flattering accounts of the importance of this city in the days of Da Gama, as, from present appearances, to be scarcely worthy of credit. The people were said to be numerous, civilized and wealthy; the city extensive and fortified, its habitations elegant, and public buildings numerous. This picture, though partly true, was probably exaggerated, like some others of the early discoveries; yet there are several heaps of ruins . . .

Songo Mnara

Within these few days we made a small party in an excursion on the main in a new direction. The tide being low, we landed at a short distance from the ship, on a flat of mud, which, at its junction with the shore, was so thickly bound with mangroves, that we had to walk above a mile, sinking to the calf of the leg, to gain a fair opening into the country . . .

The country preserves the same aspect of an uncultivated waste; man, as he exists here, seems neither to have the taste nor talent to tenant it. Yet we fancied there were faint traces of former industry and population scattered here and there, and that wars, or the detestable slave trade, had carried off the wretched inhabitants, whom it will now be impossible to replace . . .

In returning we discovered a large well, situated in an extensive copse, which had been formerly enclosed by a wall, part of which was still standing. The well seemed about twenty-five feet in depth and ten in diameter, apparently hollowed out of a soft, calcareous rock, while from the bottom grew a tree, now in a great measure decayed, affording steps by which an attendant descended, and found the water dirty, ill-tasted, and small in quantity, though bearing traces of having been formerly of much more importance. Further on, towards Pagoda Point, appeared several decayed huts, tenanted by bats and reptiles, two small burying-grounds amid a cluster of small trees, and, about a mile distant, the ruins of regular stone edifices, which, appearing unexpectedly, induced Captain B——, Mons. S——, and myself, to revisit them next day.

The first object was a small cemetery, about forty feet square, enclosed with stone, and raised two feet above the ground; the graves were convexly raised, as in Europe, with stones at the head and feet, the bodies lying east and west, but no trace that we could find of inscriptions. To the eastern end of this enclosure was attached the remains of what appeared to have been a place of worship, about twenty-three feet by twelve. The walls now remaining seemed about sixteen feet high, built of stone, cemented by mortar formed of the bastard coral, or madrepore, and in which were wedged many pieces of cocoa-nut shell, that seemed of no other use than as emblems, probably of the value of the divine gifts, as they crumbled into dust on being touched. An arched door in front, and two in the rear, formed the entrances, and a circular white stone raised above the ground may, perhaps, have received the inclined knee of many an humble suppliant for divine mercy. Behind the ruin is a steep descent to a bed of mud, thickly lined with mangroves, which, though seemingly dry, forms an island at high-water, that, at the conclusion of the first day's excursion, occasioned us some uneasiness.

Two or three hundred yards from this spot lie the ruins of a stone building, larger than any at present possessed by the Quiloans [the people of Kilwa], except the residence of the sultan. Its apartments have been numerous, some large, others smaller, and a third class, with still minuter divisions, separated by thick walls, but opening at one end into a passage common to all. The walls, at least the present remains, are broad, though not so firmly built as those of the smaller edifice, and judging from the quantity of rubbish, their height must have been considerable. Several thick trees, of a spungy texture, issue not only from among the fallen ruins, but from the substance of the walls which seem held together merely by clay. These form various convolutions, and, by a kind of heterogeneous union, living wood seems inseparably combined and coexistent with stone. Captain B—— thought he could distinguish the remains of Saxon arches; but this resemblance is probably accidental . . .

W. F. W. OWEN

After the Deluge

Captain W. F. W. Owen, Royal Navy, has a place of his own in the nineteenth-century history of the East Coast, but it refers much more to the British than the African side of it. He began his service on the Coast with the making of Admiralty surveys and noticed, as had Prior and Beaver, how sadly the seaward country had declined from a former prosperity.

[1821-1826] Quilimane [on the coast of modern Mozambique] is now the greatest mart for slaves on the east coast. They are purchased with blue dangarees, coloured cloths, arms, gunpowder, brass and pewter, red coloured beads in imitation of coral, cutlery, and various other articles . . .

The riches of Quilimane consisted, in a trifling degree, of gold and silver, but principally of grain, which was produced in such quantities as to supply Mozambique. But the introduction of the slave trade stopped the pursuits of industry, and changed those places where peace and agriculture had formerly reigned into a seat of war and bloodshed. Contending tribes are now constantly striving to obtain by mutual conflict prisoners as slaves for sale to the Portuguese, who excite these wars and fatten on the blood and wretchedness they produce. The slave trade has been a blight on its prosperity; for at present Quilimane and the Portuguese possessions in the whole colony of the Rios de Senna [i.e., the Lower Zambezi] do not supply themselves with sufficient corn for their own consumption . . .

[Of Kilwa:] A miserable village, scarcely visited or known, oc-

From Capt. W. F. W. Owen, R.N.: *Narrative of Voyages to Explore the Shores of Africa, Arabia and Madagascar* (2 vols., London: 1833).

cupies its site, and the wretched Arab hovels of the present day are blended among the ruins of the once respectable and opulent city of former years . . .

It is really melancholy to contemplate the devastations that the monopolizing spirit of mankind has produced on the east coast of Africa; wherever we went, even in the most obscure harbours, we could trace the remains of former wealth and civilization, contrasted strongly with present poverty and barbarism.

ABDULLAH BEN NASIR

Lament for Greatness

Composed between about 1810 and 1820, the *Utendi wa Inkishafi* of Abdullah ben Nasir of Pate has become the best known — or rather the least ill-known — of Swahili poems. Translated into English by Hichens as "The Soul's Awakening," the poem has been rendered anew by Dr. Lyndon Harries, from whose version I draw this extract. *Al Inkishafi* is not only a lament for the past glory of Swahili civilization but a warning to all who seek their salvation by laying up treasure on earth.

How many rich men have you seen
who shone like the sun
who had control of the weapons of war
and stored up silver and gold?

All the world paid them homage
and their world was straight ahead of them
they walked with heads held disdainfully
and eyes closed in scorn.

From Abdullah ben Nasir, *Utendi wa Inkishafi*, translated in Lyndon Harries, *Swahili Poetry* (Oxford: 1962).

Swinging their arms and arching their necks
while behind and in front crowds accompanied them
everywhere they live there are seats of honour
and troops of soldiers attend them.

Their lighted houses were aglow
with lamps of crystal and brass
the nights were as the day
beauty and honour surrounded them.

They decorated (their houses) with choice porcelain
and every goblet was engraved
and in the midst they put crystal pitchers
amongst the decorations that glittered . . .

Now they lie in a town of finger's span
with no fine curtains nor cushions
and their bodies are destroyed
for the constraint of the grave has come upon them . . .

Their lighted mansions are uninhabited
the young of bats cling up above
you hear no whisperings nor shoutings
spiders crawl over the beds.

The wall-niches for porcelain in the houses
are now the resting-place for nestlings
owls hoot within the house . . .

ARNAULD D'ABBADIE
On the Meaning of Gifts

Arnauld d'Abbadie reached Ethiopia in 1837, some sixty years after Bruce. His memoirs share much of Bruce's vivacity and savor, and make a valuable picture of the Ethiopians and their country.

One morning the Prince asked me to choose a horse from among those he daily received in tribute . . .

"In Gojam," he said to me, "every self-respecting man has a war horse except for the priests, and it is wrong that you should be without one" . . . I noticed several fine horses but by a remnant of European reticence, made no sign that any of them pleased me. I should much rather have learned how to handle them like their own cavaliers, but that was more than the Prince's liberality could do for me . . . [In the evening the Prince sent d'Abbadie an excellent horse.] My acquaintances now came to congratulate me [on receiving this horse]. I was of course grateful to the Prince for his generosity and courtesy, but as yet I did not understand their meaning, nor the eagerness of those about me who now adopted a more affectionate familiarity.

In this feudal country, however, men are united by an infinity of ties which would count for nothing in Europe. They live together in a reciprocal dependence and solidarity which they value highly and consider a matter of pride, and which influence all they do. A man freed from all subjection is in their eyes outside the social order; that is how they consider a stranger. In accepting a mule from Dedjasmatch I had already, by the customs of the country, entered into a moral obligation towards him. But in re-

From Arnauld d'Abbadie, *Douze Ans dans la Haute-Ethiopie* (Paris: 1868), vol. 1, p. 263. Translated by B. Davidson.

ceiving a war horse I became, in the eyes of his men, the man of their master; I was obliged to follow him, and at least for a certain time to share in his fortunes, bad or good. No matter how much good will they might have shown me until now, I had nonetheless been for them like a being apart, like one without any social relationship with them. But from now on I was going to share in their duties and their rights. I was no longer for them a stranger in the old and hostile sense of the word. I became their comrade, their companion . . .

MUNGO PARK
To the Niger

"My dear friend Mr. Anderson and likewise Mr. Scott are both dead, but though all the Europeans who are with me should die, and though I were myself half dead, I would still persevere; and if I could not succeed in the object of my journey, I would at least die on the Niger." Thus Mungo Park in 1805, writing back to London from the heart of West Africa before departing on the final and fatal part of his quest for the river's mouth. Of the heroes of that cataclysmic year, England has placed Nelson, dying in the battle of Trafalgar, at the head of her list; yet if courage and self-sacrifice are any test of greatness, Park surely deserves to stand beside Nelson. He had left the Gambia with forty-three Europeans; at Sansanding on the Upper Niger he had only four, and one of these was no longer fully sane. All the rest had died on the journey. Yet Park persisted. A few weeks later — or was it months? there is no means of being sure — he and his companions were also dead.

Park must have a leading place in any anthology of West African travel for the quality of his writing, the importance of what he had to say, and the initiating stimulus of what he did. In a real sense he

From Mungo Park, *Travels in the Interior Districts of Africa, etc.* (London: 1799). Long extracts are reproduced in a good cheap abridgment by the Everyman Library, 1954.

opened the nineteenth century with an unforgettable challenge to his fellow-countrymen — and hence to other Europeans — that they should at last penetrate the mysteries of inner Africa; and it is safe to say that no great traveler of the period now opening will have made his journeys without a more than occasional memory of Mungo Park to carry with him and encourage him. Park has therefore a special importance to a period in African history when the interest and influence of Europe were increasingly felt.

The following extracts are from the first of his two journeys, completed in 1797. We find him as he leaves the Gambia and proceeds eastward to what is now the Republic of Mali.

The King of Bondou

[1795] I took my interpreter with me, and followed the messenger till we got quite out of the town, and crossed some cornfields: when, suspecting some trick, I stopped, and asked the guide whither he was going. Upon which he pointed to a man sitting under a tree at some little distance, and told me that the king frequently gave audience in that retired manner, in order to avoid a crowd of people; and that nobody but myself and my interpreter must approach him. When I advanced, the king desired me to come and sit by him upon the mat; and after hearing my story, on which he made no observation, he asked if I wished to purchase any slaves, or gold: being answered in the negative, he seemed rather surprised, but desired me to come to him in the evening, and he would give me some provisions.

This monarch was called Almami, a Moorish name, though I was told that he was not a Mahomedan, but a Kafir, or Pagan. I had heard that he had acted towards Major Houghton with great unkindness, and caused him to be plundered. His behaviour, therefore, towards myself at this interview, though much more civil than I expected, was far from freeing me from uneasiness. I still apprehended some double dealing; and as I was now entirely in his power, I thought it best to smooth the way by a present; accordingly I took with me in the evening one canister of gunpowder, some amber, tobacco, and my umbrella; and, as I considered that my bundles would inevitably be searched, I concealed some few articles in the roof of the hut where I lodged, and I put on my new blue coat, in order to preserve it.

All the houses belonging to the king and his family are surrounded by a lofty mud wall, which converts the whole into a kind of citadel. The interior is subdivided into different courts. At the first place of entrance I observed a man standing with a musket on his shoulder; and I found the way to the presence very intricate, leading through many passages, with sentinels placed at the different doors. When we came to the entrance of the court in which the king resides, both my guide and interpreter, according to custom, took off their sandals; and the former pronounced the king's name aloud, repeating it till he was answered from within.

We found the monarch sitting upon a mat, and two attendants with him. I repeated what I had before told him concerning the object of my journey, and my reasons for passing through his country. He seemed, however, but half satisfied. The notion of traveling for curiosity was quite new to him. He thought it impossible, he said, that any man in his senses would undertake so dangerous a journey, merely to look at the country and its inhabitants; however, when I offered to show him the contents of my portmanteau, and everything belonging to me, he was convinced; and it was evident that his suspicion had arisen from a belief that every white man must of necessity be a trader. When I had delivered my presents, he seemed well pleased, and was particularly delighted with the umbrella, which he repeatedly furled and unfurled, to the great admiration of himself and his two attendants, who could not for some time comprehend the use of this wonderful machine. After this I was about to take my leave, when the king, desiring me to stop awhile, began a long preamble in favour of the whites, extolling their immense wealth and good dispositions. He next proceeded to an eulogium on my blue coat, of which the yellow buttons seemed particularly to catch his fancy: and he concluded by entreating me to present him with it; assuring me, for my consolation under the loss of it, that he would wear it on all public occasions, and inform every one who saw it of my great liberality towards him. The request of an African prince, in his own dominions, particularly when made to a stranger, comes little short of a command. It is only a way of obtaining by gentle means what he can, if he pleases, take by force; and, as it was against my interest to offend him by a refusal, I very quietly took off my coat, the only good one in my possession, and laid it at his feet.

In return for my compliance, he presented me with great plenty of provisions, and desired to see me again in the morning. I accordingly attended, and found him sitting upon his bed. He told me he was sick, and wished to have a little blood taken from him; but I had no sooner tied up his arm, and displayed the lancet, than his courage failed, and he begged me to postpone the operation till the afternoon, as he felt himself, he said, much better than he had been, and thanked me kindly for my readiness to serve him. He then observed that his women were very desirous to see me, and requested that I would favour them with a visit. An attendant was ordered to conduct me, and I had no sooner entered the court appropriated to the ladies, than the whole seraglio surrounded me, some begging for physic, some for amber, and all of them desirous of trying that great African specific, blood-letting. They were ten or twelve in number, most of them young and handsome, and wearing on their heads ornaments of gold, and beads of amber.

They rallied me with a good deal of gaiety on different subjects, particularly upon the whiteness of my skin, and the prominency of my nose. They insisted that both were artificial. The first, they said, was produced when I was an infant, by dipping me in milk; and they insisted that my nose had been pinched every day till it had acquired its present unsightly and unnatural conformation. On my part, without disputing my own deformity, I paid them many compliments on African beauty. I praised the glossy jet of their skins, and the lovely depression of their noses; but they said that flattery, or (as they emphatically termed it) honey mouth, was not esteemed in Bondou. In return, however, for my company or my compliments (to which, by the way, they seemed not so insensible as they affected to be), they presented me with a jar of honey and some fish, which were sent to my lodging, and I was desired to come again to the king a little before sunset.

"Broad as the Thames at Westminster"

[1796] Early in the morning we again set forward. [Park is now in the country of the Bambara, and about to reach the Niger, the great aim of his journey.] The roads were wet and slippery; but the country was very beautiful, abounding with rivulets, which were increased by the rain into rapid streams. About ten o'clock we came to the ruins of a village, which had been destroyed by war about six months before; and in order to prevent any town from being built there in future, the large Bentang tree, under which the natives spent the day, had been burned down, the wells filled up, and everything that could make the spot desirable completely destroyed.

About noon my horse was so much fatigued that I could not keep up with my companions; I therefore dismounted, and desired them to ride on, telling them that I would follow as soon as my horse had rested a little. But I found them unwilling to leave me. The lions, they said, were very numerous in those parts, and though they might not so readily attack a body of people, they would soon find out an individual. It was therefore agreed that one of the company should stay with me to assist in driving my horse, while the others passed on to Galloo to procure lodgings, and collect grass for the horses before night. Accompanied by this worthy Negro, I drove my horse before me, until about four o'clock, when we came in sight of Galloo, a considerable town, standing in a fertile and beautiful valley surrounded with high rocks.

As my companions had thoughts of settling in this neighbourhood, they had a fine sheep given them by the Dooty; and I was fortunate enough to procure plenty of corn for my horse. Here they blow upon elephants' teeth when they announce evening prayers, in the same manner as at Kemmoo.

Early next morning [July 14], having first returned many thanks to our landlord for his hospitality, while my fellow travelers offered up their prayers that he might never want, we set forward, and about three o'clock arrived at Moorja, a large town, famous for its trade in salt, which the Moors bring here in great quantities to exchange for corn and cotton cloth. As most of the people here are Mahomedans, it is not allowed to the Kaffirs to drink beer, which they call Neo-dello (corn spirit), except in certain houses. In one of these I saw about twenty people sitting round large vessels of this beer with the greatest conviviality, many of them in a state of intoxication. As corn is plentiful, the inhabitants are very liberal to strangers. I believe we had as much corn and milk sent us by different people as would have been sufficient for three times our number; and though we remained here two days, we experienced no diminution of their hospitality.

On the morning of the 16th we again set forward, accompanied by a coffle of fourteen asses, loaded with salt, bound for Sansanding. The road was particularly romantic, between two rocky hills; but the Moors sometimes lie in wait here to plunder strangers. As soon as we had reached the open country, the master of the salt coffle thanked us for having staid with him so long, and now desired us to ride on. The sun was almost set before we reached Datliboo. In the evening we had a most tremendous tornado. The house in which we lodged being flat-roofed, admitted the rain in streams. The floor was soon ankle deep, the fire extinguished and we were left to pass the night upon some bundles of firewood that happened to lie in a corner . . .

We departed from Datliboo, and about ten o'clock passed a large coffle returning from Segu with corn, hoes, mats, and other household utensils. At five o'clock we came to a large village, where we intended to pass the night, but the Dooty would not receive us. When we departed from this place, my horse was so much fatigued that I was under the necessity of driving him, and it was dark before we reached Fanimboo, a small village; the Dooty of which no sooner heard that I was a white man than he brought out three old muskets, and was much disappointed when he was told that I could not repair them . . .

We continued our journey; but, owing to a light supper the preceding night, we felt ourselves rather hungry this morning, and endeavoured to procure some corn at a village, but without success. The towns were now more numerous, and the land that is not employed in cultivation affords excellent pasturage for large herds of cattle; but owing to the great concourse of people daily going to and returning from Segu, the inhabitants are less hospitable to strangers.

My horse becoming weaker and weaker every day, was now of very little service to me; I was obliged to drive him before me for the greater part of the day, and did not reach Geosorro until eight o'clock in the evening . . . I found my companions wrangling with the Dooty, who had absolutely refused to give or sell them any provisions; and as none of us had tasted victuals for the last twenty-four hours, we were by no means disposed to fast another day, if we could help it. But finding our entreaties without effect, and being very much fatigued, I fell asleep, from which I was awakened, about midnight, with the joyful information, *"kinnenata"* (the victuals is come). This made the remainder of the night pass away pleasantly; and at daybreak, July 19th, we resumed our journey, proposing to stop at a village called Doolinkeaboo, for the night following. My fellow-travelers, having better horses than myself, soon left me, and I was walking barefoot, driving my horse, when I was met by a coffle of slaves, about seventy in number, coming from Segu. They were tied together by their necks with thongs of a bullock's hide, twisted like a rope; seven slaves upon a thong, and a man with a musket between every seven. Many of the slaves were ill-conditioned, and a great number of them women. In the rear came Sidi Mahomed's servant, whom I remembered to have seen at the camp of Benowm; he presently knew me, and told me that these slaves were going to Morocco, by the way of Ludamar, and the Great Desert.

In the afternoon, as I approached Doolinkeaboo, I met about twenty Moors on horseback, the owners of the slaves I had seen in the morning; they were well armed with muskets, and were very inquisitive concerning me, but not so rude as their countrymen generally are. From them I learned that Sidi Mahomed was not at Segu, but had gone to Kancaba for gold dust.

When I arrived at Doolinkeaboo, I was informed that my fellow-travelers had gone on, but my horse was so much fatigued that I could not possibly proceed after them. The Dooty of the town, at my request, gave me a draught of water, which is generally looked upon as an earnest of greater hospitality; and I had no doubt of making up for the toils of the day by a good supper and a sound sleep; unfortunately I had neither one nor the other. The night was rainy and tempestuous, and the Dooty limited his hospitality to the draught of water . . .

In the morning I endeavoured, both by entreaties and threats, to procure some victuals from the Dooty, but in vain. I even begged some corn from one of his female slaves, as she was washing it at the well, and had the mortification to be refused. However, when the Dooty was gone to the fields, his wife sent me a handful of meal, which I mixed with water, and drank for breakfast. About eight o'clock I departed from Doolinkeaboo, and at noon stopped a few minutes at a large *korree*, where I had some milk given me by the Foulahs. And hearing that two Negroes were going from thence to Segu, I was happy to have their company, and we set out immediately. About four o'clock we stopped at a small village, where one of the Negroes met with an acquaintance, who invited us to a sort of public entertainment, which was conducted with more than common propriety. A dish made of sour milk and meal, called Sinkatoo, and beer made from their corn, was distributed with great liberality, and the women were admitted into the society — a circumstance I had never before observed in Africa. There was no compulsion, every one was at liberty to drink as he pleased; they nodded to each other when about to drink, and on setting down the calabash, commonly said *berka* (thank you). Both men and women appeared to be somewhat intoxicated, but they were far from being quarrelsome.

Departing from thence, we passed several large villages, where I was constantly taken for a Moor, and became the subject of much merriment to the Bambarrans; who seeing me drive my horse before me, laughed heartily at my appearance. He has been at Mecca, says one, you may see that by his clothes; another asked me if my horse was sick; a third wished to purchase it, etc.; so that I believe the very slaves were ashamed to be seen in my company. Just before it was dark, we took up our lodging for the night at a small village, where I procured some victuals for myself, and some corn for my horse, at the moderate price of a button, and was told that I should see the Niger (which the Negroes called

Jolliba, or the great water) early the next day. The lions are here very numerous; the gates are shut a little after sunset, and nobody allowed to go out. The thoughts of seeing the Niger in the morning, and the troublesome buzzing of mosquitoes, prevented me from shutting my eyes during the night; and I had saddled my horse and was in readiness before daylight; but, on account of the wild beasts, we were obliged to wait until the people were stirring, and the gates opened. This happened to be a market-day at Segu, and the roads were everywhere filled with people carrying different articles to sell. We passed four large villages, and at eight o'clock saw the smoke over Segu.

As we approached the town, I was fortunate enough to overtake the fugitive Kaartans, to whose kindness I had been so much indebted in my journey through Bambarra. They readily agreed to introduce me to the king; and we rode together through some marshy ground, where, as I was anxiously looking around for the river, one of them called out, *geo affili* (see the water), and looking forwards, I saw with infinite pleasure the great object of my mission — the long sought-for majestic Niger, glittering to the morning sun, as broad as the Thames at Westminster, and flowing slowly to the eastward. I hastened to the brink, and, having drank of the water, lifted up my fervent thanks in prayer to the Great Ruler of all things, for having thus far crowned my endeavours with success . . .

Segu

Segu, the capital of Bambarra, at which I had now arrived, consists, properly speaking, of four distinct towns; two on the northern bank of the Niger, called Segu Korro and Segu Boo; and two on the southern bank, called Segu Soo Korro and Segu See Korro. They are all surrounded with high mud walls; the houses are built of clay, of a square form, with flat roofs; some of them have two stories, and many of them are whitewashed. Besides these buildings, Moorish mosques are seen in every quarter; and the streets, though narrow, are broad enough for every useful purpose, in a country where wheel-carriages are entirely unknown.

From the best inquiries I could make, I have reason to believe that Segu contains altogether about thirty thousand inhabitants. The king of Bambarra constantly resides at Segu See Korro; he employs a great many slaves in conveying people over the river, and the money they receive (though the fare is only ten cowrie shells for each individual) furnishes a considerable revenue to the king in the course of a year. The canoes are of a singular construction, each of them being formed of the trunks of two large trees, rendered concave, and joined together, not side by side, but endways; the junction being exactly across the middle of the canoe; they are therefore very long and disproportionably narrow, and have neither decks nor masts; they are, however, very roomy; for I observed in one of them four horses, and several people crossing over the river.

When we arrived at this ferry, with a view to pass over to that part of the town in which the king resides, we found a great number waiting for a passage; they looked at me with silent wonder, and I distinguished, with concern, many Moors among them. There were three different places of embarkation, and the ferrymen were very diligent and expeditious; but, from the crowd of people, I could not immediately obtain a passage; and sat down upon the bank of the river, to wait for a more favourable opportunity. The view of this extensive city; the numerous canoes upon the river; the crowded population, and the cultivated state of the surrounding country, formed altogether a prospect of civilization and magnificence, which I little expected to find in the bosom of Africa.

I waited more than two hours without having an opportunity of crossing the river; during which time, the people who had crossed carried information to Mansong, the king, that a white man was waiting for a passage, and was coming to see him. He immediately sent over one of his chief men, who informed me that the king could not possibly see me, until he knew what had brought me into his country; and that I must not presume to cross the river without the king's permission. He therefore advised me to lodge at a distant village, to which he pointed, for the night; and said that in the morning he would give me further instructions how to conduct myself. This was very discouraging. However, as there was no remedy, I set off for the village; where I found to my great mortification, that no person would admit me into his house. I was regarded with astonishment and fear, and was obliged to sit all day without victuals, in the shade of a tree; and the night threatened to be very uncomfortable, for the wind rose, and there was great appearance of a heavy rain; and the wild beasts are so very numerous in the neighbourhood, that I should have been under the necessity of climbing up the tree, and resting among the branches.

About sunset, however, as I was preparing to pass the night in this manner, and had turned my horse loose, that he might graze at liberty, a woman, returning from the labours of the field, stopped to observe me, and perceiving that I was weary and dejected, inquired into my situation, which I briefly explained to her; whereupon, with looks of great compassion, she took up my saddle and bridle, and told me to follow her. Having conducted me into her hut, she lighted up a lamp, spread a mat on the floor, and told me I might remain there for the night. Finding that I was very hungry, she said she would procure me something to eat. She accordingly went out, and returned in a short time with a very fine fish; which having caused to be half-broiled upon some embers, she gave me for supper.

The rites of hospitality being thus performed towards a stranger in distress, my worthy benefactress (pointing to the mat, and telling me I might sleep there without apprehension) called to the female part of her family, who had stood gazing on me all the while in fixed astonishment, to resume their task of spinning cotton; in which they continued to employ themselves [a] great part of the night. They lightened their labour by songs, one of which was composed extempore; for I was myself the subject of it. It was sung by one of the young women, the rest joining in a sort of chorus. The air was sweet and plaintive, and the words, literally translated, were these: — "the winds roared, and the rains fell. The poor white man, faint and weary, came and sat under our tree. He has no mother to bring him milk; no wife to grind his corn." Chorus — "Let us pity the white man; no mother has he," etc., etc. Trifling as this recital may appear to the reader, to a person in my situation, the circumstance was affecting in the highest degree. I was oppressed by such unexpected kindness; and sleep fled from my eyes. In the morning I presented my compassionate landlady with two of the four brass buttons which remained on my waistcoat; the only recompense I could make her.

A *Slave Coffle*

[1797] My clothes were by this time become so very ragged, that I was almost ashamed to appear out of doors; but Karfa, on the day after his arrival, generously presented me with such a garment and trousers as are commonly worn in the country.

The slaves which Karfa had brought with him were all of them prisoners of war; they had been taken by the Bambarran army in the kingdoms of Wassela and Kaarta, and carried to Segu, where some of them had remained three years in irons. From Segu they were sent, in company with a number of other captives, up the Niger in two large canoes, and offered for sale at Yamina, Bammakoo, and Kancaba, at which places the greater number of the captives were bartered for gold dust, and the remainder sent forward to Kankaree.

Eleven of them confessed to me that they had been slaves from their infancy; but the other two refused to give any account of their former condition. They were all very inquisitive; but they viewed me at first with looks of horror, and repeatedly asked if my countrymen were cannibals. They were very desirous to know what became of the slaves after they had crossed the salt water. I told them that they were employed in cultivating the land, but they would not believe me; and one of them, putting his hand upon the ground, said, with great simplicity, "Have you really got such ground as this to set your feet upon?" A deeply rooted idea that the whites purchase Negroes for the purpose of devouring them, or of selling them to others, that they may be devoured hereafter, naturally makes the slaves contemplate a journey towards the coast with great terror, insomuch that the Slatees are forced to keep them constantly in irons, and watch them very closely to prevent their escape. They are commonly secured by putting the right leg of one and the left of another into the same pair of fetters. By supporting the fetters with a string, they can walk, though very slowly. Every four slaves are likewise fastened together by the necks with a strong rope or twisted thongs; and in the night an additional pair of fetters is put on their hands, and sometimes a light iron chain passed round their necks.

Such of them as evince marks of discontent, are secured in a different manner. A thick billet of wood is cut about three feet long, and a smooth notch being made upon one side of it, the ankle of the slave is bolted to the smooth part by means of a strong iron staple, one prong of which passes on each side of the ankle. All these fetters and bolts are made from native iron; in the present case they were put on by the blacksmith as soon as the slaves arrived from Kancaba, and were not taken off until the morning on which the coffle departed for Gambia . . .

UTHMAN DAN FODIO
Reformation

The great upheavals of the Western Sudan in the first half of the century may be said to have begun, at least in their main part, with the rebellion of Fulani people (in modern Niger and Northern Nigeria) against their Hausa or Habe overlords. This rebellion had many social motivations but took the form, characteristic of the place and period, of jihad, a war of religion. It began in 1804 and was associated with three outstanding men in the Hausa state of Gobir: *Shehu* (or Sheikh) Uthman dan Fodio (died 1817), his brother Abdullahu (died 1829), and his son Muhammad Bello (died 1837).

These reformers wrote enormously. Many of their works have been preserved. As many as 258 surviving books and pamphlets on a wide variety of topics — Koranic study, medicine, diplomacy, rules for good government — are attributed to these distinguished men, and more

From the *Kitab al-Farq*, attributed to Uthman dan Fodio, translated by M. Hiskett in *Bulletin* of the School of Oriental and African Studies (London: 1960), part 3, p. 558.

may yet be found. Only lately have students of West African history turned their attention to this copious literature. "At present," writes H. F. C. Smith, "it is possible to say that in outline the thought of the leaders followed a classical pattern of Islamic revivalism. In their search for the ideal society and the just ruler, they looked back to a previous golden age in the history of *dar al-Islam* [*Pax Islamica* as we might call it], and their aim was to re-create in the Western Sudan the society of the rightly guided caliphate." They were trying, that is, to reconstruct the political and social order of the Western Sudan in line with the great precedents of its past. Severe moralists, they repeatedly attacked their Hausa (Habe) opponents, whom they overthrew, for "corruption and misgovernment," as the following extracts interestingly show.

Much that these men and their contemporaries had to say is historically of the highest possible interest, obscure though it may often seem. Here then are three fragments to whet the appetite for more: the first from one of Uthman dan Fodio's minor works, the second from the *Tazyin al-Waraqat* of Abdullah Ibn Muhammad, and the third from Muhammad Bello.

The Old Habe Kingdoms

One of the ways of their government [that is, of the Hausa or Habe kings] is succession to the emirate by hereditary right and by force to the exclusion of consultation. And one of the ways of their government is the building of their sovereignty upon three things: the people's persons, their honour, and their possessions; and whomsoever they wish to kill or exile or violate his honour or devour his wealth they do so in pursuit of their lusts, without any right in the Shari'a. One of the ways of their government is their imposing on the people monies not laid down by the Shari'a, being those which they call *janghali* and *kurdin ghari* and *kurdin salla*. One of the ways of their governments is their intentionally eating whatever food they wish, whether it is religiously permitted or forbidden, and wearing whatever clothes they wish, whether religiously permitted or forbidden, and drinking what beverages [*ta'am*] they wish, whether religiously permitted or forbidden, and riding whatever riding beasts they wish, whether religiously permitted or forbidden, and taking what women they wish without marriage contract, and living in decorated palaces, whether religiously permitted or forbidden, and spreading soft (decorated) carpets as they wish, whether religiously permitted or forbidden . . .

One of the ways of their governments is to compel the people to serve in their armies, even though they are Muslims, and they call it *gharghadi,* and whosoever does not go, they impose upon him a money payment, not imposed by the Shari'a. One of the ways of their government which is also well known, is that if you have an adversary (in law) and he precedes you to them, and gives them some money, then your word will not be accepted by them, even though they know for a certainty of your truthfulness, unless you give them more than your adversary gave. One of the ways of their government is to shut the door in the face of the needy. One of the ways of their governments is their forbidding to the worshippers of God part of that which is legal for them, such as the veiling of women, which is incumbent upon them, and turbans for men, which is *sunna* for them, and they call this forbidding *duka.* One of the ways of their government which is also well known is that they will not abandon the custom which they found their forebears practicing, even though it is evil. One of the ways of their government is the putting of dust upon their heads when giving a greeting, and it is an evil custom, as in *al-Kibrit al-ahmar,* where the author says "because it is a sign of excess."

One of the ways of their government is their being occupied with doing vain things (continuously) by night or by day, without legal purpose, such as beating drums, and lutes, and kettledrums. The Muslims only beat the kettledrum, and similar instruments for a legal purpose, such as wishing to gather the army together, or to signify its departure, or the setting up of camp, and its arrival, and as a sign of the advent of the festival, as the kettledrum is beaten for the advent of 'Id al-adha, and they confine themselves to what necessity requires. One of the ways of their governments is the giving of a gift to one who conducts them before the ruler. . . .

Five Rules of Government

. . . and I say — and help is with God — the foundations of government are five things: the first is that authority shall not be given to one who seeks it. The second is the necessity for consultation. The third is the abandoning of harshness. The fourth is justice. The fifth is good works. And as for its ministers, they are four. (The first) is a trustworthy wazir to wake the ruler if he sleeps, to make him see if he is blind, and to remind him if he forgets, and the greatest misfortune for the government and the subjects is that they should be denied honest wazirs. And among the conditions pertaining to the wazir is that he should be steadfast in compassion to the people, and merciful towards them. The second of the ministers of government is a judge whom the blame of a blamer cannot overtake concerning the affairs of God. The third is a chief of police who shall obtain justice for the weak from the strong. The fourth is a tax collector who shall discharge his duties and not oppress the subjects . . .

ABDULLAH IBN MUHAMMAD
Against Bad Rulers

Whose purpose is the ruling of the countries and their people
In order to obtain delights and acquire rank
According to the custom of the unbelievers and the titles of
   their sovereignty.
And the appointing of ignorant persons to the highest offices
And the collecting of concubines and fine clothes.
And horses that run in the towns, not on the battlefields.
And the devouring of the gifts of influence, booty, and bribery,

From Abdullah Ibn Muhammad, *Tazyin al-Waraqat*, edited, with translation and introductory study of the author's life and times, by M. Hiskett (Ibadan: 1963), p. 121.

And lutes and flutes, and the beating of drums.
And their activities weaken those charged with managing affairs.
And the country people make off from every side.
Their purpose is fleeing from the judge . . .
And the selling of free men, while in the market.
And some of them are posing as *qadis*, in the clothing of
   foxes . . .

MUHAMMAD BELLO
Jihad

To the Emir of Bauchi, Ya'qub bin Dadi, a thousand valedic-
tions and a thousand greetings.

After which, the reason for [this message] is to inform you of
our circumstances, and of what we are engaged in today of the important affairs of Islam and of the Muslims. That is, that we have
gone out in the direction of the North, because of the affair of the
beasts, and the foray against Tadaghaw with al-Jilani. We have
taken our equipment, consisting of tents of hide, and water-skins,
and all that is required for a journey.

We have ordered the expedition for the twentieth of Sha'ban,
and we commanded those of the brethren who adjoin us to follow
us, and to march out with us bringing their beasts and military
equipment. There is not to stay behind a single one of the owners
of beasts [*ashabu 'l-dawwabi'*], nor of the ghazis, whoever he may
be, excepting those who have embarked upon the campaign
against Banagha. The result is that we have imposed upon the
community at the present time one of two alternatives; either they
should join the ghazis on the Banagha front, and besiege it until
we arrive, if Allah so wills; or for whoever may prefer the expedi-

From Muhammad Bello, Sultan of Sokoto (1817-1837), a letter to the Emir
of Bauchi, translation of Arabic text by A. D. H. Bivar in *Bulletin* of the
School of Oriental and African Studies (London: 1960), part 2, p. 339.

tion to Tadaghaw to accompany us. As for the cattle-owning herdsmen [*al-ra'atu ashabu 'l-baqari*], not one of them must fail to join us, unless there is no help for it . . .

As for what is required of you yourself, you must follow our example — when this reaches you — and gird up your skirts for the sacred war [*jihad*] against the infidels upon your most important fronts and "let them find strength in you," and do not give way, and "do not be discouraged, for you shall have the upper hand"; or rather "a morning upon the road of Allah, or a day's march is better than this world, and what is in it." So do not turn aside from your resolve [*al-hazmi*] but be heroes of Allah [*rijjalu 'llahi*]. Incumbent on you too is the multiplication of your beasts, and the seeking out for them of grazing-grounds that are suited to them, since they are the instruments of the sacred war. Greetings.

AL HAJJI SA'ID
Muhammad Bello

The Hausa country flourished greatly under his rule. He spread respect for learning, and scholars came from different countries. He was very solicitous for their welfare . . . whether they came from east, west, south or north . . . He spent much time in writing; every time he finished one of his works he made it known to the public and had them read it, and then set himself to writing another volume . . . If anyone posed him a problem he made it at once the subject of a publication. If he found that such and such persons were in disagreement on a point, he at once composed a treatise on it . . . He supported himself by the fruits of his work, without asking for upkeep from the public purse . . . He was sym-

From al Hajji Sa'id, A *History of Sokoto*, translated here from the French version of the Arabic text of O. Houdas (Paris: 1901), p. 318. This writer was a Koranic official under Sultan Ali, son of Muhammad Bello, who reigned from 1837 to 1849. Houdas thought that Sa'id was possibly from the Masina region on the Middle Niger.

pathetic to the people and full of care for them, calm, patient, indifferent to the wealth of other men. A skillful administrator, he watched over the work of the *qadis*, quashed their judgments if these had been given under the influence of passion, never allowing them to grow slack in their work . . . Ruddy of complexion, tall, bald of head, wearing a long and tufted beard, such was his appearance . . .

THOMAS BOWDICH
At Kumasi

Early in this century the English on the Gold Coast became interested in the greatest inland power they knew, which was then Ashanti. Bowdich was sent on an official British mission to Kumasi, and saw this capital at the zenith of its wealth and influence.

[1817] We entered Kumasi at two o'clock . . . Upwards of five thousand people, the greater part warriors, met us with awful bursts of martial music . . . The smoke which encircled us from the incessant discharges of musquetry confined our glimpses to the foreground; and we were halted, while the captains performed their phyrric dance, in the centre of a circle formed by their warriors; where a confusion of flags, English, Dutch, and Danish, were waved and flourished in all directions . . . The dress of the captains was a war cap, with gilded rams' horns projecting in front, the sides extended beyond all proportion by immense plumes of eagles' feathers . . . Their vest was of red cloth, covered with fetishes and saphies in gold and silver . . . They wore loose cotton trowsers, with immense boots of a dull red leather, coming half way up the thigh . . .

From T. E. Bowdich, *Mission from Cape Coast to Ashantee* (London: 1819).

Our observations *en passant* had taught us to conceive a spectacle far exceeding our original expectations; but they had not prepared us for the extent and display of the scene which here burst upon us: an area of nearly a mile in circumference was crowded with magnificence and novelty. The king, his tributaries, and captains, were resplendent in the distance, surrounded by attendants of every description . . . More than a hundred bands burst [out] at once on our arrival, with the peculiar airs of their several chiefs; the horns flourished their defiances, with beating of innumerable drums and metal instruments, and then yielded for a while to the soft breathings of their long flutes . . . At least a hundred large umbrellas, or canopies, which could shelter thirty persons, were sprung up and down by the bearers with brilliant effect, being made of scarlet, yellow, and the most shewy cloths and silks, and crowned on the top with crescents, pelicans, elephants, barrels, and arms and swords of gold . . .

The caboceers, as did their superior captains and attendants, wore Ashanti cloths, of extravagant price from the costly foreign silks which had been unraveled to weave them in all the varieties of colour, as well as pattern; [these cloths] were of an incredible size and weight, and thrown over the shoulder exactly like a Roman toga; a small silk fillet generally encircles their temples, and massy gold necklaces, intricately wrought . . .

Four of the principal streets [of Kumasi] are half a mile long, and from fifty to one hundred yards wide. I observed them building one, and a line was stretched on each side to make it regular. The streets were all named, and a superior captain in charge of each . . . The Ashantis persisted that the population of Kumasi, when collected, was upwards of one hundred thousand . . . Perhaps [its] average resident population . . . is not more than from twelve to fifteen thousand . . . What surprised me most . . . was the discovery that every house had its cloacae, besides the common ones for the lower orders without the town. They were generally situated under a small archway in the most retired angle of the building, but not unfrequently upstairs, within a separate room like a small closet . . . the holes are of a small circumference, but dug to a surprising depth, and boiling water is daily poured down, which effectually prevents the least offense. The rubbish and offal of each house was burnt every morning at the back of the street, and they were as nice and cleanly in their dwellings as in their persons . . .

BRODIE CRUICKSHANK
Political Background

Arriving on the Gold Coast in 1834, Brodie Cruickshank remained there for eighteen years, and served as a magistrate and as British lieutenant-governor in 1853-1854. A Scottish merchant by origin and formation, he became interested in African political affairs and went to great pains, as his book reveals, to find out what they really implied and meant. His account of some forms of government in the interior and along the seaboard of the Gold Coast remains especially interesting, for it throws a broad light on the situation which had flowed from the pressures of two centuries of great involvement in the European slave trade; and it opens an early discussion on the nature of African forms of feudalism.

. . . By the treaty concluded with the king of Ashantee at the close of the war, the English [on the Gold Coast] obtained for their allies an acknowledgment of entire independence [from Ashantee overlordship]. Those countries . . . returned to the simple and original form of government, which had been in force previous to the subjection of their country by the Ashantees. It would be difficult, however, to define the nature of that government.

It was not a despotism, nor a constitutional monarchy, nor an oligarchy, nor a republic, but partook something of the qualities of each of these different forms, and depended much upon the in-

From Brodie Cruickshank, *Eighteen Years on the Gold Coast* (2 vols., London: 1853), vol. 1, p. 232.

dividual character and riches of the chief. It was, moreover, greatly modified by traditionary customs and precedents, which appear to define the extent of the chiefs' authority, as well as the privileges of the people, and to be equally binding on both. From this cause it is that we see a strange combination of despotic acts, with occasional instances of great freedom and equality, in which the authority of the chief seems nearly lost . . . But while the chief is thus checked in the general government of his country, his authority over his immediate retainers is absolute . . . The same feudal system prevails among the Denkeras . . . the Assins . . . the Abrahs . . . the Akims, Aquapims, and others . . .

Observation shows that in this country the principal source of feudal retainers has arisen from the necessity of obtaining a protector. Families and whole tribes, to avoid extirpation by war, have placed themselves under the wing of some powerful chief, who perhaps supported them in famine and shielded them in battle. Only a personal interest in the individuals whom he thus supported would have induced him to burden himself with their care; and he consequently expects, as a return for his protection, their ready and willing obedience as vassals. There are also instances of whole towns undergoing this vassalage, in return for money advanced to help them out of difficulties . . .

[Writing of the town governments of the Gold Coast seaboard, which have "an infinitely greater share of political liberty" — as did, in Cruickshank's comparison, the "free towns" of medieval Europe — he points out that] in the towns of Cape Coast, Anamaboe, Accra, and others situated under the guns of the European forts, or in the immediate vicinity of the sea, we find, as among the chiefs in the interior, an hereditary power vested in an individual, indiscriminately called king, chief, or principal cabboceer. He is the acknowledged head of the town, but has not, like the bush chief, any claim to the services of the inhabitants as vassals . . . He is, in fact, the chief magistrate of the town, presiding and assisting in council and in the judgment hall, but with a voice no whit more potential than his fellow-counselors and judges. These consist first of hereditary cabboceers, men of the principal rank in town, whose authority has been originally derived from the consequence which wealth has given to the first distinguished founder of the family . . .

In addition to the king and cabboceers, both the council and judgment seat are composed of the representatives of the people. The towns are invariably divided into departments or wards, and those residing within these divisions are formed into companies, who have each their distinctive flags, drums, and other equipments . . . There are instances of women, from some particular services, either of themselves or of their family, being promoted to the rank of captain [of a company] . . .

HEINRICH BARTH

The Western Sudan

For long years after its appearance Barth's great work was appreciated only by a handful of specialists. This curious public attitude to an outstanding explorer may probably be best explained in terms of the peculiar slant of European interest in Africa at that time, concentrated as this so greatly was on missionary enterprise. Three of the five volumes of his principal book appeared in 1857, the same year as Livingstone's *Missionary Travels*, but whereas Livingstone's single though substantial volume ran through twenty-two thousand copies in six months, Barth's first three volumes were published in an initial edition of only twelve hundred copies followed by another of one thousand, while one thousand copies were found to be enough for the fourth and fifth volumes (perhaps the most interesting and exciting of them all), which appeared in July 1858.* It may be added that Barth suffered an eclipse in Germany, his native land, as well. Even the 1952

From Heinrich Barth, *Travels and Discoveries in North and Central Africa, etc.* (5 vols., London: 1857-1858). These extracts are from vols. 2, 4 and 5. A good modern introduction to Barth, and an anthology of his writings so far as they concern Nigeria, is A. H. M. Kirk-Greene's *Barth's Travels in Nigeria* (Oxford: 1962).

* I am indebted for these figures to Longmans, Green & Co. Ltd., and John Murray Ltd., respectively the publishers of Barth and Livingstone.

edition of *Der Grosse Brockhaus,* appearing at a time when Barth's importance was widely recognized, gives him no more than fourteen lines. And we still await a complete republication of his West African travels.

Born in Hamburg in 1821, Heinrich Barth died at the age of forty-four. He traveled in North Africa and the Near East in 1845-1847, and went to the Western Sudan as a member of a British expedition in 1849, returning in 1855 with the first scholarly and comprehensive understanding of this vast region that any European had ever secured. We take up his story with his first arrival in the famous city of Kano, then known to the outside world only by vague report.

Kano in Mid-Century

[1851] Kano had been sounding in my ears now for more than a year; it had been one of the great objects of our journey as the central point of commerce, as a great storehouse of information, and as the point whence more distant regions might be most successfully attempted. At length, after nearly a year's exertions, I had reached it . . .

With regard to the growth of the town, we have express testimony that Dala was the most ancient quarter. The steep rocky hill, about 120 feet high, naturally afforded a secure retreat to the ancient inhabitants in case of sudden attack; but it is most probable that there was another or several separate villages within the wide expanse now encompassed by the wall, which rather exceeds than falls short of fifteen English miles . . .

The wall, just as it has been described by Captain Clapperton, is still kept in the best repair, and is an imposing piece of workmanship in this quarter of the world . . .

In estimating the population of the town at thirty thousand, I am certainly not above the truth. Captain Clapperton estimated it at from thirty thousand to forty thousand. The population, as might be expected in a place of great commercial resort, is of a rather mixed nature; but the chief elements in it are Kanuri or Bornu people, Hausawa, Fulbe or Fellani, and Nyffawa or Nupe; a good many Arabs also reside there, who by their commerce and their handicraft contribute a great deal to the importance of the place. The influx of foreigners and temporary residents is occasionally very great, so that the whole number of residents during the most busy time of the year (that is to say from January to April) may often amount to sixty thousand. The number of domestic slaves, of course, is very considerable; but I think it hardly equals, certainly does not exceed, that of the free men, for, while the wealthy have many slaves, the poorer class, which is far more numerous, have few or none. It would be very interesting to arrive at an exact estimate of the numbers of the conquering nation, in order to see the proportion in which they stand to the conquered. As for the town itself, their whole number, of every sex and age, does not, in my opinion, exceed four thousand; but with regard to the whole country I can give no opinion. [Barth is referring here to the Fulani and the Hausa peoples.]

The principal commerce of Kano consists in native produce, namely, the cotton cloth woven and dyed here or in the neighbouring towns, in the form of tobes or *rigona* (sing. *riga*); *turkedi*, or the oblong piece of dress of dark-blue colour worn by women; the *zenne* or plaid, of various colours; and the *rawani baki*, or black litham.

The great advantage of Kano is, that commerce and manufactures go hand in hand, and that almost every family has its share in them. There is really something grand in this kind of industry, which spreads to the north as far as Murzuk, Ghat, and even Tripoli; to the west, not only to Timbuktu, but in some degree even as far as the shores of the Atlantic, the very inhabitants of Arguin dressing in the cloth woven and dyed in Kano; to the east, all over Bornu, although there it comes into contact with the native industry of the country; and to the south it maintains a rivalry with the native industry of the I'gbira and I'gbo, while towards the southeast it invades the whole of 'Adamawa, and is only limited by the nakedness of the pagan sans-culottes, who do not wear clothing.

As for the supply sent to Timbuktu, this is a fact entirely overlooked in Europe, where people speak continually of the fine cotton cloth produced in that town, while in truth all the apparel of a decent character in Timbuktu is brought either from Kano or from

Sansandi; and how urgently this article is there demanded is amply shown by the immense circuit which the merchandise makes to avoid the great dangers of the direct road from Kano to Timbuktu traveled by me, the merchandise of Kano being first carried up to Ghat and even Ghadames [in the Northern Sahara], and thence taking its way to Timbuktu by Tawat.

I make the lowest estimate in rating this export to Timbuktu alone at three hundred camel-loads annually, worth sixty million *kurdi* in Kano — an amount which entirely remains in the country, and rebounds to the benefit of the whole population, both cotton and indigo being produced and prepared in the country.

In taking a general view of the subject, I think myself justified in estimating the whole produce of this manufacture, as far as it is sold abroad, at the very least at about three hundred million; and how great this national wealth is, will be understood by my readers when they know that, with from fifty to sixty thousand *kurdi*, or from four to five pounds sterling a year, a whole family may live in that country with ease, including every expense, even that of their clothing: and we must remember that the province is one of the most fertile spots on the earth, and is able to produce not only the supply of corn necessary for its population, but can also export, and that it possesses, besides, the finest pasture-grounds. In fact, if we consider that this industry is not carried on here as in Europe, in immense establishments, degrading man to the meanest condition of life, but that it gives employment and support to families without compelling them to sacrifice their domestic habits, we must presume that Kano ought to be one of the happiest countries in the world; and so it is as long as its governor, too often lazy and indolent, is able to defend its inhabitants from the cupidity of their neighbours, which of course is constantly stimulated by the very wealth of this country . . .

Finding the Tarikh es-Sudan

[1853] . . . I passed the time during my residence in this place [Gando] not quite uselessly, especially as I was so fortunate as to obtain here from a learned man of the name of Bokhari, a son of the late Mohammed Wani, a copy of that most valuable historical work of Ahmed Baba,* to which my friend 'Abd el Kader, in Sokoto, had first called my attention, but without being able to satisfy my curiosity; and I spent three or four days most pleasantly in extracting the more important historical data of this work, which opened to me quite a new insight into the history of the regions on the middle course of the Niger, whither I was bending my steps, exciting in me a far more lively interest than I had previously felt in a kingdom the great power of which, in former times, I here found set forth in very clear and distinct outlines, and I only lamented that I had not time enough to copy the whole.

Timbuktu

[1853] Thus the day broke which, after so many months' exertion, was to carry me [up the Niger] to the harbour of Timbuktu. We started at a tolerably early hour, crossing the broad sheet of the river, first in a northeasterly, then in an almost northerly direction, till finding ourselves opposite the small hamlet Tasakal, mentioned by Caillié, we began to keep along the windings of the northern bank which, from its low character, presented a very varying appearance, while a creek, separating from the trunk, entered the low ground . . .

We entered the branch of Korome, keeping along the grass which here grows in the river to a great extent, till we reached the village, consisting of nothing but temporary huts of reed, which, in the course of a few weeks, with the rising of the waters, were to be removed further inland. Notwithstanding its frail character, this poor little village was interesting on account of its wharfs, where a number of boats were repairing. The master of our own craft residing here (for all the boatmen on this river are serfs, or nearly in that condition), we were obliged to halt almost an hour and a half; but in order not to excite the curiosity of the people, I thought it prudent to remain in my boat. But even there I was incommoded with a great number of visitors, who were very anxious to know exactly what sort of person I was . . .

At length we lay to, and sending two of my people on shore, in

---

* Barth was mistaken. The author was es-Sa'di.

order to obtain quarters, I followed them as soon as possible, when I was informed that they had procured a comfortable dwelling for me. The house where I was lodged was a large and grand building (if we take into account the general relations of this country), standing on the very top of the mound on the slope of which the town is situated. It was of an oblong shape, consisting of very massive clay walls, which were even adorned, in a slight degree, with a rude kind of relief; and it included, besides two anterooms, an inner courtyard, with a good many smaller chambers, and an upper story. The interior, with its small stores of every kind, and its assortment of sheep, ducks, fowls, and pigeons, in different departments, resembled Noah's ark, and afforded a cheerful sight of homely comfort which had been preserved here from more ancient and better times, notwithstanding the exactions of Fulbe [Fulani] and Imoshagh [Tuareg of the Sahara].

Having taken possession of the two anterooms for my people and luggage, I endeavoured to make myself as comfortable as possible; while the busy landlady, a tall and stout personage, in the absence of her husband, a wealthy Songhay merchant, endeavoured to make herself agreeable, and offered me the various delicacies of her store for sale; but these were extremely scanty, the chief attraction to us, besides a small bowl of milk seasoned with honey, being some onions, of which I myself was not less in want than my people for seasoning our simple food; but fresh ones were not even to be got here, the article sold being a peculiar preparation which is imported from Sansandi, the onions, which are of very small size, being cut into slices and put in water, then pounded in a wooden mortar, dried again, and, by means of some butter, made up into a sort of round ball, which is sold in small pats of an inch and a half in diameter for five shells each: these are called *lawashi* in Fulfulde, or *gabu* in the Songhay language. Besides this article, so necessary for seasoning the food, I bought a little *bulanga*, or vegetable butter, in order to light up the dark room where I had taken up my quarters; but the night which I passed here was a very uncomfortable one, on account of the number of mosquitoes which infest the whole place.

Thus broke the 6th of September, a very important day for me, as it was to determine the kind of reception I was to meet in this quarter. But notwithstanding the uncertainty of my prospects, I felt cheerful and full of confidence; and, as I was now again firmly established on dry soil, I went early in the morning to see my horse, which had successfully crossed all the different branches lying between Kabara and Sarayamo; but I was sorry to find him in a very weak and emaciated condition.

While traversing the village, I was surprised at the many clay buildings which are to be seen here, amounting to between one hundred fifty and two hundred; however, these are not so much the dwellings of the inhabitants of Kabara themselves, but serve rather as magazines for storing up the merchandise belonging to the people of, and the foreign merchants residing in, Timbuktu and Sansandi. There are two small market places, one containing about twelve stalls or sheds, where all sorts of articles are sold, the other being used exclusively for meat. Although it was still early in the day, women were already busy boiling rice, which is sold in small portions, or made up into thin cakes boiled with *bulanga*, and sold for five shells each.

Almost all the inhabitants, who may muster about two thousand, are Songhay; but the authorities belong to the tribe of the Fulbe, whose principal wealth consists of cattle, the only exception being the office of the inspector of the harbour, — a very ancient office, repeatedly mentioned by Ahmed Baba — which at present is in the hands of Mulay Kasim, a sherif whose family is said to have emigrated originally from the Gharb or Morocco, but who has become so Sudanized that he has forgotten all his former knowledge of Arabic. On account of the cattle being driven to a great distance, I found that milk was very scarce and dear. The inhabitants cultivate a little rice, but have some cotton, besides *bamia*, or *Corchorus olitorius*, and melons of various descriptions.

Having returned to my quarters from my walk through the town, I had to distribute several presents to some people whom El Walati chose to represent as his brothers and friends. Having then given to himself a new, glittering, black tobe of Nupe manufacture, a new "haf," and the white bernus which I wore myself, I at length prevailed upon him to set out for the town [of Timbuktu], in order to obtain protection for me; for as yet I was an outlaw in the country, and any ruffian who suspected my character might have slain me, without scarcely anybody caring anything about it; and circumstances seemed to assume a very unfavourable aspect: for there was a great movement among the Tawarek [Tuareg] in the neighbourhood when it almost seemed as if some news of my real character had transpired.

Not long after my two messengers were gone, a Tarki* chief, of the name of Kneha, with tall and stately figure, and of noble expressive features, as far as his shawl around the face allowed them to be seen, but, like the whole tribe of the Kel-hekikan to which he belongs, bearing a very bad character as a freebooter, made his appearance, armed with spear and sword, and obtruded himself upon me while I was partaking of my simple dish of rice; notwithstanding which, he took his seat at a short distance opposite to me. Not wishing to invite him to a share in my poor frugal repast by the usual *bismillah*, I told him, first in Arabic and then in Fulfulde, that I was dining, and had no leisure to speak with him at present. Whereupon he took his leave, but returned after a short while, and, in a rather peremptory manner, solicited a present from me, being, as he said, a great chief of the country; but as I was not aware of the extent of his power, and being also afraid that others might imitate his example, I told him that I could not give him anything before I had made due inquiries respecting his real importance from my companion who had just gone to the town. But he was not at all satisfied with my argument; representing himself as a great *dhalem*, or evildoer, and that as such he might do me much harm; till at length, after a very spirited altercation, I got rid of him.

He was scarcely gone, when the whole house was filled with armed men, horse and foot, from Timbuktu, most of them clad in light blue tobes, tightly girt round the waist with a shawl, and dressed in short breeches reaching only to the knees, as if they were going to fight, their head being covered with a straw hat of the peculiar shape of a little hut with regular thatchwork, such as is fashionable among the inhabitants of Masina and of the provinces

* Targui, sing. of Tuareg.

further west. They were armed with spears, besides which some of them wore also a sword: only a few of them had muskets. Entering the house rather abruptly, and squatting down in the antechambers and courtyard, just where they could find a place, they stared at me not a little, and began asking of each other who this strange-looking fellow might be, while I was reclining on my two smaller boxes, having my larger ones and my other luggage behind me. I was rather at a loss to account for their intrusion, until I learned, upon inquiry from my landlady, that they were come in order to protect their cattle from the Tawarek, who at the time were passing through the place, and who had driven away some of their property. The very person whom they dreaded was the chief Kneha, who had just left me, though they could not make out his whereabouts. Having refreshed themselves during the hot hours of the day, these people started off; but the alarm about the cattle continued the whole of the afternoon, and not less than two hundred armed men came into my apartments in the course of an hour.

My messengers not returning at the appointed time from their errand to the town, I had at length retired to rest in the evening, when shortly before midnight they arrived, together with Sidi A'lawate, the Sheikh El Bakay's brother, and several of his followers, who took up their quarters on the terrace of my house in order to be out of the reach of the mosquitoes; and after they had been regaled with a good supper, which had been provided beforehand by some of the townspeople, I went to pay my respects to them.

It was an important interview; for, although this was not the person for whom my visit was specially intended, and whose favourable or unfavourable disposition would influence the whole success of my arduous undertaking, yet for the present I was entirely in his hands, and all depended upon the manner in which he received me. Now my two messengers had only disclosed to himself personally, that I was a Christian, while at the same time they had laid great stress upon the circumstance that, although a Christian, I was under the special protection of the Sultan of Stambul; and Sidi A'lawate inquired therefore of me, with great earnestness and anxiety, as to the peculiar manner in which I enjoyed the protection of that great Mohammedan sovereign.

Now it was most unfortunate for me that I had no direct letter from that quarter. Even the *firman* with which we had been provided by the Basha of Tripoli had been delivered to the governor for whom it was destined, so that at the time I had nothing with me to show but a *firman* which I had used on my journey in Egypt, and which of course had no especial relation to the case in question. The want of such a general letter of protection from the Sultan of Constantinople, which I had solicited with so much anxiety to be sent after me, was in the sequel the chief cause of my difficult and dangerous position in Timbuktu; for, furnished with such a letter, it would have been easy to have imposed silence upon my adversaries and enemies there, and especially upon the merchants from Morocco, who were instigated by the most selfish jealousy to raise all sorts of intrigues against me.

Having heard my address with attention, although I was not able to establish every point so clearly as I could have wished, the sheikh's brother promised me protection, and desired me to be without any apprehension with regard to my safety . . .

After a rather restless night, the day broke when I was at length to enter Timbuktu . . . It was ten o'clock when our cavalcade at length put itself in motion, ascending the sandhills which rise close behind the village of Kabara, and which, to my great regret, had prevented my obtaining a view of the town from the top of our terrace. The contrast of this desolate scenery with the character of the fertile banks of the river which I had just left behind was remarkable . . . Having traversed two sunken spots designated by especial names, where in certain years when the river rises to an unusual height . . . we approached the town: but its dark masses of clay not being illuminated by bright sushine, for the sky was thickly overcast and the atmosphere filled with sand, were scarcely to be distinguished from the sand and rubbish heaped all round; and there was no opportunity for looking attentively about, as a body of people were coming towards us in order to pay their compliments to the stranger and bid him welcome. This was a very important moment, as, if they had felt the slightest suspicion with regard to my character, they might easily have prevented my entering the town at all, and thus even endangered my life.

I therefore took the hint of A'lawate, who recommended me to make a start in advance in order to anticipate the salute of these people who had come to meet us; and putting my horse to a gallop, and gun in hand, I galloped up to meet them, when I was received with many salams. But a circumstance occurred which might have proved fatal, not only to my enterprise, but even to my own personal safety, as there was a man among the group who addressed me in Turkish, which I had almost entirely forgotten; so that I could with difficulty make a suitable answer to his compliment; but avoiding further indiscreet questions, I pushed on in order to get under safe cover.

Having then traversed the rubbish which has accumulated round the ruined clay wall of the town, and left on one side a row of dirty reed huts which encompass the whole of the place, we entered the narrow streets and lanes, or, as the people of Timbuktu say, the *tijeraten,* which scarcely allowed two horses to proceed abreast. But I was not a little surprised at the populous and wealthy character which this quarter of the town, the Sane-Gungu, exhibited, many of the houses rising to the height of two stories, and in their façade evincing even an attempt at architectural adornment. Thus, taking a more westerly turn . . . we reached the house on the other side of the street, which was destined for my residence, and I was glad when I found myself safely in my new quarters . . .

I was not allowed to stir about, but was confined within the walls of my house. In order to obviate the effect of this want of exercise as much as possible, to enjoy fresh air and at the same time to become familiar with the principal features of the town, through which I was not allowed to move about at pleasure, I ascended as often as possible the terrace of my house. This afforded an excellent view over the northern quarters of the town. On the north was the massive mosque of Sankore, which had just been restored to all its former grandeur through the influence of the Sheikh el Bakay, and gave the whole place an imposing character. Neither the mosque Sidi Yahia, nor the "great mosque," or Jingere-ber, was seen from this point; but towards the east the view extended over a wide expanse of the desert, and towards the south the elevated mansions of the Ghadamsiye merchants were visible. The style of the buildings was various. I could see clay houses of different characters, some low and unseemly, others rising with a second story in front to a greater elevation, and making even an attempt at architectural ornament, the whole being interrupted by a few round huts of matting . . .

But while the terrace of my house served to make me well acquainted with the character of the town, it also had the disadvantage of exposing me fully to the gaze of the passers by, so that I could only slowly and with many interruptions, succeed in making a sketch of the scene thus offered to my view . . . At the same time I became aware of the great inaccuracy which characterizes the view of the town as given by M. Caillié; still, on the whole, the character of the single dwellings was well represented by that traveler, the only error being that in his representation the whole town seems to consist of scattered and quite isolated houses, while, in reality, the streets are entirely shut in, as the dwellings form continuous and uninterrupted rows. But it must be taken into account that Timbuktu, at the time of Caillié's visit, was not so well off as it is at present, having been overrun by the Fulbe [Fulani] the preceding year, and he had no opportunity of making a drawing on the spot . . .

The circumference of the city at the present time I reckon at a little more than two miles and a half; but it may approach closely to three miles, taking into account some of the projecting angles . . . At present it is not walled. Its former wall, which seems never to have been of great magnitude, and was rather more of the nature of a rampart, was destroyed by the Fulbe [Fulani] on their first entering the place in the beginning of the year 1826. The town is laid out partly in rectangular, partly in winding, streets, or, as they are called here, *tijeraten*, which are not paved, but for the greater part consists of hard sand and gravel, and some of them have a sort of gutter in the middle. Besides the large and the small market there are few open areas, except a small square in front of the mosque of Yahia, called Tumbutu-bottema.

Small as it is, the city is tolerably well inhabited, and almost all the houses are in good repair. There are about 980 clay houses, and a couple of hundred conical huts of matting, the latter, with a few exceptions, constituting the outskirts of the town on the north and northeast sides, where a great deal of rubbish, which has been accumulating in the course of several centuries, is formed into conspicuous mounds . . .

The only remarkable public buildings in the town are the three large mosques: the Jingere-ber, built by *Mansa* Musa; the mosque of Sankore, built, at an early period, at the expense of a wealthy woman; and the mosque Sidi Yahia, built at the expense of a *kadhi* of the town. There were three other mosques . . . Besides these mosques, there are at present no distinguished public buildings in the town; and of the royal palace, or Ma-dugu, wherein the kings of Songhay used to reside occasionally, as well as the Kasbah, which was built in later times, in the southeastern quarter, or the "Sane-gungu," which already at that time was inhabited by the merchants from Ghadames, not a trace is to be seen . . .

The whole number of the settled inhabitants of the town amounts to about thirteen thousand; while the floating population, during the months of the greatest traffic and intercourse, especially from November to January, may amount, on an average, to five thousand, and under favourable circumstances to as many as ten thousand.

Industry and Trade

The great feature which distinguishes the market of Timbuktu from that of Kano is the fact, that Timbuktu is not at all a manufacturing town, while the emporium of Hausa fully deserves to be classed as such. Almost the whole life of the city is based upon foreign commerce, which owing to the great northerly bend of the Niger, finds here the most favoured spot for intercourse, while at the same time that splendid river enables the inhabitants to supply all their wants from without; for native corn is not raised here in sufficient quantities to feed even a very small proportion of the population, and almost all the victuals are imported by water-carriage from Sansandi and the neighbourhood.

The only manufactures carried on in [Timbuktu], as far as fell under my observation, are confined to the art of the blacksmith, and to a little leatherwork. Some of these articles, such as provision or luggage bags, cushions, small leather pouches for tobacco, and gun-cloths, especially the leather bags, are very neat but even these are mostly manufactured by Tawarek, and especially females, so that the industry of the city is hardly of any account. It was formerly supposed that Timbuktu was distinguished on account of its weaving, and that the export of dyed shirts from hence was considerable; but I have already had an opportunity of showing that this was entirely a mistake, almost the whole clothing of the natives themselves, especially that of the wealthier classes, being imported either from Kano or from Sansandi, besides the calico imported from England.

The export of the produce of Kano, especially by way of A'rawan, extends to the very border of the Atlantic, where it comes into contact with the considerable import of Malabar cloth by way of St. Louis, or Nder, on the Senegal, while the dyed shirts from Sansandi, which, as far as I had an opportunity of observing, seem to be made of foreign or English calico, and not of native cotton, do not appear to be exported to a greater distance. These shirts are generally distinguished by their rich ornament of coloured silk, and look very pretty; and I am sorry that I was obliged to give away, as a present, a specimen which I intended to bring home with me.

The people of Timbuktu are very experienced in the art of adorning their clothing with a fine stitching of silk, but this is done on a very small scale, and even these shirts are only used at home. There is, however, a very considerable degree of industry exercised by the natives of some of the neighbouring districts, especially Fermagha, who produce very excellent woollen blankets, and carpets of various colours, which form a most extensive article of consumption with the natives.

The foreign commerce has especially three great highroads: that along the river from the southwest (for lower down the river there is at present scarcely any commerce at all), which comprises the trade proceeding from various points; and two roads from the north, that from Morocco on the one hand, and that from Ghadames on the other. In all this commerce, gold forms the chief staple, although the whole amount of the precious metal exported from this city appears to be exceedingly small, if compared with a

European standard. It probably does not exceed an average of £20,000 sterling per year. The gold is brought either from Bambuk or from Bure, but from the former place in a larger quantity. The gold from the country of the Wangarawa does not reach this market, but, as it seems, at present is directly exported to that part of the southern coast which on this account is called the Gold Coast. The species of gold from Bambuk is of a more yellow colour; that from Bure is rather whitish; and that from Wangara has a greenish hue. Most of this gold, I think, is brought into the town in rings. I do not remember to have seen or heard of gold dust, or "tibber," being brought to market in small leathern bags, such as Shabini and other people describe, containing about one ounce, equal to twenty-five dollars in value. But, nevertheless, a considerable amount of this article must come into market, as most of the gold dust which comes to Ghadames and Tripoli passes through Timbuktu, while another portion goes directly from Sansandi to A'rawan.

It was evidently in consequence of the influence of the Arabs, that the scale of the *mithkal* was introduced in the trade in gold; but it is a very general term, which may signify very different quantities, and thus we find various kinds of *mithkals* used in Negroland, especially those of A'gades, Timbuktu, and Mango, the Mandingo place between Yendi and the Niger, the former of which is the smallest, and equal, as I have stated in the proper place, to one thousand shells of Hausa standard, although in the present decayed state of the town of A'gades, where all the gold trade has ceased, it possesses rather an imaginary value. The *mithkal* of Timbuktu contains the weight of twenty-four grains of the kharub tree, or ninety-six of wheat, and is worth from three thousand to four thousand shells. The *mithkal* of Mango is equal to one and one-fourth of that of Timbuktu. Besides rings, very handsome ornaments are worked of gold; but, as far as I could learn, most of this workmanship comes from Walata, which is still celebrated on this account.

The next article that forms one of the chief staples in Timbuktu, and in some respects even more so than gold, is salt, which, together with gold, formed articles of exchange all along the Niger from the most ancient times. It is brought from Tao-denni, a place whose situation has been tolerably well established by M. Caillié's journey, and the mines of which have been worked, as we know from Ahmed Baba,* since the year 1596, when the former mines of Teghaza, situated some seventy miles further to the north, were given up. These salt mines of Teghaza appear to have been worked from very remote times, or at least before the eleventh century; and there can be little doubt that the mines of Tatental, described by the excellent geographer El Bekri as situated twenty days' journey from Sijilmesa, and two from the beginning of the desert, are identical with Teghaza. Even at that time both Sijilmesa and Ghanata were provided from here, while at least the eastern and original portion of Songhay was supplied at that early period from the mines of Tautek, six days from Tademekka . . .

* That is, the *Tarikh es-Sudan*, wrongly attributed by Barth to Ahmad Baba.

MARTIN DELANY

On Slavery

The first Negro to be commissioned by President Lincoln with field rank in the United States Army, Martin R. Delany was a Harvard-trained physician who visited Africa in 1859-1860 by commission from the National Emigration Convention of Coloured Men which he had helped to form at Cleveland in 1854. With Edward Blyden, he was one of the earliest to understand the coming nationalist challenge, and to use the slogan of "Africa for the Africans." Speaking at Philadelphia in 1852, he declared that: "The claims of no people . . . are respected by any nation until they are presented in a national capacity." A century later this thought would sweep the whole African continent.

From Martin R. Delany, *Official Report of the Niger Valley Exploring Party* (New York: 1861), p. 40.

A word about slavery. It is simply preposterous to talk about slavery, as that term is understood, either being legalized or existing in this part of Africa. It is nonsense. The system is a patriarchal one, there being no actual difference, socially, between the slave (called by their protector son or daughter) and the children of the person with whom they live. Such persons intermarry and frequently become the heads of state; indeed, generally so, as I do not remember at present a king or chief with whom I became acquainted whose entire members of the household, from the lowest domestic to the highest official, did not sustain this relation to him, they calling him baba or "father," and he treating them as children. And were this not the case, it either arises from some innovation among them or those exceptional cases of despotism to be found in every country. Indeed, the term "slave" is unknown to them, only as it has been introduced among them by whites from Europe and America. So far from abject slavery, not even the old feudal system, as known to exist until comparatively recent times in enlightened and Christian Europe, exists in this part of Africa.

Criminals and prisoners of war are legally sold into slavery among themselves, just as was the custom in almost every civilized country in the world till very lately, when nothing but advanced intelligence and progressive Christianity among the people put a stop to it. There is no place, however, but Ilorin, a bona fide Mohammedan kingdom, where we ever witnessed any exhibition of these facts.

Slaves are abducted by marauding, kidnapping, depraved natives, who, like the organized bands and gangs of robbers in Europe and America, go through the country thieving and stealing helpless women and children, and men who may be overpowered by numbers. Whole villages in this way sometimes fall victims to these human monsters, especially when the strong young men are out in the fields at work, the old of both sexes in such cases being put to death, whilst the young are hurried through some private way down to the slave factories usually kept by Europeans (generally Portuguese and Spaniards) and Americans, on some secluded part of the coast. And in no instances are the parents and relatives known to sell their own children or people into slavery, except, indeed, in cases of base depravity, and except such miserable despots as the kings of Dahomi and Ashantee; neither are the heads of countries known to sell their own people; but like the marauding kidnapper, obtain them by war on others.

ROBERT CAMPBELL

Yoruba Government

Although a Jamaican by origin, Robert Campbell may count, with Delany, as one of the earliest Negro Americans to visit and report on Africa. A teacher in chemistry at the Institute for Colored Youth in Philadelphia, Campbell accompanied Martin Delany to Yorubaland in 1859-1860. He describes the politics of the Yoruba town of Abeokuta, and the importance of the Ogboni Society there. This was a device for the self-government of a community of people of different Yoruba loyalties that was typical of political development in these southern Nigerian lands, where the splintering impact of the slave trade, and the wars to which the trade had helped to give rise, had taken their full effect.*

The government of Abeokuta is peculiar, combining the monarchical, the patriarchal, and no small share of the republican. Almost every free man, woman and child is a member of the Ogboni Lodge, of which there is one in every township or chiefdom. These lodges are presided over by elders of their own election, and the elders at the decease of the chief choose his successor from his relatives, generally his brother, seldom or never among his sons . . . The successor of the king is also chosen by the chiefs

From Robert Campbell, A *Pilgrimage to my Motherland, etc.* (New York: 1861), p. 36.

* For a detailed discussion of this trend, see K. O. Dike, *Trade and Politics in the Niger Delta* (Oxford: 1956), and B. Davidson, *Black Mother* (Boston and London: 1961).

and elders combined, their act being subsequently ratified by the people, assembled en masse. It is in this that the republican element of the government of Abeokuta is recognized . . .

WINWOOD READE
In the Oil Rivers

By the middle of the nineteenth century the old but costly local prosperity of the slaving ports and little kingdoms of the Niger Delta had been replaced entirely by a still greater and altogether more acceptable prosperity from the sale of palm oil, then wanted in Europe as the only known basis for good soap. But by this time the long years of enmity, suspicion, violence and double-dealing had produced an atmosphere of bitter hostility between African and European traders. Winwood Reade was a radical-minded English landowner who traveled much in West Africa and wrote books that were widely read.

. . . We entered Bonny, the wealthiest of these rivers of corruption. Here the traders do not dare to live ashore, but inhabit the huge hulks of ancient merchantmen . . . The trade [in oil] is active enough, but from its nature is attended with much delay. The Bonny natives go to market in the interior. The oil is brought to them little by little in calabashes. This they pour off into barrels. It is then brought on board one of the hulks, and is purchased with goods of European manufacture . . . These black traders are now almost too much for the white ones in these matters of low cunning which enter so largely into commerce of a petty nature. The days have long gone by when charcoaled powder and coraline could be passed off [by European traders] upon the simple natives with impunity. A little can still be done with false weights and measures, but the good old days are gone for ever, and the natives have learnt to turn the dirty tables upon those who could

From W. Winwood Reade, *Savage Africa* (London: 1863), p. 53.

once cheat them as they chose . . . Among the whites there is no real unity: nobody trusts his neighbour. This gives the blacks a great advantage . . . Rivals as they are, they [the blacks] can always combine with that honesty which is always the best policy . . .

EDWARD BLYDEN

A West African Spartacus

Born of Negro parents in the West Indian island of St. Thomas, Edward Wilmot Blyden became one of the earliest and most distinguished spokesmen of the independent African spirit. He first went to Liberia at the age of seventeen, gained there an education at an American missionary school and, thanks to his brains and application, was awarded a professorship at the newly founded College of Liberia in 1862. Entering his adopted country's service, he became Liberian ambassador in London in 1877. Much of what he wrote is bone and sinew of the rise of West African nationalism, but a collected edition of his scattered books and papers has still to be published. What follows is an extract from his report to the governor of Sierra Leone on an expedition to the interior of that country, undertaken in 1872 during a period in British service at Freetown.

The present unsettled state of the [inland] country [of Sierra Leone] is owing to the influence of one Bilali, a native of the Kissy country, and formerly a slave among the Soosoos. About twenty seven years of age he ran away from his master, Almamy Mumineh, now residing at Kukuna, and founded a settlement be-

From Edward W. Blyden, M. A., "Report on the Expedition to Falaba, January to March 1872": *Proceedings of Royal Geographical Society* 1872-1873, vol. 17, p. 117. A masterly review of early West African nationalist thinkers such as Blyden will be found in D. Kimble's *Political History of Ghana* (Oxford: 1963).

tween the Soosoo and Limba countries, to which numerous fugitives have, from time to time, betaken themselves.

By numerous accessions of that class of person, Bilali has succeeded in forming a powerful party, and in rousing a large portion of the servile population, not only to a devotion to the idea of liberty at any price, but a strong attachment to himself and a hatred of all who hold slaves; and he is by no means scrupulous as to the price he pays for their support.

On the other hand, the slave-holding chiefs, in various parts of the surrounding country, except those of the Limba district, have formed a combination against him, alleging, when appealed to in favour of Bilali on the ground of the abstract right of every man to personal liberty, the same argument that is always used by oppressors, viz., granting that Bilali has just cause for rebellion, granting that he is wise in periling his personal ease and security for the sake of liberty, still his course (as they hold) is producing a confusion in the country, which will eventually beget a state of things much worse than that against which he and his allies have risen. Standing on the basis of this, to them conclusive argument, they are anxious to crush Bilali, but it seems that their combination is powerless against him . . .

In the neighbourhood of Kukuna, the country gives sad evidence of the dire results of war. We were surrounded by lamentable illustrations of a war which had lasted during a whole generation; and it is difficult for one at a distance to frame any clear idea of a state of society induced by this protracted contest, kept up by determined slave-holders in the vain hope of reducing to servitude a man to whom there is no equal in the country for military prowess, tact, and ability.

MARY KINGSLEY

In the Gaboon

Mary Kingsley wrote two important books which can still be read with great enjoyment for their wit and understanding: *Travels in West Africa* (London: 1897), and *West African Studies* (London: 1899). Had she not died of typhoid while nursing Boer prisoners during the South African War, she would no doubt have written other books; and all who are interested in Africa must lament their loss. More than most Europeans of her day she was free of that stifling "paternalism" which saw in Africans a curiously "childish" branch of humanity. She was shrewd and sympathetic at the same time. These extracts from her *Travels* give at least some notion of her quality. They describe her wanderings in what is now the Republic of Gabon, or, as the English have generally written it, Gaboon.

Went alone for a long walk to the bend of the mangrove-swamp river to the east. It stank severely, but was most interesting, giving one the conditions of life in a mangrove-swamp in what you might call a pocket edition. Leaving this, I made my way north-west along native paths across stretches of trees growing on rolling hills and down through wooded valleys, each of which had a little stream in it, or a patch of swamp, with enormous arums and other water plants growing, and along through Fan villages, each with just one straight street, having a clubhouse at the alternate ends. I met in the forest a hunter, carrying home a deer he had shot; in addition to his musket, he carried a couple of long tufted spears, archaic in type. He was very chatty, and I gave him tobacco, and we talked sport, and on parting I gave him some more tobacco, because he kindly gave me a charm to enable me to see things in the forest. He was gratified, and said, "You ver nice,"

From Mary H. Kingsley, *Travels in West Africa* (London: 1897).

"Good-bye," "Good-day," "So long," "Good-night," which was very nice of him, as these phrases were evidently all the amiable greetings in English that he knew. The "So long" you often hear the natives in Gaboon say: it always sounds exceeedingly quaint. They have of course picked it up from the American missionaries, who have been here upwards of thirty years.

Ascent of the Ogowé

About 9:30 we got into a savage rapid. We fought it inch by inch. The canoe jammed herself on some barely sunken rocks in it. We shoved her off over them. She tilted over and chucked us out. The rocks round being just awash, we survived and got her straight again, and got into her and drove her unmercifully; she struck again and bucked like a broncho, and we fell in heaps upon each other, but stayed inside that time — the men by the aid of their intelligent feet, I by clinching my hands into the bush rope lacing which ran round the rim of the canoe and the meaning of which I did not understand when I left Talagouga. We sorted ourselves out hastily and sent her at it again. Smash went a sorely tried pole and a paddle. Round and round we spun in an exultant whirlpool, which, in a lighthearted, maliciously joking way, hurled us tail first out of it into the current. Now the grand point in these canoes of having both ends alike declared itself; for at this juncture all we had to do was to revolve on our own axis and commence life anew with what had been the bow for the stern. Of course we were defeated, we could not go up any further without the aid of our lost poles and paddles, so we had to go down for shelter somewhere, anywhere, and down at a terrific pace in the white water we went. While hitched among the rocks the arrangement of our crew had been altered, Pierre joining M'bo in the bows; this piece of precaution was frustrated by our getting turned round; so our position was what you might call precarious, until we got into another whirlpool, when we persuaded nature to start us right end on. This was only a matter of minutes, whirlpools being plentiful, and then M'bo and Pierre, provided with our surviving poles, stood in the bows to fend us off rocks, as we shot towards them; while we midship paddles sat, helping to steer, and when occasion arose, which occasion did with lightning rapidity, to whack the whirl-pools with the flat of our paddles, to break their force. Cook crouched in the stern concentrating his mind on steering only. A most excellent arrangement in theory and the safest practical one no doubt, but it did not work out what you might call brilliantly well; though each department did its best. We dashed full tilt to-wards high rocks, things twenty to fifty feet above water. Midship backed and flapped like fury; M'bo and Pierre received the shock on their poles; sometimes we glanced successfully aside and flew on; sometimes we didn't. The shock being too much for M'bo and Pierre they were driven back on me, who got flattened on to the cargo of bundles which, being now firmly tied in, couldn't spread the confusion further aft; but the shock of the canoe's nose against the rock did so in style, and the rest of the crew fell forward on to the bundles, me, and themselves . . .

Adventures in the Forest

I watched the gorillas with great interest for a few seconds, until I heard Wiki make a peculiar small sound, and looking at him saw his face was working in an awful way as he clutched his throat with his hands violently.

Heavens! think I, this gentleman's going to have a fit; it's lost we are entirely this time. He rolled his head to and fro, and then buried his face into a heap of dried rubbish at the foot of a plan-tain stem, clasped his hands over it, and gave an explosive sneeze. The gorillas let go all, raised themselves up for a second, gave a quaint sound between a bark and a howl, and then the ladies and the young gentleman started home. The old male rose to his full height (it struck me at the time this was a matter of ten feet at least, but for scientific purposes allowance must be made for a lady's emotions) and looked straight towards us, or rather towards where that sound came from. Wiki went off into a paroxysm of falsetto sneezes the like of which I have never heard; nor evi-dently had the gorilla, who doubtless thinking, as one of his black co-relatives would have thought, that the phenomenon favoured Duppy, went off after his family with a celerity that was amazing the moment he touched the forest, and disappeared as they had, swinging himself along through it from bough to bough, in a way that convinced me that, given the necessity of getting about in tropical forests, man has made a mistake in getting his arms shortened. I have seen many wild animals in their native wilds, but never have I seen anything to equal gorillas going through bush; it is a graceful, powerful, superbly perfect hand-trapeze performance.

Advantages of Wearing a Skirt

. . . But these Fans are a fine sporting tribe, and allowed they would risk it; besides, they were almost certain they had friends at Efoua; and, in addition, they showed me trees scratched in a way that was magnification of the condition of my own cat's pet table leg at home, demonstrating leopards in the vicinity. I kept going, as it was my only chance, because I found I stiffened if I sat down, and they always carefully told me the direction to go in when they sat down; with their superior pace they soon caught me up, and then passed me, leaving me and Ngouta and sometimes Singlet and Pagan behind, we, in our turn, overtaking them, with this difference that they were sitting down when we did so.

About five o'clock I was off ahead and noticed a path which I had been told I should meet with, and, when met with, I must follow. The path was slightly indistinct, but by keeping my eye on it I could see it. Presently I came to a place where it went out, but appeared again on the other side of a clump of underbrush fairly distinctly. I made a short cut for it and the next news was I was in a heap, on a lot of spikes, some fifteen feet or so below ground level, at the bottom of a bag-shaped game pit.

It is at these times you realize the blessing of a good thick skirt. Had I paid heed to the advice of many people in England, who ought to have known better, and did not do it themselves, and adopted masculine garments, I should have been spiked to the bone, and done for. Whereas, save for a good many bruises, here I was with the fullness of my skirt tucked under me, sitting on nine ebony spikes some twelve inches long, in comparative comfort, howling lustily to be hauled out. The Duke came along first, and looked down at me. I said, "Get a bush-rope and haul me out."

He grunted and sat down on a log. The Passenger came next, and he looked down. "You kill?" says he. "Not much," say I; "get a bush-rope and haul me out." "No fit," says he, and sat down on the log. Presently however, Kiva and Wiki came up, and Wiki went and selected the one and only bush-rope suitable to haul an English lady, of my exact complexion, age, and size, out of that one particular pit. They seemed rare round there from the time he took; and I was just casting about in my mind as to what method would be best to employ in getting up the smooth, yellow, sandy clay, incurved walls, when he arrived with it, and I was out in a twinkling, and very much ashamed of myself, until Silence, who was then leading, disappeared through the path before us with a despairing yell . . .

MACEMBA

Facing Invasion

By 1890 the invasion of many coastal and near-coastal regions was in full spate. It was bitterly resisted. In southern Tanganyika the main opponents were Hermann von Wissmann, commanding the German forces, and Macemba, ruling chief of the Yao people. When the empire-building Wissmann demanded submission by this ruler, Macemba wrote him — in Kiswahili — a memorable reply, and one that was characteristic of the African response. This letter has become known only in the last few years, thanks to the opening of the German colonial archives.

I have listened to your words but can find no reason why I should obey you — I would rather die first. I have no relations

From the German version of the Kiswahili original in Archives of the *Reichskolonialamt*, No. 747, Deutschen Zentralarchiv, Potsdam, reprinted in F. F. Müller, *Deutschland-Zanzibar-Ostafrika* (Berlin: 1959), p. 455. Translated by B. Davidson.

with you and cannot bring it to my mind that you have given me so much as a *pesa* [fraction of a rupee] or the quarter of a *pesa* or a needle or a thread. I look for some reason why I should obey you and find not the smallest. If it should be friendship that you desire, then I am ready for it, today and always; but to be your subject, that I cannot be . . . If it should be war you desire, then I am ready, but never to be your subject . . . I do not fall at your feet, for you are God's creature just as I am . . . I am sultan here in my land. You are sultan there in yours. Yet listen, I do not say to you that you should obey me; for I know that you are a free man . . . As for me, I will not come to you, and if you are strong enough, then come and fetch me . . .

The Twentieth Century

A FEW SIGNPOSTS

*H*ERE WE MUST CALL A HALT. NO BRIEF GUIDE TO THE LITERATURE of the present century could be useful to the general reader, much less to the student. Far too much would have to be left out. For if books and papers about Africa become copious in the 1880s, in the years that follow they swell into a flood, and the tide is still rising. Yet the reader who has come with me as far as this may feel, as I do, the need for a rounding off and a completion of the story, even though in summary and symbolic fashion.

The first fifty years of the twentieth century may be divided into three overlapping periods. From an African standpoint these may be labeled as the periods of subjection, stagnation and liberation. The first begins really in about 1880 and continues until the end of "pacification" in about 1920. While some territories were taken without much warfare, others required a long military effort (even for the year 1915, Belgian records show as many as thirty "armed operations" against Africans in the Congo); generally it will be true to say that about forty years were required to consummate the colonial enterprise. This is worth remembering when we are told, as nowadays we sometimes are, that the establishment of the colonial system was a relatively peaceful and even benevolent affair. Three brief though painful extracts for this period will suffice. True enough, the enclosure of Africa was not always as crude and harsh as these suggest, and here and there it even brought relief to war-shattered lands; but since this book has borne frequent witness to the services of Europeans in Africa, it may be right to show at least a little of the other side of the medal.

A new political consciousness was growing up among Africans

even during the years of subjection, and Charles Domingo, our next author, is no unworthy representative of that. The Pan-African idea was also coming forth at this time, and those who want to read about its origins should turn to Colin Legum's selection of relevant documents, *Pan-Africanism* (London and New York: 1962).

During the next period, that of stagnation between about 1920 and 1945, the brutality of conquest paled, except in the Portuguese colonies and here and there elsewhere, to a dull uniformity of deprivation relieved now and then, though not often, by strenuous individual efforts at improvement. There are not many books from this period that need be remembered except for a small category of thoughtful inquiries of which Norman Leys's *Kenya* (London: 1926), remains outstanding; but there is a vast documentation in the form of official reports and correspondence, a little of which is now becoming available to public inspection. At the same time there were other men who had begun to devote their lives to scientific rediscovery. As a tribute to their work and that of their successors — often solitary, seldom recognized except by their colleagues, always demanding great physical and moral effort — I take particular pleasure in offering a fragment from my friend Théodore Monod's memoirs of Saharan travel.

Today we are still in the third period, that of liberation, which may be said to have opened in 1945, to have passed its first large milestone with the independence of Ghana in 1957, and to have begun to grapple with its second major phase, that of economic reconstruction, in the early sixties. This period is already rich in books and papers of every kind. In face of such remarkable abundance of interesting material, I conclude with three passages which point to that many-sided reassessment of the moral worth and historical validity of African culture and civilization which is now in progress, and which makes, more and more clearly, an indispensable contribution to the Africa of tomorrow.

K. SCHWABE
Colonial Conquest

The following is from an account of the conquest of southwest Africa.

In 1883-1885 the Bremen businessman Lüderitz managed to obtain important land concessions — at first in the hinterland of Angra Pequena, later named Lüderitz Bay — by means of treaties with various native chiefs. By 1884, the whole region between the Orange and the Cunene had become a German protectorate . . . [But the inhabitants objected, and this "protectorate" was soon threatened.] Then, in the twelfth hour, Captain von François began the war in the course of which, through many victorious battles, he destroyed the power of Hendrik [Witboi], and an end to which was made at last by Major Leutwein, after fortunate but difficult battles, in 1894.

The overthrow of these powerful chiefs, whose names were known far beyond the boundaries of the colony . . . nonetheless did not avert the need for new warlike expeditions every year, so as to stifle the resistance of various tribes. In 1894-1895 the Hottentots of Khauas and Simon Copperschen had to be dealt with. The year 1896 saw heavy losses in the campaign against the rebellious Eastern Hereros, Ovambandjeru and once more the Khauas Hottentots . . . Then came a period of apparent peace until the end of 1903 when serious troubles broke out in Amboland and on the Okavango as well as in the Bondelzwart region. And the Herero, who had long been systematically preparing their national uprising, used these troubles as a springboard . . .

From Captain K. Schwabe, *Der Krieg in Deutsch-Südwestafrika 1904-1906* (Berlin: 1907). Translated by B. Davidson.

[Massive operations were undertaken against the Herero, who were crushed without pity.] The Herero people, who had brought such trouble to our protectorate, were driven into the waterless sands [of the Kalahari] by a terrible though just fate. Thousands were killed and died of thirst . . .

LEO FROBENIUS

Leopold's Congo

Leo Frobenius is best known as a pioneer writer on African art, ethnography and history. Although not a liberal-minded man — "Certainly," he wrote, "one must handle the Negro with a firm hand" — he was disgusted by what he saw and experienced in the Congo Free State of King Leopold of Belgium. Time has gratefully erased much that happened then, yet the Congo Free State remains an integral part of the history of a large part of Central Africa. It was administered by a system that may be called colonialism at its worst and most wasteful. Reporting in 1919, for example, the Belgian Permanent Commission for the Protection of the Natives came to the conclusion that the population of the country had been "reduced by half" since the beginning of European occupation.* Here, from a copious Congo literature, is a passage from Frobenius, who traveled there in 1904-1906, which suggests some of the reasons why.

Everyone in the Congo State has accustomed himself to exercise an illegal private police service, so that he becomes independent. Later I will describe even worse events [than the coercion and beating of Africans which he has just related], such as when the

From L. Frobenius, *Im Schatten des Kongostaats* (Berlin: 1907), p. 95 and (for the last incident) p. 282. Translated by B. Davidson.

* Report of the Commission's third session, Leopoldville, December 8-12, 1919, reproduced in *Bulletin* of Centre d'Etude des Problèmes Sociaux Indigènes (Elisabethville: Feb. 1953), p. 197.

missionaries of Bena Makima, although they were living only two days from the government station, put the chiefs of the Bakuba in chains, because these chiefs refused to build for them; and such as when the Superior of Luluabourg caused women who had voluntarily left the mission station to be bound and brought back from the nearby government station because these women were not "free" . . .

The whole system rests upon a mean utilitarianism. While the Company [that is, the Belgian concession company in the area where Frobenius was] takes the severest measures against any of its agents who may steal from it or falsify accounts or in any way damage the company's commercial interests — while the Company is absolutely merciless in these cases, yet it is satisfied merely to dismiss those agents who are guilty of acts of violence [against Africans, such as here described] . . . On October 4, during our second stay at Kabeja, a sixth unhappy Negro, the Kaloshi Watobelle, was captured. He too was a Kapita [agent] who had failed to deliver his stipulated supply of cotton. He must have been an excellent fellow, was a Christian, and brought up at the mission of Luebo. He came in the evening and was seized next morning and held on the ground. On one side stood a Kapita, on the other a European. Each held a whip. It sounded like a mill, flip-flap, flip-flap. And when one stick was broken, so another was quickly seized so that there should be no interruption in the rhythm. I counted 53 flip-flaps, or 106 blows . . .

R. MEINERTZHAGEN
White Man's Country?

[Nairobi, Kenya, 1902] Apparently Charles Eliot, the High Commissioner, learned that Beatrice Webb is my aunt, so he asked me to dine with him this evening. My only clothes were a

From Colonel R. Meinertzhagen, *Kenya Diary*, 1902-1906 (London: 1957).

dirty old shirt and shorts. I explained my predicament and refused, but he insisted on my coming. He is not my idea of a High Commissioner; he looks more like a university don or a priest. He is a scholar, a philosopher, and a very able man with great vision. He amazed me with his views on the future of East Africa. He envisaged a thriving colony of thousands of Europeans with their families, the whole of the country from the Aberdares and Mount Kenya to the German border [i.e., of Tanganyika] divided up into farms; the whole of the Rift Valley cultivated or grazed, and the whole country of Lumbwa, Nandi to Elgon and almost to Baringo under white settlement. He intends to confine the natives to reserves and use them as cheap labour on farms. I suggested that the country belonged to Africans and that their interests must prevail over the interests of strangers. He would not have it; he kept on using the word "paramount" with reference to the claims of Europeans. I said that some day the African would be educated and armed; that would lead to a clash. Eliot thought that that day was so far distant as not to matter and that by that time the European element would be strong enough to look after themselves; but I am convinced that in the end the Africans will win and that Eliot's policy can lead only to trouble and disappointment.

CHARLES DOMINGO

The African Awakening

The roots of African nationalism lie in many fields, but one of them is certainly the Christian religion, especially in its African forms and communities. Probably born in Mozambique, Domingo became a missionary in Nyasaland. His contribution to twentieth-century national-

From Charles Domingo, "To the Pastors and Evangelists," pamphlet, Seventh Day Baptist Historical Society, 1911, quoted in G. Shepperson and T. Price, *Independent African* (Edinburgh: 1958), p. 163.

ism has been assessed in detail by George Shepperson and Thomas Price in the masterly book from which this striking statement is drawn.

[1911] Poor Resident, he thinks too much of his skin and not of his heart. What is the difference between a white man and a black man? Are we not of the same blood and all from Adam? This startles me much — is Europe still Christian or Heathen? . . . There is too much failure among all Europeans in Nyasaland. The three combined bodies, Missionaries, Government and Companies, or gainers of money — do form the same rule to look upon the native with mocking eyes. It sometimes startles us to see that the three combined bodies are from Europe, and along with them there is a title "CHRISTENDOM." And to compare or make a comparison between the MASTER of the title and his servants it pushes any African away from believing the Master of the title. If we had power enough to communicate ourselves to Europe we would advise them not to call themselves "Christendom" but "Europeandom" . . .

THÉODORE MONOD
Rediscovering Africa

For long the director and guiding spirit of the Institut Français d'Afrique Noire at Dakar, Professor Théodore Monod is one of the most eminent scholars that France has given to the Continent. Pioneer of Saharan exploration, he traversed the daunting sands of the inner desert in days when motor transport was still a rarity. His brief and modest memoirs are a delight to read. They suggest by what process of resolute and painful discovery the cultural truths of Africa have been determined.

From Théodore Monod, *Méharées, Explorations au Vrai Sahara* (Paris: 1947). Translated by B. Davidson.

[1936] Tichitt [far out on the western fringe of the true Sahara] is very interesting. I should like to stop here so as to see more and see better. But the trail is long. Back to wandering again.

Now, by way of Walata, I approach Néma whence a last leap will take me to Timbuktu . . .

More and more archeological discoveries: from the locality of Aghréjit alone I have more than a thousand prehistorical objects, among them some precious documents, for example, a splendid bone harpoon.

Excursion to Taokest . . . A hard journey but fruitful: a bone boring tool.

I follow again the great cliffs of Tichitt towards the east. After Tennegué, traversing a gorge and seeing ahead some rocks which augur badly for an eye practiced in the search for rock-drawings, I make sacrilegious vows to the gods that they should rub out any such drawings, or make it seem as though there had never been any. It's five in the evening, the night is drawing in, and the water-point is far.

A moment later I bump into a formidable site of Libyco-Berber engravings in excellent condition. What to do? Impossible to lose such fine documents, impossible also to leave the work of copying them until tomorrow.

I halt the caravan and begin copying at 17 hours 30. And under what conditions . . . At night; with a carbon lamp which suddenly decides to burn deplorably; and across a vertical face which I have to climb like a lizard on a wall, but a lizard with a drawing board at the end of its fingers instead of suction pads.

I finish the job towards midnight . . .

PLACIDE TEMPELS

Bantu Philosophy

Father Placide Tempels is a Belgian priest, long in Catholic missionary service in the Congo, whose book has become a classic demonstration of the truth that African peoples have worked out complex and coherent, though prescientific, explanations of Man and the Universe. "Within the context of this system of metaphysics, as expounded in detail by Tempels," William Fagg has written, "many traits in African culture which appear absurd and inexplicable when stated in European terms . . . are readily seen to be intelligible, reasonable and logical." * Readers interested in this angle of approach to the "myth of the Negro past" should also turn to the works of Marcel Griaule, Germaine Dieterlen, and Roger Parrinder.

———

. . . All the strivings of the Bantu [that is, of the Bantu-speaking peoples who occupy the greater part of central and southern Africa] are related to the idea of vital force. This is the fundamental notion in their concept of being . . . They consider man, *muntu*, as the central living force: the being who has life at its best and most elevated. Man is the supreme force . . . dominating animals, plants and minerals. These lower beings exist by divine decision only to be of help to man, their superior . . . [After enlarging on this idea and its associated metaphysic, Tempels concludes:] The discovery of Bantu philosophy must trouble those of us who are concerned with the education of Africans. Too often we have seen ourselves before them as confronted by a void. In our educational and civilizing mission, we have thought

From Placide Tempels, *La Philosophie Bantoue* (Paris: 1949). Translated by B. Davidson.

* W. Fagg in *The Webster Plass Collection of African Art* (British Museum, 1953).

ourselves beginning with a bare sheet from which we had only to erase valueless vanities in order to start afresh . . . We have thought we were educating children, "big children"; and this seemed an easy task. But now, suddenly, we see that we are dealing with a humanity that is adult, conscious of its own wisdom, penetrated by its own universalist philosophy. And we feel the ground slipping from beneath our feet . . .

VINIGI GROTTANELLI
Points of Arrival

Just as a few men like Father Tempels have profoundly affected modern thought about the intellectual truths of "savage Africa," so have a few others changed the approach to African art. Dr. Vinigi Grottanelli is a distinguished Italian ethnographer.

Of European art — for example, of Gothic sculpture — no criticism would have been taken seriously if it had offered explanations based on banal generalities such as primitive faith, mysticism, collectivism; yet such crudities have been nonetheless accepted as true and profound when applied to Negro sculpture . . .

African sculpture, like so-called primitive art in general, is not in itself "primitive" at all and nor were the men who created it. In considering it we are not confronted by primordial gropings, any more than by the spontaneous self-expressions of a suppositional (but nonexistent) "natural man."

On the contrary, we are looking at the outcome of ancient and most elaborate traditions. These are works not of exuberant youth, nor even less of inexpert childhood; they are the products of a

From V. L. Grottanelli, "Sul Significato della Scultura Africana," Lugard Memorial Lecture, 1961, reprinted in *Africa*, Oct. 1961. Translated by B. Davidson.

conscious and thoughtful maturity, even of old age. They are not points of departure, but points of arrival . . .

ONWUKA DIKE

African History

Several Africans turned to the major task of writing African history in what I have termed the second and third periods of the first half of the century. One thinks especially of the Ghanaian, Dr. J. B. Danquah. But I have chosen to end this anthology with something from Dr. K. O. Dike, chancellor of the University College of Ibadan, because his book on the politics of the Niger Delta is a most clear and scholarly example of the way in which the rewriting of African history from a noncolonial standpoint can free the world of many destructive misconceptions.

The pivot of Delta social organization was the "House System" or "House Rule." This peculiar constitution is common to all the trading states and was the direct result of the trade with the Europeans . . . The mixture of [African] peoples [in the Delta] often meant that African law and custom vanished and a new law and order was evolved based partly on African precedent and experience and partly on the lessons of the contact with Europe. In its full development the House became at once a cooperative trading unit and a local government institution . . .

It was in the interest of every House Head to foster and increase the trade of his people: as trade cannot flourish under conditions of terror, the Heads must have used their absolute power with great discretion and restraint . . . For the difference between the plantation slavery of the New World and the domestic

From K. O. Dike, *Trade and Politics in the Niger Delta, 1830-1885* (Oxford: 1956).

slavery as practiced in the Niger Delta lies in this: whereas in the former the slaves performed, on the whole, an indirect and impersonal service and were regarded as some form of capital goods, in the latter the wealth produced by a slave eventually set him free, for the master knew the slave intimately and the value of his work and rewarded him accordingly. It was this incentive, ever present in the House system, that made it in the nineteenth century an institution full of vitality, flexible, and in a large measure beneficial to all . . .

Acknowledgments

I SHOULD LIKE ESPECIALLY TO THANK PROFESSOR PHILIP CURTIN, Mr. Thomas Hodgkin, Mr. J. O. Hunwick and Professor George Shepperson for generous help and advice, Professor E. H. Carr for permission to quote from him, and the London Library for its unfailing and often indispensable patience. Thanks for photographs are equally due to the American Research Center in Egypt, Dr. A. D. H. Bivar, the Clarendon Press, Dr. Lyndon Harries, Mrs. F. Elwyn Jones, Professor J. Leclant, Professor R. Pankhurst, Sayed Hasan Thabit, and Mr. David Williams.

Acknowledgments are also due to the following for permission to quote copyright material:

Cambridge University Press for material from *Science and Civilisation in China*, by J. Needham; the Carnegie Institution of Washington for material from *Documents Illustrative of the History of the Slave Trade to America*, edited by E. Donnan; E. H. Carr for material from his Trevelyan Lectures; the Clarendon Press, Oxford, for material from *Trade and Politics in the Niger Delta*, by K. O. Dike; *The East African Coast, Select Documents* by G. S. P. Freeman-Grenville; and from *Swahili Poetry*, translated by L. Harries; Constable & Co. Ltd. for material from *The Land of Zinj*, by C. H. Stigand; the Controller of H. M. Stationery Office for material from Plymouth Customs accounts (Crown-copyright); the Director of National Archives, Ibadan, for material from *The Rise of the Sokoto Fulani*, by E. J. Arnett; *Lugard Lectures* (1955) by S. O. Biobaku, and *Sudanese Memoirs* by H. R. Palmer; Edinburgh University Press for material from *Independent African*, by Shepperson and Price; the editor of the *African Ecclesiastical Review* and the

374 ACKNOWLEDGMENTS

author for material from "Islam and Christianity in East Africa Before the Mid-nineteenth Century" by G. S. P. Freeman-Grenville; the editor of the *Ethiopian Observer* for material from the "Chronicle of Zara Yaqob"; the editor of the *Journal of African History* and the authors for material from "Ife and Its Archaeology" by F. Willett, "An Analysis of the Sources of Coins" by G. S. P. Freeman-Grenville, and "Maramuca" by D. P. Abraham; the editor of the *Journal* of the Historical Society of Nigeria and the author for material from "The Nok Culture in Prehistory" by B. A. B. Fagg; the editor of *Kush*, Khartoum, and the author for material from "The Decline and Fall of Meroë" by L. P. Kirwan; the editorial board of the *Bulletin* of the School of Oriental and African Studies and the authors for material from articles on dan Fodio and Muhammad Bello by M. Hiskett and A. D. H. Bivar; Chief J. V. Egharevba for material from his book *A Short History of Benin* (Ibadan University Press); the Government Printer, Pretoria, for material from *Records of South-eastern Africa* by G. M. Theal; the Hakluyt Society for material from *Europeans in West Africa*, by J. W. Blake, *The Book of Duarte Barbosa*, translated by M. Longworth Dames, and *A Journal of the First Voyage of Vasco da Gama*, translated by E. G. Ravenstein; M. Hiskett for material from his translation of *Tazyin al-Waraqat*, by Abdullah Ibn Muhammad (Ibadan, 1963); J. O. Hunwick for material from his translation of al Maghili; the Institut Français d'Afrique Noire, Dakar, for material from "Sundiata's Triumph," published in *Notes Africaines*; the International African Institute and the author for material from "Sul Significato della Scultura Africana" by V. L. Grottanelli, published in *Africa*; the Junta de Investigacoes do Ultramar, Lisbon, for material from *O Muata Kazembe* by A. C. P. Gamitto, translated as *King Kazembe* by I. Cunnison; Guy Le Prat for material from *Méharées: Explorations au Vrai Sahara* by T. Monod; Librairie Orientaliste Paul Geuthner for material from *Masalik al Absar fi Mamalik al Amsar*, translated by Gaudefroy-Demombynes; R. Mauny for material from his translation of *Esmeraldo de Situ Orbis*; Oliver & Boyd Ltd. and the author for material from *Kenya Diary* by Colonel R. Meinertzhagen; Penguin Books Ltd. and Penguin Books, Inc., Baltimore,

Maryland, for material from *The Prehistory of Southern Africa* by J. D. Clark and from Herodotus: *The Histories,* translated by A. de Sélincourt; Présence Africaine, Paris, for material from *La Philosophie Bantoue* by P. Tempels; Presses Universitaires de France for material from M. Kati, *Tarikh al-Fettash,* translated by O. Houdas and M. Delafosse; Arthur Probsthain for material from *China's Discovery of Africa* by J. J. L. Duyvendak; Routledge & Kegan Paul Ltd. for material from Ibn Battuta, *Travels in Asia and Africa,* translated by H. A. R. Gibb, and *History of the Yorubas,* by S. Johnson; the Trustees of the British Museum for material from the account of Sir John Hawkins's voyage in Cotton MS, Otho E viii, and the University of Chicago Press for material from *Ancient Records of Egypt,* by J. H. Breasted.

Index

ABBADIE, ARNAULD D', 37, 309-310
Abbas, Abu'l-, 94
Abdelkader, Ali ben, 94
Abdullahu (Sokoto reformer), 322
Abeokuta, 349-350
Abomey, 234, 236
Abraham, D. P., 142, 144-146, 374
Abrahs, 331
Abutua, 160, 161
Abyssinia, 247. (See also Ethiopia)
Accra, 178, 212, 331
'Adamawa, 334
Adanson, Michel, 30, 221-222
Adelan, Sheikh, 257-258
Aden, 135
Adulis, 25
Affonso, King, of Congo (Mbemba Nzinga), 175, 191-194
Affonso, Martin, 123
A'gades, 346
Agaja, King. See Trudo, Guadja
Agaow (Dahoman general), 236
Aghréjit, 368
Ahmadu, 267
Ajayi, J. F. Ade, 269n.
Akan, 43
Akims, 331
Akwamu, 15, 178
A'lawate, Sídi, 340, 342
Alcançova, Diogo de, 137-138, 146-150
Alexandria, 21
Algeria, 80
Ali, Chi (Songhay ruler), 92
Ali, Sultan of Sokoto 1837-1849, 327n.
Ali, Mai, Sarki of Bornu, 85

Almami, King, 311-313
Almammy, 232
Almeida, Francisco d', 105, 136
Alooma, Mai (Sultan) Idris, 89-90
Alvares, Francisco, 27
'Alwa, 54, 56
Ama-Xosa, 210
Amboland, 363
Anamaboe, 331
Anaya, Pedro d', 138
Anderson, Alexander, 310
Angola, 18, 29, 160, 161, 175, 194, 208, 210, 216-217, 227n., 274, 291, 301
Angoya, 130-131
Angra Pequena (Lüderitz Bay), 363
Anville, Jean Baptiste d', 277
Aoukar. See Wagadu
Appolonia, 225
Aquapims, 331
A'rawan, 345, 346
Ardra, 234, 235
Arguin, 334
Arkell, Anthony John, 44
Arnett, E. J., 67n., 373
Arrhenius, Captain, 231n.
Asahel, Woodage, 256
Ashanti, 19, 177, 208, 328-329, 330, 349
Assins, 331
Aswan, 44, 47, 49, 52
Asyut, 44
Atkins, John, 222-223
Authule, 247, 248
Aveiro, Joham Affom da, 99-100, 185
Axelson, E., 135n., 274n., 276n.
Axim, 218

Axum, 11, 46, 54, 118
Ayabdar, 255
Aylo, Ayto, 248, 249, 250, 251
Azambuja, Diego da, 181, 184
Azanegas, 189
Azurara. *See* Zurara

Baba, Ahmad, 24, 90-91, 336, 338, 347, 347n.
Baba-Sec, 222
Bagamoyo, 274
Bakay, Sheikh el, 340, 342
Baker, Samuel, 273, 275
Bakone, 288, 289
Bakuba, 365
Bakwains, 298
Bambara, 314, 317, 318-321
Bambugu, 77
Bambuk, 346
Bammakoo (Bamako), 321
Banagha, 326
Bantus, 12, 58, 142, 210, 369-370
Baptista, Pedro João, 291
Baraguri, 77
Barbosa, Duarte, 105, 106, 128-135, 147, 151
Barbot, James, 214n., 216-217
Barbot, John, 30, 211-213
Barea, Coque Abou, 256
Bari, 89
Baro, *Chi*, 93
Baroso, Pero, 187
Barra, Kingdom of, 226, 227
Barreto, Manoel, 148, 167-169
Barros, João de, 28, 136, 147, 152, 176
Barrow, John, 57, 278-281
Barth, Heinrich, 6-7, 37, 89, 92, 269, 273, 275, 332-347
Barwe, 145
Basuto, 283-285
Basutoland, 57, 58, 209
Battell, Andrew, 29
Battuta, Muhammad ibn Abdul-

lah ibn, 22, 64, 79-83, 86, 105, 116-117
Bauchi, Emir of. *See* Dadi, Ya'qub bin
Beaver, Captain Philip, 32, 303-304, 306
Beazley, C. R., 174
Bechuana, 278, 298, 299
Bechuanaland, 274, 297
Bekri, Abdullah Abu-Ubayd al, 22, 64, 72-73, 347
Bellefonds, Linant de, 277
Bello, Muhammad, Sultan of Sokoto, 26, 67-68, 267, 269, 273, 322, 323, 326, 327-328
Bena Makima, 365
Benametapa, 129, 130, 151, 152, 153. *See also* Monomotapa
Benin, 15, 26, 30, 64, 66, 68n., 95-100, 177, 179-180, 180n., 185, 187-188, 196-198, 213, 224-225, 241-243
Benoist, Edmond, 94n.
Benowm, 316
Berber, 79, 189, 368
Bernaldez, Joham, 182, 184
Bilali, 351, 352
Binger, L. G., 276n.
Biobaku, Saburi O., 70, 373
Bird, J., 281n.
Biri, King, 161
Biruni, abu-al-Rayhan Muhammad ibn-Ahmad al, 22
Bitou, 94
Bivar, A. D. H., 326n., 373, 374
Blake, J. W., 180, 187n., 188n., 195n., 374
Blemmyes, 55
Blomert, Samuel, 30
Blyden, Edward Wilmot, 35, 269, 269n., 347, 351-352
Boccarro, Antonio, 163-164
Bocicas, 160

Boers, 19, 57, 210, 211, 353, 286, 297, 298
Bokhari, 335
Boma, 274
Bondou, 311-313
Bonny, 227, 227n., 350
Booshuana, 279-281
Bornu, 15, 26, 89, 273, 333, 334
Bosman, William, 30, 217-221
Botelho, 292-294
Botero, 162
Botonga, 152, 161
Bowdich, Thomas, 328-330
Bradbury, R. E., 95
Brava, 104, 134
Breasted, James Henry, 5, 44, 47n., 49n., 50n., 51n., 375
Brew, Richard, 225-226
Brito, Domingos d'Abreu de, 194, 194n.
Bruce, James, 246-249, 273, 277, 309
Bry, De, 30
Bryant, A. T., 281n.
Bucutu, 163
Buganda, 18
Bugau, *Sarkin* Aujera, 85
Bulala, 89
Bunduu, *Shehu*, 85
Bure, 346
Burrom, Prince, 152
Bursale (Bursall), 202
Bursalim, 90
Burton, Richard, 6, 37, 273, 273n., 275, 291
Bushmen, 10, 12, 37, 57, 58, 211, 261-263
Butabute, 285
Butua, 152

Cabral, Pedro Alvares, 106
Cadornega, Antonio de Oliveira, 203, 203n.
Caillaud, Frédéric, 277, 277n.

Caillié, René, 272, 272n., 336, 343, 347
Cairo, 64, 75-77, 78
Calabar, 227, 227n.
Calecut, 128
Calmina, 234
Calonina, 237
Cambay, 129, 132, 133, 134, 135
Camdebo, 261
Cameron, V. L., 274n.
Campbell, Robert, 349-350
Cantore, 202
Cão, Diogo, 27
Cape Coast, 225, 234, 331
Cape Province, 259, 273-274
Capracina, King, 168
Caramansa, 182
Carr, E. H., 373
Carthage, 10, 11, 53
Casalis, Edouard, 33, 283-285
Cassan, 201
Casseneuve, John, 214-215, 216
Castros, 199, 200
Cavazzi, Father Giovanni, 33, 177, 238
Cesta, King of, 200
Chang Hsieh, 115, 115n.
Changamire, 145-146, 147, 149-150
Ch'ang-lo (Ming admiral), 22, 104
Chao Ju-kua, 104, 114n.
Chicanga, 160, 161
Chicova, 159
Chidima, 145
Chiroro, 161
Chittick, Neville, 103, 303
Churchill, A. and J., 211, 214n., 216n.
Clapperton, Hugh, 6, 67-68, 269, 272, 272n., 273, 333
Clark, J. Desmond, 57-59, 57n., 141, 374
Coelho, J. R., 187n.

Coelho, Nicolau, 126
Coetzee, Jacobus, 210
Colchians, 46
Commendo (Commenda), 212, 225
Confu, Ayto, 254
Conga, 199
Congo, 18, 27, 29, 33, 36, 123, 175, 176, 177, 191-194, 216, 227n., 237-240, 361, 364-365, 369
Cook, Captain James, 259
Copperschen, Simon, 363
Cormantine, 178
Cosmas Indicopleustes, 25
Coupland, Sir Reginald, 4
Courteille, Pavet de, 107
Couto, Diogo de, 28, 163n., 176
Cox, Captain, 228
Crone, G. R., 174
Cruickshank, Brodie, 330-332
Cuama, 131
Cugoano, Ottobah, 27
Cunnison, Ian, 291n., 292, 374
Curtin, Philip, 373
Cuvelier, Monsignor J., 29, 176, 192

DADI, YA'QUB BIN, EMIR OF BAU-CHI, 326
Dafur, 11, 44
Dahomey, 19, 177, 208, 218, 222, 234-235, 235-237, 349
Dakar, 6, 233
Dala, 333
Dalzell, Archibald, 234-235
Dambarari, 167
Dames, Mansel Longworth, 106, 128n., 151n., 374
Danquah, J. B., 371
Dapper, Olfert, 29, 179-180, 201, 259n.
Darfur, 25
Darmura, 77

Daro, 54, 56
Datliboo, 315
Dawhee, 234
Dedjasmatch, 309
Défremery, C., 79n.
Delafosse, Maurice, 73, 73n., 90n., 375
Delany, Martin, 347-349
Denham, Dixon, 6, 272-273
Denkyira (Denkera), 15, 331
Denny, A., 271n.
Denon, Vivant, 277
Diaz, Bartholomeu, 27, 120
Dieterlen, Germaine, 369
Dike, K. Onwuka, 349n., 371-372, 373
Dingaan, 298
Djenné, 24, 87, 88, 90, 91, 94-95, 177, 186, 207, 272
Dodona, 46
Domingo, Charles, 362, 366-367
Donnan, Elizabeth, 178, 215n., 225n., 226n., 227n., 228n., 230n., 373
Doolinkeaboo, 316
Duas Partes, das (Village of the Two Parts), 182
Dukkali, Sheikh Abu Sa'id Otman ed, 77
Dunqul, 44
Dussi, 85
Duyvendak, J. J. L., 103, 104, 114n., 375

EDEN, RICHARD, 196-198
Efoua, 356
Egharevba, Chief Jacob V., 64, 68n., 95-100, 180n., 374
Egypt, 10, 11, 15, 43, 45-46, 50, 51, 53, 75-77, 96
Eka, 99
Ekiti, 99
El Fasher, Sudan, 44

Elephantine. *See* Aswan
Elgon, 366
Eliot, Charles, 365
Ellenberger, D. F., 283n.
Elmina Castle, 180, 217
Engaruka, 17, 19
Equiano, Olaudah, 27, 241-243
Ere, *Ogiso*, 96
Eresoyen, *Oba*, 95
Erinmwinde, 98
Esigie, *Oba*, 99-100
Esther, Ozoro, 249, 251, 252
Estuniga, Gonzalo de, 189-190
Ethiopia, 11, 18, 25, 26, 27, 37, 45, 46, 52, 53, 106, 117-119, 154, 177, 186, 246-249, 273, 309
Evian, 97
Eweka I, *Oba* of Benin, 98
Ewuare the Great, 99
Ezana, King of Axum, 46, 54-56

FAGAN, BRIAN, 142
Fagg, Bernard A. B., 65-66, 374
Fagg, William, 369
Faggi, 85
Fanimboo, 315
Fans, 353, 356
Fantiland, 27
Faqih, Ibn al-, 81
Farrington, B., 259n.
Fartua, Imam Ahmed ibn, 89-90
Fellani, 333
Felner, A. de A., 191n.
Fermagha, 345
Fernando, Don, King of Spain, 188-190
Ferrer, Jacme, 173
Fez, 80
Fezzan, 89
Fida. *See* Ouidah
Fingos, 285
Fodio, Uthman dan, 267, 322-325

Fons (Foys, Dahomans), 234, 236-237
Foulahs, 317
François, Captain von, 363
Freeman-Grenville, Greville S. P., 5, 103, 107, 110, 110n., 111, 112, 116n., 119n., 135n., 208, 373, 374
Freetown, 351
Frobenius, Leo, 364-365
Fukien, 104
Fulah (Sosso), 73
Fulani (Fulbe), 26, 84, 243, 245, 269, 322, 333, 334, 337, 338, 339, 343
Fung, 177, 257
Fyfe, Christopher, 34-35
Fynn, Henry, 281-282

GABON, REPUBLIC OF, 353
Gallagher, J., 271n.
Galloo, 314
Gama, Paulo da, 126
Gama, Vasco da, 27, 105, 119, 122-128, 304
Gambaru, 90
Gambia, 174, 201-203, 231, 233, 310, 322
Gamitto, Captain Antonio C. P., 291-296, 374
Gando, 335
Gao, 23, 64, 77, 90, 177
Gardiner, Sir Alan, 50
Gatawa, 90
Gaudefroy-Démombynes, 75n.
George, King of Nubia, 25
Geosorro, 316
Ghadames, 335, 345, 346
Ghadamsiye, 342
Ghana, 14-15, 24, 27, 43, 70-71, 72-73, 77, 91, 141, 143, 362
Ghanata, 347
Gharb, 338
Ghat, 334, 335

Ghiaru, 73
Gibb, Sir H. A. R., 79n., 375
Gibberti, Mahomet, 249
Gillofree Port, 226, 227
Gobir, 85, 322
Gogobiri, 69
Gojam, 309
Gondar, 246, 247, 252, 254
Goree, 233
Grant, James, 273, 273n.
Greenlee, W. B., 106
Grevenbrock, Johannes de, 259n.
Griaule, Marcel, 369
Grottanelli, Vinigi L., 370-371, 374
Gufho, 255
Guillain, M., 5
Guinea, 27, 29, 30, 32, 77, 178, 185, 188-190, 195, 196, 198, 199, 207, 210, 217-221, 222, 224
Guniuswa, 145
Gusman, 162

HABE. *See* Hausa
Hakluyt, Richard, 28, 196n., 198n.
Hanzuan, 116
Harkhuf, 44, 47-48
Harries, Lyndon, 307, 307n., 373
Hasan, Abu'l-, 80-81
Hatshepsut, Queen, 25, 50
Hausa, 15, 69, 84, 269, 322, 323-324, 327, 333, 334, 344, 346
Hawkins, John, 175, 199-200
Hawkins, William, 195
Heatley, Captain, 226-227
Hereros, 363-364
Herodotus, 7, 45-46, 52-53
Herskovits, Melville, 8
Hichens, W., 307
Hirth, F., 114n.
Hiskett, M., 322n., 325n., 374

Hodgkin, Thomas, 5, 26, 68n., 180, 241n., 276n., 373
Hottentots, 58, 122, 210, 211, 259-263, 297, 363
Houdas, Octave, 90n., 92, 94n., 327n., 375
Houghton, Major Daniel, 311
Howard, C., 272n., 276n.
Hucicas, 129
Hunwick, J. O., 24, 86n., 373, 374

IBADAN, 6, 371
Ibo, 99
Iboland, 27, 241-243
Idrisi, Abu Abdullah Muhammad al, 22, 30, 103, 111, 143
Ife, 66, 96, 98
I'gbira, 354
I'gbo, 334
Igodo, *Ogiso*, 96
Iguegha, 98-99
Ihama, 98
Ikare, 99
Ilorin, 348
Imoshagh (Tuareg), 337
Inhabaze, 159
Inhambane, 161
'Iraq, 68
Iresni, 73
Irthet, 45, 47-48, 49
Isesi, 48

JACQUIN, 235
Jadin, Abbé L., 29, 176
Jaubert, P. A., 111
Jemaa, 65
Jibrila, *Sarki* of Nupe, 85
Jilani, al-, 326
João, Dom, King of Portugal, 192
Jobson, Richard, 201-203
Johnson, Samuel, 68-69, 375
Johnston, John, 230-231
Jones, Mrs. F. Elwyn, 373
José, Amaro, 291

Justinian, Emperor, 25
Juzayy, ibn, 79-80

KAARTA, 318, 321
Kabara (Kabora), 77, 338, 341
Kabeja, 365
Kader, 'Abd el, 336
Kaduna, 6
Kakuyo Komunyaka, 146
Kamal, Yusuf, 23
Kancaba, 316, 321, 322
Kanem, 15, 89-90
Kankaree, 321
Kano, 84-85, 333-335, 344, 345
Kanuri, 333
Karanga, 17, 144, 147, 208, 270, 286
Karfa, 321
Kashta, 45
Kasim, Mulay, 338
Katanga, 16, 142, 145, 291
Kati, Mahmud, 26, 90-94
Kawa, 55
Kayes, 91
Kazembe, King, 291, 294-297
Kemmoo, 314
Kenya, 18, 23, 113, 365-366
Kerimba Islands, 153
Khartoum, 45, 258
Khauas, 363
Kiewiet, C. W. de, 210*n.*, 211*n.*,
Kilimane. *See* Quilimane
Kilimanjaro, 273
Kilwa, 17, 22, 104, 105, 106, 112,
    116-117, 119, 122, 128, 130,
    131, 132, 136, 137, 138, 143,
    146, 208, 313-305, 306-307
Kimble, D., 351*n.*
Kimble, G. H. T., 186*n.*
Kingsley, Mary, 271, 276, 353-357
Kirina, 73, 74
Kirk, Sir John, 105
Kirk-Greene, A. H. M., 332*n.*
Kirwan, L. P., 54, 54*n.*, 374

Kissy, 351
Kneha, 339, 340
Kolobeng, 299
Konnté, Sangaran Danguinia, 74
Kordofan, 11
Kotoko, 26
Koulikoro, 73
Krapf, Johann, 6, 37, 273, 273*n.*
Krieger, Gert, 298
Kua, 208
Kuba, 209
Kubbel, L. E., 23*n.*
Kukawa, 69
Kukuna, 351, 352
Kukuruku, 99
Kumasi, 328-330
Kumbari, *Sarki* Muhammad, 85
Kumbi, 70, 73
Kuruman, 274
Kush, 11, 13, 25, 45-46, 51-52,
    54, 277
Kwekarynugo, 149

LAGDEN, G., 283*n.*, 284*n.*
Lambart, Nicholas, 196
Lamu, 134
Lamurudu, 69
Lander, John, 272, 272*n.*
Lander, Richard, 272, 272*n.*
Landye, John, 195
Le Prat, Guy, 374
Leakey, Louis, 9
Leclant, Jean, 44, 373
Leetakoo, 278, 281
Legum, Colin, 362
Leo Africanus, 26, 64, 90
Leopold II, King of Belgium, 36,
    276, 364
Lesuto, 285
Leutwein, Major Theodor von,
    363
Leys, Norman, 362
Liberia, 26, 35, 351
Libya, 53

Lillo, Antonio Rodriguez de, 190
Lima, Antonio Rois de, 168
Limba, 352
Limiin, 117
Linschoten, Jan Huyghen van, 29
Littmann, E., 54n.
Livingstone, David, 33, 36, 274, 274n., 275, 297-302, 332
Loanda, 194
Loango, 239
Lok, John, 175, 196n.
Lourenço, Fernã, 181
Lourenço, Francysquo, 188
Luanda, 274
Luanze, 159, 163
Ludamar, 316
Lüderitz, Adolf, 363
Luebo, 365
Luluabourg, 365
Lumbwa, 366
Lunda, 209, 291

MACEMBA, 357-358
Madagascar, 114n., 134
Madanda, 145
Mafia, 113, 119, 134, 208
Maghili, Muhammad ben Abd al-Karim al, 24, 86-89
Mahdi, 270
Mahomed, Sidi, 316
Maitfha, 257
Makuri, *Sarki* of Dussi, 85
Mali, 15, 24, 64, 73, 75-79, 79-83, 89, 91, 93, 310
Malin, 104
Malindi, 119, 120, 127, 128, 129, 130, 132, 133, 134, 208
Mambasa, 134
Mambo, 163
Mamgegar, 203
Manamotapa. *See* Monomotapa
Mandakha, 116
Mandingo, 64, 231, 346

Mangalo, 130
Mango, 346
Manica, 154, 160, 161
Manipanza, Dom Pedro, 193
Manissaba, Dom Manuel, 193
Mansong, King, 319
Mantatees, 285, 288
Manuel, King of Portugal, 150
Manura (Mavura), King of Monomotapa, 165, 166
Manzovo, 159
Manyika, 145
Maravi (Malawi), 167, 291, 292, 293, 294
Mariam, 254
Masapa, 147
Mascal, Guebra, 246-252, 254, 255
Mashonaland, 274
Masina, 327n., 339
Massapa, 159, 160, 161, 163
Massingan, 217
Mas'udi, Abdul Hassan ibn Hussein ibn Ali al, 22, 103, 107-109, 110
Matabeleland, 274
Matebele (Ndebele), 209, 286, 287, 288, 289
Matewane, 285
Matope (Rozwi king), 144-145
Matuca, 152
Matveev, V. V., 23n.
Mauny, Raymond, 174, 186n., 374
Mauretania, 189
Mayr, Hans, 135-136
Mbanza Congo (S. Salvador), 192n.
Mbire, 145
Mehmendar, Emir Abu'l 'Abbas Ahmed ben Abi'l Kaki el, 75-76
Meinertzhagen, Colonel R., 364, 374
Mekher, 47

Mello, Antonio de, 168
Memphis, 51-52
Mernere, Pharaoh, 44, 47
Meroë, 45, 46, 52-53, 54-56, 67, 70, 104, 247, 258-259, 277
Meynard, C. Barbier de, 107
Michael, Ras, of Tigre, 247-252, 254, 256
Mina. *See* Elmina Castle
Mocaranga, 160
Moffat, Robert, 286-291
Mogadishu, 104, 112, 116, 135
Mokachane, 285
Mokaranga, 167
Mokomba, 149
Mombasa, 116, 117, 120, 128, 129, 130, 132-133, 136, 137, 138, 208
Monod, Théodore, 362, 367-368, 374
Monomotapa, 17, 141, 147, 148, 150, 151, 159-163, 163-164, 164-166, 294n. *See also* Benametapa
Monteiro, Major José, 291
Montgomery, James, 38-39
Moorja, 314
Morocco, 15, 19, 27, 80, 316, 338, 341, 345
Moselekatse, Chief, 285, 286-291, 298
Moses, 26
Moshesh, King of the Basuto, 283, 284-285
Mosto, Ca' da, 174
Mozambique, 18, 111, 119, 124-125, 130-131, 141, 147, 151, 153, 154, 159, 160, 165, 208, 210, 294, 308, 366
Muhammad, Abdullah ben, 323, 325-326
Muhammad, Abu Abdallah, 24
Muhammad, Sheikh Amin ibn, of Bornu, 26

Muhammad, Askia (Askia Muhammad ben Abi Bakr Ture), 24, 86-89, 91-94
Muhammad, Sultan of Pate, 120
Müller, F. F., 357n.
Mumineh, Almamy, 351
Munhaes, 294
Murzuk, 334
Musa, *Mansa* Kankan, Emperor of Mali, 64, 75-76, 94, 344
Mutota Mwanamutapa, Rozwi king, 144, 145
Muza, 21
Myna, 185

NAIMBANNA, KING, 228-229
Nairobi, 365
Nandi, 366
Napata, 45, 51
Napoleon, 277
Nasir, Abdullah ben, 307-308
Nasir, el Malik en, Sultan of Egypt, 75-76
Natal, 275, 283, 285
Neame, A., 274n.
Needham, J., 115n., 373
Neferkere, 48
Néma, 368
Nevinson, Henry, 275
New Calabar, 227
Nguni, 19, 209
Nhaya, Pero da, 154
Niané, D. Tamsir, 70-71
Niane (town in the kingdom of Mali), 77, 80
Niger (republic), 322
Nigeria, 11, 24, 27, 65, 66, 67, 84, 93, 322, 332, 349
Noba (Nuba), 54-56
Nobatae, 55
Nok, 65-66, 66-67
Norris, Robert, 235-237
Northern Rhodesia, 142
Nubia, 25, 44, 49, 50, 55, 67

Nupe, 85, 333, 338
Nyahuma, 145-146
Nyasaland, 366, 367
Nyendael, van, 179

OAKE, HENRY, 178
Obalufon, 97
Obbah, 98
Odudua, *Oni*, 96-97
Oduduwa (ancestor of Yorubas), 69
Ogiamwen, 97-98
Ogiefa, 97, 98
Ogun (Ewuare the Great), 99
Oguola, *Oba*, 98-99
Okavango, 363
Old Lithako, 288
Oloton, 98
Omar, Sultan, 120
Omari, Ibn Fadl Allah al, 64, 75-79
Opone (Ras Hafun), 21
Orange Free State, 283
Oranmiyan, Prince, 96, 97-98
Osanego, *Onogie*, 98
Osogan, 97
Osorius, 162
Oudney, Dr. Walter, 272
Ouidah (Fida or Whydah), 218-219, 222-223, 234, 235, 237
Ovambandjeru, 363
Owen, W. F. W., 306-307
Owodo, 97
Oye-Eboe, 242
Oyo, 15, 68*n*., 69, 98, 177, 235-237

PAIVA-MANSO, VISCONDE DE, 191*n*., 194*n*., 203*n*.
Pakalita (chief of Fingos), 285
Palencia, Alonso de, 188-190
Palmer, Sir (Herbert) Richmond, 71*n*., 84, 84*n*., 89, 89*n*., 373
Palos, 189

Pankhurst, Richard, 373
Park, Mungo, 6, 272, 278, 310-322
Parrinder, Roger, 369
Pate, 23, 120-121, 134, 208, 307
Pedro, João, 292
Pemba, 113, 116, 134, 208
Penny, James, 227-228
Pepi II, 44, 49
Pepi-nakt, 49
Pereira, Duarte Pacheco, 174, 176, 186, 186*n*.
Philipe, Dom (Philip IV, King of Spain and Portugal), 166
Phillips, Captain, 178
Piankhi, 45, 51-52
Pigafetta, Philip, 162, 176
Pina, Ruy de, 174, 180-185
P'ing, Emperor, of China, A.D. 1-6, 104
Pinkerton, J., 153*n*., 221*n*., 237*n*.
Pinteado, Captain, 196, 197
Pires, Duarte, 187-188
Pires, Gonçalo, 193
Place, J., 273*n*., 276*n*.
Plumb, J. H., 272*n*.
Po-pa-li, 114
Portendic, 232
Potgieter, Hendrick, 298
Prestage, E., 174
Prester John, 125
Pretorius, Andries, 298
Price, Thomas, 366*n*., 367, 373
Prins, A. H. J., 120
Prior, James, 303-305, 306
Probsthain, Arthur, 375
Proyart, Abbé, 237-240
Ptolemy, Claudius, 21
Punt, 25, 48, 50
Purchas, Samuel, 28

QAHTAN, YA'RUB IBN, 68
Quashies Town, 230

Quilimane (Kilimane), 124, 145, 302, 306
Quiloans (Kilwans), 305
Quiteve (Chiteve), 147, 154, 156, 160, 161

RABEH, 267
Ramusio, 5, 28
Ravenstein, E. G., 122n., 374
Reade, Winwood, 350-351
Rebmann, Johannes, 37, 273, 273n.
Resende, 176
Rhapta, 21
Rhodes, Cecil, 36
Rhodesia, 16, 19, 59
Rhyne, Willem ten, 259n.
Richards, C., 273n., 276n.
Riebeeck, Jan van, 210
Ritter, E. A., 281n.
Robanna, 229
Robinson, R., 271n.
Rockhill, W. W., 114n.
Rodney, Jack, 229
Roger II, of Sicily, 111
Rozwi, 17, 142-143, 144, 148
Rozwi-Karanga, 147, 270
Ruiters, Diereck, 30
Ruwaya, 89
Ryder, A. F. C., 95-96

SABAEANS, 11
Sabia, 161
Sacina, King (Zacina), 199, 200
Sacumbe, 159
Sa'di, Abderrahman es-, 26, 91, 94-95, 336n.
Sa'id, al Hajji, 327-328
Said, Ibn, 22
St. Louis (Nder), 345
Saldanha, Antonio de, 132
Salem, 55

Sama, 71
Samagi, 85
Samory, 268
Sané, 23
Sanguinetti, B. R., 79n.
Sansanding, 310, 315, 335, 337, 338, 344, 345, 346
Santos, João dos, 147, 153-163
Sanuda, 254
Sarakolle, 14, 70, 91
Sarayamo, 338
Schapera, I, 259n., 274n.
Schwabe, K., 363
Schweinfurth, G., 273n.
Scott, George, 310
Sechele, 299
Sedanda, 156, 160, 161
Segu, 93, 315, 316, 317, 318-321
Sekeletu, 302
Selasse, Welleta, 251, 252
Seligman, C. G., 37
Selima, 44
Selimani, Sutan Ali ben, 105
Sélincourt, Aubrey de, 52n., 375
Selous, F. C., 274n.
Sena, 145, 147, 153, 159, 164, 165
Senegal, 77, 176, 221, 231, 232, 233
Sennar, 257
Sesostris, Pharaoh, 46
Setecama, King (Zetecama), 199, 200
Sethu, 47-48
Seyon, Zara, 118
Shabini, 346
Shaka, 281-282, 283, 285, 289
Sharp, Granville, 34-35, 228
Shaugu, 116
Shekkarau, Sarki, 84-85
Shendi, 54, 258
Shepperson, George, 366n., 367, 373
Shiringoma, 145

Sierra Leone, 26, 31, 34-35, 199, 228, 229, 231, 243, 251
Sigueira, Ruy de, 99
Siguiri, 77n.
Sijilmasa, 80, 347
Silva, Antonio Lobo da, 168
Simões, Diogo, 164
Slane, MacGuckin de, 72n.
Slatees, 321
Smith, H. F. C., 5, 26, 267, 267n., 269n., 323
Smith, William, 224-225
Sneeberg, 261
Soares, Pedro Vaz, 150
Soba (*Sarki* of Gobir), 85
Sobrynho, Joham, 188
Sofala, 22, 111, 117, 128-130, 131, 134, 136, 137, 138, 143, 145, 146, 147, 148-149, 150, 150n., 151, 152, 153, 154, 156, 158, 160
Sokoto, 6, 26, 273, 336
Solvyns, Baron, 36
Somalia, 25, 50, 113
Songhay, 15, 19, 24, 64, 86-89, 90, 91, 92, 93, 267, 337, 338, 344, 347
Songo Mnara, 304-305
Soosoos, 351, 352
Sosso (Fulah), 73
South Africa, Union of, 297
Southern Rhodesia, 141, 142, 143, 144, 147, 154, 274, 275, 297
Sparrman, Andrew, 231, 231n., 259-263
Speke, John Hanning, 6, 273, 273n.
Sprenger, Aloys, 107
Stanley, Henry M., 6, 18, 36, 274, 274n., 275
Stengers, J., 271n.
Stigand, C. H., 120n., 373

Stow, 57, 59
Succondee, 225
Sudan, 44, 68, 89, 91, 96, 268, 269, 270, 272. *See also* Western Sudan
Sugham, 71
Sulayman, *Mansa* (Sultan of Mali), 80-82
Sullivan, William, 278n.
Sumanguru, King of Sosso (Fulah), 73-74
Summers, Roger, 142, 143
Sundiata Keita, Mandingo ruler, 73-74
Suret-Canale, J., 70-71, 268n.
Susu, 74

TACHOMPSO, 52
Tacoodonou, King of Dahomey, 234
Tadaghaw, 326, 327
Tademekka, 347
Taharqa, 45
Tahiru, *Shehu*, 85
Talagouga, 354
Tanganyika, 18, 21, 24, 26, 103, 208, 274, 357, 366
Tangier, 79, 272
Taodenni, 347
Taokest, 368
Tasakal, 336
Tatental, 347
Tautek, 347
Tawarek (Tuareg), 339, 340, 345
Tawat, 335
Tegbesu, King (Bossa Ahadee), King of Dahomey, 235n.
Teghaza, 80, 94, 347
Teixeira, Dom João, 192, 194
Tekrur, 77
Temeh, 47
Tempels, Placide, 369-370, 375

Tenkaminen, King of Ghana, 72-73
Tennegué, 368
Tereres, 47
Tesfos, Ayto, 255, 256
Tete, 147, 153, 159, 164, 165, 167, 291, 292, 293, 301
Thabit, Sayed Hasan, 373
Theal, G. M., 136, 137n., 146n., 150n., 152n., 163n., 164n., 166n., 167n., 374
Tichitt, 368
Tigre, 118, 247, 249, 252
Tijani, Sheikh Ahmad al-, 269
Tijaniyya, 34
Timbuktu, 64, 88, 90, 91, 92, 94, 177, 186, 272, 334-335, 336-344, 344-346, 368
Tirakka, 77
Togwa, 145
Toloa, 150
Tombo, Torre do, 187n.
Toroa, 152
Torwa, 145
Touré, Samory, 267
Towerson, William, 175, 198n.
Trater, Pieter, 278n.
Tripoli, 334, 346
Trudo, Guadja (King Agaja), 234-235, 236, 237
Tuat, 94
Ture (Touré). *See* Muhammad, Askia
Tuthmosis III, 50
Tylden, 57

Uganda, 16, 273
Ugato (Gwato), 185
Ugha (Okha), 98
Ughoton (Benin), 100
Uhe, 96
Umar, al Hajj, 267, 268-269

Usama, 98
Usumbura, 273
Uteve, 145
Utonga, 145
Uwaiñokun, 99

Vai, 26
Vanhuisen, Jasper, 178
Vassa, Gustavus. *See* Equiano, Olaudah
Vealanga, 148-149
Velten, C., 105
Ventris, Michael George Francis, 45

Wadström, C. B., 231-234
Wagadu, 70, 72
Walata, 80, 346, 368
Walati, El, 338
Walker, John, 112
Wangara, 346
Wani, Mohammed, 336
Wassela, 321
Wawat, 45, 47-48, 49, 50
Webb, Beatrice, 365
Weebaigah, 234
Western Sudan, 6, 15, 18-19, 23, 26, 34, 37, 67, 86, 90-91, 177, 267, 269, 272, 322, 332-347. *See also* Sudan
Whydah. *See* Ouidah
Wilberforce, William, 35
Willett, Frank, 66-67, 374
Williams, David, 373
Williamson, J. A., 195n., 199n.
Windham, Thomas, 175, 196n.
Winterbottom, Dr. Thomas, 31-32, 243-245
Wissmann, Hermann von, 357
Witboi, Hendrik, 363
Woggora, 252
Wolfson, F., 276n.
Wolof (Oualof, Jolof), 186, 221

Woolley, 202

Xosa. *See* Ama-Xosa.

Yafous, Kefla, 254
Yaga, 29
Yakubi, al, 71
Yam, 44, 47, 48
Yamina, 321
Yamvo, *Muata*, 291
Yanbu, 116
Yao, 357
Yaqob, Zara, 117-119
Yauri, 68
Yhoma, 199
Yoruba, 66, 67-68, 68-69, 70, 96, 97, 235, 349-350
Yufi, 117
Yu-yang-tsa-tsu, 114

Zacina, King (Sacina), 199, 200
Zaga, 77
Zaghawa, 11, 67
Zagun, 77
Zair (Congo), 216
Zanj, 22, 93, 107-109, 116-117
Zanzibar, 112, 115, 132, 134, 208
Zarquatabana, 77
Zassa, 236, 237
Zayyati, Hassan ben Muhammad el Wazzan es, 26
Zetecama, King (Setecama), 199, 200
Zimbabwe, 17, 141, 147, 148, 149, 217
Zimbaoe, 154
Zulu, 19, 209, 281-282, 283, 286, 289, 298
Zurara, 27, 174